A COURSE OF LECTURES

ON THE

CONSTITUTIONAL JURISPRUDENCE

OF THE

UNITED STATES;

DELIVERED ANNUALLY IN COLUMBIA COLLEGE, NEW YORK,

BY

WILLIAM ALEXANDER DUER, LL.D.,

LATE PRESIDENT OF THAT INSTITUTION.

THE SECOND EDITION,

REVISED, ENLARGED, AND ADAPTED TO PROFESSIONAL AS WELL AS GENERAL USE.

Est omnibus necessarium nosse Rempublicam. — Cic.

THE LAWBOOK EXCHANGE, LTD.
UNION, NEW JERSEY
1999

ISBN 1-58477-020-1

Printed in the United States of America
On Acid-Free Paper

The Lawbook Exchange, Ltd.
965 Jefferson Avenue
Union, New Jersey 07083-8605

Please see catalogue at rear of this volume
or our website www.lawbookexchange.com
for a selection of our other reprints.

Library of Congress Cataloging-in-Publication Data

Duer, William Alexander, 1780-1858.
A course of lectures on the constitutional jurisprudence of the United States : delivered annually in Columbia College, New York / by William Alexander Duer.
p. cm.
Originally published : 2nd ed., rev., enl. Boston : Little, Brown, 1856.
Includes bibliographical references and index.
ISBN 1-58477-020-1
1. Constitutional law—United States. I. Title.
KF4550.D8 1999
342.73—dc21 99-16385
CIP

A COURSE OF LECTURES ON THE CONSTITUTIONAL JURISPRUDENCE OF THE UNITED STATES;

DELIVERED ANNUALLY IN COLUMBIA COLLEGE, NEW YORK,

BY

WILLIAM ALEXANDER DUER, LL.D.,
LATE PRESIDENT OF THAT INSTITUTION.

THE SECOND EDITION,

REVISED, ENLARGED, AND ADAPTED TO PROFESSIONAL AS WELL AS GENERAL USE.

Est omnibus necessarium nosse Rempublicam. — Cic.

BOSTON:
LITTLE, BROWN AND COMPANY.

RIVERSIDE, CAMBRIDGE:
PRINTED BY H. O. HOUGHTON AND COMPANY.

ADVERTISEMENT.

The favorable reception given to the former edition of the following work, has encouraged the author to devote to its revision the health and leisure vouchsafed to his declining years. By a more frequent and extensive citation of authorities, he has endeavored to impart to it a more professional aspect and authentic character. He has added the most important subsequent decisions upon constitutional questions, both of the Federal and State Courts, down, as nearly as possible, to the present time, and included many earlier cases not noticed on the former occasion as not falling within a plan adapted merely to a particular and limited purpose. Thus has he attempted to render the production more acceptable to the judicial, as well as more useful to the general scholar, and to afford indeed to all, and especially to those foreigners who may desire information in regard to our political institutions, the means of acquiring it in a compendious and convenient form.

If in this he has succeeded, he trusts he may in some measure have discharged the debt which, according to Lord Coke, every man owes to his profession,—in this case, the double duty of the Lawyer and the Teacher.

INGLEWOOD, near Morristown, N. J.,
August 1, 1856.

DEDICATION OF THE "OUTLINES," PUBLISHED PREVIOUSLY TO THE LECTURES AT LARGE.

TO JAMES MADISON.

To you, Sir, as the sole surviving member of the august assembly that framed the Constitution, and of that illustrious triumvirate, who, in vindicating it from the objections of its first assailants, succeeded in recommending it to the adoption of their country; to you, who, in discharging the highest duties of its administration,—proved the stability and excellence of the Federal Constitution, in war, as well as in peace,—and determined the experiment in favor of republican institutions, and the right of self-government; to you, who in your retirement, raised a warning voice against those heresies in the construction of the Constitution which, for the moment, threatened to impair it; to you, Sir, as alone among the earliest and the latest of its defenders, this brief exposition of the organization and principles of the National Government, intended especially for the instruction of our American youth, is most respectfully, and, in reference to your public services, most properly, inscribed.

W. A. DUER.

Columbia College, N. Y., August 1, 1833.

DEDICATION OF THE FIRST EDITION OF THE LECTURES.

TO JAMES KENT, LL.D.

MY DEAR SIR,

Relying for forgiveness upon "an uninterrupted possession" of your friendship "of more than twenty years, under color" at least "of title," I venture, without your knowledge or consent, to inscribe to you a Treatise on the Constitutional Jurisprudence of the United States. In this act, I do but make restitution of your own property, or, perhaps, to express myself more properly,—tender payment for the use of it; for you will soon discover that, next to the contemporaneous expositions of the authors of "The Federalist," I have drawn my materials more largely and freely from your "Commentaries," and the lucid and deep investigations of the late Chief Justice Marshall, than from any other sources. And although the responses of that great oracle of the Constitution have ceased, yet, may we hope that the inspiration will not be withdrawn, — whilst your corresponding adjudications and opinions shall be quoted as authority in the Court wherein he so long and auspiciously presided.

That you may continue, my dear Sir, to enjoy to the last the same vigor and activity of mind and body which distinguishes you at an age approaching the utmost limit assigned to man's earthly pilgrimage, is the fervent prayer of

Your faithful, constant, and hereditary[1] friend,

W. A. DUER.

Morristown, N. J., May 1, 1843.

P. S. Since the publication of the former edition of these Lectures, the venerable and profound Jurist to whom they were dedicated, has

[1] See Appendix D.

departed this life, and joined, as we may humbly hope, his great contemporary in the Courts above. His declining years were spent in dignified retirement, in the consciousness of a well-spent life, and the exercise of those Christian virtues, and the performance of those Christian duties which promised him an immortality far more glorious than that which will attend his works.

It will not, it is trusted, be deemed incompatible with the character of this work to subjoin what was intended, by an anonymous author, as an Epitaph for the late Chief Justice of the United States,—followed by some other verses from the same hand,—the concluding triplet of which might serve the same purpose for the former Chancellor of the State of New York.

"Beneath this stone, within this narrow grave,—
In hope that God's free grace his soul will save,—
Lies what was mortal of as pure a mind,
As e'er illumed an age, or blest mankind:
Wise, and accomplished in all human lore,
Yet ever prompt his frailty to deplore;
Born to instruct, to rear, uphold a State,
And teach that Justice stamps a People great,
MARSHALL'S ambition was his Country's weal,
And on her legal code to fix his seal:
As self-unconscious he obtained renown,
Disclaiming worth or merit of his own,
So, for acceptance in the Courts above,
He vouched his Maker's word, his Saviour's love.

Another still survives, worthy alone
To bear the mantle of the one that's gone;
Though now retired in dignity and ease,
And full of years, his body no disease,
His mind no torpor knows, nor amorphy;
Both active still, and active still to be.
Free from the crowd, the bustle, and the strife,
He hails the passing hour, awaits a better life:
Ah! who would wish a nobler monument,
Than that which rises from a life well spent,
And bears for Epitaph the name of KENT?"

TO JOHN DUER, LL.D.

In dedicating this edition of a Treatise on Constitutional Law to you, my brother, I am determined not less by what is due to your Judicial character, than by the friendship and affection that, for more than threescore years and ten, has existed unbroken between us.

W. A. DUER.

Inglewood, August 1, 1856.

PREFACE

TO THE FIRST EDITION.

IN submitting the following work to the public, there seems a necessity, as well as a propriety, in offering a preliminary explanation of its character and design; especially as he whose name it bears claims neither the merit of originality for his production, nor the title of author for himself. The present publication consists substantially of the Course of Lectures on the Constitutional Jurisprudence of the United States, delivered annually to the Senior Class in Columbia College, while he had the honor of presiding in that venerable and noble institution. The "OUTLINES" of those Lectures were published some years ago, at the request of "THE AMERICAN LYCEUM," an association consisting principally of persons engaged in the practical duties of instruction, who conceived that the study of our national Constitution might be introduced with advantage into the general system of public education. That little treatise, accordingly, appeared in a form adapted to the views of those who had suggested its preparation: which were, fitness as a text-book for lecturers, a class-book for academies and common schools, and a manual for popular use. Except, therefore, "as to method and arrangement," as was observed in issuing it from the press, "there could be little scope for originality in a work of which the essential value must depend on the fidelity with which the provisions of the Constitution, the Legislative enactments for giving it effect, and the Judicial construction which both have received, are stated and explained." The same remark may be repeated in reference to the present publication, and a similar disclaimer made as to its pretensions to originality. On the present occasion the author has again "implicitly followed those guides, whose decisions are obligatory and conclusive, upon such points as have been definitively settled" by judgments of the Supreme Courts of the United States; while "upon questions which have arisen in public discussion, but have neither been presented for Judicial determination nor received an approved practical construction from the other branches of the Government, he has had recourse to those elementary writers whose opinions are acknowledged to possess the greatest weight, either from their intrinsic value, or their conformity with the general doctrines of the authoritative expounders of the Constitution; and in the absence of both authority and disquisition, he has ventured to rely on his own reasonings, and has advanced his own opinions so far only as he conceives them to be confirmed by undeniable principles, or established by analogous cases."

The remaining sources drawn from on that occasion, have been resorted to again; and he now repeats the acknowledgment of his obligations, not only to the illustrious triumvirate whose combined labors were embodied in "THE FEDERALIST," to Chief Justice Marshall, and to Chancellor Kent, but also to Mr. Rawle's "View of the Constitution," and to the elaborate and voluminous "Commentaries" of the learned, ingenious, and indefatigable Mr. Justice Story.[1] The same observation may be repeated as to the different views taken in this work, as well as in its precursor, from those exhibited in the elementary treatises of the two former; with regard, in the one case, to the *supremacy*, and, in the other, to the *perpetual obligation* of the Federal

[1] The author has also to acknowledge his obligation to Joseph Blunt, Esq., for this historical sketch of the Constitution in his Annual Register.

Constitution. On both these important points the author still adheres to principles more favorable, as he believes, to the powers and stability of the National Government. He did not, however, at that time, nor does he now, venture to differ from such eminent jurists, without being supported by the opinions of some of the most distinguished statesmen of the day, of different parties — by the author of the celebrated Proclamation of President Jackson against the anti-federal proceedings in South Carolina, and the speeches of Mr. Webster *in vindication of its doctrines*; nor without being sanctioned by the judicial authority of the late Chief Justice — expressly upon one of the points in question, and virtually upon the other, by his affirmance of principles which it involves, and by which its decision must eventually be governed.

In again referring to the venerated name of Chief Justice MARSHALL, the author can but reiterate his former wish to be "understood, on this and all other occasions, as adopting his individual opinions, not less from deference to their official authority, than from the conviction wrought by the luminous and profound reasonings by which they are elucidated and supported. As this eminent and revered judge has himself declared it auspicious to the Constitution and to the country that the new government found such able advocates and interpreters as the authors of 'THE FEDERALIST,'[1] so it may be regarded as one of the most signal advantages attending its career, that its principles should have been developed and reduced to practice under a judicial administration so admirably qualified, in every respect, to expound them truly, and firmly to sustain them." Since this feeble tribute to his wisdom and virtues, this great judicial magistrate has been summoned to the bar of a higher than any earthly tribunal, there to receive, we may be certain, that justice, tempered with mercy,

[1] To the American reader it cannot be necessary to name them. But *for the benefit of others, their names* are added. Alexander Hamilton, James Madison, and John Jay.

which was the exemplar of his own administration; and to obtain, as we may hope, from the favor of his God, the reward due to his public services and private worth. There needs no monument to perpetuate the memory of his virtues but the record of his services. These, too, may serve as the fairest monument of the great political party of which he was the ornament and the boast. But if to designate the spot of earth consecrated to his remains, a tablet be required, let it be as simple and massive as was his mind, and let it be inscribed, "HERE LIES THE LAST OF THE FEDERALISTS."

Since the period referred to, the statesman to whom the work was dedicated — the last surviving member of that august assembly that formed the Constitution, and sole remaining luminary of that bright constellation of genius and talent, which, in vindicating that instrument from the objections of its first assailants, succeeded in recommending it to the adoption of the people; he who, in discharging the highest duties of its administration, proved the stability and excellence of the Constitution in war as well as in peace, and determined the experiment in favor of Republican institutions and the right of self-government; and, in his retirement, raised a warning voice against heresies in the construction of the national compact, which, for a moment, threatened to overthrow it — has also disappeared from among us, full of years and honors. The enumeration of such services recalls the name of Madison; and great as were those services, honored as was that name, the brightest glory that attends them both springs from the association of his genius, his learning, and his labors, with those of his once kindred spirits, HAMILTON and JAY. "*Vita enim mortuorum, vi unita fortior, in memoria vivorum est posita.*"

Morristown, N. J., May 1, 1843.

ANALYSIS.

Introduction.

I. Definition and origin of political Constitutions, as derived,

1. From tradition, or the act of the Government itself.
2. From written fundamental compacts.

Either of which may be formed,

1. On a simple principle of
    1. Monarchy.
    2. Aristocracy.
    3. Democracy.
2. Or combine these three forms in due proportions, by means of the principle of representation, applied,
    1. To the powers of Government; which are,
        1. The Legislative.
        2. The Executive.
        3. The Judicial.
    2. To the persons represented in the Government.

II. Foundations of representative Governments were laid,

1. *Partially*, in the British Colonies, in which were established,
    1. Royal Governments.
    2. Proprietary Governments.
2. *Universally*, in the American States, upon the establishment of independent Governments, which secured the enjoyment of,
    1. The inalienable natural rights of individuals.
    2. The political and civil privileges of the citizens, designed for maintaining, or substituted as equivalents for, natural rights.

III. The same fundamental principles were recognized and adopted upon the establishment of a Federal Government by the people of the several States.

1. In regard to the principle of representation, as applied,
    1. To the three great departments of Government.
    2. To the individual citizens of the United States, and to the several States of the Union.
2. In regard to the distribution of the powers of Government, as the Constitution of the United States contains,
    1. A general delegation of the Legislative, Executive, and Judicial powers to distinct departments; and,
    2. Defines the powers and duties of each department respectively.

OUTLINES of that branch of Jurisprudence which treats of the principles, powers, and construction of the Constitution, are therefore to be traced,

FIRST. With regard to the particular structure and organization of the Government.

SECOND. In relation to the powers vested in it, and the restraints imposed on the States.

I. Of the structure and organization of the Government, and the distribution of its powers among its several departments.

1. Of the Legislative power, or Congress of the United States.
    1. Of the constituent parts of the Legislature, and the modes of their appointment.
        1. Of the House of Representatives.
        2. Of the Senate.
    2. Their joint and several powers and privileges.
    3. Their method of enacting laws, with the times and modes of their assembling and adjourning.
2. Of the Executive power, as vested in the President,
    1. His qualifications; the mode and duration of his appointment, and the provision for his support.
    2. His powers and duties.
3. Of the Judicial power.
    1. The mode in which it is constituted.
    2. The objects and extent of its jurisdiction.

3. The manner in which its jurisdiction is distributed.
   1. Of the Court for the trial of Impeachments.
   2. Of the Supreme Court.
   3. Of the Circuit Courts.
   4. Of the District Courts.
   5. Of the Territorial Courts.
   6. Of powers vested in State Courts and Magistrates by laws of the United States.

II. Of the nature, extent, and limitation of the powers vested in the National Government, and the restraints imposed on the States, reduced to different classes, as they relate,

1. To *security from foreign danger*; which class comprehends the powers,
   1. Of declaring war, and granting letters of marque and reprisal.
   2. Of making rules concerning captures by land and water.
   3. Of providing armies and fleets, and regulating and calling forth the militia.
   4. Of levying taxes and borrowing money.
2. To intercourse with foreign nations; comprising the powers,
   1. To make treaties, and to send and receive ambassadors and other public ministers and consuls.
   2. To regulate foreign commerce, including the power to prohibit the importation of slaves.
   3. To define and punish piracies and felonies committed on the high seas, and offences against the laws of nations.
3. To the maintenance of harmony and proper intercourse among the States, including the powers,
   1. To regulate commerce among the several States, and with the Indian tribes.
   2. To establish post-offices and post-roads.
   3. To coin money, regulate its value, and to fix the standard of weights and measures.
   4. To provide for the punishment of counterfeiting the securities and public coin of the United States.
   5. To establish a uniform rule of naturalization.

6. To establish uniform laws on the subject of bankruptcies.
7. To prescribe, by penal laws, the manner in which the public acts, records, and judicial proceedings of each State shall be proved, and the effect they shall have in other States.

4. To certain miscellaneous objects of general utility; comprehending the powers,
   1. To promote the progress of science and the useful arts.
   2. To exercise exclusive legislation over the district within which the seat of Government should be permanently established; and over all places purchased by consent of the State Legislatures for the erection of forts, magazines, arsenals, dockyards, and other needful buildings.
   3. To declare the punishment of treason against the United States.
   4. To admit new States into the Union.
   5. To dispose of, and make all needful rules and regulations respecting the territory and other property of the United States.
   6. To guarantee to every State in the Union a republican form of government, and to protect each of them from invasion and domestic violence.
   7. To propose amendments to the Constitution, and to call conventions for amending it, upon the application of two thirds of the States.
5. To the Constitutional restrictions on the powers of the several States; which are,
   1. *Absolute* restrictions, prohibiting the States from,
      1. Entering into any treaty of alliance or confederation.
      2. Granting letters of marque and reprisal.
      3. Coining money, emitting bills of credit, or making any thing but gold or silver coin a lawful tender in payment of debts.
      4. Passing any bill of attainder, *ex post facto* law, or law impairing the obligation of contracts.

5. Granting any title of nobility.

2. *Qualified* limitations; prohibiting the States, *without the consent of Congress*, from,

1. Laying imposts on imports or exports, or duties on tonnage.
2. Keeping troops or ships of war in time of peace.
3. Entering into any agreement or compact with another State, or with a foreign power.
4. Engaging in war, unless actually invaded, or in such imminent danger as will not admit delay.

6. To the provisions for giving efficacy to the powers vested in the Government of the United States; consisting of,

1. The power of making all laws necessary and proper for carrying into execution the other enumerated powers.
2. The declaration that the Constitution and laws of the United States, and all treaties under their authority, shall be the Supreme Law of the land.
3. The powers specially vested in the Executive and Judicial departments, and particularly the provision extending the jurisdiction of the latter to all cases arising under the Constitution.
4. The requisition upon the Senators and Representatives in Congress; the members of the State Legislatures; and all Executive and Judicial officers of the United States and of the several States, to be bound by oath or affirmation to support the Constitution of the United States.
5. The provision that the ratifications of the Conventions of nine States should be sufficient for the establishment of the Constitution between the States ratifying the same.

Conclusion.

CONTENTS.

LECTURES

ON

CONSTITUTIONAL JURISPRUDENCE.

LECTURES.

LECTURE I.

INTRODUCTORY.

A KNOWLEDGE of the history, organization, and principles of the government under which he lives, must be beneficial to every man, wheresoever he may dwell, and under whatsoever form of government his lot may have been cast. It may, indeed, be regarded as peculiarly advantageous in free states, where every citizen must possess an interest, if not an influence in the administration of public affairs, and it is obviously indispensable where the political rights of all are equal, and the obscurest individual has a voice in the election of his rulers, and is himself eligible to the highest office in the state.

It was, therefore, with reason, considered a defect in the prevailing systems of education, that the study of our Constitutional Jurisprudence should have been either altogether omitted, or deferred to that period of life when our youth are called on to participate in the active duties of society; or that it should have been regarded as necessary only to lawyers and politicians. For, essential as is a profound knowledge of the Constitution to statesmen and jurists, some acquaintance with its principles and details must, in the opinion of all who entertain liberal views of public education, and correctly estimate their privileges as citizens, be requisite, even, for those whose ambition rises no higher than the mere exercise of those privileges at elections of their representatives in the government, without desiring political influence or public station for themselves.

It is gratifying, however, to find that of late years a greater interest has been manifested among the more intelligent portion of the community, with regard to the origin, structure, and principles of our political institutions. This certainly evinces that one class, at least, of our citizens appreciates their value, and that so far, therefore, they are better understood. But both reason and common sense suggest that such information cannot be too soon acquired, while experience teaches us that it cannot be too widely diffused. The public interest and welfare, if not the stability of the system itself, not less than the safety and happiness of individuals, and the security it affords to their persons and property, require that, in common with other important branches of education, the knowledge in question should be extended to every portion, and, if possible, to every member of the body politic.

Until lately, it was a reproach to this College, that it sent forth its graduates more familiar with the Constitution of the Roman Republic, and the principles of the Grecian confederacies, than with the fundamental laws of their own country. To remedy the evil, it was proposed to ingraft this new branch of study upon the general course pursued in the Institution; but in preparing the Lectures we are now commencing, I have not lost sight of their possible usefulness to others than yourselves, and especially to foreigners, in their publication, at some future day, subsequent to their completion and delivery in this place. For it will hardly be denied that more accurate information in regard to the organization and powers both of Federal and State governments, is desirable in European statesmen, ministers, and lawyers, while their want of it is not only mortifying to our national pride, but prejudicial to our national interests. Much vexatious difficulty, groundless misunderstanding, and fruitless negotiation would, doubtless, have been prevented, and much needless embarrassment and delay avoided, had the public men of Great Britain and France been better informed with respect to them.

A rapid sketch of the origin and progress of the American Confederation, until it reached a result so auspicious as the establishment of the present Constitution, seems proper as an introduction to the study upon which we are now to enter; and this historical review will prove, it is trusted, the more useful, as it will not only serve to exhibit the genius and practical excellence of the Government, but also to facilitate the proposed investigation of its organization and powers.

While the American people were subjects of the British crown, and the elder of these States were as yet British colonies, it was perceived that their union was essential to their safety and prosperity. Both general and partial associations were accordingly formed among them for temporary purposes, and on sudden emergencies, long before their permanent union, to resist the claims and aggressions of the mother-country, a measure which produced the Revolution, and ended in the acknowledgment of the Colonies as free and independent States. The common origin and interests of the New England provinces, the similarity of their manners, laws, religious tenets, and civil institutions, naturally led to a more intimate connection among themselves, and induced, at a very early period, the habit of confederating together for their common defence. These colonies, as far back as the year 1643, apprehending danger from the warlike and formidable tribes of Indians by which they were surrounded, entered into an offensive and defensive league, which they declared should be firm and perpetual, as well as that its members should thenceforth be distinguished as "The United Colonies of New England." In this transaction, the provincial governments, who were parties to it, acted, in fact, as independent sovereignties; and circumstances enabled and encouraged them to assume an exemption from the control of any superior power.

By the charters from the crown, under which they had been founded, and which prescribed their respective forms of government, and settled their fundamental principles, the people of those colonies were authorized, by the suffrages of the freemen of the several towns, to elect, not only their immediate representatives in the popular branch of their legislatures, but also the chief executive magistrate, or governor, and his *assistants*, or councillors, who formed a second and coördinate branch of those provincial assemblies. The supremacy, therefore, of the British crown or Parliament over the colonies in question had, at all times, been little more than nominal, in comparison with the authority exercised over those provinces, where the governors and councillors were appointed by the Crown, and held their offices at its pleasure, and which in other respects, also, were kept in closer and more immediate subjection. The civil war in which Great Britain was at that time plunged, occupied, moreover, her whole attention; and this measure of her colonies, tending so directly to future independence, was suffered to pass without much notice, or any animadversion.

From the terms of this association, it may justly be regarded as the first step towards the establishment of independent government in America; with some occasional alterations, it subsisted for nearly half a century, and for a part of that time with the countenance of the British government; nor was it dissolved until the charters of the New England provinces were, in effect, annulled by James the Second. Subsequently, however, to that arbitrary procedure, congresses of governors and commissioners from the other colonies, as well as from New England, were held from time to time, to consult on matters relative to their common welfare, and to adopt measures for the protection of the frontiers. An assembly of this description took place at Albany in 1722. But a more general and memorable convention was held at the same place in 1754, consisting of commissioners from all the New England colonies, and from the provinces of New York, Pennsylvania, and Maryland.

This Congress was called at the instance of the government in England; and although the object of the ministry in proposing it was merely to promote and facilitate the negotiation of treaties with the Indians, the colonial legislatures, who promptly acceded to the proposal, evidently entertained more extensive views.

Two of the provinces expressly instructed their delegates to enter into articles of confederation with the other colonies for their general security in time of peace, as well as in war; and one of the first acts of the commissioners, when they assembled, was a unanimous resolution that a union of the colonies was absolutely necessary for their preservation. After rejecting several proposals for the division of the colonies into separate confederacies, they agreed to a plan of federal government for the whole, consisting of a President-General, to be appointed by the Crown, and a General Legislative Council, to meet once in every year, and to be composed of delegates chosen triennially, by the provincial assemblies.

This celebrated plan of union was drawn up by Doctor Franklin, who attended as a delegate from Pennsylvania, and is to be found in the more recent editions of his works, with an exposition of the reasons and motives which guided him in forming it. The confederacy was to embrace all the then existing colonies; and the rights of war and peace, in respect to the Indian nations, were to be vested in the General Council of the confederates, subject to the immediate negative of the President-General, and the ultimate approval of the Crown. It was to possess the further power "to raise troops and build forts for the defence of the colonies, and to equip vessels of war to guard the coasts and protect commerce;" and for these purposes the General Council was to have power to levy such general imposts and taxes as should seem most just and equal.

Besides the venerable name of Franklin, there were enrolled among the delegates to this Congress some others of the greatest distinction in our colonial history. In the course of their proceedings, these enlightened men asserted and promulgated those principles, the reception of which, in the minds of the people of this country, prepared them for future independence, and laid the foundations of our present national government. But the times were not yet propitious—the season had not yet arrived, nor were public sentiment and intelligence sufficiently matured for so comprehensive and liberal a proposition. The master-minds who governed that assembly had gone before their age; and their bold project of continental union had the singular fate of being rejected, not only in England, but by every provincial legislature. By the mother-country, it was probably supposed that union would soon reveal to her colonies the secret of their strength, and afford them the opportunity and the means of giving it effect; while on the part of the colonies, a dread of the preponderating influence of the royal prerogative, in the operation of the proposed system, condemned them to remain for some years longer, separate and insignificant communities, emulous in their obedience to the parent state, and in devotion to her interests, but jealous of each other's prosperity; gradually estranged by conflicting pretensions and narrow views of local policy; and, in some instances, kept apart by mutual prejudices, or dissimilarity in their institutions and manners. The necessity of union had, nevertheless, been felt; its advantages perceived; its principles explained, and the way to it clearly pointed out; and at length, the sense of common danger and oppression brought the colonies once more together, and led them to adopt the same measures of defence and security, not, indeed, against the vexatious and irregular warfare of the savage tribes, but in resistance to the formidable claims, and still more formidable power, of the mother-country.

When the first attack was made by Parliament upon the chartered privileges of the colonists, and their inherent rights as subjects of the English law, by the celebrated Stamp Act of 1763, a congress of deputies from all the colonial assemblies was recommended by the popular branch of the Massachusetts Legislature; and in the month of October, in that year, delegates from most of the provinces assembled at New York. Without delay or hesitation, they published a declaration of the rights and grievances of the colonists, in which they asserted their title to the enjoyment of all the rights and privileges of British subjects, and especially the exclusive power of taxing themselves. They complained more particularly of the act of Parliament imposing stamp duties, and other direct taxes in the colonies; and their remonstrances were so far successful that this obnoxious measure was rescinded, although its repeal was accompanied by a declaratory assertion of the power of Parliament to tax the colonies in all cases whatever.

This reservation, however, of the abstract right gave little umbrage to the colonists, who regarded it merely as a *salvo* for the offended pride of Great Britain, and verily believed that no new attempt would be made to reduce the principle to practice. But it was soon discovered that they had reposed too much faith in the intelligence, prudence, and moderation of the British statesmen of that day. Before two years had elapsed, the very men who had consented to the repeal of the Stamp Act brought into Parliament a bill equally objectionable in principle, though less odious in its features and oppressive in its operation; and this bill, levying taxes on the colonists without their consent, by a legislature in which they were not represented, became a law, almost without opposition. After a long course of patient remonstrance and constitutional resistance to the execution of this new act, a general congress was proposed at town meetings in New York and Boston, and more formally recommended by a majority of the members of the Virginia Assembly, upon the dissolution of that body in consequence of its opposition to the claims of Parliament. The committees of correspondence established in the several colonies, selected the city of Philadelphia as the place, and appointed the tenth of September, 1774, as the time of meeting of the first Continental Congress.

The members of that illustrious body were in general elected by the colonial legislatures; but in some instances a different method was pursued, which, for the most part, was adopted from necessity. In New Jersey and Maryland, the elections were made by committees chosen in the several counties for that purpose; and in New York, where the royal party being the stronger, it was improbable that a legislative act authorizing the election of representatives in Congress could be obtained, the people themselves assembled in those places where the spirit of opposition prevailed, and elected delegates, who were readily received as members of the Congress. The powers with which the deputies of the several colonies were invested were of various extent. Some were limited to special objects, notwithstanding the recommendations for their appointment had been expressed in the most general and comprehensive terms, and requested that they should be clothed with "authority and discretion to meet and consult together for the *common welfare*." Most generally, they were empowered to consult and advise on the means most proper to secure the liberties of the colonies, and restore the harmony formerly subsisting between them and the parent state. In some instances, the powers conferred seemed to contemplate only such measures as would operate on the commercial connection between the two countries; in others, the discretion of the delegates was unlimited.

Deputies from eleven of the provinces appeared at Philadelphia on the day appointed, and took into immediate consideration the calamitous aspect of public affairs; and especially the sufferings of those colonies which had been foremost and most active in resistance to the oppressive measures of the mother-country. By a series of declaratory resolutions, they asserted what they deemed to be the absolute and inalienable rights of the colonists, as men, and as free subjects of Great Britain; pointed out to their constituents the systematic aggression which had been pursued, and the impending violence premeditated against them; and enjoined them, by their regard to honor, and their love of country, to renounce commerce with Great Britain, as the most effectual means of averting the dangers with which they were threatened, and of securing those liberties which they derived from the bounty of their Creator, or claimed as an inheritance from their fathers.

This requisition received prompt and universal obedience; and the *Union* thus formed, and confirmed by these resolutions, was continued by successive elections of delegates to the General Congress, and maintained through every period of the Revolution which immediately ensued, and every change in our Federal and State governments, and is revered and cherished by every true American as the source of our national prosperity, and the only solid foundation of our national independence.

In the month of May, 1775, a new Congress, consisting of delegates from twelve provinces, clothed with ample discretionary powers, met at Philadelphia; and soon after it assembled, the accession of Georgia completed the confederation of the Thirteen Colonies of North America. These delegates were instructed to "concert and prosecute such measures as they should deem most fit and proper to obtain a redress of grievances;" and, in more general terms, corresponding with the *formula* of classic antiquity, to "take care of the liberties of the country." Charged thus solemnly with the protection of the common rights and interests, the representatives of the American people prepared for resistance, sustained by the confidence, and animated by the zeal, of their constituents. They published a declaration of the causes and necessity of resorting to arms, and proceeded to levy and organize forces by land and sea; to contract debts and emit a paper currency, pledging the faith of the Union for its redemption; and, gradually assuming all the powers of national sovereignty, this Congress at length declared the United Colonies free and independent States.[1]

Preparatory to this momentous and uncompromising measure, by which our Revolution may be said to have been consummated, an important preliminary step had

[1] *Vide* Appendix A.

been taken by Congress, which in itself was considered decisive of the question of independence. It had previously recommended to particular colonies to establish temporary institutions for conducting their affairs during the contest with the mother-country; but when independence was perceived to be the inevitable result, it was proposed by Congress, to the respective assemblies and conventions of the provinces where no government adapted to the exigencies of the crisis had already been formed, to adopt such Constitutions as should be most conducive to the happiness and safety of their immediate constituents, as well as of the nation at large. The provincial assemblies acted on this recommendation; and the several colonies, already contemplating themselves as independent States, adopted the principle, then considered visionary in Europe, of limiting the constituted authorities by a written fundamental instrument; and thus the doctrine of the "Social Contract," hitherto advanced merely as an ingenious theory, or regarded as a bold and fanciful speculation, was first actually exemplified, and successfully reduced to practice.

To secure and perpetuate these State institutions, it was deemed expedient, while these measures were maturing, to explain more fully, and by a formal instrument, the nature of the federative compact, and to define both the powers vested in the General Government, and the residuary sovereignty of the States. But the measure was attended with so much embarrassment and delay, that, notwithstanding they were surrounded by the same common danger, and were together contending for the same inestimable principles and objects, it was not until late in the following autumn that the discordant interests and prejudices of these thirteen distinct commonwealths could be so far blended and compromised as to induce their agreement to the terms of the proposed Federal Union; and when submitted to the State legislatures for ratification, the system was declared by Congress to have been the result of impending necessity, consented to, not for its intrinsic excellence, but as the best that could be adapted to the circumstances of the States respectively, and, at the same time, afford any reasonable hope of general assent.

These "Articles of Confederation" met with still greater obstacles in their progress through the States. Most of the State legislatures, indeed, ratified them with a promptitude which evinced a due sense on their part of the necessity of preserving the Confederacy, and of the duty, to that end, of exercising a liberal spirit of accommodation. But some of the States withheld their assent for several years after the Declaration of Independence; and one, in particular, persisted so long in its refusal, as to injure the common cause, afford encouragement to the enemies, and depress the hopes of every friend of America. The perception of these consequences at length induced the State in question to abandon its objections; and on the first of March, 1781, these articles of Union received, upon the accession of Maryland, the unanimous approbation of the States.[1]

By the terms of this compact, cognizance and jurisdiction of foreign affairs, the power of declaring war and concluding peace, and authority to make unlimited requisitions of men and money, were exclusively vested

[1] *Vide* Appendix B.

in Congress; and a compliance with these powers, when exercised by that body, was rendered obligatory upon the several States. But these rights of political supremacy, extensive as they were, had been conferred in an insufficient manner, and under a most imperfect organization. The articles, indeed, were but a written digest, and even a limitation of the discretionary powers which had been delegated to Congress in 1775, and which had always been freely exercised, and implicitly obeyed. The powers themselves, now formally enumerated and defined, might, nevertheless, have proved competent for all the essential purposes of union, had they been duly distributed among the several departments of a well-balanced government, and brought to bear upon the individual citizens of the United States by means of a federal Executive and Judicial, as well as Legislative authority. Congress, as then constituted, was, in fact, an improper and unsafe depository of political power, since the whole national authority, in one consolidated mass of complicated jurisdiction, was vested in a single body of men; while, in imitation of all former confederacies of independent sovereignties, the decrees of the federal council affected the States only in their corporate capacity, as contradistinguished from the individuals of whom they are composed. This was considered by the ablest statesmen of that day as the radical defect of the first Confederation; "and although this vicious principle did not," as one of them has justly remarked, "run through all the powers delegated to the Union, yet it pervaded and governed those on which the efficacy of the rest depended."[1] Except as to the rule of appor-

[1] By Mr. Hamilton, in the 15th Number of "The Federalist." See also "The Federalist," No. 9, by Mr. Madison, for further exam-

tionment, Congress had an indefinite discretion to make requisitions for men and money; but they had no authority to raise either the one or the other by regulations extending to the individual citizens of the States. Like the warrior magician of the great dramatic poet, they could "call up spirits from the vasty deep," but none would "come when they did call." The consequence was, that though in theory the resolutions of Congress were equivalent to laws, yet in practice they were found to be mere recommendations, which the States, like other irresponsible sovereigns, observed or disregarded, according to their own good-will and gracious pleasure.

The next most palpable defect, therefore, in the system, was the absence of all power in Congress to compel obedience to their decrees; or, in legal *parlance*, the total want of a *sanction* to their laws. There was no express delegation of authority to use force against delinquent members of the Confederacy, and no such right could be ascribed to the federal head, as resulting from construction, or derived by inference from the nature of the compact, inasmuch as Congress was actually restricted from any assumption of implied powers, however essential to the complete exercise of those which were expressly given. Fortunately for the country, there was then too much public virtue in that body to assume a power not warranted by the Constitution. Had its members possessed less wisdom and integrity, and stretched their authority under the plea of an imperious necessity, which might often have been alleged on stronger and more plausible grounds than at any subsequent period,

ples; and an observation on the subject by Mr. Jefferson, in his "Notes of Virginia," p. 105. Pennington & Gould's Ed., N. Y., 1801.

it would have been usurpation; and had they been clothed with the power of enforcing their constitutional requisitions, it might, from the accumulated jurisdiction vested in them, have proved fatal to public liberty. The only remedy, therefore, for a violation of the compact, was war upon the refractory party, by such others of the Confederacy as might think proper to resort to it. But the application of this remedy would probably have produced dismemberment, and thus have proved worse even than the disease itself.

The want of a mutual guarantee of the State governments to protect them from internal violence and rebellion; the principle by which the contributions of the States were made to the common treasury; the want of a power in Congress to regulate commerce; the right of equal suffrage possessed by the States in Congress, as well as the omission of distinct and independent Executive and Judicial departments, were also regarded as fundamental errors in the Confederation. In these leading particulars, and in some others of inferior importance, it had proved totally incompetent to fulfil the ends for which it had been devised. Almost as soon as it was finally ratified, the States began to fail in prompt and faithful observance of its provisions. As the dangers incident to revolution and war receded, instances of neglect and disobedience became more gross and frequent; and, "by the time peace was concluded," as was observed by one of our constitutional jurists,[1] "the *disease* of the government had displayed itself with alarming rapidity." The inequality in the application of the principle of contributions produced

[1] Chancellor Kent.

delinquencies in many of the States; and the delinquencies of one State became the pretext or apology for those of another, until the project of supplying the pecuniary exigencies of the nation by requisitions upon the individual States, was discovered to be altogether delusive in its conception, and hopeless in its execution.

The Continental government being destitute, as we have seen, of power to adopt regulations of commerce binding on the States, each State established its separate system on such narrow and selfish principles, and executed it in so partial and unequal a manner, that the confidence of foreign nations in our commercial integrity and stability, and the mutual harmony and freedom of intercourse among the States themselves, were impaired, if not destroyed. The national engagements, indeed, seem, in most cases, to have been abandoned; and, in the indignant language of "The Federalist,"[1] "each State, yielding to the voice of immediate interest or convenience, successively withdrew its support from the Confederation, until the frail and tottering edifice was ready to fall on the heads of the people, and crush them beneath its ruins."

In the most persuasive and manly remonstrances, Congress had endeavored to obtain from the States the right of levying, for a limited time, a general impost on goods imported from abroad, for the exclusive purpose of providing for the discharge of the national debt. But it was impracticable to unite so many independent sovereignties in this or any other measure demanded for the safety and honor of the Confederacy. Disas-

[1] No. 15, by Mr. Hamilton.

trous, however, as their refusal appeared at the time, and deeply regretted as it was by every intelligent friend of the Union, it may now be deemed providential that the State legislatures withheld from Congress the power solicited; for, had it then been granted, it is the opinion of the constitutional jurist to whom I have already referred, that "the subsequent effort to amend the system of federal government would never, probably, have been made, and the people of this country might have continued to this day the victims of a feeble and incompetent Confederacy." The necessary tendency of affairs at that period, was either to an entire annihilation of the national authority or to a civil war in order to maintain it. Universal poverty and distress were spreading dismay throughout the land. Agriculture, as well as commerce, was crippled; private confidence, as well as public credit, was destroyed; and every expedient was resorted to by men of desperate fortunes to inflame the minds of the people, and cast odium upon those who labored to preserve the national faith, and establish an efficient government. Notwithstanding the sufferings of the people and the imbecility of the government, there were many citizens, of high respectability and undoubted patriotism, who still adhered to the old Confederation; and, from their preference or their possession of State authority, and their jealousy of federal power, could see nothing in the proposed renovation of the Union but oppression and tyranny. They apprehended, indeed, nothing less than the entire destruction of the State governments by the overwhelming influence of the national institutions, and determined to resist the contemplated change. But a large majority of those who had conducted the country in safety through the

Revolution, united their influence to put an end to the public calamities, by establishing a political system which should be adequate to the exigencies of national union, and act as an efficient and permanent government on the several States. The foremost among these patriots was Washington. At the close of the revolutionary war, he had addressed a circular letter to the governors of the several States, urging an indissoluble union as essential to the well-being, and even to the existence, of the nation; and now, from his retirement, he strove, in all his intercourse and correspondence with his fellow-citizens, to impress upon the public mind the necessity of such a measure. At his seat at Mount Vernon, in the year 1785, it was agreed by certain commissioners from Virginia and Maryland, whose visit had reference to far inferior objects, to propose to their respective governments the appointment of new commissioners, with more extensive powers in regard to the commercial arrangements between these States. This proposal was not only adopted by the Virginia Legislature, but so enlarged as to recommend to all the other States to unite in the appointment of commissioners from each, to meet and consult on the general subject of the commercial interests and relations of the Confederacy. And this measure, thus casual and limited in its commencement, terminated in a formal proposition for a General Convention to revise the state of the Union.

When the period arrived for the meeting of this body, the objects of its assembling had been carried much further than was at first expressed by those who perceived and deplored the complicated and increasing evils flowing from the inefficiency of the existing

Confederation. Representatives from New York, New Jersey, Pennsylvania, and Delaware were all that assembled on this occasion, in addition to those from Virginia and Maryland; and upon proceeding to discuss the subjects for which they had convened, it was soon perceived that a more general representation of the States, and powers more extensive than had been confided to the delegates actually attending, would be requisite to effect the great purposes in contemplation. This first Convention, therefore, broke up without coming to any specific resolution on the particular matters referred to them; but, previously to adjourning, they agreed to a report to be made to their respective States, and transmitted to Congress, representing the necessity of extending the revision of the federal system to all its defects, and recommending to the several Legislatures to appoint deputies to meet for that purpose, in Convention, at Philadelphia, on the second of the ensuing May.

On receiving this report, the Legislature of Virginia immediately appointed delegates for the object specified in the recommendation; and within the year, every State except Rhode Island had acceded to the proposal, and elected delegates with power to carry that object into full effect. The General Convention, thus constituted and empowered, met at Philadelphia on the day appointed; and having chosen General Washington (whose name was first on the list of the deputies from his native State) for their President, proceeded, with closed doors, to deliberate on the momentous and extensive subjects submitted to their consideration. The crisis was most important in respect to the welfare and prosperity of America, if not of the whole civilized world. The fruits of our glorious Revolution, and, perhaps, the final destiny of Republicanism itself, were involved in the issue of this experiment to reform the system of our National Government; and, happily for the people of America — auspiciously for the liberties of mankind — the Federal Convention comprised a rare assemblage of the best experience, talents, character, and information which this country afforded, and it commanded that universal public confidence at home and abroad which such qualifications were calculated to inspire. With regard to the great principles which should constitute the basis of their system, not much contrariety of opinion is understood to have prevailed; but on the application of those principles, in their various forms and intricate modifications, an equal degree of harmony was not to have been expected. Eventually, however, the high importance attached to the preservation of the Union triumphed over local interests and personal feelings; and after several months of arduous deliberation, the Convention finally agreed, with unexpected and unexampled unanimity, on that plan of government which is contained in the CONSTITUTION OF THE UNITED STATES.[1]

The new system was directed by the Convention to be laid before Congress, to be by them transmitted to Conventions to be chosen by the people in each State, for their assent and ratification. It was, moreover, provided in the Constitution itself, that, as soon as it should be ratified by nine States, it should be carried into operation among them, in a mode prescribed by a separate act of the Federal Convention; and in their letter,

[1] *Vide* Appendix C.

transmitting it to Congress, they declared the Constitution to be "the result of a spirit of amity, and of that mutual deference and concession which the peculiarity of their political system rendered indispensable."

The course pointed out by the Convention was pursued by Congress, and the request formally communicated to the State legislatures. The People were, accordingly, invited to choose delegates to meet in each State, for the purpose of deliberating and deciding on the National Constitution. Besides the solemn and authoritative examination of the subject in these assemblies, the new scheme of government was subjected to severe scrutiny and animated discussion, both in private circles and in the public prints. But neither the intrinsic merits of the Constitution itself, nor the preponderating weight of argument and character by which it was supported, gave assurance to its advocates that it would be eventually accepted. It contained provisions for the preservation of the public faith and the support of private credit which interfered with the views, and counteracted the interests and designs, of those by whom public and private credit were equally disregarded; and against the jealous opposition of such objectors the powers of reason were exerted in vain, because their real motives could not be avowed. There were, however, among the opponents of the new Constitution, individuals of a different character, upon whom the force of argument, it was hoped, might make its due impression. Men of influence and authority were to be found in every State, who, from an honest conviction of its justice and policy, were desirous of retaining, unimpaired, the sovereignty of the States, and reducing the Union to a mere alliance between kindred nations.

Others supposed that an irreconcilable opposition of interests existed between different parts of the Continent, and that the claims of that portion to which they themselves belonged had been surrendered without an equivalent; while a more numerous class, who felt themselves identified with the State institutions, and thought their ambition restrained to State objects, considered the government now proposed for the United States, in some respects, a foreign one; and were, consequently, disposed to measure out power to the National Legislature with the same sparing hand with which they would confer authority on agents neither chosen by themselves nor accountable to them for its exercise.

The friends and opponents of the Federal Constitution were therefore stimulated in their exertions by motives equally powerful; and during the interval between its publication and adoption, every faculty of the superior minds of both the parties was strained to secure the acceptance or rejection of the new system. The result was for some time extremely doubtful. The amendments proposed by several of the States as conditions of their accession show with what reluctance their assent was given, and clearly evince that the dread of dismemberment, rather than sincere approbation of the Constitution, had in many instances induced its adoption. Nevertheless, the cause of political wisdom and justice at length prevailed. Within one year from its promulgation, the new Government was assented to by eleven of the States, and ratified by Congress. Delaware was the first to accede to it; and the assent of New Hampshire, as the ninth State, rendered it certain that the Constitution would be carried into effect by the States which had already adopted it. The important States of Virginia and New York, in each of which its fate remained uncertain, were probably determined in its favor by the previous ratification of New Hampshire;[1] so that, by the spring of 1789, the Federal Government was duly organized under the new Constitution, and went immediately into full and successful operation, without the concurrence of Rhode Island or North Carolina, who were afterward admitted, in succession, into the Union.

The final establishment of this admirable system of government, so well adapted to the genius, character, and circumstances of the people, and to the situation and extent of the country; so skilfully ingrafted upon the preëxisting institutions, amid all the difficulties and impediments which have been exhibited, affords a signal example of the benignant influence of peaceful deliberation and calm decision, combined with a spirit of moderation and mutual conciliation, not only beyond all precedent, but, when we reflect on the fate of similar attempts in other countries, almost beyond the hope of imitation. And while the felicitous issue of this experiment, and the universal acknowledgment of its hitherto successful results, constitute lasting proofs of the wisdom and patriotism of the founders of our Government, we must ever venerate their names, adhere to their principles, and cherish the remembrances of services, which are entitled equally to the gratitude and admiration of their posterity. We shall never, it is devoutly to be hoped, disregard or undervalue the blessings which, under Providence, they secured to us, nor forget the dangers and evils which were averted by their persever-

[1] *Vide* Appendix D.

ing and devoted efforts — dangers and evils to which the people of these States would again be exposed, in every degree and form of aggravation, should the wisdom and energy of the fathers of our country be rendered abortive by the madness and folly of their sons. If threatened with such a reverse, may we ever be ready to respond to the sentiments called forth in a happy hour from one of our late chief magistrates, that at every sacrifice, except of the inalienable rights and liberties which the Constitution was intended to perpetuate, "THE UNION MUST BE PRESERVED."[1]

[1] *Vide* Appendix E.

LECTURE II.

FUNDAMENTAL PRINCIPLES OF THE CONSTITUTION.

HAVING, in the former Lecture, presented a rapid sketch of the origin and progress of the American Confederation, down to the establishment of the present Constitution, I now propose to treat more particularly of the fundamental principles on which the Federal Government was formed, and exhibit a general view of its organization and powers. This statement of the subjects of discussion comprises a definition of the terms by which they are designated; for by a *constitution* is meant, not only the form in which a government is organized, but the principles upon which it is founded; and that branch of jurisprudence — which treats of those principles, of the practical exercise of the powers of government in conformity with them, and the construction to be given to them in such their application — has been denominated by jurists "CONSTITUTIONAL LAW."

It has been justly observed by a writer on this subject,[1] that "the origin of political constitutions is as various as their forms. In a pure and unmixed monarchy, we seldom hear," he remarks, "of a constitution; in a despotism, never. The subjects or the slaves of

[1] Mr. Rawle.

such governments may nevertheless be roused or driven to the vindication of their natural rights; and the absolute king or the obdurate tyrant may be compelled to adopt fixed, if not liberal principles of administration, or they may voluntarily concede them in favor of their subjects. So, too, a successful conqueror may, from motives of policy, establish certain forms and principles for the government of a people whom he may have subdued. In any of these cases, if the government obtained be the result of general consent, whether actually expressed or fairly to be implied, such nation or people may be said to possess a constitution. The same may be affirmed of an *aristocracy*, if the people at large agree to deposit all the powers of government in a select few; as it may also be said of a *democracy*, in which the people retain, under such modifications as they conceive most conducive to their own safety and liberty, all sovereignty within their own control. The great difficulty, however, in every such case, is to regulate the subdivisions of authority granted, so that the portion of it vested in one department or body of men, shall bear a due proportion to that vested in another. Each branch of the government should be sufficient for its own support in the exercise of its appropriate functions, yet all should be made to harmonize and coöperate.

To alter and amend an existing system, by adding new parts to the old machinery, and particularly to attempt to infuse a new spirit into the existing government, contrary to its original genius, produces an irregular and jarring combination, discordant in its elements, and confused in its operation. An exemplification of this idea is afforded by the late *reform* of the Parliament in England, where, although the elective branch has been rendered a more perfect representative of the Commons, the members of the upper house continue to sit in their individual right, and still constitute an hereditary and permanent body. We Americans may be pardoned for considering that the best mode of forming a political community is the voluntary association of a sufficient number of individuals, *on the ground of an original contract*, specifying the terms on which they are to be united, and thus to establish a new constitution or plan of government adapted to their situation, character, exigencies, and prospects. Indeed, this may be asserted to be the only true origin and firm basis of a republic.

The constitution of a government on a single principle, whether of monarchy, aristocracy, or democracy, is undoubtedly the most practical and easy, from its greater simplicity. But a constitution may embrace any two of those principles, as that of ancient Rome and those of some of the Grecian States, and, in more modern times, those of Geneva and some of the smaller communities of Italy; or a constitution may, like that of England, unite the three simple forms; a government of which description, although antiquity afforded no example of it, was pronounced by Cicero to be, if rightly organized and justly balanced, the most perfect. Modern times and our own country have shown that all the power conceded to an hereditary monarch may be safely vested in the elective head of a Democratic Republic, and that all the advantages arising from the unity of the executive power may be secured, without necessarily incurring the evils of an hereditary succession. These ends are effected by the application of that great discovery of modern politics *the principle of representation.*

By the proper distribution of the powers of government among several distinct branches, according to this fundamental principle, each of them becomes, in its respective sphere, the immediate and equal representative of the people, as the direct source of its authority, and sole ultimate depository of the sovereign power.

By the "Powers of Government," I mean those distinguished from each other, as appertaining to the Legislative, Executive, and Judicial departments; which division, founded as it is on moral order, cannot be too carefully preserved. In the wise distribution of these powers, and the application of proper aids and checks to each, consists the *optima constituta Respublica*, contemplated by the Roman orator as an object of desire and admiration, rather than of hope.

Should these three powers be injudiciously blended—for instance, should the Legislative and Executive, or the Legislative and Judicial branches be united in the same hands, the combination would be dangerous to public liberty, and the evils to be apprehended would be the same, whether the powers in question were devolved on a single magistrate, or vested in a numerous body. If, moreover, the principle of representation be applied only to a part of the government, where other parts exist independently of that principle, with an equal or superior weight to that constituted in conformity to it, the benefits of the one must obviously be partial, and the danger to be apprehended from the others, in proportion to their predominance.

As representation may thus be partial in respect to the powers of the government, so it may be confined to a portion only of the governed; and in this case, the restriction is objectionable in exact proportion to the number of those excluded from representation, or from the exercise of a free and intelligent voice in the choice of their rulers. In some countries possessing a constitution, the right or power of election is variously limited. In Venice, it was formerly, and in some of the aristocratical republics of Switzerland, it still is, the exclusive privilege of a few families. In the limited or mixed monarchies of England, Holland, and Belgium, it is confined to persons possessing property of a certain description or amount. With us, the rights of representation and suffrage are, according to the theory of the Constitution, universal; but in practice they both are qualified—without, however, impairing the general principle.

It is in defining the limits of the three great departments of government, and, by proper checks and securities, preserving the principle of representation in regard both to the exercise of the power and the enjoyment of the right, that a written constitution possesses great and manifest advantages over those which rest on traditionary information, or which are to be collected from the acts of the government itself. If the people can refer only to the ordinances and decrees of their rulers to ascertain their rights, it is obvious that, as every such act may introduce a new principle, there can be no stability in the Constitution. The powers of the representative and of the constituent are inverted; and the Legislature is, from its omnipotence, enabled to alter the Constitution at its pleasure. Nor can such laws be questioned by individuals, or declared void by the Courts of Justice, as they may with us, where the power of the legislature itself is controlled by the Constitution.

A written constitution, therefore, which may thus be

appealed to by the people, and construed and enforced by the judicial power, is most conducive to the happiness of the citizen, and the safety of the Commonwealth; and it was reserved for the present age, and the citizens of this country, fully to appreciate and soundly to apply the great principle of popular representation, and to afford the first practical example of a "SOCIAL CONTRACT." In England, one only of the coördinate branches of Government is supposed by the Constitution to represent the people; and the Provincial Constitutions of the American Colonies (with but few exceptions) had, at the period of our Revolution, been modelled in conformity with the same theory. Their charters were originally framed, or subsequently modified, so as to exclude the principle of representation from the Executive department, of which, as in England, the Judicial was considered as a subordinate branch. The solid foundations of popular government had, nevertheless, been laid; and the institutions received from the mother-country were admirably adapted to prepare the way for a temperate and rational Democratical Republic.

As the discoveries which had been made in America by European navigators, were deemed to confer the exclusive right of occupancy upon their respective sovereigns, those parts of the Continent which had been claimed as the reward of English enterprise, were appropriated as British colonies, either by extensive grants of territory and jurisdiction to favored individuals, or by encouraging settlers at large by limited territorial grants, reserving the eminent domain of the Province to the Crown, and providing for the exercise of the whole jurisdiction, under its authority. Hence two sorts of

Provincial Governments had arisen; first, those denominated *Royal* Governments, in which the general domain continued in the Crown; and, secondly, *Proprietary* Governments, in which both the territory and jurisdiction were granted by the King to one or more of his subjects. In the former case, the Chief Executive Magistrate was appointed by the Crown; in the latter, by the Proprietaries; in both, the Legislative Power was vested, wholly or partially, in the People; subject, in the one case, to the control of the King in Council; in the other, to that of the Proprietary. In some few of the colonies, indeed, the power of legislation was uncontrolled, as we have seen, by the parent state; so that, previously to the Revolution, the colonists had long been accustomed to elect representatives to compose the more numerous branch of their Legislature, and, in some instances, the second, or less numerous branch, and even their chief Executive magistrate. No hereditary powers had ever existed in the colonial governments, and all political power exercised in them was derived either from the People or from the King.

The powers of the Crown being abrogated by the successful assertion of our Independence, the *People* remained the only source of legitimate authority; and when the citizens of the several States proceeded to form their respective Constitutions, the materials in their possession, as well as their former habits, and modes of thinking and acting on political subjects, were peculiarly favorable to governments representative in all three departments; and, accordingly, such governments were almost universally adopted. Under various modifications and forms, produced in a great degree by ancient habits, the same general principles were established in every State. In general, the Legislative, Executive, and Judicial powers were kept distinct, with the manifest intention of rendering them essentially independent of each other. The Legislature was, for the most part, divided into two branches; and all persons holding offices of trust or profit were excluded from it. The Supreme Executive Magistrate was also made elective; and a strong jealousy of his power was everywhere apparent. The Superior Judges received their appointments from the Legislature or Executive, and, in most instances, the tenure of their offices was "during good behavior."

These principles formed the common and original basis of the American republics, and were adhered to in the Federal Constitution, which, while it unites them as one Nation, guarantees their separate, subordinate, and residuary sovereignty. The same fundamental principles have also been recognized and adopted in the new States since erected from the territory ceded by individual States for the common benefit, or acquired by negotiation or purchase, and subsequently admitted into the Union. There were, however, several departures from this general outline, which, in most instances, have been superseded by subsequent amendments, but in some retained in the original Constitution, and imitated in some of those which have been more recently established. In some cases, the Legislature consisted of a single body; but this peculiarity has since been abandoned. In some of the States, the tenure of Judicial office is for a term of years. In others, the Judges are elected by the People; as in Connecticut, until the adoption of a new Constitution in 1818, where they also formed one branch of the Legislature. Such, also, was the case in Rhode Island, whose Colonial Charter has even been copied, in the first of these particulars, by some of the younger members of the National Union, although, in Rhode Island itself, this provision, and the Charter containing it, have since been abrogated, and a Legislature, consisting of two branches, established by a new Constitution. The qualifications requisite to confer the privileges of an elector, and to constitute eligibility to office, are also various; and the second branch of the Legislature is, in many instances, differently constituted in different States. In some, a greater, in others, a less effort is discernible to render that body an effectual check upon the more numerous or popular branch, either by prolonging the term for which its members are elected, or requiring higher qualifications in them or their constituents.

In constituting the Executive Power, there appears at first to have been equal variety. It is now, however, uniformly vested, either in whole or in part, in a single person. In some States, he is elected for longer, in others, for shorter periods. In some, he is not eligible for two successive terms; in others, there is no such restriction. By the Constitutions of some of the States, he is invested with a qualified negative upon the Acts of the Legislature, which in others is withheld from him. In some few instances, he is intrusted with power to make appointments to certain offices — either absolutely, or, more generally, subject to the confirmation of a Council, or of the second branch of the Legislature; whilst, in most of the States, that power is exercised exclusively by the two branches of the Legislature in conjunction. In some States, the Chief Executive Magistrate is enabled to pursue the dictates of his own unbiased judgment; and in others, he is divested of all actual responsibility—either directly, by being placed under the control of a Council, or indirectly, from his being chosen by the Legislative body, or its more numerous branch. In general, however, the ancient institutions which the Provinces had derived by Charter from the Crown of Great Britain, were, at the change of government, so far preserved as was compatible with the abolition of royal or metropolitan authority and colonial dependence.

Among the most valuable of the institutions retained by the States on the change of Government, was that system of jurisprudence by which the absolute and inalienable rights of the People were recognized and secured, the relative rights of individuals, and their civil privileges regulated and maintained; and offences against public justice investigated and punished. It was held as a fundamental maxim, that the colonists, as English subjects, were entitled to the benefits and protection of the Common Law of England, and of such parts of the Statute Law of Great Britain as were applicable to their situation. This system of jurisprudence prevailed in all the colonies. It was brought from England by the original settlers, in those planted under her authority, and had been gradually and silently extended to those Provinces which had been conquered by her arms; so that, before the Revolution, it had been universally established as their municipal code, so far as it was adapted to their circumstances; and it was claimed by the Congress of 1774, as a branch of those "indubitable rights and liberties to which the respective colonies were entitled."

The most essential of these privileges were those

natural rights which are, indeed, common to all mankind, but which, in virtue of *Magna Charter*, and other fundamental laws of the mother-country, were deemed to be the peculiar birthright and inheritance of British subjects. These, according to Sir William Blackstone, comprise that *residuum* of natural liberty which is not required by the laws of society to be sacrificed to public convenience, as well as those civil privileges which society engages to provide in lieu of those natural liberties so given up by individuals for the public good. In the first class, the learned commentator comprehends, 1. The right of personal security; 2. The right of personal liberty; and 3. The right of private property.[1] The other privileges of the same character, but subordinate in degree, to which, as English subjects, the colonists were entitled, were, 1. The constitution, powers, and privileges of their Provincial Legislatures; 2. The limitation of the King's prerogative by certain and notorious bounds; 3. The right of applying to the Courts of Justice for the redress of injuries,—the most valuable incidents to which privilege, were the right of *Trial by Jury*,[2] and the benefit of the writ of

[1] A statute vesting a certain freehold in A. without judgment in law, has frequently been held in the Federal, as well as State Courts, to be void as against common right, and *Magna Charta*. 2 *Peters*, 268; 2 *Dallas*, 310; 1 *Bay*, 252; *Harper*, 200; *Cooke*, 214; 1 *Dev.* 1; 5 *Heym.* 106; 1 *Yeates*, 260; 5 *Cowen*, 346.

[2] The phrase "Common Law," in the 7th Amendment of the Constitution of the United States, providing for the trial by jury, is used in contradistinction to Equity, and Admiralty, and Maritime jurisdiction. It means not only suits which the old Common Law recognized among its settled proceedings, but all suits in which *legal* rights are to be determined in contradistinction to *equitable* rights, and cases of *Admiralty*, &c., jurisdiction. 3 *Peters*, 433. A Territorial law, direct-

Habeas Corpus; the right of petitioning the King, or either branch of the imperial or provincial Legislature, for the redress of grievances; and 5. That of keeping arms for defence; which was, indeed, a public allowance, under certain restrictions, of the natural right of resistance and self-preservation.[1]

In these several articles are contained what are emphatically termed "the Liberties of Englishmen." To their enjoyment, the colonists were entitled by birthright as British subjects; and to vindicate that right they first took up arms against the parent state, and ultimately withdrew from her dominion. Upon that separation, and the subsequent establishment of Governments of their own choice, they were careful to provide for the secure and permanent enjoyment of these their natural rights, and of the civil privileges designed for their maintenance, or substituted as their equivalents. As additional safeguards for their protection, they established, moreover, those great engines of modern opinions, *freedom of speech, and of the press,* uncontrolled by any but proper moral restraints. But while some of the States expressly recognized, and others tacitly accepted, as part of their municipal code, those portions of the Common Law which had previously been in force in

ing a Court of Common Law to decide matters of fact, is inconsistent with this provision of the Constitution. 11 *Howard*, 437.

[1] As the Constitution of Kentucky declares that "the right of the citizens to bear arms, in defence of themselves and the State shall not be questioned," a statute "to prevent persons from wearing concealed arms," was held to be void. 3 *Marshall*, 73. Also a statute of the same State, subjecting free persons of color to corporal punishment "for lifting hands in opposition" to a white person. *Ibid.* But see 2 *Blackford*, 229.

the Colonies, and were now further modified by the change of government, they universally abolished, either by their Constitutions, or by statutes deemed fundamental, that feature of the English system of real property, which, in its character of a mere civil regulation, is, nevertheless, like most others of the same feudal origin, powerfully and essentially political in its effects,—I mean *the right of primogeniture.* This harsh and inequitable rule of descent, which, indeed, is not peculiar to England, but prevails in most of the feudal monarchies of Europe, was rejected in all the American States, and each enacted its own law of descents, differing, indeed, in detail, but agreeing in the general principle of equal distribution.

The frequent violation of the natural and political rights of the colonists by both King and Parliament, and their repeated denials of redress, were set forth in the Declaration of Independence as the cause and justification of dissolving the mutual ties of sovereignty and allegiance, which bound them to each other; and upon forming the State Constitutions, those rights were, in some form or other, and with a greater or less degree of particularity and precision, enumerated, declared inalienable, and reserved inviolably to every citizen.

Such were the institutions of the several States, and such the rights of their individual citizens, when the States and their respective citizens, became, conjointly, parties to the National Compact. The same great principle of *representation* which had been embodied in the State Constitutions, was adopted as the foundation of the Government established for the Union; and the same national, political, and civil rights and privileges which had been declared to be the inalienable inheritance of the people, as citizens of the several States, were asserted to belong to them as citizens of the United States. Among these, as we have seen, are comprehended such provisions of the Common Law as were applicable to their situation and circumstances. By the AMENDMENTS insisted upon by some of the States, as conditions of their ratification of the Federal Constitution, and eventually adopted by all, it is declared that "the right of the people to be secure in their persons, houses, papers, and effects shall not be violated;" that "no warrant shall issue but upon probable cause, supported by oath or affirmation, and particularly describing the place to be searched, and the persons or things to be seized;" that "no person shall be held to answer for a capital, or otherwise infamous crime, unless on presentment or indictment of a grand-jury, except in cases arising in the land or naval forces, and in the militia when in actual service in time of war, or public danger;" that "no person shall be subject, for the same offence, to be twice put in jeopardy of life and limb,[1] nor be compelled, in any criminal case, to be a witness

[1] This provision means, that no person shall be tried a second time for the same offence, after a trial by a competent and regular jury, upon a good indictment, whether there be a verdict of acquittal or conviction. 2 *Sumner*, 19; 18 *Johnson's Rep.* 187; 5 *Lett.* 139. And it was held by STORY, J., in 2 *Sumn.* 19, that the Circuit Courts of the United States could not grant a new trial, in a capital case, even after *a verdict of conviction* rendered on a sufficient indictment. DAVIS, Dis. Judge, dissenting. In Mississippi, this Amendment has been held to bind the State Courts, as well as those of the United States. *Walker*, 134. But see 2 *Sumn.* 19; 19 *Cowen*, 820; *Ibid.* 701; 8 *Wendell*, 100; 12 *Cowen*, 243, and many other decisions of the State Courts to the same effect.

against himself; nor be deprived of life, liberty, or property, without due process of law;" that "private property shall not be taken for public use, without just compensation;" that "in all criminal prosecutions, the accused shall enjoy the right to a speedy and public trial by an impartial jury in the State or district wherein the crime shall have been committed,—which district shall have been previously ascertained by law,—to be informed of the nature and cause of the accusation,—to be confronted with the witnesses against him, and to have compulsory process for obtaining witnesses in his favor, and the assistance of counsel for his defence;" that, "in suits at Common Law, where the value in controversy shall exceed a certain small amount, the right of trial by jury shall be preserved;" that "no fact tried by a jury shall be otherwise reëxamined in any Court of the United States, than according to the rules of the Common Law;" and that "excessive bail shall not be required, nor cruel and unusual punishments inflicted."[1]

But these Amendments apply only to the United States, and not to the States severally; and the rights secured by them are subject, in their assertion, to some modifications and restrictions. Thus, private property cannot be taken by the public for merely *ornamental* purposes. The purpose must be "*necessary and useful.*"[2] It may be taken by a military commander to prevent it from falling into the hands of an enemy, or for the purpose of converting it to the use of the public; but the danger must be immediate and impending, and the

[1] Amendts. to Const. U. S. 4, 5, 6, 7, 8.

[2] 7 *Peters*, 243; 8 *Wend.* 85; 12 *Pickering*, 48.

necessity urgent—such as will not admit delay, and where the action of the civil authority would be too late in providing the means which the occasion calls for. Nor can such officer take possession of private property for the purpose of securing the success of an expedition upon which he is about to march; nor justify the trespass by showing the order of his superior officer. If it were committed without the limits of the United States, an action for it may be maintained in the Circuit Court of any district in which the offender may be found, where the citizenship of the respective parties gives jurisdiction to the Court.[1] Again: where the Legislature authorize the taking of such private property, the compensation must be previously settled, either by stipulation between the Legislature and the proprietor, or by Commissioners mutually agreed on by the parties; or by the intervention of a jury;[2] and until just indemnity be afforded, the power of taking the property cannot be exercised.[3] It is, however, sufficient if the indemnity be secured. The principle upon which this doctrine is founded, is that the owner of the land takes it subject to the right of *eminent domain* in the State, for public purposes.[4] The power in question is incident to the sovereignty of every Government, which, moreover, must judge of the necessity or expediency of its exercise.

With respect to the right of trial by Jury, the Amendment on that subject has been held to be restricted to suits not of Equity or Admiralty jurisdiction; although

1 2 *Dall.* 313.

2 2 *Johns. Ch. Rep.* 162; 1 *Baldwin*, 205; 4 *Washington, C. C.* 601.

3 13 *Howard*, 115.

4 3 *Yerg.* 41; 2 *N. and M.* 387; 2 *Bay*, 38.

admitted to embrace all others, whatever peculiar form they may assume, to settle legal rights.[1]

It has been a subject of much discussion whether the United States, in their national capacity, have actually adopted the Common Law; and to what extent, if at all, it may be considered as forming a part of the National Jurisprudence. But however doubtful it may be whether, in its broadest sense, and to the same extent, *mutatis mutandis*, that it prevails in England, and in some of the States, that code is recognized as the Common Law of the Union, it cannot be denied that it forms the *substratum* of the laws of all its original members, and, consequently, of the new States formed from their subdivision; nor, that the Constitution of the United States, as well as the Constitutions and laws of the several States, was made in reference to the pre-existing validity of the Common Law in the Colonial and State Governments. In many instances, the language of these public acts would be inexplicable without recourse to the Common Law of England; and, not only is the existence of that system supposed by the Constitution of the United States, but it is constantly appealed to for the construction of powers granted to the Federal Government. The general question, however, as to the application and influence of the system in reference to our National institutions, has not been settled upon clear and definite principles, and may still be regarded, especially in civil cases, as open for further judicial investigation. The prevailing opinion, at present, seems to be, that under the Federal

[1] 1 *Baldw.* 221; 1 *Ham.* 247, 249; 4 *Ibid.* 253; 2 *Greenleaf*, 5, 255; 3 *Ibid.* 97; 7 *Ibid.* 273; 3 *Watts*, 294; 7 *Mass. Rep.* 395; 2 *Bailey*, 321; *Miner*, 75; 3 *Steward*, 42.

Government, the Common Law, considered as a *source of jurisdiction*, was never in force; but considered merely as *a means or instrument* of exercising the jurisdiction conferred by the Constitution, it does exist in full validity, and forms a safe and beneficial portion of our National Code.

The Constitution erected on this basis, and from these materials, is declared by its preamble, to be "ordained and established by *the People of the United States*, in order to form a more perfect union, establish justice, insure domestic tranquillity, provide for the common defence, promote the general welfare, and secure the blessings of liberty to themselves and their posterity." By the terms, therefore, of this compact, the States are no longer known to each other merely in their sovereign and corporate capacities; but, without destroying their previous separate organization, *the People* of the respective States united with each other in founding a new Government operating directly on themselves as individuals, for the attainment of objects for which neither the States separately, nor the former Confederation had been found competent. The principle of representation is applied in it, not only to the individual citizens of the respective States as citizens of the United States, but also to the individual States themselves; and it pervades the three great departments of which the Government consists.

Besides a general delegation of the Legislative, Executive, and Judicial powers to distinct departments, so far as was necessary to effect the purposes of National Union, the Constitution specially defines the powers and duties of each of those branches of the Government. This was essential to peace and safety in a Government, invested with specific powers for national objects, and formed from the union of several independent States, as well as of the individuals composing them; each of the former yielding, for that purpose, the requisite portion of its sovereignty, while it retained the exclusive control of its local concerns.

In analyzing the Federal Constitution, it may, therefore, be considered, as has been already indicated, under two principal points of view, viz:—

First. With regard to the particular structure and organization of the Government, and the distribution of its powers among the several branches; in reference to which, the necessary provisions for their organization into separate departments,—for making, executing, and expounding the laws,—for rendering efficient those powers,—and for confining them to their respective spheres, as well as for ascertaining the limits between the National and State jurisdictions,—are all contained in that instrument.

Secondly. With regard to the nature, extent, and limitation of the powers conferred on the Government of the Union, and the restraints imposed on the State governments.

As different views and interests have at different times prevailed, different theories for the construction of the Constitution have been advanced. It has sometimes been regarded as a mere confederacy or alliance between the States, implying no surrender of their sovereign power or character; but this opinion is manifestly inconsistent with the nature of the Federal compact, as explained by judicial interpretation of conclusive authority, as will be seen hereafter. Some jurists and politicians, however, who, although they admit that it constitutes a *Government*, contend that, inasmuch as it establishes a Government of limited powers, it should be construed strictly; whilst others have asserted that, from the extensive and high objects to be accomplished by the exercise of those powers, the most liberal interpretation should be allowed. As, on the one hand, a strict adherence to the letter, without regarding the spirit, or pursuing the manifest sense of the instrument, can only proceed from groundless jealousy, or concealed hostility to the system, so, on the other, a liberal construction may, from the possession or desire of power under it, be carried to a pernicious extreme. Limitations and restrictions may be conceived to exist by some, which would render nugatory the National authority, and were, therefore, never meant to be imposed; while concessions of power may be imagined or assumed by others, incompatible with the sovereignty retained by the States, if not unnecessary to give effect to the Federal supremacy. The true rule of interpretation seems to be no other than that which is applied in all cases of correct and impartial exposition, viz: to deduce the meaning of the contract from its known design and entire language,—to reconcile, and, if possible, to give effect to every part of the instrument, and at the same time, to preserve the unity and harmony of the whole, in due regard to the expressions, as well as to the intentions, of the parties.

As was observed by Mr. Justice Story, in delivering the opinion of the Court in a leading and important case,[1] "it will be probably found, when we look to the character of the Constitution itself, that the objects

[1] In Prigg *v.* The Commonwealth of Pennsylvania, 16 *Peters*, 539.

which it seeks to attain, the powers which it confers, the duties which it enjoins, and the rights which it secures, as well as to the known historical fact that many of its provisions were matters of compromise of opposing interests and opinions, that no uniform rule of interpretation can be applied which may not allow, even if it does not positively demand, many modifications in its actual application to particular clauses. Perhaps," said he, "the safest rule of interpretation, after all, will be found to be to look to the nature and objects of the particular powers, duties, and rights, with all the lights and aids of contemporary history, and to give to the words of each, such operation and force, consistent with their legitimate meaning, as to fairly secure and attain the ends proposed."

On many questions which have already arisen, we have the benefit of equally learned elucidations of the judicial departments of the General Government, and of many of the State Governments; and wherever the Supreme federal tribunal has pronounced its solemn decision, its authority must be deemed conclusive; because that Court, and that Court alone, possesses ultimate and final jurisdiction upon all points of controversy arising under the Constitution of the United States. But where a guide so certain and authoritative cannot be found, we must endeavor, with the aid of inferior lights, to discover the true, but latent meaning of a Constitution, which, in the language of that venerable and accomplished jurist, the late Chancellor of New York, "must always be more admired, as it is more considered, and better understood."

LECTURE III.

OF THE LEGISLATIVE POWER.

THE first general point of view in which it was proposed to consider the Federal Constitution, was "*with regard to the particular structure and organization of the Government, and the distribution of its powers among its several branches.*"

I have already had occasion to advert to the rule inculcating the separation of the Legislative, Executive, and Judicial departments, and to remark that it had been substantially adhered to in framing our National Government. These different branches, however, have not, in all cases, been kept entirely distinct; and it therefore becomes necessary to ascertain, *in limine*, the meaning of a political apothegm, of which none is of more intrinsic value, or stamped with the approbation of a more enlightened authority.

From the sense in which the maxim in question was first applied by Montesquieu to the English Constitution, as well as from the mode in which it has been practically acknowledged in our State Constitutions, it is evident that it was never understood to require that the three departments should be wholly unconnected with each other. On the contrary, it has been satisfactorily shown by the authors of "The Federalist,"[1] that

[1] In No. 47, by Mr. Madison.

unless they be so far connected and blended as to give to each a constitutional control over the others, the degree of separation which the rule requires, cannot be maintained. It is, indeed, obvious, that the powers properly belonging to one of the departments ought not to be directly and completely administered by either of the others. It is equally clear that, in reference to the others, neither branch should possess, directly or indirectly, an overruling influence in the exercise of their peculiar powers; and although, in our Governments, each department derives its authority from the same source, and equally represents the People, yet the Legislative branch, as its constitutional powers are at once more extensive, and less susceptible of precise limitation than either of the others, must necessarily possess a greater preponderance in the political system, and act with greater force upon the public mind. In order, therefore, to maintain in practice the requisite partition of power, the internal structure of the Government should be so contrived as to render its constituent parts, by their mutual relations, the means of keeping each other within their proper spheres of action.[1]

[1] There is nothing, however, in the Constitution of the United States which forbids the Legislature of a State to exercise Judicial functions; and, accordingly, in some of the States, where no such restraint exists, it has been the practice for the Legislature to grant appeals and new trials in civil suits. But a State Legislature cannot annul the jurisdiction of the Federal Courts; nor, as it seems, authoritatively declare what the law is, or *has been*, but only what it *shall be*. 2 *Peters*, 413; 2 *Root*, 350; 2 *Dall.* 419, *note;* 3 *Ibid.* 309; 3 *Greenl.* 334; 2 *Cranch*, 272; 5 *Ibid.* 115; 4 *Pick.* 23. But this must be understood to be meant when exercising Judicial powers. See 2 *Peters*, 660; 19 *Mass. Rep.* 328; 1 *N. H.* 199; 4 *Ibid.* 572; 4 *Serg. & Rawle*, 435; *Walker*, 258; 4 *Munro*, 91–381; 6 *Ibid.* 594; 10

The great security against a gradual concentration of the several powers of government in the same hands, consists in giving to the persons who administer them in one department, the necessary constitutional means and personal motives to resist encroachments from the others. A dependence on the people is, no doubt, the primary control over the Government; but experience had shown to the framers of our Constitution, the necessity of auxiliary precautions; and the remedy they adopted for the natural predominance of the Legislative authority, was the division of the Legislative body into two branches, and rendering them, by different modes of election, and principles of action, as little connected with each other as the nature of their common functions, and their dependence on the people, would admit. The comparative weakness of the Executive branch, on the other hand, was fortified by investing it with a qualified negative upon the Acts of the Legislature, and connecting it with the weaker branch of that stronger power, by allowing the latter to participate in certain Executive duties; while the Judicial department was deemed to be equally secure, from the nature of its constitutional powers, the permanency of its character, and the independent tenure by which its functionaries hold their offices. Thus the mutual participation, to a limited extent, of the several branches of the Government in each other's powers, is rendered subservient to their mutual independence, and the apparent violation of a fundamental principle of the Constitution, converted into a security for its preservation.

I now proceed to examine and explain the organiza-

Yerg. 59; 3 *Greenl.* 326; 4 *Ibid.* 140; 2 *Chipm.* 77; 1 *Ack.* 314; *Hardin*, 856.

tion of these separate departments in their order, and commence with a review of the *Legislative Power;* under which title I shall consider:—

First. The constituent parts of the Legislature, with the mode of their election, or appointment.

Secondly. Their joint and several powers and privileges.

And, *Thirdly,* Their method of enacting laws, with the times and modes of their assembling and adjourning.

I. All Legislative powers *granted by the Constitution,* are vested in a CONGRESS OF THE UNITED STATES, consisting of a SENATE, and a HOUSE OF REPRESENTATIVES.[1] The terms conferring the Legislative authority import its limitation to the objects specified in the Constitution. And besides the end already stated to have been proposed by the division of the Legislature into two branches, another important object is accomplished by it, and that is the preventing of the evil effects of excitement and precipitation, which had been found, by sad experience, to exert a powerful and dangerous sway in single assemblies. No portion of the political history of mankind, according to the elder President Adams, in his celebrated Defence of our American Constitutions, is more full of instructive lessons on this subject, or contains more striking proofs of the factious instability and turbulent misery of States under the dominion of a single unchecked Legislature, than the annals of the Italian Republics of the middle ages. They arose in great numbers, and with dazzling, but transient splendor, in the interval between the falls of the Western and Eastern Empires, and were

[1] Const. U. S., Art. I. Sect. 1.

all constituted with a single unbalanced Legislative Assembly. They were alike wretched in existence, and all ended in similar disgrace. At the commencement of the first French Revolution, many of their speculative politicians seem to have been struck with the *simplicity* of a Legislature, consisting of a single *Chamber*, and concluded that more was useless and expensive. This led that veteran statesman to write and publish, during his diplomatic residence in Europe, his great work entitled "*A Defence of the Constitutions of Government of the United States*," in which he vindicates, with great learning and ability, the advantage and necessity of dividing the Legislature into two branches, and of distributing the powers of government among distinct departments. He reviewed the history, and examined the Constitutions, of all the mixed and free governments which had existed from the earliest records of time, in order to deduce, with more certainty and force, his great practical truth, that single Legislatures without check or balance, or a Government with all authority collected in one centre or department, were violent, intriguing, corrupt, and tyrannical dominations of majorities over minorities, uniformly and rapidly terminating their career in profligate despotism; and the correctness of his deduction was amply confirmed by the subsequent example of France.

The visionary notion of a single Assembly was embodied in the Constitution adopted in that country in 1791; and the same false and vicious principle continued for some time, to prevail with the sublimated theorists of that period. A single chamber was again established in the plan of government published by the Convention of 1793. But their own sufferings, at length, taught the French people to listen to that oracle of wisdom, the experience of other nations and other ages, which, amid the tumult and violence of the passions that influenced them, they had utterly disregarded, and which, under any circumstances, their national vanity would probably have led them to despise. "No people," said *Boissy d'Anglas*, one of their greatest orators, "can testify to the world, with more truth and sincerity than the French, the dangers inherent in a single Legislative body, and the point to which the faction may mislead an assembly without check or counterpoise." We find, accordingly, that in the next of their ephemeral Constitutions, which was brought forth in 1797, there was a division of the Legislature into two branches, and the *idea* of two chambers has never been abandoned, either under the military despotism of the first Empire, in the Charters obtained upon the restoration of the Monarchy—in the subsequent revolution and change of dynasty—or upon the revival of a second despotic Empire.

Our country had, indeed, afforded more than one instance in point, in which, fortunately, however, the evil consequences were by no means so great as those experienced in France. The Legislatures of Pennsylvania and Georgia consisted originally of a single House, but the instability and passion which marked their proceedings, far short as these were of the least of the atrocities of the French National Convention, were the subject of much public animadversion at the time; and in the subsequent reforms of their Constitutions, the people of those States were so sensible of this defect, and of the evils they had suffered from it, that a Senate was introduced into the amended Constitution of each.

There was a further reason for a division of the Legislative powers in the Government of the United States, arising from its federative character, and which, from its peculiar importance, deserves a fuller explanation. On those just principles of public polity on which our Constitution is founded, it is essential that in communities thoroughly incorporated into one nation, the inhabitants of every geographical district, or territorial subdivision, should have their *proportional* share in the National Government; whilst, among independent sovereign States, bound together by a simple league, the several parties, however unequal in respect to territory and population, should have an *equal* share in the Federal Councils. It was, therefore, reasonable and proper, that in a Republic partaking of both the National and Federal characters, the Government should be founded on a union of both those principles of representation. Hence, in the constitution of the Legislative Power, the House of Representatives was constructed on the principle of *proportional*, and the Senate on that of *equal* representation; and although this equality in the latter was evidently the result of a compromise between the larger and smaller States, yet, as it afforded a convenient and effectual mode of applying the rule of combined representation to that coördinate branch of the Legislature, and necessarily induced a separation of the two bodies of which Congress is composed, its adoption was the more strongly recommended.

1. The House of Representatives was accordingly founded on the principle of *proportional* representation—yet not purely and abstractedly so; but with as much conformity to that principle as was practicable. It is

composed of representatives of the people *of the several States*, not of the people *of the United States collectively and at large;* and, in this respect, it partakes of the *federative* quality. Neither are the qualifications of its electors uniform, inasmuch as great variety of opinion and practice exists concerning them in the several States. The Representatives in Congress are chosen every second year by the people of the several States, who are qualified to vote for the most numerous branch of their State Legislature. No person can be a representative until he has attained the age of twenty-five years, and has been seven years a citizen of the United States; nor unless he is an inhabitant of the State for which he is chosen. When vacancies happen from death or resignation in the representation of any State, its Executive authority is directed to issue writs of election to fill them, either at a general or special election.[1]

The general qualifications of the electors of the most numerous branch of the State Legislatures are, that they be past the age of twenty-one years, free resident citizens of the State in which they vote, and have paid taxes thereto. In some of the States, they are required to possess property of a certain description or amount, and in others, to be *white* as well as free citizens. These different qualifications are, in some instances, differently combined, or restricted, and modified; and, in most others, are so large as to include all persons who are of competent discretion, and interested in the welfare of the Government; liable to perform any of its duties, or bear any of its burdens; so that, upon the whole, the House of Representatives may be said very fairly to represent the aggregate body of the American People.

[1] Const. U. S., Art. I. Sect. II. 4.

Several of the State Constitutions have prescribed the same, if not higher, qualifications in the elected than in the electors, and some of them require a religious test; but the Constitution of the United States requires no evidence of property in the Representative, nor any declaration of his religious belief. He is merely required to be a citizen of competent age, and free from undue bias or dependence, by not holding any office of trust or profit under the United States. The term for which he is elected to serve is not so short as to prevent his obtaining a comprehensive acquaintance with his duties, nor so long as to tempt him to forget his dependence on the approbation of his constituents. For, as on the one hand, frequent elections tend to diminish the importance of the office, and to render the electors indifferent to the exercise of their right; so, on the other, long intervals between the elections are apt to produce too much excitement, and, consequently, to render the periods of their return, a season of more severe competition and conflict, and of more serious disturbance of the public tranquillity. The Constitution has not, certainly, deviated to the latter extreme in the establishment of biennial elections. Considering not only the present extent and situation of the country, but also the probability of its future enlargement, the medium adopted seems to combine as many advantages, and avoid as many difficulties, as any other term which might have been chosen.

The Representatives are directed to be apportioned among the States according to numbers; which are determined in each State by adding to the whole number of free persons, exclusive of Indians, not taxed, three fifths of all other persons. This rule of apportionment is obnoxious to the objection that three fifths of the slaves in those States where slavery exists are computed in settling the representation. But this provision, which thus enables those States to swell their representative population, and thereby increase their political weight and influence, was the result of a compromise, without which, the Federal Union, if formed at all, would not have comprehended the States in question; and the same rule that apportions the Representatives in Congress, extends to the apportionment of direct taxes; so that while their slaves give to those States an increased representation, they contribute also to increase the amount of their taxes, when the direct mode of levying them is resorted to. The mischief, however, is, that the undue preponderance thus obtained in the public councils has hitherto prevented, and may in future always prevent, a recourse to that species of taxation, except during a part of those brief periods in which the country has since been, or may hereafter be, engaged in foreign war.

The Constitution directed an actual enumeration of the people to be made within three years after the first meeting of Congress, and provides that one be taken, in virtue of Acts passed for that purpose, within every subsequent period of ten years.[1] The number of Representatives cannot exceed one for every thirty thousand; but each State is entitled to at least one Representative. Upon the return of the first *Census*, it was conceived by Congress that, without invading the Constitution, the principle of apportionment might, with advantage, be so modified as to prevent the loss in

[1] Const. U. S., Art. I. Sect. II. 3.

the number of Representatives arising from the fractional parts produced by the application of the *ratio* of representation to the representative population of *the respective States.* The aggregate number of the representative population of *the United States*, as ascertained by that census, was accordingly divided by the *ratio* adopted in the bill, which was thirty thousand, and the operation was found to produce the quotient of one hundred and twenty; whereupon that number of Representatives was apportioned among the several States, until as many Representatives as it would give were assigned to each State, and then the residuary or surplus number was distributed among the States having the highest fractional numbers, until the whole number of one hundred and twenty was exhausted. After much debate, and strong opposition, this bill passed both Houses of Congress; but the correct and independent mind of President Washington could not reconcile its provisions with the Constitution, and he returned the bill to the House of Representatives, in which it had originated, with this objection, "that the Constitution had provided that the number of Representatives should not exceed one for every thirty thousand, which *ratio* was to be applied to the respective numbers of the States;[1] whereas the bill allotted to several of the States more than one Representative for every thirty thousand of its population." As there was not a Constitutional majority to pass the bill, notwithstanding the objections of the President, it was consequently rejected. A new one was immediately brought in and passed, adopting the *ratio* of thirty-three thousand, applying it to the numbers of the

[1] Const. U. S., Art. I. Sect. II. 3.

States respectively, and without providing for the representations of the fractional remainders. This course was pursued on every subsequent occasion, until the last; although, on the return of the fifth census, a proposal for the representation of the fractional parts, similar in principle to the former one, was adopted in the Senate, but rejected by the House. In this case, although the *ratio* adopted exceeded thirty thousand, and was fixed by an amendment in the Senate at forty-seven thousand, yet this *ratio* was applied, as before, to the aggregate number of the representative population of the United States in order to obtain the number of Representatives, who were then, in like manner, apportioned among the several States, and the residuary members distributed among those having the highest fractions exceeding twenty-five thousand. In this last respect, therefore, the amendment in question was liable to the objection of assigning a Representative to a less number than thirty thousand.

The principle upon which this objection was founded seems, however, to have been disregarded in the last Act of Congress on the subject; the provisions of which, to a certain extent, assume a permanent character. It provides that the House of Representatives shall hereafter consist of two hundred and thirty-three members, to be apportioned among the several States by the Secretary of the Interior, who is directed upon the return of the census, to ascertain the number of the representative population of the United States, and divide it by two hundred and thirty-three, the products of which division, rejecting fractions, is declared to be the *ratio*, or rule of apportionment of Representatives among the several States. He is then to ascertain the representative population of each State, and divide it by the *ratio* already determined by him; the product of which last division gives the number of Representatives apportioned to such State. The loss in the number of members caused by the fractions remaining in the several States is compensated by assigning an additional member to so many of the States having the largest fractions as may be necessary to make the whole number of Representatives two hundred and thirty-three. If, after the apportionment, a new State be admitted into the Union, the Representative assigned to it is to be added to the above number; but this excess is to continue only until the next succeeding apportionment.[1]

It will be observed that this elaborate plan is open to the objection interposed by President Washington to the first apportionment bill, in which he was sustained by Congress, inasmuch as, in assigning the deficient members to the States having the highest fractions, it does not provide that each fraction shall exceed thirty thousand — the number required by the Constitution to entitle a State to more than one Representative.

To guard against a refractory disposition, should it ever appear in any of the States, in the neglect or refusal to exercise the right vested in them by the Constitution, of prescribing the time, places, and manner of holding elections of Representatives, Congress is empowered, at any time to make or alter such regulations.[2]

[1] The subsequent admission of California into the Union, with two Representatives, makes the whole number of the present House of Representatives, two hundred and thirty-five. The *ratio* of representation for the next House, is one Representative for every 93,420 of representative population.

[2] Const. U. S., Art. I. Sect. IV. 1.

This power was, for the first time, exercised by the twenty-fifth Congress, by an Act directing the State Legislatures to divide their respective States into as many districts for the election of their Representatives in Congress, as there are Representatives to be elected in each; and that each district shall consist of contiguous territory, and contain an equal number of persons, as nearly as may be, without dividing counties, or other similar subdivisions. Several of those States in which the principles of anti-federalism and *nullification* prevail, demurred in carrying this regulation into effect, and at last yielded only a reluctant consent.

2. THE SENATE of the United States consists of two Senators from each State, chosen by its Legislature, for six years, and each Senator has one vote.[1] If a vacancy happen during a recess of the Legislature, the Executive power of the State may make temporary appointments until the next meeting of the Legislature, when the vacancy must be filled in the ordinary manner. Each State, therefore, has its equal voice and weight in the Senate of the Union, without regard to disparity of population, wealth, or territory. The number of two Senators would, however, have been found inconvenient if the votes in the Senate had been taken, as in the Congress of the Confederation, by States. There, if the delegates of a State were equally divided, its vote was lost; and this, of course, rendered an uneven number preferable. But from the numerical vote taken *per capita* upon all questions in the Senate, a division of opinion between the Senators of a particular State has no such influence on the general result.

[1] Const. U. S., Art I. Sect. III. 1.

The election of Senators in Congress by the State Legislatures has the double advantage of favoring a select appointment, and of giving to the State Governments such an essential agency in the organization of the General Government as recognizes and preserves them, in their sovereign character, living and active members of the federal body. Whether the choice of Senators should be made by the joint or concurrent vote of the two branches of the State Legislatures, the Constitution does not direct. Hence, difficulties have arisen as to its meaning. The difference between the two modes of election is, that, on a joint vote, the members of both branches of the Legislature assemble together for the purpose, and vote *numerically;* while a concurrent vote is taken by each House separately, and the decision of one is subject to the approval of the other. The difficulties alluded to, have arisen in cases of their disagreement; but as the Legislatures may prescribe the manner, as well as the times and places, of choosing Senators, it has been considered in several of the States, that the Legislature may direct them to be chosen by the joint vote or ballot by both Houses assembled together for the purpose, in cases of non-concurrence; and then, of course, the weight of the least numerous branch is dissipated and overcome by the heavier vote of the other. This construction has been found the most convenient, and has been too long settled by the repeated recognitions of Senators so elected to be now disturbed; but were the question an open one, I think it might be maintained that where the Constitution directed the Federal Senators to be chosen in each State "by the Legislature thereof," it meant the *Legislature* in the true technical sense of the term — consisting of two branches, acting in their separate organized capacities, with the ordinary constitutional negative on each other's proceedings, and not the members of the two Houses *per capita.*

The smaller number and longer duration of the Senate were intended to render it a safeguard against those paroxysms of heat and passion which occasionally prevail in more popular assemblies. The characteristic qualities of the Senate, in the intendment of the Constitution, are wisdom and experience. The legal presumption, therefore, is that it will entertain more enlarged views of public policy, feel a higher and juster sense of national character, and a greater regard for permanence and stability in the administration of the government, than a more numerous and changeable body. These qualities, indeed, may be found in the other branch of the Legislature, but its constitutional structure is not so well calculated to produce them; for, as the House of Representatives comes more immediately from the people, and its members hold their seats for a much shorter term, they are presumed to partake, with a quicker sensibility, of the prevailing temper and irritable disposition of the times, and to be in much more danger of adopting measures with precipitancy and changing them with levity, than the more sage and experienced members of the more select and less numerous body. In order, therefore, to counteract these propensities, to maintain a greater confidence in the Government, and to insure its safety at home and its character abroad, it was necessary that another body of men, coming likewise, though mediately, from the people, and equally responsible to them for their conduct, but resting on a more permanent basis, and constituted with stronger tendency to moderation in debate, and tenacity of purpose, should be placed as a check upon the natural intemperance of the younger and more popular branch.

The Senate, at its first organization, was divided, in the mode pointed out in the Constitution, into three classes. The rotation intended to be produced by that division was originally determined by lot, and the seats of one of the classes become vacant at the expiration of every second year; so that one third of the Senate is regularly chosen every two years.[1] This provision was borrowed from some of the State Constitutions, of which that of Virginia gave the first example; and it is admirably well calculated, on the one hand, to infuse into the Senate renewed confidence and vigor, and on the other, to retain a large portion of experienced members, duly initiated into the general principles of national policy, and the forms and course of legislative business.

II. The House of Representatives possesses the sole power of *impeachment*, or of presenting accusations against public officers of the United States for malversation in their offices.[2] It has also the exclusive right of originating all bills *for raising revenue*;[3] and this is the only privilege which that House possesses, that is not equally shared with the other; and even these revenue bills are amendable by the Senate at its discretion; so that in all business pertaining to legislation, each House is an entire and perfect check upon the other. The pro-

[1] Const. U. S., Art. I. Sect. III. 2.

[2] *Ibid.*, Art. I. Sect. II. 5.

[3] *Ibid.*, Art. I. Sect. VII. 1.

ceedings of the House of Representatives are conducted with open doors, except on very special occasions. This publicity affords the people early and authentic information of the progress, reason, and policy of measures pending before Congress, and is, moreover, a powerful stimulus to industry and research, and to the cultivation of talent and eloquence in debate. These advantages, indeed, are doubtless acquired at the expense of much useless discussion, and much valuable time; yet the balance of utility is greatly in favor of open deliberation, and it is very certain, from the opposition made to the experiment of the first Senate to sit with closed doors, that such a practice, by any legislative body in this country, would not be endured.

The Senate has the sole power of trying impeachments.[1] The first recognition in the Federal Constitution, of a court for that purpose, is in the Article we are now examining, which declares that "the House of Representatives shall have the sole power of impeachment," and that "the Senate shall have the sole power to try all impeachments." The term is thus introduced into the Constitution, as of a known and definite signification; and a well-constituted court for the trial of impeachments was considered by the authors of "The Federalist"[2] as an object not more to be desired than difficult to be obtained, in a government wholly elective. The delicacy and magnitude of a trust which so deeply concerns the political reputation and existence of every one engaged in the administration of public affairs, may be readily perceived; as will, also, the difficulty of

[1] Const. U. S., Art. I. Sect. III. 6.

[2] No. 65, by Mr. Hamilton.

placing it rightly in a government in which the most conspicuous persons are the leaders, and too often the instruments of party, and can, therefore, hardly be expected to possess the neutrality requisite in regard to those whose conduct may be submitted to their scrutiny. It would be improper, too, to commit the cognizance of those offences which are the objects of impeachments to the ordinary courts of justice, as the complexities and variety of political delinquencies are too numerous and artful to be anticipated by positive enactment, and sometimes too subtle and mysterious to be fully detected and exposed in the limited period of ordinary investigation. A peculiar tribunal seems, therefore, useful and necessary,—an institution of a liberal and comprehensive character; confined as little as possible to strict forms; enabled to continue its sessions as long as the nature of the case before it may require; qualified to view the charge in all its bearings and dependences, and to appreciate, on sound principles of public policy, the defence of the accused.

To compose this Court of persons wholly distinct from the other branches of the Government, and forming a permanent body for the single purpose of exercising this jurisdiction, would have been as inconvenient as to appoint and collect temporary judges whenever an impeachment may be determined upon. The Convention that formed the Constitution thought it most fit and safe to make the Senate the depository of this important trust; and upon a review of all the departments of the Government, no other could have been found so suitable for such a jurisdiction. The model from which the institution was borrowed, was the British House of Peers, which had been previously followed in some of the State Constitutions. Besides the reasons already suggested against intrusting its exercise to the ordinary courts, there remains this further consideration, that the punishment consequent upon conviction, is not the only one to which the offence is liable. The judgment in cases of impeachment, extends no further than removal from office, and disqualification to hold in future any office of trust or profit under the United States. But the party convicted is, nevertheless, subject to prosecution, according to the usual course of administering the law; and it would obviously be improper, if not in a high degree dangerous, that the same tribunal that had already disposed of the fame and character of the accused, and of his most valuable political rights as a citizen, should, in another trial for the same offence, be also the arbiter of his life, liberty, or property.

The only persons liable to impeachment with us, are those, as we have seen, who are, or have been, in public office. But a construction has been given to the Constitution, by which a member of the Senate was held not to be liable to impeachment. The deliberations of the Court being had in secret, we can only infer from the arguments urged at the bar, that the term "officers" used in the Constitution was held not to include Senators; and on the same principle members of the House of Representatives would also be exempt from liability to this jurisdiction. The grounds of the distinction may probably have been that the power of impeachment was intended merely as a check given to the Legislative upon the other two departments; and that, as each House of Congress was the judge of its own members, all the ends of justice might be attained by the expulsion of a delinquent member.

When sitting as a Court for the trial of impeachments, the Senators are put under oath or affirmation, faithfully and impartially to discharge their judicial functions. No person can be convicted but with the concurrence of two thirds of *the members of the Court;* the Vice-President of the United States, as President of the Senate, being a "member of the Court," with a constant, instead of a contingent vote, presides in it, except when the President of the United States is tried, on which occasion the Chief-Justice presides.

The Senate, moreover, in its exclusive connection with the Executive department, has a negative upon the nomination by the President of all officers whose appointment is not otherwise provided for in the Constitution; and the advice and consent of two thirds of the Senators present are requisite to all treaties, which are submitted to the consideration of the Senate alone. The Senate, however, is not consulted in the first instance; but when a treaty is agreed upon by the agents employed in its negotiation, the President, unless he disapprove it, submits it to the Senate, and renders to them, from time to time, such information relative to it as they may desire, unless the public good requires it to be withheld. The Senate may wholly reject a treaty, or they may ratify it in part, or recommend additional or explanatory articles which, if the President approve, become the subject of further negotiation with the foreign power. When the whole receives the sanction of the Senate, the ratifications are exchanged, and the treaty becomes obligatory upon both nations. Although not required by the Constitution, yet, from the fitness and exigency of the case, the proceedings of the Senate on these occasions are always with closed doors; and the contents of the treaty, and the information connected with it are, from motives of delicacy and good policy, kept secret until the publication or other termination of the negotiations in regard to it, render such reserve no longer necessary.

From the superior weight and delicacy of the trusts thus confided to the Senate, the Constitution requires that a Senator be thirty years of age, nine years a citizen, and, at the time of his election, an inhabitant of the State for which he is chosen.

Although no express power is given by the Constitution to either House of Congress to provide for contempt, except when committed by one of its own members, yet such power is necessarily implied with respect to others who commit contempts in its presence; and extends to the imprisonment of the guilty party. Without this power, either House would be exposed to any indignity and interruption that rudeness or caprice, or even conspiracy, might perpetrate or meditate against it. But the imprisonment must, at all events, terminate with the adjournment of Congress, or the periodical dissolution of the House of Representatives inflicting it.

III. Each House is the judge of the elections, returns, and qualifications of its own members; and a majority of each constitutes a quorum for the transaction of business; but a smaller number may adjourn from day to day, and may compel the attendance of absent members, in such manner, and under such penalties, as it may provide. Each determines the rules of its proceedings, punishes its members for disorderly behaviour, and, with the concurrence of two thirds, may expel a member. It is obligatory upon each to keep a journal of its proceedings, and, from time to time, to publish the same, excepting such parts as may in its judgment require secrecy; and the yeas and nays of its members must, at the desire of one fifth of the members present, be taken and entered on its journal.[1] The members of each House receive a compensation for their services, provided by law, and paid out of the treasury of the United States.[2] In all cases, except treason, felony, and breach of the peace, they are privileged from arrest during their attendance, and going to and returning from the sessions of their respective Houses; nor can they be questioned in any other place, for any speech or debate in either.[3]

The rules of proceeding in each House are substantially the same; and are such as are essential to the transaction of business with order and safety. The House of Representatives chooses its *Speaker*,[4] or presiding officer, from among its own members; and it also chooses its other officers. But the Vice-President of the United States is, *ex officio*, President of the Senate, having, however, no vote therein, unless the Senators be equally divided. The Senate chooses its other officers; and a President *pro tempore*, from its own body, in the absence of the Vice-President, or

1 Const. U. S., Art. I. Sect. v. 1, 3.

2 *Ibid.*, Art I. Sect. vi. 1.

3 *Ibid.*, Art. I. Sect. vi. 1.

4 The title is taken from that of the presiding member of the British House of Commons, and derived from his addressing or *speaking* to the Crown on behalf of its "faithful Commons," when soliciting its confirmation in their privileges, its assent to bills, its acceptance of grants, or upon presenting addresses upon any other subject or occasion.

when he executes the office of President of the United States.

Bills, or the original drafts or projects of laws, are introduced into both Houses respectively, either upon the order of the House on the Report of a *standing* or of a *select* committee, or upon leave granted to an individual member on motion, after due notice of his intention to move the House to grant it. Standing Committees are appointed for the session upon all the usual subjects of ordinary legislation, and upon the general matters incident to the proceedings of each House respectively. Select Committees are appointed from time to time upon special subjects as they arise; and their powers cease upon the performance of the temporary duties assigned to them, or upon their discharge from the consideration of the subject referred to them. Both standing and select committees are appointed, in the House of Representatives, on the nomination of the Speaker, and in the Senate, generally by ballot, but sometimes, and in some special cases, on the nomination of the President of the Senate.

Bills are introduced by standing committees, upon the order of the House, upon subjects embraced by the general objects of their appointment, either accompanied by a report upon those general objects, or upon a particular object relative thereto, or specially referred to them; or upon the mere motion of the Chairman, or any other member of the Committee under its direction, without previous notice. Bills are, in like manner, introduced by Select Committees, upon the order of the House on a report relative to the special matter referred to them, or upon motion, without previous notice, for leave to report by bill.

Every bill must receive three readings before it can be passed by either House; and these several readings must be on different days, unless upon a special order made by the unanimous consent of the House, to the contrary; which is usually given or tacitly assumed so far as to permit the first and second reading on the same day. No bill can be committed or amended, until it has been read twice; and upon its second reading, it is declared to be ready for commitment or engrossment. If committed, it is either to a standing or select committee, or to a committee of the whole House; or if the bill, instead of being committed, be ordered to be engrossed, the House appoints the day on which it shall be read a third time. If a bill be committed to a Committee of the whole, the House determines on what day the committee shall consider it; and when the House resolves itself into such committee, the Speaker leaves the chair, after appointing another member to preside as Chairman of the Committee; when the Speaker may take part in the debates of the committee as an ordinary member. In the Senate, the Committee of the whole is called a *quasi* committee, because the President of the Senate, in virtue of one of its rules, acts as Chairman of the Committee.

Important bills are usually referred to a Committee of the whole House; and every motion or proposition for a tax or charge upon the people, or for a variation in the sum or *quantum* of a tax or duty, and for an appropriation of money, is required first to be discussed there. The object of referring these, or any other matters to this Committee, is to allow greater latitude and freedom in discussing its merits, and settling the details, than is generally allowed by the rules of either House, when the proceeding is in the House itself.

After commitment and report to the House, and at any time before its passage, a bill may be recommitted at the pleasure of the House; and when a bill, either upon a report of a Committee, or after full discussion and amendment in the House, stands for the next stage of its progress, the question is, whether it shall be engrossed for its third reading? and this is the proper time for those who are opposed to the principle of the bill to take their stand against it, as it is now supposed to be as perfect, or as little exceptionable, as it can be made. When a bill has been engrossed for a third reading, and upon being read a third time, has passed one House, it is transmitted for concurrence to the other, where it is subjected to similar forms of examination and discussion. If it be altered or amended, or agreed to without amendment, or totally rejected in the House to which it has been so transmitted, it is, in either of these cases, returned to the House in which it originated, with a message communicating the result. If amendments made in one House are not agreed to in the other, a message to that effect is sent to the former, which may either *recede from*, or *insist on* its amendments; and if the two Houses cannot agree, they appoint committees of conference, and upon receiving their report, either House may *recede* from its amendment, or from its vote of concurrence, or accept a compromise suggested by the Committee; or it may *adhere* to its former vote of disagreement, in which case the bill falls to the ground.

These checks and formalities, which are intended to

guard against surprise or imposition, were originally borrowed, although much contracted and simplified, from the proceedings of the British Parliament. They prevailed substantially in the Colonial Assemblies, from which they were *immediately* adopted by the State Legislatures, and from them, by Congress; and in their application and interpretation, recourse is frequently had to the precedents afforded by the practice and decisions of the body whence they are derived.

When a bill, or any vote or resolution, to which the concurrence of both Houses is necessary, (except the adjournment of Congress,) is passed by both branches of that National Legislature, it is required by the Constitution[1] to be presented to the President of the United States for his approval. If he approve, he signs it; but if not, he must return it with his objections to the House in which it originated, which must enter the objections at large on its journal, and proceed to reconsider it. If, after such consideration, two thirds of that House agree to pass the bill or resolution, it must be sent, together with the objections, to the other House, by which it must likewise be reconsidered; and if approved by two thirds of that House also, it becomes a law, notwithstanding the objections of the President. In all such cases, the votes of both Houses must be determined by *yeas* and *nays*, or openly ascertained; and the names of the persons voting for, or against the bill or resolution entered on the journal. But if it be not returned by the President within ten days (Sundays excepted) after it is presented to him, it becomes a law, in like manner as if he had signed

[1] Const. U. S., Art. I. Sect. VII. 3.

it — unless Congress, by adjournment, prevents its return.

The Constitution directs that Congress shall assemble at least once in every year, and that such meeting shall be held on the first Monday in December, unless another day be appointed by law.[1] So that until the time fixed either by the Constitution or the law, the action of Congress cannot commence, unless the President, in the exercise of his constitutional power, shall, on extraordinary occasions, convene it sooner. Congress, also, by concurrent resolution, to which, in this case, the assent of the President is not, as we have seen, necessary, fixes the time of its own adjournments. But, during a session, neither House, without the consent of the other, can adjourn for more than three days, nor to any other place than that in which it is sitting.[2]

Although Congress may be convened by the President, and in cases of disagreement may be adjourned by him to such time as he may think proper,[3] yet our National Legislature possesses this advantage over others, that may be adjourned or dissolved at the pleasure of the Executive authority; that, if in the opinion of Congress itself, the public good may require it, it may continue uninterruptedly in session until the expiration of the term for which the House of Representatives is chosen; and it may appoint as early a day as it thinks proper for the meeting of the next Congress; and as the term for which the House, and one third of the Senate are elected expires at the end of

[1] Const. U. S., Art. I. Sect. IV. 2.
[2] *Ibid.*, Art. I. Sect. V. 4.
[3] *Ibid.*, Art. II. Sect. III.

every second year, Congress must of necessity adjourn at the expiration of that period, as it is, in fact, dissolved by the joint operation of the Constitution and the law, as it stands at present, on the third day of March in every alternate year. And among the benefits of our written Constitution, it may be accounted as one of the most valuable, that no Act of Congress can prolong its own existence, beyond the time fixed by the fundamental law.

LECTURE IV.

OF THE EXECUTIVE POWER.

In the construction of a Republican Government, there is no point more difficult of adjustment than the proper constitution of the Executive Power. The object of this department being the execution of the laws, good policy requires that it should be organized in the mode best calculated to effect that end with precision and fidelity. In the proceedings of the other branches of the Government, deliberation is necessary. Both in making and expounding the laws, caution and consultation are implied as indispensable duties. But when laws are duly made and promulgated, they only remain to be executed. No discretion is vested in the Executive officer in regard to their wisdom or expediency. What has been declared under the forms of deliberation prescribed by the Constitution to be the meaning and intention of the Legislature should be carried into prompt execution, and due effect given to it by the Executive department, until repealed by the Legislative power, or pronounced unconstitutional by the Judiciary; in which latter case, the act of the Legislature is ascertained to be void, and neither public officers nor private citizens are responsible for its neglect or violation.

But every individual is bound to obey a constitutional law, however objectionable, in other respects, it may appear to him; and whosoever refuses or withholds obedience to a law, on the ground even of its unconstitutionality, does so at his peril. For if the question be judicially decided by a competent tribunal, in favor of its validity, he is liable to all the legal consequences of disobedience. The presumption, moreover, is always in favor of a law passed in accordance with the forms of the Constitution; and where the Chief Executive Magistrate has a negative upon the Acts of the Legislature, that presumption is, of course, the stronger against him, especially as to Acts passed under his own administration, and which must, therefore, have received his official approval. For in such case, the existence alone of the law is evidence of his admission of its constitutionality, if the negative he possesses be absolute, and if qualified, it shows that his objections, if made, were overruled. If the law to which he objects were passed under a former administration, his official, if not his personal obligation, is not less absolute and peremptory. For the negative vested in him is a legislative and not a judicial power; and to allow a contrary doctrine would be to admit in the Executive department a right to repeal laws without the intervention of the Legislature. As, therefore, the Executive power is bound, not only to obey, but to carry into effect the law, the essential qualities requisite in that department are *promptness*, *vigor*, and *responsibility*.

A prompt submission to the law, and immediate preparation to enforce it, are absolutely necessary in respect to the authority whence it emanates. In regard also to its effect,—whenever the time for acting on a law has arrived, its operation should be immediate and decisive; otherwise the sense of its protection and control will be weakened, and its power unfelt or forgotten. On general principles, therefore, as delay is reprehensible, *promptness* is a duty, the non-performance of which, in certain cases, enables the transgressor to escape punishment. For this reason, it is both wise and humane that the execution of the law should be speedy, and that no unnecessary interval should be allowed between its violation and the adoption of measures for enforcing it.

For this purpose, the Executive Magistrate should be endowed with sufficient *energy*. A feeble Executive department implies a feeble execution of the law, which is but another name for a bad execution; and a government in which the laws are not faithfully executed, whatever it may be in theory, must, in practice, be a bad government. A vigor of action, duly proportioned to the exigencies which arise, must be imparted to the Executive power. But for this purpose, the proportion of power vested to the occasions that may be expected to require its exercise, should be as exact as possible; for if the power fall short of the end proposed, the evils already adverted to will ensue; and if it exceed the due proportion, the liberties of the people would be endangered. It is difficult, however, in a written Constitution, to adopt general expressions precisely descriptive of the proper extent and limitation of this power. To guard, therefore, against its abuse, as well as to insure a faithful execution of the general trust reposed in this department, it is requisite that it should be held *responsible* to the people for official delinquencies.

Now these three qualities of promptness, vigor, and responsibility, are certainly more likely to exist where the

Executive authority is limited to a single person, moving at the discretion of a single will. But in some republics, the fear of danger from such a head, has led to the introduction of councils, and other subdivisions of the Executive power; and the consequent imbecility and distractions of these governments have probably contributed to the preference given in Europe to monarchies. It was falsely conceived that to vest the Executive power in a single person was inconsistent with the nature and genius of a Republic; or that a Republic thus constituted could long maintain its freedom. But during the American Revolution, neither the fervor of republican principles, nor resentment towards the monarchy then arrayed against us, overpowered the deliberate judgments of our statesmen; and upon the establishment of independent governments, almost all the States adopted the principle of UNITY in the Executive power. The experience of more than half a century has evinced that, under proper limitations, no abuse of the power is to be apprehended merely from its *unity;* while every government, ancient or modern, constituted upon the scheme of compound Executive authority, has suffered from the evils of division, indecision, and delay, and the public interests have been sacrificed or have languished under a feeble and irregular management. In those States of our Union where Executive Councils have been tried, this weakness and inefficiency have been strikingly exemplified. In most instances where they were at first adopted, they were speedily abandoned, and a single person substituted in accordance with the lights afforded to the States in question by their own experience, or the institutions of their neighbors.[1]

[1] Pennsylvania and Georgia.

Unity not only increases that efficiency which is necessary to preserve tranquillity at home, and command respect abroad, but it is requisite to secure the *responsibility* of the Executive power. Where there is but one agent, every act can be traced and brought home to him; nor can there be any concealment of the real author, and, generally, none of the true motives of public measures, where there are no associates to divide or mask responsibility. The eyes of the people will be constantly directed to a single conspicuous object, and, for these reasons, De Lolme considers it a sound maxim of policy, that the Executive power is more easily confined where it is one and indivisible. "If," he observes, "the execution of the laws be intrusted to a number of hands, the true cause of public costs is hidden. Tyranny, in such States, does not always beat down the fences that are set around them, but it leaps over them. It mocks the efforts of the people, not because it is invincible, but because it is unknown."[1]

In accordance with these principles, the Federal Constitution vests the Executive power in a single person, who is styled "THE PRESIDENT OF THE UNITED STATES." The qualifications and election, the powers and duties of this high officer, will now be the subject of consideration.

I. His qualifications, and the mode of his election.

1. The Constitution requires that the President should be a natural-born citizen, or a citizen of the United States at the time of its adoption; that he should have attained the age of thirty-five years, and have been fourteen years resident within them.[2] Considering the magnitude of the trust, and that the Executive depart-

[1] On the Const. of England, p. 111.

[2] Const. U. S., Art. II. Sect. I. 5.

ment is the ultimate efficient power in the Government, these restrictions will not appear useless or unimportant. The qualification required of citizenship, was intended to prevent ambitious foreigners from intriguing for the office, and to cut off all those inducements from abroad, to corruption, *intervention*, and war, which have frequently and fatally harassed the elective monarchies of Europe. The age required in the President is sufficient to have formed his public and private character; and the previous term of domestic residence is intended to afford his fellow-citizens the opportunity of gaining a correct knowledge of his principles and capacity, and to enable *him* to acquire habits of attachment and obedience to the laws, and practical devotion to the public welfare.

2. The mode of his appointment presented one of the most difficult problems solved by the Convention; and if ever the tranquillity of this nation is to be disturbed, and its peace jeoparded by a struggle for power among ourselves, it is the opinion of some of our wisest, both of our departed and of our living statesmen, that it will be on this very subject of the choice of the President. It is therefore the more remarkable, that this was almost the only part of the federal system, of any importance, which escaped the severest censure, or received the slightest mark of approbation from its opponents. By the authors of "The Federalist,"[1] the manner of choosing the President was affirmed to be "if not perfect, at least excellent," and "to unite, in an eminent degree, all the advantages of which the selection and association were to be desired." It was, nevertheless,

[1] No. 68, by Mr. Hamilton.

considered by Mr. Chancellor Kent as "the question which is to try the strength of the Constitution," and that "if we are able for half a century hereafter to continue to elect the Chief Magistrate of the Union, with discretion, moderation, and integrity, we shall undoubtedly stamp the highest value on our national character, and recommend our republican institutions, if not to the imitation, yet certainly to the esteem and admiration of mankind." [1]

The experience, both of ancient and modern Europe, as this eminent jurist observes, has certainly been unfavorable to the practicability of the fair and peaceable election of the Executive of a great nation. It was found impossible to guard such elections from the mischiefs of foreign intrigue and domestic turbulence — from violence or corruption; and men have generally sought refuge from the dangers of popular elections, in hereditary Chief Magistrates, as the lesser evil of the two. Archdeacon Paley[2] condemns all elective monarchies, and thinks nothing gained by a popular choice, with the dissensions, tumults, and interruptions of regular industry with which it is inseparably connected. But these consequences rarely attend our elections; and no such evils as he describes have ever been experienced in our elections of a President by the *Electors;* although, on one memorable occasion, of which I shall speak hereafter, much riotous and violent conduct was exhibited in the House of Representatives, when, upon an equality of electoral votes between two of the persons voted for, the choice devolved upon that body. Nor can any danger be apprehended in future from a

[1] 1 Comm. 256. 1st Ed.

[2] Moral and Political Philosophy, p. 345.

similar occurrence, from the nature of the precautions so happily concerted to prevent them,—in addition to the nature, extent, and duration of his power,—by a change in the manner of electing the President. The question, too, was different with us, from the wisdom or policy of preferring an hereditary to an elective monarchy, as the same restraints do not exist in Europe on the Executive authority to diminish its value in the estimation of competitors, where different orders and ranks are established in their communities, and large masses of property are accumulated in the hands of individuals,—where ignorance and poverty are widely diffused, and standing armies are maintained to preserve the stability of the government. The state of society and property in this country, and the moral and political training and habits of the people have enabled us to adopt the republican principle in relation to the Chief Executive Magistrate, and to maintain it hitherto with signal success. From the peculiar character of our Federative Union, in which the concerns only of the NATION, as such, are confided to the General Government, and those of a local description, to the States,—from the nature of the civil and municipal institutions of the States, which favor the exertions of industry by the certainty of adequate rewards and secure enjoyment, but discourage and prevent the accumulation of overgrown estates,—from the spread of knowledge and the prevalence of moral and religious habits, we may reasonably hope that the checks which the Constitution has provided against the dangerous propensities of our system,—although sometimes contemned by ambitious popular leaders,—will prove continually and ultimately successful. The election, however, of a Supreme Magistrate for a whole nation, affects so many interests, addresses itself so strongly to popular passions, and holds forth such powerful temptations to ambition, that even under the most favorable circumstances and wisest regulations, it necessarily becomes a formidable trial to public virtue, and sometimes hazardous to the public tranquillity. The framers of our Constitution, from an enlightened view of all the difficulties of the case, did not think it safe or prudent to refer the election of the President immediately to the people, but confided it to a small body of ELECTORS appointed in each State, under the direction of its Legislature; and in order to close the door as effectually as possible against negotiation, intrigue, and corruption, they declared that Congress might determine the day on which the election should be held, and that the day of election should be the same in every State.

It was essential that the sense of the people should operate in the choice of a person to whom so important a trust was to be confided; and this end is answered by committing the right of election, not to any preestablished body, but to men chosen by the people for the special purpose, and under such circumstances as would best insure the freedom and purity of the election. It was also desirable that the immediate election should be made by men capable of analyzing the qualities adapted to the station, and who should act under circumstances favorable to deliberation, and to a judicious combination and comparison of all the reasons and inducements proper to govern their choice; and it was fairly and reasonably supposed that a small number of persons, selected by their fellow-citizens from the general mass, would be most likely to possess the information and discernment requisite to such an investigation. It was, moreover, peculiarly desirable to afford as little opportunity as possible to tumult and disorder, and it was, therefore, considered that the choice of *several* to form an intermediate body of electors, would be much less apt to convulse the community with any extraordinary and violent emotions, than the choice of *one*, who would himself be the first object of the public wishes; and, by requiring the Electors chosen in each State to assemble and vote in the State in which they are appointed, it was intended that they should be less exposed to heats and ferments communicated to them from the people, than if they were all to be assembled at the same place.

Nothing was more to be desired, and nothing was more anxiously attempted, than that every practical obstacle should be opposed to cabal, intrigue, and corruption. These deadly foes to republicanism were naturally expected to make their approaches from more than one quarter; but chiefly from abroad,—from the desire of foreign powers to gain an improper ascendency in our public councils; and it was apprehended that they might effect this, by raising a creature of their own to the Chief Magistracy of the Union. The Convention, therefore, guarded against all danger of this sort, with the most provident and judicious attention. Another, and not less important object, was that the President should be independent for his continuance in office on all but the people themselves. This object, also, was designed to be secured by making, as we have seen, his reëlection depend upon a special body of representatives, deputed by the nation for the single purpose of his election, instead of permitting his continuance in office to depend on the will of Congress,—to whose favor he might, in that case, be tempted to sacrifice his duty and official dignity.

Such were the advantages intended to be combined and secured by the plan as devised by the Convention. Whether they have been altogether realized, we shall hereafter have occasion to inquire; for the present, it may be as well to suggest that the contest alluded to, which arose in 1801, has not been imitated, at least by none of equal violence, since the adoption of an amendment of the Constitution intended to prevent its recurrence.[1] It has, nevertheless, been deemed advisable by some of our ablest and most experienced statesmen, to propose a further amendment, disqualifying the President from reëlection.

The Constitution ordains that each State shall appoint, in such manner as its Legislature may direct, a number of Electors equal to the whole number of Senators and Representatives which the State is entitled to send to Congress;[2] and to prevent the President in office at the time of the election from having an improper influence on his reëlection by his ordinary agency in the government, it is declared that no Senator or Representative, nor any person holding an office of trust or profit under the United States, shall be appointed an Elector. In no other respect has the Constitution defined the qualifications of the Electors. In several of the States, the Electors were formerly chosen by the Legislature, in a mode prescribed by law; and this method still prevails in Delaware and South Carolina. But it is to be presumed that there will be less

[1] Amendments to Const. U. S. XII.

[2] Const. U. S., Art. II. Sect. I. 2.

opportunity for dangerous coalitions,—for ambitious, selfish, or party purposes, were the choice of the Electors referred, as, according to the clear sense of public opinion, it now almost universally is, to the people.

The Electors are directed by the Constitution to meet in their respective States on the same day, as we have seen, throughout the Union, which, in pursuance of the discretionary power vested in Congress, has been fixed by law on the first Wednesday in December, in every fourth year succeeding the last election. The place of meeting resting in the discretion of the State Legislatures, is usually at the seat of the State Government. When thus assembled, and fully organized by filling up vacancies occurring from the death or absence of any of their number, the Electors proceed to vote by ballot for two persons, one of whom, at least, must not be an inhabitant of the same State with themselves. According to the original Constitution, they were not to designate which of the two they voted for as President, and which for Vice-President; the latter of whom was, nevertheless, to be elected at the same time, in the same manner, with the same qualifications, and for the same term as the President. It was merely provided that the person having the greatest number of votes should be the President, if such number were a majority of the whole number of Electors chosen; and if there were more than one having such majority, and an equal number of votes, the House of Representatives were immediately to choose by ballot, one of them for President; and if no person had a majority, then, from the five highest on the list, the House were, in like manner, to choose the President. After the choice of the President, the person having the next greatest number of votes of the Electors, should be the Vice-President; but if there should remain two or more having equal votes, the Senate was to choose from them by ballot, the Vice-President. But in thus choosing the President, the votes were to be taken by States; the Representation from each State having one vote, and a quorum for the purpose was to consist of a member, or members from two thirds of the States; and a majority of all the States was necessary to a choice.

After the difficulty already alluded to in procuring a constitutional choice, in consequence of an equality in the Electoral votes, between Mr. Jefferson and Colonel Burr, the two highest on the list of persons voted for by the Electors, the Constitution was so amended as to require the Electors to name in distinct ballots the persons voted for respectively as President and Vice-President. They are then directed to make distinct lists of all voted for as President, and as Vice-President, and the number of votes given to each respectively. These lists they are to sign, certify, and transmit sealed, to the seat of Government of the United States, directed to the President of the Senate, before the first Wednesday in January next ensuing the election.[1] An Act of Congress passed in March, 1792, requires that body to be in session on the second Wednesday in February, next ensuing the election, when the President of the Senate, in the presence of both Houses of Congress, opens the certificates received, and the votes are counted. It is not explicitly declared by whom the votes are to be counted, and the result proclaimed; but the practice has been for the President of the Senate to appoint a joint

[1] Amendment to Const. U. S., XII.

committee of the two houses to perform the first of those duties, and himself to perform the last, the two Houses being present as spectators, to witness the fairness and accuracy of the proceeding.

The person having the greatest number of votes for President, if a majority of the whole number of Electors appointed, is declared to be elected to that office; and if no person have such majority, then from those having the highest numbers not exceeding *three*—instead of *five*, as was required by the Constitution—on the list of those voted for as President, are immediately to choose the President in the manner directed in the Constitution, the same number of States being requisite to form a quorum, and the same majority of them necessary to a choice. The amendment then declares that the person having the greatest number of votes for Vice-President—if a majority of the whole number of Electors appointed—shall be the Vice-President; and if no person have such majority, then from the two highest *numbers* on the list, the Senate shall choose the Vice-President; a quorum for the purpose to consist of two thirds of the whole number of Senators. But no person constitutionally ineligible to the office of President shall be eligible to that of Vice-President.

Although the Constitution directs that when no person is found to have a majority of the Electoral votes, the choice shall be *immediately* made by the House of Representatives, yet it is not held obligatory upon that House to proceed to the election directly upon the separation of the two Houses; but that it may proceed either at that time and place, or omit it until afterwards. This construction was adopted before the amendment in question, and there can now be no doubt of its correctness, as the amendment expressly declares the choice of the House to be valid, if made before the fourth of March following the day on which the Electoral votes are counted. Accordingly, in 1825, when there was again no choice by the Electors, the House of Representatives retired to their own chamber, and on this, as well as upon the occasion already mentioned, the Senators were allowed to be present as spectators only of the proceeding, and witnesses of the result. In case no choice of President be made by the House of Representatives before the time limited for their action, it is declared that the Vice-President shall act as President, as in the case of the death or constitutional inability of the President.

The Constitution, as thus amended, does not prescribe specifically when or where the Senate is to choose the Vice-President, in case no choice be made by the Electors, and no case has occurred to form a precedent; but from analogy to the provision and practice in regard to the President, it is presumed that the Senate may elect one at any time before the ensuing fourth of March. With respect to the day to which the secondary election is in both cases limited, it is to be remarked that it was adopted in reference to the law existing previously to this amendment of the Constitution, which had declared, as we have seen, that the term of four years for which the President and Vice-President are elected, should commence on the fourth day of March next succeeding the day on which the votes of the Electors are given. The effect of this amendment, therefore, is to render the provisions of the Act of Congress, relative to the specific times appointed for the performance of the several duties enjoined by the Constitution, thus amended, in regard to the election of President and Vice-President, as permanent as the Constitution itself.

Although the wisdom and policy of this amendment has been doubted by some of our ablest statesmen and jurists, there are others who consider it an improvement, not only with respect to voting separately for President and Vice-President, but in reducing the number of candidates from which the Congressional selection of a President is to be made from five to three, while the Senate, in their choice of a Vice-President, is confined to the two highest *numbers* of those voted for by the Electors. In another particular, also, the amendment may be considered beneficial. By the former mode of proceeding, the Senate was restrained from acting until the House had made its selection of a President, which, if parties ran high, might be indefinitely delayed. By the amendment, the Senate may proceed to choose a Vice-President, in case one be not chosen by the Electors, immediately upon the declaration of that result. Under the original mode, if the House of Representatives, in the event of no choice by the Electors, did not choose a President by the fourth of March, and the provision that Congress is authorized to make by law for supplying the vacancy of the office, should fail, it must have remained vacant, unless, as it has been contended, the Vice-President then in office was to act as President for the next official term; so that, notwithstanding the public confidence may have been wholly withdrawn from him, he would actually become President for the ensuing four years, when he had been chosen by the Electors, in reference, not in form, but in fact, to the Vice-Presidency, and that, too, for the preceding term; whereas, on the plan now in force, if no President be chosen, either by the Electors, or the House of Representatives, the Vice-President then to fill the office of President, will have recently received the suffrages of the Electors, as well as of the Senators. After all, however, it may be doubted whether a greater evil has not been introduced by the amendment in the greater facility it affords to party organization, and the selection of mere party leaders, which was the very evil intended to be guarded against by the former regulation, besides insuring the election of two persons, either of whom would be competent for the higher office.

From a review of these various provisions, the mode of electing the Supreme Magistrate of the Union appears to be well calculated to secure a discreet choice, and to avoid those evils which the partizans of monarchy have ascribed, and the experience of past ages have shown to belong to popular election. It must, nevertheless, be acknowledged, that the large and elevated views of the men who planned the Constitution, and the expectations of those who defended this portion of it, upon the refined theoretical reasoning I have adverted to, have not been realized in its practical operation and effects. It was supposed that the election of the President would be committed to men not likely to be swayed by party or personal bias; who would act unfettered by previous commitment, uncontrolled by combinations or discipline, and be subject neither to intimidation nor corruption; and it was thought that the choice of an intermediate body of Electors, consisting of several members, would be much less apt to agitate and convulse the community than the election of a single person, who was himself the first object of their wishes. Perhaps those views and expectations were founded on too exalted an estimate of human nature; and that, making due allowance for human frailty and imperfection, they have not been altogether frustrated. Experience, however, has proved that the Electors do not, in fact, assemble for a strictly free exercise of their own judgments, but for the purpose of giving a constitutional sanction to the choice of a particular candidate, previously designated by their party leaders. In some instances, the principles on which they are constituted have been so far forgotten, that the individual opinion of the Elector has submitted to the dictation of those by whom he was chosen; and in others, the Electors have even pledged themselves beforehand to vote for a candidate prescribed to them by the managers of their party; and thus, the whole foundation of the elaborate theory on which this part of the Constitution was built, has been subverted in practice. The essential ends of the Constitution have, nevertheless, in a measure been attained; and in a government in which parties must ever exist, that system may be deemed salutary in its operation, which results in the election of the most eminent, or, even the most popular statesman of the most numerous party.

Had any other mode of election been adopted, it would have been impossible, in a Republican Government, to have excluded party considerations, interests, and feelings. The great objects were to preserve purity as well as harmony in the election, and to secure integrity as well as independence in the Executive Power. Had the choice of President been referred in the first instance to Congress, it would, without excluding party views and motives, have rendered him too dependent on the immediate authors of his elevation to comport with the requisite energy of his department, and have tempted him to indulge in intrigues and manœuvres utterly subversive of the fairness of the election, and the purity of his own character. He would then no longer consider himself responsible to the People, but would be prone to obey, and fearful to offend a power which, in that case, would have shown itself greater than the People themselves.

Whether greater ferments and commotions would accompany a general election of the President by the whole body of the People, than have hitherto attended the elections by Electors,—and, certainly, these have, as yet, excited no real alarm,—or whether that mode of election would, with regard to the prescribed *ratio* of representation, be conveniently practised, remains, indeed, to be ascertained. It has been objected that such a measure would "lead to an entire consolidation of the Government, and the annihilation of the State sovereignties, so far as concerns the organization of the Executive Department." But if the difference should consist merely in the form, and not the objects of the election,—nor in the authority that orders and controls it,—if, for instance, the People in their several States, instead of voting for Electors, should, in the same manner, at the same time and places, and under the same regulations, vote directly for the President and Vice-President, and the number of votes to which the State is entitled under the existing provisions of the Constitution, should be computed as given to the persons receiving the highest vote from the people for these offices respectively, I must confess my inability to discover any greater danger to the sovereignty of the States than exists under the present system. Nor, as the Electors are now avowedly chosen in direct reference to the persons for whom they are expected, if not pledged to vote, can I conceive any sound objection to such an amendment. On the contrary, I think there is much to recommend it, especially if accompanied by a provision superseding the ultimate reference to Congress, in case of no choice by the Electors, by a secondary resort to the latter body. Such an alteration has, indeed, been actually proposed and urged in Congress with great force of argument, particularly the substitution of a final election by Electors, instead of the House of Representatives, in cases where no choice of a President is made by the People.

From the example of the illustrious individual who first held the office, a practice has arisen, and seems now to be permanently established, for the President to decline a second reëlection. As this precedent has never been, as yet, and probably never will be, departed from, it has in effect limited the period of service to eight years, subject to an intermediate election. But to render the President more independent, the administration and its policy more stable, and the People more secure, it would be better that this practice should be sanctioned and legalized by being incorporated in the system; and such an amendment of the Constitution, in connection with that already suggested, has been actually brought forward, and appeared to have been favored by some of the most intelligent and upright of our public men.

Having fully explained the manner in which the Supreme Executive office is constituted, and the mode of electing the President and Vice-President, I proceed to consider —

II. The powers with which the President is invested.

1. The first of these which offers itself to observation, has already been adverted to in reviewing the Legislative departments, and its connection with the Executive power, for the preservation of their mutual independence,—I mean the *qualified negative* of the President upon the concurrent acts of Congress, or his right of returning Bills and Resolutions, with his objections to them, to the House in which they originated, for reconsideration; whereby they are prevented from taking effect as laws, unless again passed by two thirds of the members present in each House respectively.

The propensity of the Legislative department to intrude upon the rights and absorb the powers of the other weaker branches of the government, and the consequent necessity of furnishing the latter with constitutional arms for their defence, have already been the subject of remark. From clear and indubitable principles it has been shown that, without this control over the proceedings of Congress, the Executive department would be unable to sustain itself against the encroachments of the Legislature. The President might gradually be stripped of his authority by concurrent Resolutions of Congress, or so weakened as ultimately to be annihilated by a single vote of the more popular branch of the Legislature; and by the one mode or the other, the Legislative and Executive powers might speedily be united in the same hands. Indeed, if no tendency had ever been manifested in Legislative bodies to invade the rights of the Executive power, just reasoning and theoretic propriety would of themselves teach us, that the one ought not to be left at the mercy of the other, but should be endowed with a constitutional and effectual power of self-defence.

But the power in question has a further use. It not only serves as a shield to the Executive authority, but affords an additional security against the enactment of improper laws. It establishes a salutary guard upon the Legislative power, well calculated to defend the community against the effects of faction, precipitancy, or any impulse hostile to the public good, which may happen for the moment to influence a majority of Congress.[1] The propriety of vesting such a power in the Chief Magistrate has been sometimes combated on the ground of its presuming that a single individual was possessed of more wisdom and virtue than a numerous assembly. The question, however, does not depend upon the supposition of superior wisdom and virtue in the President, but upon the presumption that the Legislature, though possessed of those qualities in the highest degree, would still be fallible; that the love of power would sometimes dispose them to acts injurious to the rights of the other members of the Government; that a spirit of faction might sometimes pervert their deliberations, and that momentary impressions sometimes impel them to measures which, upon mature

[1] A prerogative has, of late years, been claimed in favor of majorities, similar to that vested by the English Constitution in the Crown, viz: that *they* "*can do no wrong.*" But this was not the doctrine of Mr. Madison, and the other founders of our Constitution. That great republican statesman defined "any number of citizens, *whether amounting to a majority* or a minority of the whole, united and actuated by some common impulse of purpose or interest adverse to the rights of other citizens, or to the permanent and aggregate interests of the community," to be "a *faction.*" See "The Federalist," No. 10.

reflection, they would themselves condemn. Thus the *primary* inducement of conferring this power on the President is to enable him to defend himself; the *secondary*, to increase the chances in favor of the community against the passage of bad laws by Congress, through haste, inadvertence, or design.

2. The President is constituted *Commander-in-chief* of the army and navy of the United States, and of the militia of the several States, when called in the service of the Union.[1]

The command and direction of the public force, to execute the laws, maintain peace and tranquillity at home, and resist invasion from abroad, are powers so obviously of an executive nature, and so peculiarly demand the exercise of the qualities characteristic of that department,—these duties have been so uniformly appropriated to it in every well-organized government, and are so consonant to the precedents of the State Constitutions, that little is necessary to explain or enforce them. Of all the cares or concerns of government, the management of war, which implies the direction of the public force, demands most peculiarly the exercise of power by a single hand; and even those of our States which have, in other matters, coupled their Chief Magistrate with a Council, have, for the most part, concentrated the military authority in him alone.

3. The President has the sole power of *granting reprieves and pardons* for offences against the United States, except in cases of impeachment.[2]

The necessity of such an authority in every government, arises from the infirmities incident to the admin-

[1] Const. U. S., Art. II. Sect. II. 1.

[2] *Ibid.* 3.

istration of human justice. And were it possible, in every case, to maintain a just proportion between the crime and the penalty; were the rules of evidence, and the mode of trial, so perfect as to preclude every possibility of mistake or injustice, still, policy would sometimes require the remission of a punishment strictly due for a crime clearly ascertained. Both humanity and policy dictate that this benign prerogative of mercy should be as little as possible fettered and embarrassed, and suggests as plainly the expediency of vesting it exclusively in the President.

As the sense of responsibility is always stronger in proportion as it is undivided, it may justly be inferred that one man will be more ready to recognize the force of motives and reasons for mitigating the rigor of the law, and least apt to yield to inducements calculated to shelter a fit object from its exemplary visitation; while, on the other hand, as men generally derive confidence from their numbers, it may, with equal justice be apprehended, that they might often encourage each other in acts of obduracy, and be less sensible to the dread of censure for an injudicious or affected clemency. The power of *pardon* vested in the President is not, however, without limitation. He is precluded, as we have seen, in cases of impeachment, from screening public officers, with whom he may have formed a daugerous or corrupt coalition, or who may frequently be his favorites and dependents.

4. The President has power, by and with the advice and consent of the Senate, *to make treaties*, provided two thirds of the Senators present concur.[1]

[1] Const. U. S., Art. II. Sect. II. 4.

Much difference of opinion seems to prevail among writers on Government upon the question whether, in the natural distribution of power, the authority to negotiate and conclude compacts and arrangements with foreign nations, is properly of Legislative or of Executive cognizance. As treaties are declared, by the Constitution of the United States to be a part of the supreme law of the land,—as by means of these national engagements, new relations are formed, and new obligations contracted, it seems more consonant to the principles of our Government to consider the right of entering into them as falling within the jurisdiction of the Legislature. On the other hand, the preliminary negotiations which may be required, and the secrecy and dispatch proper to take advantage of a sudden and favorable turn in public affairs, render it expedient to place this power in the hands of the Executive. The framers of the Constitution were influenced more by the latter, than the former consideration. But although the power in question, if we carefully attend to its operation, will be found to partake more of the Legislative than of the Executive character, yet it does not seem to fall strictly within either department. The essence of the Legislative power is to prescribe laws for the regulation of the Commonwealth; while the execution of those laws, and the employment of the public force, either for that purpose, or for the common defence, comprise all the proper functions of the Executive magistrate. The power of making treaties relates neither to the execution of subsisting laws, nor to the making of new ones. Its objects are *contracts*, which have, indeed, the force of laws, but derive that force, not from legislation, but from the obligations of good faith. They are not rules prescribed by the supreme legislative power to the citizens of the State, but agreements between sovereign and independent States. This power, then, forms a distinct department, and the Constitution has wisely confided it, in its preliminary stages, to the President.

The qualities indispensable to the management of international intercourse and negotiation, point to the President as the most fit organ of communication with foreign powers, and the efficient agent in the conclusion of treaties; while the vast importance of the trust, and the operation of treaties as laws, strongly recommend the participation of a portion, at least, of the Legislative power in the office of making them. The Senate was most judiciously selected for that purpose, not only as the deposit of the power in that body imparts additional strength and security to it, as the weaker branch of the Legislature, but because, from its smaller number and greater permanence, it may be more readily convened, and is moreover governed by steadier and more systematic views of public policy, and enabled to act with due promptitude and firmness.

5. The President is invested with the power *to nominate, and, with the advice and consent of the Senate, to appoint* Ambassadors, and other public Ministers, and Consuls, Judges of the Supreme Court, and all other officers of the United States whose appointments are not otherwise provided for, and which shall be established by law. But Congress may vest the appointment of such inferior officers as they may think proper, in the President alone, in the Courts of Law, or in the Heads of Departments.[1]

[1] Const. U. S., Art. II. Sect. II. 5.

The exercise, by the people at large, of this power of appointing the subordinate officers of the government would be impracticable; and a *concurrent* right of nomination by the Legislature, or any other select body, would afford great temptation and opportunity to intrigue, favoritism, and corrupt cabals, besides releasing the appointing power from all responsibility. No plan, probably, could have been devised better calculated, upon the whole, to promote a judicious choice of men to fill the public offices, than that which was adopted. The power of selecting *the Heads of Departments*, who, by the way, are not otherwise recognized in the Constitution, but are established by law to aid the President in the discharge of his Executive duties; of nominating agents to whom the immediate conduct of international affairs, and the negotiation of foreign treaties are confided; and of selecting the proper men for the highest judicial stations, is with peculiar propriety vested in the President, as he is held responsible for those acts of his immediate assistants and confidential advisers which receive his sanction, is charged with the management of foreign affairs, and bound to see both the treaties and the laws faithfully executed.

The association of the Senate with the President in the exercise of this power, is an exception to the general delegation of the Executive authority, which, were it not accompanied by the provision vesting in him the exclusive right of nomination, would be attended by the evils already adverted to. But this power of nomination is, for all useful purposes of restraint, equivalent to a power of absolute appointment; and imposes upon the President the same vivid sense of responsibility, and the same necessity of meeting the public approbation or censure; while the advice and consent of the Senate, which are necessary to render the nomination effectual, can never be attended with mischievous consequences, and must, at all times, prove a check upon the misinformation or errors of the President. To prevent the inconvenience which would arise from occasional vacancies in office when the Senate is not in session, the President has power to fill up those which happen during a recess, by granting commissions which expire at the end of the next session of Congress.[1]

6. The remaining duties of the President consist in giving information to Congress of the state of the Union; and recommending to their consideration such measures as he shall judge necessary or expedient. He may, on extraordinary occasions, convene both Houses of Congress, or either of them, and, in case of disagreement between them, may, as we have seen, adjourn them to such time as he may think proper. It is his duty to *receive* ambassadors, and other public ministers from abroad,—to commission all officers of the United States, and generally and comprehensively to take care that the laws be faithfully executed.[2]

Such are the powers vested by the Constitution in the President; and so far as they are derived from that instrument, he is beyond the control of any other branch of the government, except in the mode it prescribes,—by impeachment. But it by no means follows that every officer in every subdivision of the Executive departments, is under the exclusive control of the President. Congress has created certain subordinate officers to assist the President in the discharge of his duties,

[1] Const. U. S., Art. II. Sect. II. 5.

[2] *Ibid.*, Art. II. Sect. III.

and has organized the several "Departments," of which it has constituted those officers the "Heads."[1] Through these, the President speaks and acts in relation to the subjects appertaining to their respective duties. For certain duties are imposed upon each of them by law, to be discharged under the direction of the President. It would, nevertheless, be an alarming doctrine that Congress cannot impose upon any Executive officer any duty it may think proper, not repugnant to any right secured by the Constitution, and render such duty, and his responsibility for its discharge, subject to the control of the law, and not the direction of the President,— especially when the duty enjoined is of a merely ministerial character. Such a doctrine would invest the President with a dispensing power, which has no countenance for its support in any part of the Constitution, and enable him to control the legislation of Congress, and paralyze the administration of justice.

In general, however, the official duties of these Heads of Departments are not mere ministerial duties. In the administration of the various and important business of their offices, they are continually required to exercise judgment and discretion. They must use their judg-

[1] There are, at present, 1. "The Secretary of State," to whom is committed the charge of foreign affairs. 2. "The Secretary of the Interior," having charge of domestic concerns, and Indian affairs. 3. "The Secretary of the Treasury," superintending the revenue and financial affairs of the government. 4. "The Secretary at War," charged with the management of military affairs. 5. "The Secretary of the Navy," having charge of the naval affairs of the Union. 6. The Postmaster-General, as superintending the management of postal concerns, both in regard to finance and the transportation of the mails. 7. The Attorney-General, as "Head" of the recently created "Law Department."

ment in expounding the laws and resolutions of Congress, under which they are, from time to time, required to act. In cases of doubt, the Secretaries have a right to call upon the Attorney-General to assist them with his counsel; and it would be difficult to imagine why a legal adviser should have been provided by law for the other Heads of Departments, as well as for the President himself, unless their duties were regarded, in some instances, as such in which judgment and discretion were to be exercised.

If a suit should come before the courts of the United States, which involved the construction of any law imposing duties on the Head of a Department, the judges certainly would not be bound by the construction he may have given to it. If they held his decision to be wrong, they would, of course, pronounce judgment accordingly. But the judgment of the court upon its construction of the law, must be given in a case in which it has jurisdiction; and in which it is its duty to interpret the Act of Congress in order to ascertain the rights of the parties. The Supreme Court cannot entertain an *Appeal* from a decision of one of the Heads of Departments, nor revise his judgment in any case where the law authorizes him to exercise his discretion or judgment; nor can it, by *mandamus*, act directly upon the officer, or guide and control his judgment or discretion, in matters committed to his care in the ordinary discharge of his official duties. The interference of the courts with the performance of the ordinary duties of the Executive Departments of the government, would be productive of nothing but mischief, and this power was never intended to be given to them.[1]

[1] 12 *Peters*, 524; 14 *Ibid.* 497; 1 *Howard*, 120.

III. The support of the President, which is the next subject of examination, is secured by a provision in the Constitution, which declares that he shall, at stated times, receive for his services a compensation which shall neither be increased nor diminished during the period for which he was elected; and that he shall not receive, within that time, any other emolument from the United States, or any of the States.[1] This provision was intended to strengthen and preserve the proper independence and energy of the Executive Department. It would be in vain to declare that the different departments of the government should be separate and distinct, if the Legislature possessed a control over the salaries of the Chief Executive Magistrate and the Judicial officers. This, indeed, would be to disregard the voice of experience, and the operation of invariable principles of human conduct. The former Constitution of Virginia, for instance, considered it as a fundamental maxim of government, that the three great Departments should be kept distinct, so that neither of them should exercise the powers properly belonging to another. But without taking any precautions to preserve this principle in practice, it rendered the Governor dependent upon the Legislature for his annual existence and support. The result was, as Mr. Jefferson informs us, "that during the whole session of the Legislature, the direction of the Executive by that body was habitual and familiar."[2]

The Constitution of Massachusetts discovered more wisdom, and afforded the first example of a constitu-

1 Const. U. S., Art. II. Sect. 1. 7.

2 Notes on Virginia.

tional provision for the support of the Executive Magistrate, by declaring that the Governor should have a salary of a fixed and permanent value, amply sufficient, and established by standing law. Those State Constitutions which have been made or amended since the adoption of the Constitution of the United States, have generally followed the example which that instrument happily set to them in this, as well as in many other particulars; and, it has been well observed by one of our ablest jurists, that "we may consider it as one of the most signal blessings bestowed on this country, that we have such a fabric as the Federal Constitution constantly before our eyes, not only for national protection, but for local imitation and example.[1]

The appointment of an extraordinary person as Vice-President of the United States, and *ex-officio* President of the Senate, was originally objected to as superfluous, if not mischievous. But it was justified principally on two considerations; the first was, that to secure, at all times, a definite resolution of the Senate, it was necessary that the President of that body should have a casting vote; and to take a Senator from his seat as Senator, and place him in that of the presiding officer, would be, in regard to the State from which he came, to exchange a constant, for a contingent vote. The other consideration was, that as the Vice-President may occasionally become a substitute for the President in the supreme Executive office, all the reasons which recommend the mode of election prescribed, in the first instance, for the one, apply with great, if not with equal force to the other.

[1] By Mr. Chancellor Kent, in his "Commentaries."

The powers and duties of the President devolve, as we have seen, on the Vice-President, not only when no choice is made by the Electors, or the House of Representatives, but also in case of the President's removal from office, or of his death, resignation, or inability to discharge his duties; and Congress is authorized to provide by law for the case of vacancies in the offices of both President and Vice-President.[1] In pursuance of this power, it has been enacted that in the event of such vacancies, the President of the Senate *pro tempore*, and, in case there should be no such President of the Senate, that the Speaker of the House of Representatives for the time being, shall act as President of the United States until the vacancy be supplied.

The evidence of a refusal to accept, or of a resignation of the office of President or Vice-President, is declared by the same Act of Congress to be a declaration in writing, filed in the office of the Secretary of State.

As it might become a question who would be the person to serve, if the office of President should devolve on the Speaker of the House of Representatives, after the Congress for which the last Speaker was chosen had expired, and before the new Congress has met, it is usual for the Vice-President to withdraw from the Senate shortly before the adjournment of the session, in order to afford that body the opportunity to choose a President, *pro tempore*, from among those of its members whose terms of service continue over the next session of Congress; and if *he* should die or resign during the interval or recess, and a casual vacancy occur in the

[1] Const. U. S., Art II. Sect. I. 6.

offices of President and Vice-President, the former Speaker would probably be deemed the person upon whom the office was intended to devolve. If the Vice-President succeed to the office of President, he continues in it until the expiration of the term for which the President was elected. If both offices are vacant, it is made the duty of the Secretary of State to take measures under the Act of Congress, for the election of a President. But as that Act was passed before the amendment of the Constitution, directing the Electors to vote separately for the President and Vice-President, and as that amendment omitted, perhaps intentionally, to provide for the case, a Vice-President cannot be elected, in the event of a vacancy in that office, until the next regular period.[1]

In addition to all the other precautions to prevent abuse in the Executive trust, in the mode of the President's appointment, in the limitation of his term of office, and in the precise and definite restrictions on the exercise of his powers, the Constitution provides that, before he enter on the execution of his office, he shall take an oath or affirmation faithfully to execute the same; and, to the best of his ability, to preserve, protect, and defend the Constitution; and it renders him amenable to justice for mal-administration.[2] The President, as well as all other officers of the Government, may be impeached, as we have seen, for treason, bribery, and other high crimes and misdemeanors, and, upon conviction, removed from office.

[1] Const. U. S., Art. II. Sect. I. 6. Amend. XII. Mr. Justice Story, in his Commentaries, §§ 14–77, hints a doubt, whether the Act in question be constitutional.

[2] Const. U. S., Art. II. Sect. II. 8, and *Ibid.* Sect. IV.

The inviolability of the Supreme Magistrate, as maintained in the English law, is incompatible with the theory of our government, as well as with the principles of retributive justice; and if neither the sense of duty, the force of public opinion, nor the transitory nature of his power, prove sufficient to secure the faithful discharge of the Executive office,—if a President of the United States will use the authority of his station to violate the Constitution and laws, even he, as easily and as promptly as any subordinate officer, may be arrested in his course by an impeachment.

Considering the nature and extent of the authority necessarily incident to the station, it was difficult to constitute the office of President so as to render it equally safe and efficient, by combining, in the structure of its power, a due proportion of energy and responsibility. The former is necessary to maintain a firm administration of the laws; the latter, to preserve inviolate the rights of the People and of the States. "The authors of the Federal Constitution," says the eminent jurist I have so frequently quoted, "appear to have surveyed these two objects with profound discernment, and have organized the Executive Department with consummate skill."[1]

[1] 2 Kent's Comm. Part. 2d, Sect. 13.

LECTURE V.

OF THE JUDICIAL POWER.

As the personal security and private property of every individual depend on the wisdom, stability, and integrity of the Courts of Justice, the Judicial power interferes more directly and uniformly than either of the other departments, with all the concerns of social and private life. No Government can be complete in its form, or perfect in its principles of organization, without this power. To make laws and execute them, are the respective objects of the other two departments, and are, indeed, the two principal operations of government. But laws cannot be fully and correctly executed unless there be a power in the State to expound and apply them. This power being auxiliary to the Executive authority, partakes, in some degree, of its nature. But its office is, in some cases, to control the exercise of Executive power; and those acts of the latter, which are judicially declared to be unconstitutional or unlawful, are thereby rendered inoperative and void. The Judicial department may also be said to participate in the Legislative power, as its construction of Legislative acts is binding and conclusive; although this does not prevent the Legislature from repairing defects, or explaining ambiguities, by subsequent laws operating on subsequent cases.

A higher function, moreover, appertains to this department, under a written Constitution, founded upon true principles of representation, and establishing a just separation of the three branches of Government, and that is, to expound the Constitution, and thereby test the validity of the acts of the Legislature, as well as those of the Executive department, *in all cases where the question as to their construction arises in a suit at law or in equity.* Hence the more imperious and absolute necessity of securing, by fundamental provisions, the independence of the Judicial power. A Constitution which omitted to establish an adequate Judicial power, could not successfully be carried into effect; and if, instead of being rendered independent, that power be united with one or both of the other departments, or if those charged with its administration were made dependent on either of them, its dignity and utility would be destroyed.

The Judicial power in every government must be coextensive with the power of legislation. Were there no power to interpret, pronounce, and enforce the laws, the Government, if it did not perish by its own weakness, would be corrupted by the usurpation of new powers by the Legislature, to the subversion of public liberty. But the Judicial authority cannot, by the force of language, be made to exceed the Legislative power, for such excess would be inconsistent with its nature; and if, by express terms, it should, on the other hand, be so restricted as to embrace a part only of the subjects of actual legislation, the integrity and efficiency of the whole system would, in proportion, be materially impaired. The Constitution, therefore, establishes the Judicial power as a substantive, integral, and independent branch of the Government; and this was the more necessary, from the extraordinary complications of the authority of the United States with that of the several States, resulting unavoidably from the nature of the Federal Union. The Judicial power of the National Government is accordingly vested "in one Supreme Court, and in such Inferior Courts as Congress may, from time to time, ordain and establish."[1] A Chief Justice is recognized in the article which provides that when the President shall be impeached, "the *Chief Justice*" shall preside at the trial; and the existence of other Judges is contemplated by the provision which prescribes the manner of their appointment. The complete organization, however, of the Supreme Court, as well as the establishment of inferior and subordinate Courts, is provided for by statute.

In the survey which I propose to take of this interesting and important branch of the Federal Government, I shall consider, *First*, the manner in which it is constituted; and *Secondly*, the extent and distribution of its authority. The first point embraces these several objects, viz: The mode in which the Judges of the several Courts of the United States are *appointed;* the *tenure* by which they hold their offices; the provision for their *support;* and the precautions to secure their *responsibility.*

I. The manner in which the Judicial power of the United States is constituted; and 1st. As to the mode in which the Judges are appointed.

The mode of appointing public officers, by the President and Senate, I have already spoken of as generally

[1] Const. U. S., Art. III. Sect. 1.

advantageous; and it seems peculiarly fit and proper with respect to the Judicial department. The just and vigorous investigation and punishment of every species of fraud and violence, and the compelling every man punctually to fulfil his contracts, are duties, not, certainly, of the most popular character, although their faithful discharge will always command the approbation of the candid and judicious. The fittest men would probably possess too much reserve, and too much severity of morals, to secure an election depending on universal suffrage; nor would the mode of appointment by a large deliberative assembly be entitled to unqualified approbation. There are too many occasions, and too many temptations for intrigue and the operation of party prejudices, and too much scope for the interference of local interests to permit such a body to act, in such cases, with a sufficiently single and steady regard for the public welfare.

2. The Judges, both of the Supreme and inferior Courts, hold their offices *during good behavior.* This tenure, as a standard for the duration and continuance in office of the Judicial Magistracy, is considered by the authors of "The Federalist,"[1] as "one of the most valuable of modern improvements in the practice of government. In a Monarchy, it is a necessary barrier against the despotism of the Prince. In a Republic, it is no less essential as a defence against the encroachments of the Executive and Legislative powers; and it is the best expedient that can be devised, in any Government, to secure a steady, upright, and impartial administration of the laws." This principle, which has

[1] No. 78, by Mr. Hamilton.

been the subject of much deserved eulogy, is one of the many benefits derived from the land of our forefathers, where the Judges anciently held their seats at the pleasure of the Crown, as does the Chancellor to this day. It is easy to conceive what a dangerous influence this must have given to the King in the administration of justice in those cases where the claims or pretensions of the Government were made to bear on the rights of a private individual. And, although in the reign of James I., the Barons of the Exchequer,—the Court in which jurisdiction is taken of all matters relative to the revenues and property of the Crown,—were created during good behavior; and, although the commissions of the other Judges were made so to run at the restoration of Charles II., it still remained at the pleasure of the Crown to prescribe the form of the commission, until the statute of William and Mary established the commissions of all the Common Law Judges to be *quam din bene se gesserint.* The excellence of this provision has recommended its adoption by other nations of Europe, and it prevails in many of our State Constitutions; but in some, under modifications more or less extensive and injurious.

Whoever attentively considers the different departments of power, must perceive that in a Government in which they are separated from each other, the Judiciary, from the nature of its functions, will always be the least dangerous to the political rights secured by the Constitution, because it will have the least capacity to invade or injure them. The Executive power not only dispenses the honors, but wields the sword of the community. The Legislature not only holds the public purse, but prescribes the rules by which the rights and duties of every citizen are to be enjoyed and regulated. But the Judicial power has no command over the sword or the purse;—no direction, either of the strength or the wealth of the society, and can take no active resolution whatsoever. It has been truly and emphatically said to have "neither force nor will, but merely judgment;"[1] and even for the practical exercise of this faculty, it must depend on the protection and support of the Executive arm. This view of the subject shows, in the first place, that the Judicial is, beyond all comparison, the weakest of the three departments of power; that it can never attack, with success, either of the others; and that all possible care is required to defend it from attacks by them. It also shows that, although individual oppression may, now and then, proceed from the Courts of Justice, yet the general liberty of the People can never be endangered from that quarter,—so long as the Judicial remains truly distinct from the Legislative and Executive powers; and lastly, it shows, as a consequence of these previous deductions, and bearing immediately upon the point we are considering, that nothing can contribute so much to the firmness and independence of the Judicial power, as permanency in office. This quality, therefore, may justly be regarded as an indispensable ingredient in its constitution, and as rendering it the great security of public justice, liberty, and safety.

3. In addition to the tenure by which the Judges hold their offices, the permanent provision for their *support* is admirably adapted to secure their independence. It tends, also, to secure a succession of learned

1 "The Federalist," No. 78.

men for the bench, who, in consequence of a certain fixed support, are induced to relinquish the lucrative pursuit of their practice at the bar, for the duties of a more important and honorable station. The Constitution declares, on this subject, that all the Judges of the United States "shall, at stated times, receive for their services, a compensation which shall not be diminished during their continuance in office;"[1] and this provision was considered an improvement upon the previously existing Constitutions of the States. It was ordained in the Constitution of Massachusetts, that permanent and honorable salaries should be established by law for the Judges. But this was not sufficiently precise and definite, and the more certain provision in the Federal Constitution has been wisely followed in the subsequent Constitutions of several of the individual States.

The complete and perfect independence of the Judiciary is peculiarly requisite in a limited Constitution like that of the United States, which contains certain specific restrictions upon the Legislative authority both of the Federal and State Governments, such, for instance, as that "Congress shall pass no bills of attainder, or *ex post facto* law," and that "no State shall coin money, emit bills of credit, or pass laws impairing the obligation of contracts." Limitations of neither of these kinds can be preserved in practice in any other way than through the instrumentality of Courts of Justice; and it is a wise and necessary principle of our Government, as I shall show more fully hereafter, that the Acts both of the Federal and State Legislatures are subject to the severe scrutiny and impartial inter-

[1] Const. U. S., Art. III. Sect. I.

pretation of tribunals who are bound to regard the Constitution as the paramount law, and the highest evidence of the will of the People; and, consequently, to declare void all acts contrary to its tenor. Without this power, not only all the limitations and restrictions such as I have specified, but all the reservations of rights and privileges, either to the several States, or their individual citizens, would be ineffectual and nugatory.

4. But while the Constitution has thus rendered the Federal Courts independent of undue influence from the other departments of the Government, it has adopted a precaution for their *responsibility*, by rendering them amenable for any corrupt violation of their trust; and the Judges of the United States may be held to answer upon an impeachment; and, if convicted, they may be removed from the bench, and be disqualified from holding any office in the Government. This, perhaps, is the only provision consistent with the necessary independence of the Judicial character in a Government of the complex nature of that of the United States, and is the only one to be found relative to the subject in the Constitution.

The want of a provision for removing the Judges on account of inability, or upon the address of the Legislature, which exists not only in England, but in some of the States of this Union, afforded ground of objection when the Federal Constitution was under discussion in the State Conventions. But the most wise and considerate men of that period believed that such a provision could not be reduced to practice, or, in a Government like ours, would be more liable to abuse than productive of good consequences. A provision similar to that in the first Constitution of New York, which limited the duration of the highest Judicial officers to the age of sixty years, was also complained of as an omission in the Federal Constitution; but it was admirably replied by Mr. Hamilton,[1]— one of the ablest and most illustrious defenders of that instrument, that "in a Republic where fortunes are not affluent, and pensions not expedient, the dismission of men from stations in which they have served their country long and usefully,— on which they depend for subsistence, and from which it will be too late to resort to any other occupation, should have some better apology to humanity than is to be found in the imaginary danger of a superannuated bench."

II. The Federal Judiciary being established, as I have explained, on principles essential to maintain that department in a proper state of independence, and to secure a pure and vigorous administration of the law, the Constitution proceeds to designate the objects of its jurisdiction. It extends the Judicial power of the Union to all cases in Law and Equity, arising under *the Constitution and laws of the United States*, and *treaties* made under their authority; to all cases affecting *Ambassadors, other public Ministers, and Consuls*;[2] to all cases of *Admiralty and Maritime Jurisdiction;*[3] to controversies to which *the United States are a party;* to controversies between *two or more States;* between *a State when*

[1] In "The Federalist," No. 79.

[2] A State Court cannot claim jurisdiction of civil suits against foreign Consuls. 7 *Peters*, 276.

[3] But the grant of this jurisdiction does not take away the authority of the several States to regulate their *fisheries*, and punish those who violate such regulations. 4 *Washington C. C.* 383.

plaintiff and citizens of another State; between *citizens of the same State, claiming lands under grants from different States;* and to controversies between *citizens of the United States, and foreign States, citizens, or subjects.*[1]

A citizen of one State having title to lands in another, is not disabled from suing for those lands in the Courts of the United States by the fact that he derives his title from a citizen of the State in which the lands lie.[2] And if the controversy is founded on conflicting grants of different States, the Judicial power of the Federal Courts extends to the case.[3] A citizen of one State has a right to sue upon the bond of a Sheriff of another, and to use the name of the Governor to whom the bond is given, although the parties to the bond, the Sheriff, and the Governor are all citizens of the same State, *provided the parties for whose use the suit is brought* is a citizen of a different State.[4] A citizen of one State can sue a Corporation which has been created by, and transacts business in another,—the suit being brought in the latter,—although some of the members of the Corporation are not citizens of the State in which the suit is brought, and although the State itself may be a member of the corporation.[5]

As the Constitution originally stood, the Judicial power of the United States extended to suits prosecuted against an individual State by a citizen of another State of the Union, or by citizens or subjects of any

[1] Const. U. S., Art. III. Sect. II. 1.
[2] 1 *Peters*, 263.
[3] 1 *Wheaton*, 415; 3 *Condensed Rep.* 580.
[4] 2 *Howard*, 9.
[5] *Ibid.* 497.

foreign State. The States, however, were not willing to be arraigned as defendants before the Federal Courts, at the instance of private persons; — and it was subsequently declared by an Amendment, that the Judicial power of the United States should not be construed to extend to any suit of law or equity commenced or prosecuted against one of the States by citizens of another State, or by citizens or subjects of any foreign State.[1]

The object of this Amendment was to inhibit the commencement or prosecution of a suit against a State by the citizens of another State, or the subjects of a foreign power. Where the record of a judgment obtained by a State, in its own courts, against an individual, is removed to the Supreme Court of the United States, *by writ of error*, for the purpose of examining the question — Whether that judgment be in violation of the Federal Constitution, or a law of Congress, and not for the purpose of asserting a claim or demand against the State, it is not embraced by the prohibition of this Amendment. For a writ of error is only in the nature of a suit or action where the object is to restore the possession of something withheld from the party obtaining it, and not where its operation is wholly defensive.[2]

A motion to dismiss a cause pending in a Court of the United States, for want of jurisdiction, may be made at any stage of the proceedings. It is not analogous to a plea to the jurisdiction of a Court of Law, or Equity, in England, where the Superior Courts have a general jurisdiction over all persons within the realm,

[1] Amendments Const. U. S., XI.

[2] 6 *Wheat.* 264; 5 *Cond. Rep.* 90.

and all causes of action between them. The rule prevailing there, in reference to a Court of general jurisdiction, is, that a party claiming exemption from its process, must set out the reason by a special plea in abatement, and show that some inferior Court of Law or Equity has exclusive cognizance of the case; otherwise, the Superior Court must proceed in virtue of its general jurisdiction; but as the Courts of the United States are of a special and limited original jurisdiction, their action must be confined to the particular cases, controversies, and parties, over which the Constitution and laws have authorized them to act,—any proceeding without the limits prescribed, is *coram non judice*, and their action a nullity; and wherever the want of power is objected to by a party, or is apparent to the Court, it must surcease its action, or proceed extra-judicially.[1]

Nor can the local laws of the States confer jurisdiction on the Courts of the United States. They can only furnish rules to ascertain the rights of parties; and thus assist in the administration of the proper remedies where the jurisdiction is vested by the laws of the United States.[2] Neither can State laws confer any authority upon the Federal Courts in the exercise of their jurisdiction, by the use of State process to reach persons or property which could not be reached within the meaning of the law establishing the jurisdiction.[3]

The propriety of vesting the jurisdiction, as it now stands, in the Judicial department of the United States, seems to result necessarily from their union as one nation; and its exercise by the national tribunals may be considered requisite to the existence of the Federal

[1] 12 *Peters*, 657. [2] 11 *Ibid.* 175. [3] 12 *Ibid.* 300.

Government. It may be profitable, however, at the present moment, to view this branch of our subject somewhat in detail, in particular reference to questions arising under *the Constitution and laws of the United States.*

The fitness of extending the jurisdiction of the Federal Courts to cases arising under the *Constitution*, in contradistinction to those arising under the laws passed in virtue of its authority, results from the obvious necessity of a constitutional method of giving efficacy to those provisions of the national compact which neither require nor admit of an act on the part of the national legislature to sanction or enforce them. What, indeed, would avail the restrictions on the States, without some constitutional mode of compelling their observance? The individual States are prohibited, for instance, from the performance of a variety of acts, some of which are incompatible with the objects and interests of the Union, and others with the principles of good policy. The imposition, by State authority, of duties on imported articles, is an example of the first, and the emission of bills of credit, a specimen of the second. Now, in the face of the experience afforded under the former Confederation, it will hardly be pretended that such prohibitions would be scrupulously regarded without some effectual power in the General Government to restrain or correct their violation. The power must be either a direct negative on the State laws vested in the Executive authority of the Union, (which, indeed, was proposed as the alternative in the General Convention,) or an authority in the Federal Courts, to overrule such laws of the several States as contravene the National Constitution.[1] The latter expedient was preferred by the Convention, and was, unquestionably most acceptable to their constituents; and there is no third course that can be imagined short of the modern heresy of *nullification*, which assumes a power in any one State, to suspend, if not to subvert, within its own limits, the acts and operations of every department of the Federal Government, although every other member of the Union admit their validity, and submit to their authority.

As to extending the jurisdiction of the National Courts to all cases arising under *the laws* of the United States, it seems impossible, by any argument or illustration, to render its propriety clearer than it appears from the mere statement of the question. If there be such things as political *axioms*, or truths in the science of government too plain to be disputed, the principle already stated, that "the Judicial power must be coextensive with the power of legislation," must certainly be one of them; and in Governments formed from the union of the People of so many separate and independent States, as well as of those States themselves, as one Nation, organized under a written compact, the mere necessity of uniformity in the interpretation of the national laws is sufficient to decide the question.

[1] It has accordingly been held by the Supreme Court, that its exposition of the Federal Constitution is conclusive upon the State Courts. 3 *Marsh.* 423; 8 *Pick.* 196; 6 *Conn.* 493; 3 *Binn.* 84; 6 *Ibid.* 272; 3 *Monr.* 55; 5 *Ibid.* 294. But it seems it has no authority on a writ of error from a State Court to declare a State law void by reason of its collision with *the State Constitution.* 3 *Peters,* 289; 2 *How.* 236; 4 *Gill & Johns.* 519.

If the Courts of the United States have not this paramount jurisdiction, it must remain without control in the tribunals of the States; and between thirty and forty independent judicatures, with final jurisdiction over the same kind of causes, arising under the same laws, would present a monstrous anomaly in judicial organization and procedure, from which nothing but contradiction and confusion could ensue.

The People of the United States have declared that the Constitution, laws, and treaties of the United States shall be the supreme law of the land, and that the Judges in every State shall be bound by them, "any thing in the Constitution and laws of any State to the contrary notwithstanding."[1] Congress, no more than the State Legislatures, have power to pass laws repugnant to the Federal Constitution, because that Constitution is not only the *paramount*, but also the *fundamental law;* and those laws, only, which are passed in pursuance of the Constitution, are declared to be *supreme* in reference to the Constitutions and laws of the several States. Every act, therefore, of Congress, as well as of the State Legislatures, and every part of the Constitution of any State, which is repugnant to the Constitution of the United States, is necessarily void. This we must regard as a clear and settled principle of our National Jurisprudence, — unalterable by any authority but that from which the National compact is derived; and not liable to any change, even by that authority, except in the mode prescribed by the instrument itself. Now, as the Judicial power of the Union is declared to extend to *all cases* arising under the

[1] Const. U. S., Art. VI. 2.

Constitution, to that power it must necessarily belong, in cases where the question is judicially presented for decision, to determine what *is* the *Supreme Law;* and the judgment of the Federal Supreme Court must be final and conclusive, because the Constitution invests that tribunal with the power to decide, and gives no appeal from its decision. If an Act of Congress be repugnant to the Constitution, it is *ipso facto* void; and the Courts have the power, and it is their duty so to declare it. But if it admit of two interpretations, one of which brings it within, and the other presses it beyond the constitutional authority of Congress, it is the duty of the Courts to adopt the former construction, because a presumption ought never to be indulged that Congress meant to exercise or usurp any unconstitutional authority. Nor will the Courts ever pronounce an Act of Congress void, except in a very clear case.[1]

[1] For cases, both in the Federal and State Courts, in which Acts of Congress and State Constitutions and laws have been declared void as against the Constitution, laws, or treaties of the United States, see 2 *Peters*, 522; 12 *Wheat.* 270; 3 *Dall.* 309; 4 *Ibid.* 18; 6 *Cranch*, 128; *Charlt.* 175; *Ibid.* 235; *Walker*, 146; 1 *Blackf.* 206; 1 *Breese*, 209; *Ibid.* 70; 2 *Porter*, 303; 1 *Marsh.* 290; 2 *Litt.* 90; *Pr. Dec.* 64; *Ibid.* 89; 4 *Monr.* 43; 1 *Hayw.* 28; *Ibid.* 272; *Cooke*, 217; 4 *Yerg.* 202; 9 *Ibid.* 490; 1 *Rep. Const. C.* 267; 3 *Desauss.* 476; 1 *McCord*, 238; *Harper*, 385; 1 *Car. Law Rep.* 246; 1 *Murphy*, 58; 6 *Rand.* 245; 1 *Virg. Cas.* 20; 1 *Binn.* 491; 5 *Ibid.* 355; 2 *Yeates*, 493; 2 *Pennsyl.* 184; 3 *Serg. & Raw.* 169; 19 *Johns. Rep.* 58; 1 *Cowen*, 550; 1 *South.* 192; 2 *Ibid.* 466; 1 *Har. & J.* 236; 7 *Gill & Johns.* 7; 1 *Ibid.* 463; 10 *Conn.* 522; 4 *Ibid.* 225; 3 *Verm.* 507; 1 *Chip.* 237; *Ibid.* 257; 1 *Aick.* 314; 3 *N. H.* 473; 4 *Ibid.* 16; 7 *Ibid.* 65; 3 *Greenl.* 326; 4 *Ibid.* 140; 6 *Ibid.* 412; *Ibid.* 112; 9 *Ibid.* 60; 2 *Fairf.* 118; 11 *Mass.* 396; 15 *Ibid.* 447; 7 *Pick.* 460; 13 *Ibid.* 60. So also Statutes which violate the plain and obvious principles of common right, and common reason, have been declared by the Courts to be null and

Some perplexity, indeed, existed at first, in regard to the rights of Courts of Justice to pronounce Legislative acts void on the ground of their repugnancy to the Constitution. It arose from apprehension that the doctrine would establish a superiority of the Judicial, over the Legislative power; and notwithstanding the numerous cases above referred to in support of the principle, difficulties, at least, if not doubts on this subject, have been since revived in some of the States, and among a particular class of politicians. The question, therefore, having of late assumed great practical importance, a rapid survey of the grounds on which the affirmative was maintained by some of the most eminent of the statesmen who framed the Constitution, cannot be disadvantageous or misplaced, especially as it exhibits a contemporaneous construction of that part of the instrument of the highest authority.

"There is no position," say the illustrious authors of "The Federalist," "which depends on clearer principles, than that every act of a delegated authority contrary to the commission under which it is exercised, is void."[1] No Legislative act, therefore, contrary to the Constitution, which is the commission whence every department of the Government derives its authority from the People, can be valid. To deny this, would be to affirm that the deputy is superior to his principal; that the servant is above his master; that the representatives of the People are greater than the People themselves; and that persons acting in virtue of a delegated authority, may not only assume what their powers do

void. 1 *Bay*, 98. But see 3 *Dall.* 398; 1 *Bald.* 74; 1 *Har. & J.* 249; 2 *Rawle*, 374.

[1] No. 78, by Mr. Hamilton.

not authorize, but what they expressly forbid. If it be alleged that Legislative bodies are themselves the constitutional judges of their own powers, and that their own construction of them is conclusive upon the other departments of the Government, it may be answered that this cannot be the natural presumption, where it is not to be collected from the particular provisions of the fundamental compact. Without such express provision, it is not to be intended to enable the representatives of the People to substitute their own will in the place of that of their constituents; it is far more rational to conclude that the Courts of Justice were, equally with the other departments, intended to represent the sovereignty of the People, in a coördinate and independent one; and in that capacity, to act as an intermediate body between the People and the Legislature, in order, among other things, to keep the latter within the limits assigned to its authority.

The interpretation of the laws is the proper and peculiar province of the Courts; and the Constitution is, in fact, and must be regarded by them as a fundamental law. It must, therefore, belong to them to ascertain *its* meaning, as well as the meaning of any particular act proceeding from the Legislative body. If there should happen to be an irreconcilable variance between the two, that which has the superior obligation ought, of course, to be preferred. In other words, the Constitution ought to be preferred to the statute, — the intention of the People, to the intention of their agents. Nor does this conclusion, by any means, suppose a superiority of the Judicial to the Legislative power. It only presumes that the power of the People is superior to both; and where the will of the Legislature, declared in the statute-book, stands opposed to the will of the People declared in the Constitution, the Judges are to be governed by the latter, rather than the former, and ought to regulate their decisions by that fundamental law over which the Legislature has no control, rather than by those which it may, at any time, alter or repeal, and which derive their validity and effect from the Constitution alone. It can be of no weight to say that the Courts of Justice, under the pretence of a repugnancy between a law and the Constitution, may substitute their own pleasure instead of the constitutional intentions of the Legislature, for this supposition not only involves a petition of the question, but might as well happen in the case of two contradictory statutes, or upon every separate adjudication upon the same statute. The Courts are bound to declare the meaning of the law; and, if they should be disposed to exercise *will* instead of *judgment*, the consequence in the one case, as well as in the other, would be the substitution of their own pleasure in lieu of the pleasure of the Legislature. The objection therefore, if it proved any thing, would prove that there should be no Judges distinct from the Legislative body. But the danger of intrusting Judicial and Legislative powers in the same hands has already been pointed out; and it has been shown, I think, that the object of their separation was not only to create a distinct and independent body to expound the laws, but also to erect a bulwark to defend a Constitution, limited in its powers, against Legislative encroachments or Executive usurpation, while it was itself restrained within its proper bounds by corresponding checks, in the hands of the other departments, or inherent in its own constitution.

The design of this separation of the Judicial power from the other departments, and of the precautions for maintaining its independence, was, moreover, to afford protection to the Federal Government, in the exercise of its acknowledged powers, against the inroads or influence of the State sovereignties; and all the requirements and illustrations adduced in support of the right and duty of the Federal Courts, in the ordinary administration of their authority, to declare void those acts of Congress which, in their judgment, are repugnant to the Constitution, apply with equal, if not greater force, to establish a more extensive power in regard to the acts and proceedings of the State Governments. We have seen that the People of the several States, in their adoption of the Federal Constitution, acknowledged that Constitution, and the laws and treaties made in pursuance of its authority, to be the *supreme law of the land*, and as of paramount obligation, therefore, to the *Constitutions*, as well as of the laws, of any of the States. So far, then, from admitting each party to the National compact to interpret that instrument for itself, those very parties, by declaring that the Judicial power of the Union should extend to all cases arising under it, vested in the proper department authority to determine its construction *in every case in which a question should judicially arise, whether directly, between the parties to the suit, or collaterally, between the parties to the "social contract."*[1]

The Courts of the United States have no jurisdiction derived from the Common Law to define and punish

[1] The Supreme Court refuses to take up cases that involve constitutional questions, when the Court is not full. 9 *Peters*, 85.

criminal offences.[1] Congress, by an Act passed in 1825, provided that all crimes committed in places within the exclusive jurisdiction of the United States, which are not defined by any law of the United States, should be punished in the same manner as such crimes were punished by the laws of the particular States where they were committed. This Act is held to be limited to the laws of the several States as they existed at the time of its enactment. An offence, therefore, neither against the Common Law, nor against any State statute in force at the time the Act of Congress was passed, cannot be punished in the Federal Courts in virtue of that Act.[2] Neither can an offence against a temporary statute be punished in those Courts, after the expiration of the Act, unless a particular provision be made by law for that purpose.[3]

[1] 7 *Cranch*, 52; 1 *Wheat.* 416; 3 *Ibid.* 336; 2 *Cond. Rep.* 405; 3 *Ibid.* 585–590.

[2] 6 *Peters*, 141.

[3] 7 *Wheat.* 551; 6 *Cranch*, 203; 2 *Cond. Rep.* 346; 5 *Ibid.* 343.

LECTURE VI.

OF THE DISTRIBUTION OF THE JUDICIAL POWER AMONG THE FEDERAL COURTS.

We now proceed to ascertain in what manner the Federal jurisdiction has been distributed among the several Courts, either by the Constitution, or the Acts of Congress carrying the system into complete effect. It may be observed generally, that the disposition of this power, except in a few specified cases, is left to Congress; and that the Courts cannot exercise jurisdiction in every case to which the Judicial power extends, without the intervention of Congress. Congress, moreover, is not bound to enlarge the jurisdiction of the respective tribunals to every subject which the Constitution warrants, although the whole Judicial power ought, at all times, to be vested in some of the Courts created under the authority of the United States.

It is laid down as a rule, in the eighty-second number of "The Federalist,"[1] that the State Courts retained all preëxisting authority,—or the jurisdiction which they had before the adoption of the Constitution of the United States,—except where it was taken away either by an exclusive authority granted in express terms to the Union by that instrument, or in a case

[1] By Mr. Hamilton.

where a particular authority is granted to the Union, and the exercise of a like authority is prohibited to the States, or in the case where an authority is granted to the Union, with which a similar authority in the States would be incompatible. A concurrent jurisdiction in the State Courts was admitted in all such cases; but this doctrine is applicable only to those descriptions of causes of which the State Courts had previous cognizance, and not to cases growing out of the new Constitution.

Congress, in the course of its legislation, may commit the decision of cases arising under its own laws, to the Federal Courts exclusively; but unless the State Courts were expressly excluded by the Act of Congress, they would, of course, take concurrent jurisdiction of the causes to which those acts may give birth, under the qualifications mentioned. And before the adoption of the Constitution, it was asserted and maintained by its ablest commentators, that in all cases of concurrent jurisdiction, an appeal would lie to the Supreme Court of the United States; and that, without such appeal, the concurrent jurisdiction of the State Courts in matters of National concern, would be inadmissible, because, in that case, it would be inconsistent with the authority and efficiency of the National Government. The practice of that Government has been conformable to this doctrine; and the exclusive and concurrent jurisdiction conferred upon the Federal Courts by the Acts of Congress, are clearly distinguished and marked in correspondence with it.

It is, nevertheless, manifest, that the Judicial power of the United States may, in all cases which it comprehends, be made exclusive of State authority, at the election of Congress. Hence, the concurrent jurisdiction of the State tribunals depends altogether upon the pleasure of the National Legislature, and whenever Congress thinks proper, it may be revoked and extinguished in every case which can constitutionally be made cognizable in the National Courts; but without an express provision to the contrary, the State Courts retain a concurrent jurisdiction in all cases of which, previous to the Federal Constitution, they possessed the jurisdiction. But Acts of Congress giving the State Courts jurisdiction of suits on the penal laws of the United States, have in some of the States been declared unconstitutional;[1] although it is admitted that a State magistrate may commit for further examination touching a crime against the United States.[2]

The State Courts, moreover, may, in the exercise of their ordinary original jurisdiction, take cognizance *incidentally* of cases arising under the Constitution, laws, and treaties of the United States; and the Courts of one State have power to decide on the validity of the Legislative acts of another, with respect to the Constitution of the United States, when the question arises in a case within their jurisdiction; but, in all these cases, the Judicial power of the Union extends by means of its appellate jurisdiction.[3]

In order to ascertain to what extent, and in what manner, the Federal jurisdiction, both *original* and

1 7 *Conn.* 239, 244; 17 *Johns. Rep.* 4, 261; 1 *Virg. Cases*, 321; 2 *Ibid.* 34; 1 *Dana*, 442. *Contrâ*, 11 *Serg. & Rawle*, 193. See also 4 *Dall. Appendix* XXVI.; 2 *Atk.* 89; 5 *Har. & J.* 317; 2 *Bailey*, 44.

2 2 *Cowen*, 273.

3 5 *Binn.* 355; 8 *Pick.* 194. But see 12 *Serg. & Rawle*, 203.

appellate, has been disposed of, either by the Constitution itself, or by Act of Congress, we must review, as we proposed, the various Courts established by the one, or ordained by the other.

I. THE SUPREME COURT OF THE UNITED STATES, although created by the Constitution, received its organization from the Judiciary Act of 1789, and the several supplementary statutes which have at different times, subsequently, been passed in relation to it. The Constitution had merely declared that there should be a Supreme Court, with certain original and appellate powers; it is only to be implied from that instrument that "The Chief Justice of the United States" should preside in it, with other Judges to be associated with him.[1] By the existing Act of Congress, it consists of the Chief Justice and eight associate Judges, any five of whom constitute a *quorum*. It holds one term annually, at the seat of the General Government, commencing on the first Monday in January; and although the presence of five Judges is required for the general business of the Court, yet any one or more of them may make all necessary orders in a suit, preparatory to the hearing or trial; and it is made the special duty of the Chief Justice to attend at Washington on the first Monday in August, annually, for the same purpose.

The Supreme Court has, by the Constitution, *exclusive* original jurisdiction of all controversies of a *civil* nature, where a State can be made a party, except in suits by a State against one or more of its citizens, or against citizens of other States, or against aliens; in which cases it has *original* but not exclusive jurisdiction.

[1] Const. U. S., Art. III. Sect. II. 1.

It has, also, *exclusively* such jurisdiction of suits or proceedings *against* ambassadors, or other public ministers, or their domestics, as a Court of Law can exercise consistently with the Law of Nations; *original*, but not *exclusive* jurisdiction of all suits *brought by* ambassadors, or other public ministers, or in which a Consul or Vice-Consul may be a party.[1]

If a foreign Minister, or Consul, sued in a State Court, omit to plead his privilege of exemption, and afterwards, upon removing the suit from an inferior to a higher Court, he claims the privilege, such omission is not a waiver of it. Were it viewed only as a personal privilege, there might be grounds for an opposite conclusion; but it cannot be so considered. It is the privilege of the Country or Government which the Minister or Consul represents. This is the light in which foreign *Ministers* are viewed by the Law of Nations; and our Constitution and laws seem to regard *Consuls* in the same light in this respect.[2]

The Constitution also confers on the Supreme Court an *appellate* jurisdiction, under such exceptions or regulations as Congress may prescribe; and by the first Judiciary Act,[3] it is declared that appeals shall lie to this Court from the *Circuit Courts* of the United States, and, in certain cases, from the highest Courts of the several States. Final judgments and decrees in civil actions, and suits in Equity in the Circuit Courts, whether brought there by original process, or removed thither from the State Courts, or by appeal from the

1 Const. U. S., Art. III. Sect. II. 2.

2 7 *Peters*, 276.

3 Passed Sept. 24, 1789.

District Courts of the United States,—where the matter in dispute exceeds a specified sum, may be reëxamined, and reversed or affirmed by the Supreme Court; and final judgments or decrees of the Circuit Courts, in cases of Admiralty and Maritime jurisdiction,—and in questions of prize or no prize, where the matter in dispute exceeds the same amount, may be reviewed on appeal in the Supreme Court; and in these cases, new evidence is admitted on the appeal, conformably with the general doctrines and usages of appellate Courts of Admiralty.[1] So, also, a final judgment or decree of the highest Court of Law or Equity in a State, may be brought up on the allegation of error in point of law, to the Supreme Court of the United States—if the validity of a treaty or of an Act of Congress, or of an authority exercised under the Government of the United States was drawn in question in the State Court, and the decision was *against* that validity; or if the validity of any State law or authority was drawn in question on the ground of its repugnancy to the Constitution, laws, or treaties of the United States, and the decision was *in favor* of its validity; or if the construction of any clause of the Constitution, or of a treaty, or statute of the United States, or of a commission held under them, was drawn in question, and the decision was *against* the title, right, privilege, or exemption especially claimed under the authority of the Union. Upon these appeals from the decision of a State Court, however, no other error can be assigned, or regarded in the Supreme Court than such as appears on the face of the record, and immediately respects the question of the

[1] 7 *Cranch*, 107; 2 *Cond. Rep.* 434.

validity, or construction of the Constitution, treaties, statutes, commissions, or authority in dispute.[1]

1. *The original jurisdiction* of the Supreme Court, or that cognizance which it takes of causes in their initiatory proceedings, is, as may have been perceived, of a very limited character. It is confined by the Constitution to those cases which affect ambassadors, and other public ministers, and consuls, and those in which a State can be made a party; and it has been made a question whether the original jurisdiction was intended to be exclusive of the inferior Courts of the United States, or of the State tribunals. The Act of 1789, seems to have considered it competent for Congress to vest concurrent jurisdiction in the above specified cases, in other Courts than the Supreme Court; for it gives a concurrent jurisdiction in some of them to the Circuit Courts; and it has been held that the word "original," was not here to be taken to imply *exclusive* cognizance of the cases enumerated.[2] But an opinion of the Supreme Court, in another case, goes far towards establishing the principle of exclusive jurisdiction in that Court, in all these cases of original jurisdiction; and although this last decision was subsequently considered as shaking the first, yet the question was afterwards left in doubt by the Court, and a decision upon it purposely waived.[3]

Admitting, then, that this original jurisdiction can be shared by other Courts, in the discretion of Congress, it has been decided that it cannot be enlarged; and that

[1] 4 *Wheat.* 311; 4 *Cond. Rep.* 465.

[2] 2 *Dall.* 297.

[3] 1 *Cranch*, 177; 5 *Serg. & Rawle*, 545; 11 *Wheat.* 467.

the Supreme Court cannot be invested with an original jurisdiction by Act of Congress, in cases other than those described in the Constitution. Congress has no authority to give it original jurisdiction, where the Constitution has declared that it shall be appellate, nor appellate where the Constitution has declared it shall be original.[1] Nor can Congress impose upon Judicial officers, duties not strictly of a Judicial character.[2]

The Constitution gives to the Supreme Court original jurisdiction in those cases in which a State shall be a party, and the Supreme Court has laid down as a rule that it must be a case in which a State is either nominally or *substantially* the party, and that it is not sufficient that the State may be consequentially affected.[3] But although a State cannot be made a defendant, a suit may be maintained against its officers and agents intrusted with the execution of a law granting *a franchise*. Jurisdiction is neither given nor taken away by the relative situation of the parties *concerned in interest*, but of those *named in the record;* consequently, the operation of the amendment to the Constitution affecting the question is limited to those suits in which a State is a party on the record. For the jurisdiction of the Federal Courts is not *ousted* by any incidental or consequential interest which a State may have in the decision. Unless, therefore, the interest of the State is to be determined by the inspection of the record, to ascertain whether it be a party, the Constitution has given no rule by which this interest is to be measured. If the Courts of the United States were required to fix a test or standard, the curious anomaly would be pre-

[1] 1 *Cranch*, 137. [2] 2 *Dall.* 409. [3] 3 *Ibid.* 411.

sented of a Court examining the whole testimony in the cause,—inquiring into, and deciding upon the State's interest, without having, it may be, any jurisdiction in the case. If the authority of the English decisions were to determine the question, it is believed that no case can be adduced from the English books where any person has been considered a party to a suit, who was not a party to the record. Where a State is not a party to the record, and the Court has jurisdiction over those who are, the true question is not one of jurisdiction, but whether, *in the exercise* of its jurisdiction, it ought to make a decree against the parties defendant, whether they are to be considered as having a real interest, or as being only nominal parties; and, where there is a personal responsibility which might be enforced by an action, the parties must certainly have a real interest at stake.[1]

And although the Judicial power of the Union extends to controversies between a State and foreign States, citizens, or subjects, and the Constitution gives original jurisdiction to the Supreme Court in all cases in which a State shall be a party, yet it was held in the celebrated case of the Cherokee Indians that they were not a foreign nation, within the meaning of the Constitution.[2] They were, indeed, considered to be a political community or State; and have been uniformly treated as such since the first settlement of the country. The numerous treaties with them by the United States recognize them as a people capable of maintaining the relations of peace and war; as being responsible in

1 6 *Wheat.* 264; 5 *Cond. Rep.* 90.

5 *Peters*, 1; 1 *Cond. Rep.* 6.

their political character for any violation of their engagements, or any aggressions upon our citizens by any individual of their tribe; laws have been enacted in the spirit of those treaties, and the Courts are held to be bound by those acts of the Government, which have thus plainly recognized this nation of Indians as a State.

The condition of the Indian tribes, in regard to their connection with the United States, bears little resemblance to the relations between any other two people in the world. In general, nations not owing a common allegiance are *foreign* to each other. But the relation of the Indians to the Government of the United States is marked by a peculiar and cardinal distinction. The Cherokees are acknowledged to have an unquestionable, and, until that controversy arose, an unquestioned right to the lands they occupied, until that right was extinguished by voluntary cession to the Federal Government. It was, nevertheless, doubted whether they, or any of the tribes residing within the acknowledged boundaries of the United States, could with accuracy be denominated *foreign* States. They may more correctly be called domestic, dependent nations, occupying a territory over which our Government asserts a right independent of their will, and which must take effect in point of possession when their right of occupancy ceases. In the mean time, their relation to the United States resembles that of a ward to his guardian,—they look to the Federal Government for protection, rely on its kindness, and appeal to its sympathies, for the relief of their wants.

Under these circumstances, the Cherokees sought to restrain the State of Georgia, within whose territorial limits their lands were situate,—from the forcible exercise of Legislative power over them, claiming their independence as a separate and neighboring people,—their right to which the State denied. The Court held its power to interpose for their protection to be, at least, doubtful; but intimated that the mere question of right might, perhaps, be settled in a proper case with proper parties. But it was asked on that occasion, to do more than decide the title; it was called on to control the Legislature of Georgia, and to restrain the exertion of its physical force; and the propriety of such an interposition might well be questioned, as it savored too much of the exercise of political power to be within the province of the Judicial department; and it refused to interfere.

In cases in which the Court has original jurisdiction, the form of proceeding is not regulated by Act of Congress, but by the rules and orders of the Court, which are framed in analogy to the practice of the English Court of Chancery. But the Supreme Court does not follow this practice where it would embarrass the case by unnecessary technicality or defeat the purposes of Justice.[1]

Before the adoption of the eleventh Amendment of the Constitution,[2] a suit might have been brought against a State by the citizens of another State;[3] but since the ratification of that Amendment, the Supreme Court can exercise no jurisdiction in any case, whether pending at that time, or afterwards commenced, in

[1] 17 *Howard*, 478.
[2] 2 *Dall.* 419.
[3] 3 *Ibid.* 378; 1 *Cond. Rep.* 169.

which a State is sued by citizens of another State, or by citizens or subjects of a foreign State.[1] This amendment, however, does not affect the right of a State to assert, as a plaintiff, any interest it may have in a subject which forms a matter of controversy.[2] And where a State is not necessarily a defendant, the mere suggestion of its title to property in the possession of an individual cannot arrest the proceedings, or prevent the Court from looking into the suggestion, and examining the validity of the title.[3]

It was once made a question, as we have seen, whether the jurisdiction of the Supreme Court is not only *original* but *exclusive*, in cases affecting Ambassadors, and other public Ministers, and Consuls, according to the true construction of the second Section of the third Article of the Constitution, and the better opinion seems now to be that it is.[4]

Thus much for the *original* jurisdiction of the Supreme Court. We now proceed to that which is *appellate*.

2. It is the appellate power of the Supreme Court of the United States which gives to it its greatest dignity and efficacy, and renders it a constant object of solicitude and attention to the Government and People of the several States. We have seen that, by an Act of Congress, a final judgment or decree of the highest Court of Law or Equity in a State, may, in certain cases, under various circumstances, be reviewed, and

[1] 5 *Cranch*, 115; 2 *Cond. Rep.* 202.

[2] *Ibid.*

[3] See cases cited above.

[4] 11 *Wheat.* 467; 6 *Ibid.* 264; 6 *Cond. Rep.* 394; 5 *Ibid.* 90; 2 *Dall.* 297.

reversed or affirmed in the Supreme Court of the Union. In cases of reversal, the cause may be remanded to the State Court for final judgment, to be rendered in accordance with the opinion of the Supreme Federal tribunal; or that Court may, at its discretion,—if the cause have once before been remanded,—proceed itself to a final decision, and award execution of its judgment or decree. Under this authority, it has been declared by the Supreme Court, that if the highest Court in a State reverse the judgment of a subordinate Court, and on an appeal, the judgment of the higher Court be, in its turn, reversed by the Supreme Court of the United States, it becomes a mere nullity; and the mandate for execution may issue directly from that Court to the inferior State Court.[1]

But in a subsequent case, a writ of error from the Supreme Court of the United States was directed to the Court of Appeals in Virginia, being the highest Court in that State, upon a judgment entered on appeal from an inferior State Court, against a right claimed under the treaty with Great Britain, and the judgment of the Court of Appeals was reversed by the Supreme Court; the cause was remanded, and the Virginia Court of Appeals was required to cause the original judgment, which had been reversed in that Court, to be carried into due execution. The Court of Appeals, when the case came back to it, resolved that the appellate power of the Supreme Court did not extend to the State Courts; that the Act of Congress to that effect was not warranted by the Constitution; and that the proceedings of the Supreme Court were

[1] 3 *Dall.* 341.

invalid in relation to the Court of Appeals,—which consequently declined obedience to the mandate of the former.[1] A new writ of error was awarded upon this refusal, and the case came up again before the Supreme Court, as a case in which the Court below drew in question and denied the validity of the Act of Congress authorizing an appeal from a State Court. In the luminous opinion delivered on that occasion, by the venerable and learned Chief Justice Marshall, he gave a full, argumentative, and conclusive exposition of the powers and jurisdiction vested in the Supreme Court, either by the Constitution or the Acts of Congress, upon every point in which they have been called in question.

He began by observing that the Judicial power of the United States had been declared by the Constitution to extend to *all* cases arising under treaties made under the authority of the United States; which was an absolute grant of jurisdiction in those cases; and that it was competent for the People to invest the General Government with that, or any other powers which they might deem necessary and proper, as well as to prohibit the States from the exercise of any powers which in their (the People's) judgment, were incompatible with the objects of the general compact. Congress was bound by the injunctions of the Constitution to create inferior Courts, in which to vest all that Judicial jurisdiction which was exclusively vested in the United States, and of which the Supreme Court cannot take other than appellate cognizance. The whole Judicial power must, at all times, be vested either in an original

[1] 7 *Cranch*, 603.

or appellate form, in some Courts created under the authority of the United States. The grant of the Judicial power was thus declared to be absolute; and it was held to be imperative upon Congress to provide for the appellate jurisdiction of the Federal Courts in all cases in which the Judicial power was granted exclusively to the United States by the Constitution, and not already given, by way of original jurisdiction to the Supreme Court.

This eminent and statesmanlike Judge in entering upon his examination of the Judicial power, took a distinction between the two classes of enumerated cases, and held that the Constitution intended that the Judicial power, either in an original or appellate form, should extend absolutely to all cases in law or equity arising under the Constitution and laws of the United States, and the treaties made under the authority of their Government; to ALL cases affecting Ambassadors, other public Ministers, and Consuls, and to *all* cases of admiralty and maritime jurisdiction, because those cases were of vital importance to the sovereignty of the Union, entered into the public policy, and affected the national rights, and the law and comity of nations. The original or the appellate jurisdiction ought, therefore, in these cases, to be commensurate with the mischiefs and policy in view. But in respect to another class of cases, the Constitution had designedly dropped the word "*all*," so as not absolutely to extend the jurisdiction of the Federal Judiciary to *all* controversies, but merely to *controversies* in which the United States were a party, or between two or more States, or between citizens of different States, or foreign States, citizens, or subjects, leaving it to Congress to qualify the jurisdiction, original, or appellate, in such manner as public policy might dictate.[1]

But whatever weight may be due to this distinction, it is manifest that the Judicial power was unavoidably, in some instances, exclusive of all State authority, and in all others might be made so at the discretion of Congress. The Act of 1789 assumed that, in all the cases to which the Judicial power of the United States extended, Congress might rightfully vest exclusive jurisdiction in their own Courts. The criminal and admiralty jurisdiction must be exclusive; and it is only in those cases where, previously to the Constitution, the State tribunals possessed jurisdiction independently of national authority, that they can now constitutionally exercise a concurrent jurisdiction. But unless Congress had provided a rule to regulate the proceedings of the Supreme Court, as to its appellate jurisdiction, that Court could not have exercised it; and where such rule has been provided by Congress, the Court cannot depart from it.[2]

The appellate jurisdiction is not limited by the Constitution to the Supreme Court, but Congress may create a succession of inferior tribunals, in each of which it may vest appellate as well as original jurisdiction. The appellate jurisdiction of the Supreme Court, in cases where it has not original jurisdiction, being by the Constitution subject to such exceptions

[1] The Supreme Court has jurisdiction to ascertain and establish the boundaries between different States. For although the Constitution does not, in terms, extend the Judicial power to *all* controversies between two or more States, yet it, in terms, excludes none, whatever may be their nature or object.

[2] 2 *Peters*, 657.

and regulations as Congress may prescribe, it remained in its discretion to provide for the exercise of the Judicial power in all the various forms of appeal. The right, therefore, of *removing* a cause from a State Court by a defendant entitled to try his right, or assert his privilege in the National *Forum*, is, in fact, the exercise of an appellate power, as that power may exist as well before as after judgment,—and by availing himself of it at an early stage of the proceeding, the defendant is enabled to save much of the time, and avoid much of the expense, of litigation. Nor is the right limited to cases pending in the Courts of the United States. Had it been so limited, it would necessarily have followed, that the jurisdiction of the Federal tribunals must have been exclusive of the State Courts, in all the cases enumerated in the Constitution; and inasmuch as the Judicial power of the United States embraces all those cases, the State Courts cannot, consistently with the express terms of the Federal Constitution, entertain any jurisdiction of them without the right of appeal to the Federal tribunals. For if the State Courts were allowed to exercise a concurrent jurisdiction in those cases free from such control, the appellate jurisdiction of the Union would, as to the cases in question, have no existence; which would be contrary to the manifest intent of the Federal Constitution.[1]

The appellate power of the Federal Courts must, therefore, continue to extend to the State Courts so long as the latter entertain any concurrent jurisdiction over the cases which the Constitution has declared to

1 Consent of parties cannot confer jurisdiction on the Supreme Court. 16 *Peters*, 525.

fall within the Judicial cognizance of the United States. It is clear that the Constitution contemplated that such cases would not only arise in the State Courts, in the ordinary exercise of their concurrent jurisdiction, but that those tribunals would *incidentally* take cognizance of questions of which the Courts of the United States have exclusive jurisdiction. Inasmuch, therefore, as the Judicial power of the Union extends to both the above specified classes of cases, it follows as a necessary consequence, that the appellate jurisdiction of the Federal Courts must, and does, extend to every case within the Federal Judicial power. All the enumerated cases of Federal cognizance are those which touch the safety, peace, and sovereignty of the Union, or in which it may be presumed that State attachments, prejudices, jealousies, or interests might sometimes obstruct or control the regular administration of justice. To all such cases the appellate power is applied on the plainest principles of policy and wisdom; and this is requisite to fulfil effectually the great and beneficial ends of the Constitution; and, especially to give efficacy to the power of deciding in all cases of conflict between the several States, or collision between powers claimed by a State, and those claimed by the General Government; and especially to maintain the declared supremacy of the Constitution, Laws, and Treaties of the United States, over the Constitution and Laws of the respective States. The existence of such a power was, moreover, deemed necessary to preserve uniformity of decision throughout the Union, upon all subjects within the purview of the Constitution; and to prevent the mischiefs of opposite constructions and contradictory decisions in the several States on these points of general concern.

The appellate power of the Federal Judiciary over the State tribunals does not, however, extend to a final judgment in a State Court on a question arising under the authority of the Union, *although a State be a party;* because that jurisdiction was given to the Federal Courts only in two classes of cases; in the one, it depends on *the character of the cause*, whoever may be the parties; in the other, it depends entirely on *the character of the parties*, and then the subject of the controversy is wholly unimportant. In the celebrated case of the Georgia missionaries,[1] where the validity, or, at least, the construction of the treaty made by the United States with the Cherokee Indians, had been drawn in question in the highest Court of that State, and the decision had been, if not "against the validity,"—against a "right, privilege, and exemption claimed under them," and where, also, had been drawn in question the validity of a law of Georgia, on the ground of its being repugnant to the Constitution, Treaties, and Laws of the United States, and the decision had been in favor of its validity,—it was considered by the Supreme Court too clear for controversy that the Judiciary Act of Congress had given it the power, and, of course, imposed on it the duty, of exercising an appellate jurisdiction in the case, *notwithstanding it arose upon a criminal prosecution in the State Court, founded upon an Act of the State Legislature.* The law of Georgia was held to be repugnant to the Constitution, Laws, and Treaties of the United States; and Chief Justice Marshall, who delivered the opinion of the Court, declared that its jurisdiction was no less clear in that case than

[1] 6 *Peters*, 515.

in civil cases. He considered the parties not less interested in the operation of this unconstitutional law, than if it had affected their property ; nor less entitled to the protection of the General Government when the judgment of the State Court affected their personal liberty, and inflicted a disgraceful punishment. The Court, therefore, ordered the proceedings against the missionaries to be annulled, and that they should be released from their imprisonment. The special mandate issued to the Court below to carry that judgment into effect, was not obeyed, and compulsory proceedings were in progress to enforce it, when the matter was compromised by the discharge of the missionaries upon their withdrawing the suits they had commenced against the State officers for their detention.

In order to give the Supreme Court jurisdiction in a case brought before it on a writ of error, or an appeal from a State Court, three things must concur, viz: —

1. The validity of a statute of the State must be drawn in question.

2. It must be drawn in question on the ground that it is repugnant to the Constitution, Laws, or Treaties of the United States.

3. The decision of the State Court must be in favor of the validity of such statute.

Where, therefore, the decision of the State Court is against the validity of the statute, the Supreme Court of the United States has no jurisdiction.[1] Neither has it jurisdiction to revise the judgment of a State Court, when the only questions involved in the case depend on the construction and validity of a State law.[2] Nor has

[1] 14 *Peters*, 56 ; 5 *Howard*, 64, 343 ; 5 *Peters*, 505 ; 16 *Ibid.* 149.

[2] 11 *Peters*, 167.

it authority to declare a State law void on account of its collision with the State Constitution.[1]

In a former case, the Supreme Court had observed that if the State Legislatures might annul the judgments of the Courts of the United States, and the rights thereby acquired, the Constitution becomes a solemn mockery, and the Nation would be deprived of the means of enforcing its laws by its own tribunals. So fatal a result must be deprecated by all; and the People of every State must feel a deep interest in resisting principles so destructive to the Union, and averting consequences so fatal to themselves.[2]

If two citizens of the same State, in a suit in a State Court, claim title under the same Act of Congress, the Supreme Court of the United States has appellate jurisdiction to revise the judgment or decree, under the twenty-fifth section of the Judiciary Act of 1789; upon the ground that the Act intended to give the Court the power of rendering uniform the construction of the laws of the United States, and the decisions upon the rights or titles claimed under those laws.[3]

The Supreme Court is also clothed with that superintending authority over the subordinate Courts of the United States, which should always be deposited in the highest tribunal and last resort of the People for Justice. It has power to issue *prohibitory* writs to the *District Courts* when proceeding as Courts of Admiralty and maritime jurisdiction; and *mandatory* process in cases warranted by the principles and usages of law, to any Courts established, or persons holding office under the

[1] 3 *Peters*, 280.
[2] 12 *Ibid.* 357.
[3] 4 *Cranch*, 382; 2 *Cond. Rep.* 149.

authority of the United States. The Supreme Court, and all the Federal Courts, have power to issue all writs, not specially provided by statute, which may be necessary for the due exercise of their respective jurisdictions, and conformable to the principles and usages of law; and the individual Judges of all of them may, by writ of *Habeas Corpus*, relieve all persons from all manner of unjust imprisonment or restraint occurring under or by color of the authority of the United States. But the Supreme Court has no *original* jurisdiction to award this writ to bring up the infant child of a Petitioner alleged to be unlawfully detained from him.[1] The jurisdiction exercised by the Court upon the return of the writ, is clearly *appellate*, being the revision of a decision of an inferior Court by which a citizen has been committed to prison. The question brought forward on the *Habeas Corpus* is always distinct from that involved in the cause itself. The question whether an individual shall be imprisoned, is distinct from the question whether he shall be convicted or acquitted of the charge upon which he is to be tried, and, therefore, may be decided by different Courts; and as the decision that the individual shall be imprisoned must always precede the application for his discharge, the jurisdiction exercised by the Supreme Court must be of an appellate, and not of an original character, which is not conferred by the Constitution.[2] This jurisdiction, therefore, is not affected by the circumstance that the commitment was made by a Court having power to commit and bail;[3] and the Supreme Court may award the writ

[1] 2 *Howard*, 65.

[2] 4 *Cranch*, 75; 2 *Cond. Rep.* 33; 5 *Ibid.* 225; 7 *Wheat.* 38.

[3] 3 *Dall.* 17.

to revise the effect of the process of a Circuit Court of the United States, under which a prisoner is detained.

Although the prohibition in the Constitution against the imposition of excessive fines is mandatory upon the Courts of the United States, yet the Supreme Court cannot reverse such a sentence, notwithstanding the excess of the fine may be apparent upon the face of the record. It cannot, therefore, on a *Habeas Corpus*, discharge a prisoner in custody for non-payment of such fine. Nor will it grant a *Habeas Corpus ad subjiciendum* where a party has been committed for a contempt by a Court of competent jurisdiction. The laws of the United States have not confided to the Supreme Court an appellate jurisdiction for the trial of criminal cases; and it has no authority to exercise it indirectly. It holds, as we have seen, that there is always a distinction between the question brought before it on a *Habeas Corpus*, and that involved in the trial; but there is no distinction between the case of a contempt, and an application for the writ after judgment upon an indictment for an offence within the jurisdiction of the same Courts. For when a party is committed for contempt, the adjudication of the Court is a conviction, and the commitment in consequence of it, is an execution of the judgment.

Thus was the law settled in England, in the celebrated case of Brass Crosby, Lord Mayor of London,[1]—an authority approved by the Supreme Court.[2] In the equally famous case of Thomas W. Dorr, who had been convicted of treason against the State of Rhode Island, and sentenced by a Court of that State to im-

[1] 3 *Wils.* 188.

[2] 7 *Wheat.* 38.

prisonment for life, the Supreme Court of the United States held that it had no power to grant the writ of *Habeas Corpus*, as it possessed no jurisdiction of the subject derived from the Common Law. It was not a case, either, in which the Constitution had conferred upon the Court original jurisdiction; and, under the provisions of the Judiciary Act, the only case where any Court or Judge of the United States could issue the writ to bring up a prisoner in custody under a sentence or execution of a State Court, was where he was to be used as a witness. It is immaterial whether the imprisonment be under civil or criminal process. As the law stands, an individual in custody under the authority of a State is beyond the reach of the Federal Courts, although he may be indicted before them for treason against the United States.[1]

The Judiciary Act authorizes the Supreme Court, as we have seen, to issue writs of *Prohibition* to the District Courts when proceeding as Courts of admiralty and maritime jurisdiction, and writs of *Mandamus* in cases warranted by the principles and usages of law,—to any Courts appointed, or persons holding office, under the authority of the United States; and it should be noted, that a *Mandamus* to *an inferior Court*, is in the exercise of appellate jurisdiction,—to *an officer*, in that of original jurisdiction.[2]

But a Superior Court will never by *Mandamus* direct in what manner the discretion of an inferior one shall be exercised; although, in a proper case, it will require it to decide. The writ in question is subject to the

[1] 3 *Howard*, 103.

[2] 12 *Wheat.* 561; 6 *Cond. Rep.* 644.

discretion of the Court, and should not be issued in cases of doubtful right. It is, however, the only adequate relief where an inferior tribunal refuses to act upon a subject properly brought before it.[1] And although the Supreme Court will not order an inferior one to render judgment for or against either party, yet, in a proper case, it will order it to proceed to judgment.[2] Should the Court before whom a case ripe for judgment is pending, perseveringly refuse to terminate the cause, the Supreme Court, without indicating the character of the judgment, would order the rendition of some judgment; but to justify such a mandate, a plain case of refusing to proceed by the inferior Court must be made out.[3]

The Supreme Court has no power from the Constitution,—nor can Congress confer it,—to grant a new trial in a Court below, *by a reëxamination of facts tried by a Jury;* as it would violate that part of the seventh Amendment of the Constitution which declares that

1 6 *Peters*, 661.

2 8 *Ibid.* 291.

3 The Circuit Court of the United States for the District of Columbia has a right to award a *Mandamus* to an officer of the United States, to enforce the performance of a merely ministerial act which he has no authority to deny or control; or where there is no room for the exercise of discretion, official, or otherwise. But, in such cases, the writ issues in virtue of the Common Law, as it was in force in Maryland when the cession of that part of the State, now within the District of Columbia, was made to the United States; and it must be considered as it was at Common Law, with respect to its object and purpose, varying only in form as required by the different characters of the Governments of the United States and England. A *Mandamus* will not lie against the Secretary of the Treasury, at the instance of an officer to enforce the payment of his pay. 6 *Howard*, 92.

"no fact tried by a Jury shall be otherwise reëxaminable in any Court of the United States, than according to the rules of the Common Law." The only modes known to the Common Law for reëxamining such facts, are the granting a new trial *by the Court in which the issue was joined*, or to which the record was properly returnable; and by the award of a *venire facias de novo* by an appellate Court, for some error of law intervening in the proceedings.[1]

To sustain the appellate jurisdiction of the Supreme Court, under the Judiciary Act of 1789, the value in controversy must exceed two thousand dollars; and to ascertain that value, recourse must be had to the foundation of the original suit, or the matter in dispute when it was instituted. Where the law gives no rule, the demand of the plaintiff must furnish one. But where the law gives the rule, the legal cause of action, and not the plaintiff's demand, must be regarded.[2] If the judgment of the Court below be for the plaintiff, that judgment ascertains the value of the matter in dispute; but where the judgment below is for the defendant, the Supreme Court has not fixed the mode of ascertaining the value.[3] It may, however, be presumed that, as in the case where the plaintiff's demand gives no rule, recourse may be had to the foundation of the controversy, so, in the case of the defendant, recourse may, in like manner, be had to the value of the matter in dispute when the suit was instituted.[4]

But, notwithstanding the cases cited in the margin,

1 3 *Peters*, 433.

2 3 *Dall.* 401; 1 *Cond. Rep.* 105.

3 1 *Cranch*, 13; 2 *Cond. Rep.* 103.

4 See cases last cited.

according to the practice since established by the Supreme Court, its jurisdiction, in this respect, depends upon the sum or value in dispute between the parties, *as the case stands upon the writ of error in that Court.* Whatever may have been the amount claimed by the plaintiff in the Court below, if the judgment in his favor is for less than two thousand dollars, and the writ of error is sued out by the defendant below, the Supreme Court has no jurisdiction. But if the writ of error be brought by the plaintiff below, provided the amount claimed in his declaration exceed two thousand dollars, the Court has jurisdiction, because, should the judgment be reversed, he may still recover what he claimed.[1] But this appellate jurisdiction is not limited by the value of the matter in dispute in cases arising under the Constitution, laws, and treaties of the United States; and it extends to a case where both parties claim a right under the same Act of Congress, and the decision is *against* the right or title claimed by either.[2]

There is no mode of proceeding by which the Federal Government can bring into review the decisions of the Supreme Court upon a question of boundary between two States. Justice therefore requires that the United States, which represent the rights and interests of the other States, should have an opportunity of being heard before the boundary is established. The Attorney-General files an *Information*, stating that the interests of the United States are involved in the establishment of the boundary line, and has a right to appear, and adduce proofs in support of the boundary claimed by them to be the true one, and to be heard on

[1] 2 *Howard*, 73; 16 *Peters*, 234.

[2] 8 *Wheat.* 312; 5 *Cond. Rep.* 445.

the argument. The United States will not by this proceeding become a party in a technical sense, and no judgment will be rendered for or against them. But the evidence and arguments offered in their behalf will be considered by the Court in deciding the matter in controversy.[1]

The power vested in Congress of creating Courts of inferior jurisdiction, necessarily implies the power of limiting the jurisdiction of those Courts to particular objects; and when such a Court is created, and its operations defined, it can, with no propriety, assume to itself a more extended jurisdiction, which might be indefinite in its nature, applicable to a variety of subjects, varying in every State in the Union, and with regard to which, there may be no definite criterion of distribution between the several inferior Courts which might be created.[2]

Under the power granted for the purpose by the Constitution, two descriptions of inferior Courts, differing materially in the nature and extent of their respective jurisdictions, have been established by Congress. The United States, exclusive of the District of Columbia, are divided by law into a number of Judicial *Circuits*, corresponding with the number of the Judges of the Supreme Court,—each "Circuit" consisting of one or more *Districts*. Each "District," for the most part, comprises an entire State; but some of the larger and more populous States are divided into two Districts.

[1] 17 *Howard*, 478.

[2] 7 *Cranch*, 32; 2 *Cond. Rep.* 405. The plaintiff in the Supreme Court may assign as error his own admissions in the pleadings in the Court below, when they go to the jurisdiction. 2 *Cranch*, 126; 1 *Cond. Rep.* 370.

Some Districts are not embraced within any Circuit, and have only "District Courts," which, however, are invested with the powers of a "Circuit Court," within their respective Districts, except in cases of error and appeal. In the "District of Columbia," which consists of the territory ceded to the United States for the seat of the General Government, there is both a Circuit and a District Court specially and differently organized for that District. The former is composed of a Chief Justice and two associate Judges, from whose decisions writs of error and appeals lie to the Supreme Court of the United States. The jurisdiction vested in these Courts respectively, corresponds with that of the Circuit and District Courts established throughout the States,—which we now proceed to explain.

II. The Circuit Courts of the United States are held annually, or oftener, in each District, by a Justice of the Supreme Court assigned by law to the particular Circuit, and the Judge of the District for which the Court is held. But the Supreme Court may, in cases where special circumstances render it, in their judgment, necessary, assign two Justices of the Supreme Court to attend the Circuit Court. It was once made a question whether the Justices of the Supreme Court could sit as Circuit Judges without a distinct commission, but it was decided that they might lawfully do so, as a contemporaneous construction of the Constitution, acquiesced in, and practised from the first organization of the Judiciary system, had fixed the construction.[1]

If a vacancy happen by the death of the Justice of the Supreme Court to whom the Circuit is allotted, the

[1] 1 *Cranch*, 299; 1 *Cond. Rep.* 316.

District Judge may, under the Act of Congress, discharge all the duties of the Circuit Court for his District, except that he cannot sit upon a writ of error, or upon an appeal from his own Court; and where the District Judge is absent, or has been of counsel, or is interested in the cause, the Circuit Court may be holden by the Justice of the Supreme Court alone.[1] If an opposition of opinions between the Justice of the Supreme Court and the District Judge occur in a case in which the Circuit Court has original jurisdiction, the point on which they disagree is directed by law to be certified to the Supreme Court; whereupon the cause is removed into that Court for final judgment or decree. But in all cases of appeal or removal from a District to a Circuit Court, judgment is to be rendered in the latter according to the opinion of the Justice of the Supreme Court, presiding at the Circuit. A division of opinion between the Judges of the Circuit Court on a motion for a new trial, is not, however, such an one as is required to be certified to the Supreme Court for its decision, under the sixth section of the Judiciary Act of 1802.[2] Nor can the Supreme Court take jurisdiction of a question upon which the opinions of the Judges of a Circuit Court are opposed to each other, where the division of opinion arises upon some proceeding subsequent to the decision of the cause in that Court.[3]

But where the whole cause, and not a point, or points arising in it, is adjourned to the Supreme Court on a

[1] Where the District Judge does not judicially sit in a cause in the Circuit Court, he is considered absent in contemplation of law, although he be personally present on the bench. 3 *Dall.* 19.

[2] 6 *Wheat.* 542; 5 *Cond. Rep.* 134.

[3] 3 *Wheat,* 600; 4 *Cond. Rep.* 522.

certificate of division of opinion, the case will be remanded to the Circuit Court. Congress intended to provide for divisions of opinion upon single points, which frequently occur in the trial of a cause, and not to enable a Circuit Court to transmit an entire cause to the Supreme Court before a final judgment of the former. A construction authorizing such a transfer, would counteract the policy which forbids writs of error or appeals, until the judgment or decree of the Court below be final. If an interlocutory judgment or decree could be brought into the Supreme Court, the same case might again be brought up after a final decision in the Circuit Court, and all the delay and expense incident to a repeated revision of the same cause would be incurred. So, if the whole cause, instead of an insulated point, could be adjourned, the judgment or decree finally given by the Circuit Court, might be again brought up, and the whole subject reëxamined. Were the Supreme Court, moreover, to decide the case upon such a certificate of division of opinion, it would be the exercise of original, rather than appellate jurisdiction.[1]

The Circuit Courts, organized as stated, are invested with *original* and *exclusive* jurisdiction,—except in certain cases hereafter mentioned,—of all crimes and offences cognizable under the authority of the United States, exceeding the degree of ordinary misdemeanors,[2]

[1] 4 *Peters*, 392; 9 *Ibid.* 297; 12 *Ibid.* 238.

[2] Under this provision, the Circuit Courts of the United States take cognizance of crimes committed on the high seas. A vessel lying in the open roadstead of *a foreign country*, is upon the "high seas," within the eighth section of the statute. 5 *Wheat.* 200; 1 *Gall.* 624; 2 *Sumn.* 482. But see *contrà*, as to offences committed in a

and of those they have *concurrent* jurisdiction with the District Courts. They have original cognizance, concurrently with the Courts of the several States, of all suits of a civil nature at Common Law, or in Equity, where the matter in dispute exceeds a certain specified sum, and the United States are plaintiffs, or an alien is a party, or the suit is between a citizen of the State where it is brought, and a citizen of another State. But when both parties are aliens, the Courts of the United States have no jurisdiction; and a citizen of the District of Columbia is not a citizen of *a State*, in the sense of the Constitution, and entitled to sue, as such, in the Federal Courts.[1] And in relation to aliens, it should be noted, that they have a right to sue only while peace exists between their country and ours. For if war break out, and they thereby become *alien enemies*, their right to sue is suspended until the return of peace.[2]

The jurisdiction of the Circuit Courts having once vested, in a suit between citizens of different States, cannot be devested by a subsequent change of domicile of either of the parties.[3] And where an alien is a party, or the suit is between a citizen of the State where the

bay entirely land-locked and enclosed by reefs. 4 *Mason*, 307; 5 *Ibid.* 290; 1 *Wash. C. C.* 463; 4 *Ibid.* 383; 4 *Dall.* 426; 1 *Sumn.* 168; *Bee*, 266. No writ of error, or appeal, lies to the Supreme Court, from the judgment or decree of a Circuit Court in a civil action, which was carried from the District to the Circuit Court, under the 21st section of the Judiciary Act of 1789. 7 *Cranch*, 168; 2 *Cond. Rep.* 424; 2 *Wheat.* 395.

[1] 4 *Cranch*, 46; 2 *Ibid.* 448; 1 *Cond. Rep.* 444.

[2] 1 *Kent's Comm.* 64–68.

[3] 2 *Wheat.* 290; 9 *Ibid.* 537; 5 *Cond. Rep.* 666; 8 *Peters*, 1; 12 *Ibid.* 165.

suit is brought, and a citizen of another State,[1] if the suit be joint, each distinct interest should be represented by persons, all of whom are entitled to sue or be sued in the Federal Courts,—that is, where the interest is joint, each of the persons concerned in it must be competent to sue or be sued in those Courts.[2]

Where the plaintiff is an alien, and sues not in his own right, but as a trustee, if the trust devolve upon him by operation of law, the Courts of the United States entertain jurisdiction;[3] but not where the trust arises from the act of a party who could not sue in those Courts.[4] Although in a case between citizens of the same State, if the plaintiff be only a nominal party, suing officially for the use of an alien, the Federal Courts have jurisdiction.[5] The jurisdiction of the Court, in other cases, has been held to be determined by the condition of the party who has the legal interest, and not by that of the party having simply a beneficial interest.[6]

The Circuit Courts have also original jurisdiction in Equity, and at Law, of all suits arising under the Acts of Congress relative to copyrights, and the rights growing out of inventions and discoveries; and concurrent

[1] The constitutional privilege which a citizen of one State has to sue the citizens of another, cannot be taken away by the erection of a Corporation by the laws of the State in which the latter reside. The Corporation itself may, therefore, be sued as such. 16 *Howard*, 314.

[2] 3 *Cranch*, 267; 1 *Wheat.* 91.

[3] 4 *Cranch*, 306; 2 *Cond. Rep.* 116; 8 *Wheat.* 642.

[4] 6 *Cranch*, 332.

[5] *Ibid.* 303.

[6] 14 *Peters*, 293; 3 *Howard*, 374.

jurisdiction with the District Courts of the United States, and with the Courts and Magistrates of the several States, where the United States, or an officer thereof, sues under the authority of an Act of Congress, however small the amount, except in cases of admiralty and maritime jurisdiction.[1]

The Circuit Courts of the United States have *appellate* jurisdiction in all final judgments and decrees of the District Courts, only in cases of admiralty and maritime jurisdiction; and if any suit be commenced in a State Court, against an alien, or by a citizen of the State in which the suit is brought against a citizen of another State, the defendant, as we have seen, on giving security, may remove the cause to the Circuit Court for the District in which the suit is brought.[2] In order to maintain a suit in the Circuit Court, jurisdiction must appear on the record; as, if the suit is between citizens of different States, the citizenship of the respective parties must be set forth.[3] A citizen of a "Territory" cannot sue a citizen of a State in the Federal Courts; nor can those Courts take jurisdiction from the circumstance of other parties being joined who are capable of suing in them; for the jurisdiction, as we have seen, cannot be sustained unless each individual party be entitled to claim it.[4]

[1] The Circuit Courts have jurisdiction in Writs of Right where the property demanded exceeds $500 in value; and if upon the trial the demandant recover less, he is not to be allowed his costs, and, in the discretion of the Court, may be adjudged to pay costs. 8 *Cranch*, 229; 3 *Cond. Rep.* 179.

[2] 5 *Peters*, 1.

[3] 6 *Wheat.* 250.

[4] 1 *Ibid.* 91; 3 *Cond. Rep.* 490.

An appeal from the District to the Circuit Courts, in admiralty cases, suspends the sentence altogether; and the matter is not considered *res judicata* until the final sentence of the appellate Court is pronounced.[1] And it is the constant practice of appellate Courts of admiralty, so to modify the decree of the inferior Court, as the justice of the case may seem to require,—or, in other words, to render such a decree as the latter should have done.[2]

The Circuit Courts have no authority to issue a *Certiorari*, or other compulsory process to the District Courts for the removal of causes from that jurisdiction before a final decree or judgment is pronounced in the latter; and, in case of the exercise of such power by the former, the District Court may, and should refuse obedience to the process; and either party to the suit may move the Circuit Court for a *Procedendo*, after the transcript of the record is removed to that Court, or pursue the cause in the District Court, as if the record had not been removed.[3] But if, instead of taking advantage of this irregularity, at the proper time, and in a proper manner, the defendant enters his appearance to the suit in the Circuit Court, makes his defence, and joins issue upon the pleadings, it is too late, after a verdict, to object to the irregularity. The Supreme Court, as we have seen, will consider the suit as an original one in the Circuit Court, made so by consent of parties.[4]

The power of the Circuit Courts to issue the writ of

1 5 *Cranch*, 281; 6 *Ibid.* 329; 3 *Peters*, 57; 2 *Cond. Rep.* 256; *Ibid.* 388.

2 3 *Dall.* 54; 1 *Cond. Rep.* 21.

3 2 *Wheat.* 221.

4 4 *Cond. Rep.* 98.

Mandamus, is confined exclusively to those cases in which it may be necessary to the exercise of their jurisdiction. Had the eleventh section of the Judiciary Act covered the whole ground of the Constitution, there would be much reason for exercising this power in many cases where some ministerial act is necessary to the completion of an individual right arising under the laws of the United States; and the fourteenth section would have authorized the issuing of the writ for the purpose. But although the Judicial power of the United States extends to all cases arising under their laws, Congress has not thought proper to delegate the power in question to the Circuit Courts, except in certain specified cases.[1]

When we find Congress withholding from its own Courts the exercise of this controlling power over the ministerial officers of the Government, the inference clearly is, that all violations of private right resulting from the acts of such officers, were meant to be left subject to actions for damages, or for the recovery of specific property, according to circumstances, in a Court of competent jurisdiction.[2] And inasmuch as the whole of this power has not been communicated by law to the Circuit Courts, it remains a dormant power, not yet called into action.[3]

A Circuit Court, although an inferior Court in the language of the Constitution, is not so in the sense which the Common Law attaches to the term; nor are its proceedings subject to the narrow rules which apply

[1] 7 *Cranch*, 504; 3 *Cond. Rep.* 4.

[2] 6 *Wheat.* 591; 3 *Cond. Rep.* 197.

[3] 12 *Peters*, 524.

to inferior Courts of Common Law, or Courts of special jurisdiction. On the contrary, the Circuit Courts of the United States are Courts of original and durable jurisdiction, and as such entitled to liberal intendments in favor of their powers. They are, nevertheless, Courts of *limited* jurisdiction, and have cognizance, not of causes generally,—but only of a few, under special circumstances, amounting to a small proportion of the cases which an unlimited jurisdiction would embrace; and the legal presumption is, that a cause is without their jurisdiction until the contrary appears.[1]

III. THE DISTRICT COURTS are derived from the same Constitutional power of Congress as the Circuit Courts. They hold annually four *stated* terms, and *special* Courts, at the discretion of the respective Judges.

The District Courts of the United States have, *exclusively* of the State Courts, cognizance of all lesser crimes and offences against the United States, committed within their respective Districts, or upon the high seas, and which are punishable by fine and imprisonment, to a small amount, and for a short term. They have, also, *exclusive original* cognizance of all civil cases of admiralty and maritime jurisdiction; of seizures under the impost, navigation, and trade laws of the Union, where the seizures are made on the high seas, or in waters within their District navigable from the ocean by vessels of ten or more tons burden; and of all suits for penalties or forfeitures incurred under those laws.

[1] A Circuit Court of the United States has not jurisdiction to enjoin proceedings in a State Court. 4 *Cranch*, 179.

They have, moreover, *concurrent* jurisdiction with the Circuit Courts of the United States, and of the States Courts, of causes in which an alien sues for the violation of a right accruing to him under the Law of Nations, or a treaty of the United States; and of all suits at Common Law in which the United States are plaintiffs, and the matter in dispute is of a certain small amount. They have jurisdiction, likewise, *exclusive* of the State Courts, of all suits against Consuls, or Vice-Consuls, except offences of a higher degree than those which have been mentioned. They have, also, *exclusive* cognizance of proceedings to repeal patents obtained surreptitiously, or upon false suggestions; and of complaints, by whomsoever instituted, in cases of capture made within the waters of the United States, or within a marine league of their coasts.

By an Act of Congress passed in 1851, provision is made for the appointment of a board of Commissioners to settle private land claims in California, and for transferring cases decided by them to the District Court of the United States, by way of appeal. This law was held by the Supreme Court to be constitutional; that the board of Commissioners was not a *Court* under the Constitution invested with Judicial powers, and that the commencement of the suit in the District to which it was transferred, must be regarded as an original proceeding. It could, therefore, hear additional evidence to that adduced before the Commissioners.[1]

The seventh Amendment of the Constitution excludes the jurisdiction of Admiralty over contracts regulated by Common Law.[2] This jurisdiction is founded, for

[1] 17 *Howard*, 525.

[2] 1 *Bald.* 544.

the most part, on the subject-matter of the contract, and not solely on the place where it is made.[1] If the subject-matter of the contract relate to navigation of the sea, though it may be made on land, Admiralty has jurisdiction.[2] It has jurisdiction, also, over all roadsteads, havens, and rivers, which are not within the body of a County.[3] As to *contracts*, their jurisdiction depends on the subject-matter,—whether maritime as above explained, or not. As to *torts*, it depends on the locality, viz: whether committed on the high seas, or in ports within the flow and reflux of the tide, or not.[4]

The Continental Congress, before the ratification of the Articles of Confederation, had authority to institute a Court of Appeal in Prize causes, and invest it with power to revise and correct the judgments of the State Courts of Admiralty; and its decisions in cases falling within its jurisdiction were final and conclusive.[5] Since

1 1 *Peters's Adm. Rep.* 231; *Gilpin*, 477; *Paine*, 621.

2 1 *Wash. C. C.* 453.

3 1 *Dall.* 49.

4 2 *Gallis*, 465; 2 *Sumn.* 1; 1 *Gilpin*, 529. For further cases on the subject of admiralty and maritime jurisdiction, see 1 *Peters's Adm. Rep.* 60–67, 78, 87, 97, 233, 244; 2 *Ibid.* 288, 309, 406; *Bee*, 51, 116, 199, 369, 378, 419, 433; *Addis.* 63; 1 *Wheat.* 96, 238, 402; 2 *Ibid.* 1; 3 *Ibid.* 246; 4 *Ibid.* 98; 8 *Ibid.* 394; 9 *Ibid.* 362; 10 *Ibid.* 418, 428, 473; 12 *Ibid.* 487, 611; 5 *Peters*, 465; 7 *Ibid.* 324; 10 *Ibid.* 118; 11 *Ibid.* 175; 1 *Dall.* 50; 2 *Ibid.* 118; 3 *Ibid.* 54, 121, 133, 297; 2 *Wend.* 64; 1 *Gallis.* 75; 2 *Ibid.* 191, 325, 349, 398; 2 *Cranch*, 406; 3 *Ibid.* 334; 4 *Ibid.* 2, 112, 320, 443; 9 *Ibid.* 102, 289; 1 *Yeates*, 55; 2 *Ibid.* 252; 1 *Mason*, 508; 3 *Ibid.* 6, 161, 242; 4 *Ibid.* 380; 5 *Ibid.* 465; 1 *Bald.* 543–547; *Gilpin*, 1, 3, 24, 191, 203, 478, 505, 516, 526, 532; 1 *Sumn.* 73, 157, 400, 551; 2 *Ibid.* 589; 1 *Wash. C. C.* 293; 2 *Ibid.* 148; *Paine*, 620, 671; 17 *Amer. Jur.* 51; 1 *Brock*, 383; 4 *Call.* 372.

5 3 *Dall.* 54; 5 *Cranch*, 115; 1 *Cond. Rep.* 21; 2 *Ibid.* 202.

the adoption of the present Constitution, the consequent abolition of the Courts of Admiralty, and the establishment under it of the Federal Judicial system, every District Court of the United States possesses all the powers of a Court of Admiralty, whether considered as an Instance or a Prize Court;[1] and they may sustain a libel to carry into effect a decree of the Continental Court of Appeals, either by enforcing its specific execution, or awarding damages for the nonperformance.[2]

The Courts of the United States being invested with *exclusive* original cognizance of all seizures by land or water, and of all suits for penalties and forfeitures incurred under the laws of the Union, whenever a revenue officer of the United States has a right to seize for a supposed forfeiture, the question whether that forfeiture has been incurred, belongs exclusively to the Federal Courts, and cannot be drawn to another *forum*. And it depends on the final decree of those Courts, proceeding *in rem*, whether the seizure is to be adjudged rightful, or not. If sentence of condemnation be pronounced, it is conclusive that such forfeiture has been incurred; if sentence of acquittal, that is equally conclusive against the forfeitures having been incurred, and, in neither case, can the question be litigated elsewhere.[3]

As questions of prize belong exclusively to Courts of Admiralty, Courts of Common Law have no jurisdiction to determine them; where property, therefore,

1 Act of Conf. IX., Sect. I.

2 3 *Dall.* 6, 54; 1 *Cond. Rep.* 10, 21; 2 *Ibid.* 4; 3 *Ibid.* 136; 4 *Ibid.* 322; 4 *Cranch*, 2; 8 *Ibid.* 110; 3 *Wheat.* 546.

3 3 *Wheat.* 346; 2 *Ibid.* 1; 4 *Cond. Rep.* 1, 244.

has been captured as prize, no action lies at Common Law, before adjudication, to recover it from any person into whose hands it may have fallen.[1] And where provision is made for a forfeiture under the laws of the United States, no State authority can interfere to take possession of the property seized, and prevent the exercise of exclusive jurisdiction by the Federal Courts; and if the property be wrongfully withdrawn, those Courts may enforce its redelivery.[2]

The District Courts, however, have no jurisdiction to entertain a suit, by way of libel, to enforce the payment of duties. The revenue-jurisdiction of those Courts, proceeding *in rem*, extends only to cases of seizure for forfeiture under the laws of impost, navigation, and trade.[3] But proceeding as Courts of admiralty and maritime jurisdiction, they have cognizance of maritime *torts in personam*, as well as *in rem;* and though the trespass complained of were piratical, the civil remedy does not merge in the crime. Whatever may have been the barbarous doctrine of antiquity about converting goods piratically taken into *droits* of admiralty, the day has long gone by since it gave way to a more rational and equitable rule; and the party dispossessed is now sustained in his remedy to reclaim the property as not devested by the piratical capture. If the party may thus recover his property, there is no reason why he should not recover the value of it from any goods of the offender within reach of the Admiralty Courts. The doctrine of *merger* has, indeed, no application to

1 3 *Dall.* 19; 1 *Cond. Rep.* 13.
2 2 *Wheat.* 1; 3 *Ibid.* 246; 6 *Cond. Rep.* 593.
3 12 *Wheat.* 486; 6 *Cond. Rep.* 593.

such a case, for even at Common Law, it was confined to felonies; and piracy was not deemed felony by that code.[1]

The Admiralty and maritime jurisdiction granted to the Federal Government is not limited to tide waters; but extends to all public navigable lakes and rivers where commerce is carried on between different States, or with a foreign nation. And the Act of Congress, extending the jurisdiction of the District Courts to certain cases upon particular lakes, and the navigable waters connecting them, does not rest upon the power to regulate commerce, but upon the ground that those lakes and waters are within the scope of Admiralty jurisdiction, as known and understood within the United States when the Constitution was adopted.[2] The District Courts, however, have no jurisdiction over vessels employed in *purely internal* navigation, in cases of dispute between part-owners; nor to enforce payment of wages due to the crew.[3]

The Courts of this country have no jurisdiction to redress any supposed *torts* committed on the high seas on the property of its citizens by a cruiser regularly commissioned by a foreign and friendly power, except where such cruiser has been fitted out in violation of its neutrality. The injured neutral must, in other cases, seek redress in the Courts of the captor.[4] Nor is the jurisdiction of the neutral Court enlarged by the fact

[1] 10 *Wheat.* 473; 6 *Cond. Rep.* 191.
[2] 12 *Howard*, 299.
[3] 11 *Peters*, 175.
[4] 10 *Wheat.* 473; 6 *Cond. Rep.* 191.

that the subject continues no longer within the power of the captor.[1]

As the laws of the United States have made no provision for an appeal from the judgments or decrees of the District Courts to the Circuit Courts, except in cases of Admiralty and maritime jurisdiction,—where a new jurisdiction is conferred upon the former, and a special mode provided for its exercise, there is no right of appeal to the latter; and if an appeal be entertained in such a case, by the Circuit Court, and its judgment or decree be taken to the Supreme Court, that Court will annul and reverse the proceedings of the Circuit Court as wholly unauthorized, but it can take no further proceeding in the cause; it cannot remand it to the Circuit Court, because the Circuit Court has no jurisdiction; and it cannot retain the cause for further proceedings, because it can exercise no appellate jurisdiction not conferred by statute.[2]

The grant of Admiralty powers in the Constitution to the Courts of the United States, was not intended to be confined to such cases as belonged to the Admiralty jurisdiction in England, at the time of the adoption of that instrument. Such a limitation would be inconsistent with the extent of the Admiralty jurisdiction exercised by the Colonies,—with a just interpretation of the Constitution,—and with its contemporaneous construction.[3]

Where the Judge of a District Court, acting in his Judicial capacity, has determined that there is not

[1] 1 *Wheat.* 228; 6 *Cond. Rep.* 558.
[2] 6 *Peters*, 470.
[3] 5 *Howard*, 441.

sufficient evidence to authorize him to proceed in a case before him, the Supreme Court will not, as has been already intimated, issue a *mandamus*, and thus in effect compel him to decide contrary to the dictates of his own judgment;[1] nor will it issue one to compel him to grant any application resting in his discretion.[2] For a Superior Court will never, as we have seen, direct in *what manner* the discretion of an inferior shall be exercised; though, in a proper case, it will require it to decide.[3]

The Judges of the District Courts have, in cases where the party has not had reasonable time to apply to the Circuit Court, as full power as is exercised by the Justices of the Supreme Court to grant writs of injunction in Equity causes, to operate within their respective Districts, and continue in force until the next sitting of the Circuit Court.

IV. THE COURTS OF THE "TERRITORIES" OF THE UNITED STATES have been created, from time to time, by the several Acts of Congress establishing *Territorial* Governments in those vast regions in the western part of the continent which were either ceded by individual States for the common benefit, upon condition that the proceeds of sales of the public lands therein should be applied to the payment of the national debt incurred during the revolutionary war, or obtained by treaty from foreign powers, and never included within the boundaries of any of the original members of the Union.

1 6 *Peters*, 216, 661; 7 *Ibid.* 637.

2 *Vide ante.*

3 It has been shown above, in treating of the Circuit Courts, in what Districts the District Court possesses the powers of a Circuit Court, and to what extent they may be exercised.

These *Territories*,—as they are politically, as well as geographically termed,—are not, in either case, considered distinct political societies, known to the Constitution as *States;* but Congress has always assumed to exercise over them supreme powers of sovereignty; and has generally adopted for that purpose the principles of the Ordinance established under the Confederation, in 1787,[1] for governing the territory Northwest of the River Ohio, which now contains the States of Ohio, Indiana, Illinois, Michigan, Wisconsin, and Iowa, and the Minnesota and Northwest *Territories*. This Ordinance was formed upon sound and enlightened principles of civil jurisprudence, and the Judges appointed in that original *Territory*, held their offices during good behavior. The Territory of Florida having since been admitted as a State, into the Union, and California coming into it already organized as such, the remaining Territories, besides Minnesota, and "Northwest," are Oregon, soon to be admitted as a State, Washington, set off from it, Nebraska and Kansas, formerly portions of the French Province of Louisiana, and New Mexico and Utah, acquired with California from Mexico. These are all organized after the model of the Ordinance of 1787; and in each of them, the Governor and members of the Legislative Council, as well as the Judges, are appointed by the President and Senate, but are removable at the pleasure of the President,[2] but subject to such removal, the Governor holds his office for three years, and the Judges for four.[3]

[1] Appendix G.

[2] The power of the President to remove a Territorial Judge has been questioned and discussed, but not as yet decided. 17 *Howard*, 284.

[3] The Legislative power in these *Territories* is vested in the Gov-

The "*Superior* Courts" in these Territories have exclusive cognizance of all capital offences, and the trial by Jury is secured, together with many other great fundamental principles of civil liberty. They have, within their limits, the same jurisdiction, in all cases arising under the Constitution and laws of the United States, which is vested in the District Courts of the United States, in those Districts in which the latter have the powers of a Circuit Court; and writs of error and appeals from their decisions may be taken to the Supreme Court of the United States, in the same cases, and under the same regulations, as from the Circuit Courts of the Union.

Admiralty jurisdiction, as we have seen, can be exercised in the several States in those Courts only which are established in pursuance of the third Article of the Federal Constitution; but this limitation does not extend to the Territories. The Courts are not *constitutional* Courts in which the Judicial power conferred on the General Government by the Constitution can be vested. They are Legislative Courts created in virtue of the general right of sovereignty existing in the Government of the Union, or in virtue of that clause of the Constitution which enables Congress to make all needful rules and regulations respecting the territory belonging to the United States. Hence Admiralty

ernor, and a Legislative Council consisting of nine members, appointed by the President and Senate, to continue in office for five years, and of a House of Representatives chosen by the inhabitants biennially. These Legislatures are prohibited from interfering with the primary disposal of the soil, or from taxing land belonging to the United States, or from imposing higher taxes upon land belonging to non-resident proprietors, than on those of residents.

jurisdiction may be vested in Courts created by a Territorial Legislature.[1] The Acts of Congress, therefore, vesting the Superior Court of a Territory with jurisdiction in "all cases arising under the laws and Constitution of the United States," does not embrace cases of Admiralty and maritime jurisdiction.

From these various regulations, it appears that Congress possesses supreme power in regard to all these Territories,—depending solely on the exercise of its sound discretion. A Territory, no more than the District of Columbia, is a *State* within the meaning of the Constitution, or entitled to claim the privileges secured to the members of the Union.[2] Nor will a writ of error, or an appeal lie from a Territorial Court to the Supreme Court of the United States, unless there be a special statutory provision for the purpose.[3]

It was observed by the late Chancellor Kent, in his valuable "Commentaries," that, "if the Government of the United States should carry into execution the project of colonizing the great valley of the Oregon west of the Rocky Mountains, it would afford a subject of grave consideration, what would be the future civil and political destiny of that country. It would be a long time," he thought, "before it would be populous enough to be created into one or more independent States; and in the mean time, upon the doctrine taught by the Acts of Congress, and the Judicial decisions of the Supreme Court, the colonists would be in a state of complete subordination, and as dependent upon

[1] 1 *Peters*, 511.
[2] 2 *Cranch*, 445; 1 *Wheat.* 91.
[3] 1 *Cranch*, 212; 3 *Ibid.* 159.

the will of Congress as the people of this Country would have been upon the King and Parliament of Great Britain, if they could have enforced their claim to bind us in all cases whatsoever. Such a state," he continues, "of absolute sovereignty on the one hand, and of absolute dependence on the other, is not at all congenial with the free and independent spirit of our native institutions; and the establishment of distant Territorial Governments, ruled according to will and pleasure, would have a very natural tendency,—as all proconsular Governments have had,—to abuse and oppression."[1]

The hand that traced these lines has long lain cold in death; but their learned and estimable author lived to see not only the "project" they refer to realized in the organization of Oregon as a Territory, but the establishment of Territorial Governments in other and more remote portions of the continent, some of which had not as yet been acquired; and had his already lengthened life been prolonged for a few years more, his fears would have subsided as he witnessed the erection of some of those Territories into States. So rapid, indeed, has been the increase and settlement of the National domain, that our political geography becomes obsolete at home, before it is known abroad.

V. The State Courts and Magistrates are, in some instances, invested by Congress with cognizance of cases arising under the laws of the United States. It seems, indeed, as we have already had occasion to mention, that Congress, in the course of its legislation upon the subjects intrusted to it, may commit the de-

[1] Comm., Part 2d, § 17.

cision of causes arising under a particular Act, solely, if deemed expedient, to the Courts of the Union; but in every case in which the State Courts are not expressly excluded, they may take cognizance of causes growing out of an Act of Congress. And although Congress cannot confer jurisdiction upon any Courts but such as exist under the Constitution, and its own laws, yet the State Courts may exercise it in cases authorized by the laws of the State, and not prohibited by the exclusive jurisdiction of the Federal Courts.[1]

Various duties have been imposed by Congress on the State Courts and Magistrates; and they have been invested with jurisdiction in civil suits, and in complaints and prosecutions for fines, penalties, and forfeitures accruing under the laws of the United States. In civil suits, the State Courts entertain such jurisdiction; but in criminal and penal cases they have, in several instances, declined it. In what cases, and to what extent, they will exercise criminal jurisdiction under the laws of the Union, and under what circumstances, and how far, the Judges of the State Courts have power to issue a *Habeas Corpus*, and decide on the validity of a commitment or detainer under the authority of the National Government, are questions which have been variously determined in the States, and never definitively settled in the Supreme Court of the United States, where the ultimate right of determining them resides.[2] The doctrine, however, seems to be admitted, that Congress cannot compel a State to entertain jurisdiction in any case. It only permits such of those tribunals as are competent, and have inherent jurisdic-

[1] 5 *Wheat.* 1.

[2] *Vide ante.*

tion adequate to the case, to entertain such suits in given cases; and they do not thereby become Inferior Courts in the sense of the Federal Constitution, because they are not ordained and established by Congress.[1] The State Courts are left to consult their own duty, from their State authority and organization; but if they do voluntarily entertain jurisdiction of causes cognizable under the authority of the United States, they do it upon the condition that the appellate jurisdiction of the Federal Courts shall apply. Their jurisdiction of Federal causes must, nevertheless, be confined to civil actions for civil demands, or to enforce penal statutes. They cannot hold criminal jurisdiction over offences *exclusively* against the United States; for every criminal prosecution must charge the offence to have been committed against the sovereign whose Court sits in judgment upon the offender, and whose authority can pardon him.

In concluding the subject of the Judicial Power, a few supplementary observations upon the general system, gathered from the adjudications of the Supreme Court, seem to be requisite. The extent to which the modes of proceeding in the Courts of the United States are regulated by the various State laws, is determined by the several Acts of Congress passed at different times for that purpose.[2] *Ex proprio vigore*, they have no operation whatever. They are only obligatory upon the National Courts, so far as they have been adopted and applied to them by Congress.[3] The section of the

1 14 *Johns. Rep.* 95.

2 In 1789, 1792, and 1828.

3 10 *Wheat.* 1, 51; 6 *Cond. Rep.* 1, 22; 9 *Peters*, 129; 16 *Ibid.* 89; 1 *Howard*, 301.

Judiciary Act of 1789,—which provides that "the laws of the several States shall be regarded as rules of decision in trials at Common Law, in the Courts of the United States, in cases where they apply," includes only civil cases at Common Law, and not criminal offences against the United States. It has no application to the practice of the Court, or the conduct of its officers in the service of an execution. This section is merely the recognition of a principle of universal law,—that contracts are to be governed by the law of the *forum*, in reference to which they were made.[1]

The process Act of 1789, expressly adopted the forms, writs, and modes of process in the State Courts, then in use in suits at Common Law. The Act of 1792 adopts the forms of writs, executions, and other process, and the forms and modes of proceeding in Courts of Common Law then in force in the Courts of the United States, under the former Act, "subject to such alterations and additions as the said Courts respectively, in their discretion, deem expedient, or, to such regulations as the Supreme Court of the United States shall think proper, from time to time, to prescribe to any Circuit or District Court, concerning the same." This delegation of power to the Judiciary by Congress, is held to be "perfectly constitutional;"—a general superintendence over the subject seeming to be properly within the Judicial province, and having been always so considered.[2] The power to alter and add to the forms of process, and modes of proceeding in a suit embraces its whole process, and every transaction in it from its commencement to its termination by the satisfaction

[1] 10 *Wheat.* 1.

[2] See cases last above cited.

of the judgment. Nor can such power be limited to formal, as contradistinguished from substantial alterations; but is to be understood as vesting in the Courts of the United States authority to frame and mould the process so as to adapt it to the purposes intended. Thus, these Courts may so vary the effect and operation of final process as to reach property not liable by the State laws as they stood in 1789, to be taken in execution; or it may exempt property, not then, but since exempted by the State laws.[1]

The Act of Congress of 1828, repeals all rules made by the Courts of the United States for the regulation of final process in all the Districts, and adopts the execution laws of the several States, as they then stood,—giving, however, to the Federal Courts power to alter final process by rules, so far only as to adapt the same to any subsequent change of the State law. The effect of this Act was to adopt the State laws then existing, as to bail, and exemption from arrest on final process; and a rule of a Circuit Court of the United States, providing that "no individual shall be kept in prison on mesne or final process, who has been released from imprisonment for such demand, by the Insolvent law of the State," is held to be fully authorized by this Act of Congress.[2]

Although this power of the Courts of the United States, under the Act in question, extends partially to the future legislation of the States, they can adopt the State law only as the Legislature has made it. They cannot adopt it in part, or alter it in any respect.[3] Nor

[1] 10 *Wheat.* 51; 1 *Peters*, 604; 13 *Ibid.* 45.

[2] 9 *Peters*, 329.

[3] 13 *Peters*, 45; 2 *Howard*, 608.

have the Federal Courts authority under the Act to adopt by rule, any provision of a State law incompatible with the positive enactments of Congress relative to the jurisdiction, practice, or proceedings of those Courts.[1]

No rule of construction is better established, or more familiar to jurists, than "if two statutes conflict with each other, the Courts must decide on the operation of each, and endeavor, if possible, to harmonize their provisions."[2] If an Act of Congress admit of two interpretations, one of which brings it within, and the other presses it beyond the constitutional authority of the Courts, they will adopt the former construction; as the presumption should never be indulged that Congress meant to exercise or usurp any unconstitutional authority,—unless, indeed, that conclusion is forced upon the Courts by language altogether unambiguous.[3]

But in the construction of State statutes, the Federal Courts are guided by the decisions of those of the State. This course is founded upon the principle universally recognized, that the Judicial department in every Government where such department exists, is the appropriate organ for construing the laws. A fixed and received construction by a State Court of its statute-laws, make a part of such laws, and must furnish the rule of decision to the Federal Courts, so far as is consistent with the Constitution of the United States,—in all cases arising within the State enacting them. And it is immaterial whether the decisions of the State Court are grounded upon a statute of the State, or

[1] 16 *Peters*, 89; 2 *Howard*, 241.

[2] 1 *Cranch*, 137; 1 *Cond. Rep.* 267.

[3] 12 *Peters*, 72.

form a part of the unwritten law, which has become a fixed rule of property.[1] So where the policy of a State, on any given subject, is manifest and settled, the Courts of the United States are bound to notice it as a part of its code; and to declare all contracts, made in the State, repugnant to it, illegal and void.[2] The evidence, however, of such a fixed policy must be clear, before the Federal Courts will set aside a contract on the ground of such a repugnancy.[3]

The fourteenth section of the Judiciary Act of 1789, which provides that "the laws of the several States, except where the Constitution, statutes, or treaties of the United States shall otherwise require,—shall be regarded as rules of decision in trials at Common Law, in the Courts of the United States, in cases where they apply," has never been applied to State laws, *not strictly local*; *that is to say, to none but positive* statute-laws, and the construction of them adopted by the local tribunals, or rights and titles to things having a permanent locality, such as the rights and titles to real estate and other matters immovable and intraterritorial in their character. It does not extend to questions of a more general nature, not at all dependent upon local statutes, or usages;—as, for example, to the construction of ordinary contracts, and other written instruments, especially those of a commercial nature,—

[1] 1 *Peters*, 351, 476; 5 *Ibid.* 151; 6 *Ibid.* 283; 11 *Ibid.* 1; 12 *Ibid.* 32; 2 *Ibid.* 85; 3 *Ibid.* 127.

[2] 5 *Cranch*, 22; 9 *Ibid.*, 87; 3 *Cond. Rep.* 386, 570; 4 *Ibid.* 132; 2 *Ibid.* 179; 5 *Ibid.* 18; 6 *Ibid.* 47, 385, 489; 1 *Wheat.* 115 279; 2 *Ibid.* 316; 6 *Ibid.* 119; 10 *Ibid.* 152; 11 *Ibid.* 361; 12 *Ibid* 153.

[3] 15 *Peters*, 446.

which last are to be interpreted upon the general principles and doctrines of commercial jurisprudence.

The Courts of the United States, under the Constitution and laws of the Union, have, moreover, *Equity Jurisdiction;* and unless the general principles of Equity have been modified by the laws and usages of a particular State, those general principles will be carried out everywhere in the same manner; and the same Equity jurisprudence prevail in all the States, when administered by the Federal Courts. Hence, the decision of a State Court in a case which involved only general principles of Equity, and was not controlled by local law or usage, is not binding as authority upon the Courts of the United States.[1]

Equity jurisdiction is conferred on the Federal Courts under certain limitations, under which the usages of the High Court of Chancery in England, which have been adopted by the rules of the Supreme Court, furnish the Equity-law exercised by the United States Courts in all the States, even in those where no Chancery system exists. Under this system, therefore, where relief can be given by the English Chancery, it may be given by the Courts of the Union.[2]

Although, on all questions arising under the Constitution and laws of the United States, the Supreme Court may exercise a revising power, and its decisions are final and obligatory upon all other tribunals,—State, as well as Federal,—yet a State Court has a right to examine and determine any such questions; but its decisions must conform to those of the Supreme Court; otherwise the corrective power of the latter

[1] 13 *Howard*, 268. [2] *Ibid.* 579.

must be exercised. The case, however, is very different when the question arises under the local law. In those cases the decision of the highest Judicial tribunal of the State should be considered final by the former,—not because the State Court has any power to bind the Federal tribunal, but because, in the language of the Supreme Court, "a fixed and received construction by a State, in its own Courts, makes a part of its statute-law."[1]

The same reason that influences the Supreme Court in adopting the construction given to a strictly local law by the State Courts, in the first instance, is not less strong in favor of following it, should the State tribunal change its construction, inasmuch as the rule is settled, not by a single adjudication, but by a series of decisions. A refusal to adopt the change would establish in the State two rules of property. And the same reasons which would render a change in the construction of a law of the United States by the Supreme Court obligatory upon the State tribunals, induce the Courts of the United States to give effect to the latest exposition of the local law by the State Courts. It is, emphatically, the law of the States, which the Federal Courts, sitting within the State, and the Supreme Court, when the case is brought before it, are called on to enforce. For, if the construction of the highest tribunal of a State, forms a part of its statute-law, as much as an Act of its Legislature, the Courts of the United States can make no distinction between them. The Supreme Court, therefore, has no hesitation in modifying its decisions so as to conform them to any alteration

[1] 11 *Wheat.* 361.

of the State law, and applying the same rule where the Judicial branch of the same Government, in the exercise of its acknowledged functions, gives, by construction, a different aspect to a statute, from that which had, at first, been given to it. The charge of inconsistency might be made with more force and propriety, against the Federal Courts, for a disregard of this rule, than for conforming to it.[1]

Where the construction of a will has been settled by the highest Court of a State, and long acquiesced in as a rule of property, the Federal Courts will, for that reason, follow it. But the mere construction by a State Court does not, like its construction of a statute, constitute a rule of construction for the Courts of the United States.[2] Nor are they governed by the decision of a State Court upon the construction of a deed, as to matters and language belonging to the Common Law, and not to any statute of the State.[3]

Where English statutes, such, for instance, as the statutes of limitation, and the statute of frauds, have been ingrafted into our legislation, the known and settled construction of those statutes by the English Courts, has been, either silently incorporated in our Codes, or received with all the weight of authority.[4] The rule uniformly observed by the Supreme Court, in construing statutes, is to adopt the construction of the Courts of the country, by whose Legislature the statute was enacted. This rule may be subject to some modification when applied to British statutes adopted in any of the States. By adopting them, they become our

[1] 6 *Peters*, 291. But see 5 *Howard*, 134.
[2] 3 *Howard*, 464. [3] 4 *Ibid.* 353. [4] 2 *Peters*, 1.

own as entirely as if enacted by the Legislature of the State. The construction, therefore, which British statutes had received in England, at the time of their adoption, in this country,—indeed, from the time of its separation from the mother-country,—may very properly be considered as accompanying the statutes themselves, and forming an integral part of them. But, however subsequent decisions of the English Courts may be respected here,—and, certainly, hey are entitled to great respect,—their absolute authority is not admitted. If those Courts vary in their construction of a statute, ours do not hold themselves bound to fluctuate with them.[1]

From the survey, which I have now completed, of our Federal Judicial establishment, it will have been perceived that the leading features of the system are to be found in the Act of 1789, so often referred to, passed at the first session of the first Congress under the present Constitution. It is understood to have been drawn up by Mr. Oliver Ellsworth, then a Senator from Connecticut, and afterwards Chief Justice of the United States. It has stood the test of severe experience since that time, with very little alteration or improvement,—a fact that affords the strongest evidence of the wisdom of the plan, and its skilful adaptation to the interests and convenience of the country. It was, evidently, the result of much profound reflection, and great legal knowledge; and the system thus formed and reduced to practice, has been so successful and beneficial in its operation, that the administration of justice in the

[1] 5 *Peters*, 264.

Federal Courts, has, upon the whole, been constantly rising in influence and reputation. In this review of the most important points which have arisen with respect to the constitutional powers of the Judicial department, we have seen that it is competent, not only to construe the Constitution, and thus pronounce on the constitutionality of the laws of the United States, and on the validity of the Constitutions and laws of the several States, and to declare either of the latter void, if repugnant to the Federal Constitution, or to a law, or treaty of the Federal Government,—but also to revise the judgments of the State Courts enforcing any ordinance contrary to the provisions of the National compact. We have seen, moreover, that the Federal Courts must either possess exclusive jurisdiction in all cases affecting the Constitution, laws, and treaties of the Union, or they must have power to review the judgments rendered on all such questions by the State tribunals; and, so far as the latter power has hitherto been controverted, it has been sustained by the Supreme National Tribunal with great ability and success, and with equal learning, dignity, and discretion.

LECTURE VII.

OF THE POWERS VESTED IN THE FEDERAL GOVERNMENT, RELATIVE TO SECURITY FROM FOREIGN DANGER.

We are now to enter upon the second general division of our subject, which relates to "the nature, extent, and limitation of the powers vested in the Federal Government, and the restraints imposed by the Constitution on the States."

The powers conferred on the National Government may be reduced, as I have already mentioned, to different classes, as they relate to the following different objects, viz:—

First. Security from foreign danger.

Second. Intercourse with foreign nations.

Third. Harmony among the States.

Fourth. Miscellaneous objects of general utility.

Fifth. Restrictions on the powers of the States; and,

Sixth. Provisions for giving efficacy to the powers vested in the Union.

As *security from foreign danger* is one of the primary objects of civil society, so it was an avowed and essential purpose of the union of the States; and, accordingly, the powers requisite to attaining it were effectually confided to the National Government, and consist,

1*st.* Of the powers of declaring war, and granting letters of marque and reprisal.

2*d.* Of making rules concerning captures by land and water.

3*d.* Of providing armies and fleets, and of regulating and calling forth the militia of the States; and, as connected with these, the substantive and distinct power of levying taxes and borrowing money.

I. The right of self-defence is a part of the law of our nature, and it is the indispensable duty of civil society to protect its members in the enjoyment of their rights, both of person and property. This is a fundamental principle of every social compact; and it is laid down by all approved writers on public law, that on this principle, an injury done or threatened to the perfect rights of a nation, or any of its members, and susceptible of no other redress, is just cause of war. But as the evils of war are certain, and its results doubtful, both wisdom and humanity require that every possible precaution should be taken, and every necessary preparation made, before engaging in it. It was formerly usual to precede hostilities by a public declaration communicated in form to the enemy; but in modern times this practice has been discontinued; and the nation proclaiming war now confines itself to a declaration within its own territory, and to its own people.

The power of declaring war is vested by the Constitution of the United States in Congress; without whose consent no State can engage in war, unless actually invaded, or in such imminent danger of invasion as will not admit delay. So that this power of Congress is not only of its own nature *exclusive*, but its concurrent exercise is expressly prohibited; nor is it easy to conceive where else but in Congress it could be properly and prudently deposited. Although Congress alone, by its solemn act, passed, like other laws, according to the forms of the Constitution, can subject the nation to the hazardous events of war, yet the interposition of a smaller portion of the Government has power to restore peace. Hostilities may be terminated by a *truce*, which may be made by the President alone, as Commander-in-chief of the military forces of the Union, and of which the duration may be indefinite; while *treaties*, by which peace is completely restored, may be made, as we have seen, by the President and Senate, without the intervention of the House of Representatives.

As delay in making war may be sometimes detrimental to individuals who may have suffered from the depredations of foreign powers, Congress is invested also with the power of issuing letters of marque and reprisal; the latter signifying a "taking in return;" the former, "passing the frontier in order to such taking."[1] This power is, in all cases, plainly derived from that of making war. It induces, indeed, only an incomplete state of hostilities, but generally ends in their formal denunciation. By the law of nations, letters of marque and reprisal may be granted whenever the subjects of

[1] This is the *literal* meaning of the terms; but the only *practical* distinction seems to be the one given in the note to Mr. Duponceau's valuable edition of *Bynkershoeck*, p. 183, which is between *Letters of Marque*, and *Letters of Marque and Reprisal*. The latter, he says, is "the old technical expression for what we now call a privateer's commission; the former is applied to a vessel fitted out for war and merchandise, and armed merely for defence." To the honor, and in proof of the progressive civilization of the age, privateering has been generally discouraged, if not wholly suppressed, in the war now raging in Europe; and will probably never be revived.

one State are oppressed and injured by those of another, and justice is denied by the State to which the oppressor belongs. They are in the nature of a commission granted by the Government to particular citizens, authorizing them to seize the bodies or goods of citizens of the offending nation, wherever they may be found, until satisfaction be made. And although this procedure seems to be dictated by Nature herself, yet the necessity is obvious, of calling on the sovereign power to determine when it may be resorted to; as, otherwise, every private individual might act as a judge in his own cause, and, to avenge his private injury, involve the nation to which he belongs in war.

II. *The power of making "rules concerning captures on land and water,"* which is superadded to the constitutional power of declaring war, is not confined to captures made beyond the territorial limits of the United States, but comprehends rules respecting the property of an enemy found within those limits. It is an express grant to Congress of the power of confiscating such property, as an independent substantive power, not included in the power of declaring war; and when a war breaks out, the question as to the disposition of enemy-property in the country, is a question of policy for the consideration of the National Legislature, and not proper for the consideration of the Judicial power, which can only pursue that course in regard to such property as Congress may direct.[1] According to the best writers on the law of nations, a declaration of war by the sovereign power of one State against another, implies that the whole nation declares war; and that

1 8 *Cranch*, 109.

all the subjects of the one are enemies to all the subjects of the other. But although a declaration of war has this effect with regard to individuals, and thus gives to them those mutual and respective rights under the law of nations which a state of war confers, yet the mere declaration does not, by its single operation, produce any of those results which are usually effected by the ulterior measures of the Government, consequent upon the declaration of war. By a strict interpretation, indeed, of the ancient public law, war gives to a nation full right to take the persons and confiscate the property of its enemy, wherever found; and the mitigation of this rule which the policy of modern times has introduced into practice, although it may affect its exercise, can never impair the right itself; and whenever the Legislature chooses to bring it into operation, the Judicial department must give it effect.

Until the Legislative will, however, is distinctly declared, no power of condemnation can exist in the Courts; and, from the structure of our Government, proceedings to condemn enemy's property found in the country at the declaration of war, can be sustained only on the principle of their having been commenced in execution of an existing law. An Act of Congress simply declaring war, does not, by its own operation, so vest such property in the Government as to support Judicial proceedings for its seizure and condemnation; but vests merely a right of which the assertion depends on the future action of the Legislature.[1]

In expounding the Constitution of the United States, a construction should not lightly be admitted, which

[1] 8 *Cranch*, 109.

would give to a declaration of war an effect in this country, which it does not possess elsewhere; and which would fetter that entire discretion respecting enemies' property, which may enable us to apply to the enemy the rule that he applies to us. That a declaration of war has only the effect of placing the two nations in a state of hostility, but not of operating by its own force any of those results,—such as a transfer of property,—which are usually produced by ulterior measures of Government, is fairly deducible from the enumeration of the power now in question. It would be restraining the clause "to make rules concerning captures on land and water," within narrower limits than the words themselves import, to say that its meaning is confined to captures which are *extra-territorial.* It extends to rules respecting enemies' property *found within* the territory; and is an express grant to Congress of the power in question, as an independent, substantive power, not included in that of declaring war. A declaration of war, therefore, is not *per se* a confiscation of enemies' property.[1]

III. *The power of raising armies and equipping fleets* seems to be involved in the power of declaring war; and to have left it to be exercised by the States, under the direction of Congress, as was the case under the Confederation, would have inverted a primary principle of the new Constitution, and, in practice, transferred the care of the common defence from the Federal head to the individual members of the Union. The various inconveniences which would attend the system of a separate organization of the national force must be

[1] 8 *Cranch*, 109.

obvious. They had been experienced during the war of our Revolution, and had proved that such a system was oppressive to some of the States, and dangerous to all. Under our present Constitution, sufficient reasons have appeared to induce an apprehension that the State Governments are naturally prone to rivalship with the Government of the Union; and if, in addition to this, their ambition were stimulated by the separate and independent possession of military forces, too strong a temptation and too great a facility would be given them to subvert the constitutional authority of the Union. The liberties of the people would, moreover, be less safe under such an arrangement than under that which leaves the national forces in the hands of the National Government. So far as an *army* may be likely, in this country, to become an instrument of ambition or power, it had better be at the disposal of that power of which the people are most apt to be jealous; for it is a truth which the experience of ages has attested, that the people are commonly most in danger when the means of invading their rights are at the command of those of whom they are the least suspicious.

Standing armies, in time of peace, have, indeed, been objected to as dangerous to our free institutions; but there can scarcely be ground for such apprehension, from the nature of the Federal Government; while the impolicy of restraints on its discretion with respect to raising forces by land or sea, is manifest, from the consideration that the efficiency of the power depends on its being indefinite, and upon its extending to the maintaining them in peace as well as in war; for with no show of propriety could the force requisite for defence be limited by those who have no power to limit the strength and power of offence possessed by an enemy; nor unless our Government could set bounds to the ambition, injustice, or exertions of other nations, could restraints be safely imposed upon its discretion, or limits prescribed to it for self-preservation. Besides, a readiness for war, in time of peace, is not only necessary for self-defence, but affords the most certain means of preventing aggression, by exhibiting such resources and preparations for repelling it as may discourage or deter an enemy from attempts which, from that very circumstance, would probably prove unavailing. A prohibition, therefore, against raising and maintaining armies and fleets in time of peace, would not only exhibit the extraordinary spectacle of a nation incapacitated by its Constitution from preparing for defence before it was actually invaded, but would be altogether inconsistent with the public safety, and the exigencies of self-protection, unless by its Constitution it could in like manner prohibit the preparations and limit the establishments of every hostile power. The means of security can only be regulated by the means, probabilities, and dangers of attack; and it would be worse than useless to oppose constitutional barriers to the impulse of self-preservation, because it would embody in the Constitution the temptation, if not the necessity of resorting to usurpations of extraordinary power, every precedent of which would be the excuse for unnecessary and multiplied repetitions of measures far more dangerous to public liberty than a standing army, in a country with a population and under a Government like ours.

The jealousy which would abolish our military establishments in time of peace, may be traced to those habits of thinking which the inhabitants of the United States derived from the people from which they sprung, and upon the prevailing sentiments on the subject at the period of our Revolution. As incident to the undefined and unrestricted power of making war, it was the acknowledged prerogative of the British Crown to maintain, by its own authority, regular troops in time of peace. The abuse of this prerogative, among others, led to the public execution of one king, and the expulsion of another; and to guard for the future against the exercise of power so dangerous, the *Bill of Rights*, framed by the Convention-Parliament, and acceded to by King William, at the revolution of 1688, declared that "raising or keeping a standing army in time of peace, unless with the consent of Parliament, was against law."[1] The events which led to our own Revolution quickened the public sensibility on every point connected with the security of popular rights; and the principles which taught our fathers to be jealous of the power of an hereditary monarch, were afterward extended to their own representatives. In the Constitutions of Pennsylvania and North Carolina, prohibitions of military establishments in time of peace were introduced; and in those of New Hampshire, Massachusetts, Delaware, and Maryland, a declaration was inserted similar to that of the English Bill of Rights, although that declaration was inapplicable to any of the State Governments; for the power of raising and keeping on foot standing armies could by no possible construction be deemed, at that time, to reside anywhere else than in the Legislatures themselves. It was therefore super-

[1] 1 *William and Mary*, Stat. 1. Ch. 1.

fluous, to say the least of it, to declare that a measure should not be adopted without the consent of that body which alone had the power of adopting it.

Those State Constitutions which have been most approved are silent on the subject; and the only direct restriction on Congress in regard to the exercise of its military powers, is contained in an amendment to the Federal Constitution, which declares that "no soldier shall, in time of peace, be quartered in any house without the consent of the owner; nor in time of war but in a manner to be prescribed by law."[1] Even in those State Constitutions which seem to have meditated a total interdiction of military establishments during peace, the expressions used are *monitory* rather than *prohibitory;* and the ambiguity of their terms appears to have resulted from a conflict between the desire of excluding such establishments, and the conviction that the measure would be unwise and hazardous. The union of the States under the National Constitution removes every pretext for a military establishment in any of the States which could be dangerous; while our distance from the powerful nations of Europe affords sufficient security that the Federal Government will never be able to persuade or delude the people into the support of large and expensive peace establishments. The danger, indeed, is the other way; and it is rather to be feared that mistaken notions of economy, if not of jealousy, will always tend to render our military force not merely too weak for the protection, but reduce it too low even for the preservation of our forts and arsenals. *The Union* itself, however, is our best protec-

1 Amendment to Const. U. S., Art. III.

tion and defence, and our principal security against danger from abroad, internal commotion, or domestic usurpation. It may, moreover, be numbered among the blessings vouchsafed to our country, *that the Union itself* is the great source of our maritime strength; while the palpable necessity of a *navy*, and its proved efficiency as an arm of national defence, have silenced the jealousy or the scruples which at one period prevented due attention to fostering it in time of peace. It has since fought its way to the patronage of the Government, and it always enjoyed the favor of the people.

Although no State can establish a permanent military government, yet it may use its military power to put down an armed insurrection too strong to be controlled by the civil authority; and the State must determine for itself, what degree of force the crisis demands. After it has declared *martial law*, a military officer may lawfully arrest any person whom he has reasonable grounds to believe was engaged in the insurrection; or he may order a house to be forcibly entered for the purpose. But no more force should be used than is necessary for the accomplishment of the object; and if the power is exercised for the sake of oppression, or any injury be done wilfully to person or property, the party by whom, or by whose order it is committed, would undoubtedly be answerable.[1]

IV. *The power of regulating the militia*, and commanding its services in cases of insurrection or invasion, are incident to the duties of superintending the common defence, and of watching over the internal peace of the Union.

[1] 6 *Howard*, 1.

Uniformity in the organization and discipline of the militia must evidently be attended with the most beneficial results whenever they are called into service, as it enables them to discharge their duties with mutual intelligence and concert. This desirable uniformity could only be accomplished by confiding the regulation of the militia of the several States to the General Government. It was therefore essential that Congress should have authority, not only "to provide for calling forth the militia to execute the laws of the Union, to suppress insurrections, and repel invasions," but also "to provide for organizing, arming, and disciplining them; and for governing such parts of them as may be employed in the service of the United States."[1]

The President is constituted, as we have seen, Commander-in-chief of the militia when called into the actual service of the Union; and he is authorized by law, in cases of invasion, or imminent danger thereof, to call forth such numbers of the militia most convenient to the scene of action, as he may judge necessary. The militia so called forth are subject to the rules of war; and the law imposes a fine on every delinquent who disobeys the summons, to be adjudged by a court-martial composed of militia officers only, and held and conducted according to the articles of war. During the war of 1812, the authority of the President over the militia of the several States became the subject of doubt and difficulty between the Federal Government and some of the States. It was the opinion of the Connecticut Government, not only that the militia could not be called out at the requisition of the General Government except in a case founded upon

1 Const. U. S., Art. I. Sect. VIII.

the existence of one of the specified exigencies, to be judged of by the State Government; but that, when called out, they could not be taken from the command of the officers duly appointed by the State, and placed under the immediate command of an officer of the United States army; nor could the United States, in the opinion of that Government, lawfully detach a portion of the privates from the body of their company. Similar difficulties arose between the Federal authorities and the Government of Massachusetts; the Governor of which State, as well as the Governor of Connecticut, refused to furnish detachments of militia for the defence of the maritime frontier, on an exposition of the Federal Constitution, which they, no doubt, believed to be sound and just. In Connecticut, the claim of the Governor to judge whether the exigency existed to authorize a call of the militia of the State, or any portion of it, into the service of the Union, and the claim on the part of the State to retain the command of them, when duly ordered out, against any subordinate officer of the United States army, were submitted to the consideration of the State Legislature, and received the strong and decided sanction of that body. In Massachusetts, the Governor consulted the Judges of the Supreme Court of that State as to the true construction of the Constitution on both those points. The Judges were of opinion that it belonged to the Governors of the several States to determine when any of the exigencies contemplated by the Federal Constitution existed to require them to transfer the militia, or any part of it, to the service of the Union, and command of the President. It was supposed that the Constitution did not give the power of judging as to the existence of the exigency, by any express terms, to the President or to Congress; and that, inasmuch as it was not prohibited to the States, the right of deciding upon that point was, of course, reserved to them. A different construction would, it was alleged, place all the militia, in effect, at the will of Congress, and produce a military consolidation of the States. The Act of Congress vested in the President the power of calling forth the militia when any one of the exigencies existed; and if to that were superadded the power of determining the *casus fœderis*, the militia would, in fact, be under the President's control.

As to the question how the militia were to be commanded when duly called out, the Massachusetts Judges were of opinion that the President alone, of all the officers acting under the United States, was authorized to command them; and that he must command them as they were organized under officers appointed by the State, as they could not be transferred to the command of any officer, not of the militia, except the President. But these learned Judges, acting as councillors, did not undertake to determine how the militia were to be commanded in case of the absence of the President; or of a junction of militia with regular troops; or whether they were to act under their separate officers, but in concert, as foreign allies; or whether the officer present of the highest rank, either of the militia or of the regular army, was authorized to command the united forces; these were found, it seems, to be questions too difficult and perplexing for *extra-judicial* decision.

Mr. Madison, one of the most prominent members of the Convention which formed the Constitution, and one of its ablest defenders, was, at the time of these disputes, President of the United States, and as such declared that these constructions of the constitutional powers of the General Government over the militia were "novel and unfortunate." In a message to Congress, to which they gave occasion, he observed that, "if the authority of the United States to call into service, and to command the militia, could thus be prostrated, we were *not one* people *for* the purpose most of all requiring that we should be united." Since that period, many and deeply interesting questions arising on the powers of the Union have been investigated and decided in the Federal Courts; and the progress of public opinion, as well as the tenor of those decisions, have been favorable to a much more liberal and enlarged construction of the Constitution than that which was adopted by the States in question; so that the doctrines of the General Government, as now understood, fully support the claim of Mr. Madison, as President of the United States, to judge, exclusively of State authority, of the existence of the exigency upon which the militia may be called into the service of the Union. The Acts of Congress already referred to, as well as the Act for establishing a uniform militia throughout the Union, were considered by the Supreme Court of the United States, in the first case[1] that came before them on the subject, as covering the whole ground of Federal legislation in regard to it. By the Act of Congress, the manner in which the militia are to be organized, armed, disciplined, and governed, is fully prescribed; provision is made for drafting, detaching,

[1] 5 *Wheat.* 1.

and calling forth the State *quotas* when required by the President; his orders are to be given to the Chief Magistrate of the State, or to any inferior militia officer he may think proper; neglect or refusal to obey his orders is declared to be a public offence, and subjects the offender to trial and punishment by a court-martial; and the mode of proceeding is perspicuously detailed. The question before the Court was whether it was competent for a court-martial, deriving its jurisdiction under State authority, to try and punish militiamen drafted, detached, and called forth by the President into the service of the United States, and who had refused and neglected to obey the call. The court decided that the militia, when called into the service of the United States, were not to be considered as being in that service until they were mustered at the place of rendezvous; and that, until then, the State retained a right concurrent with the United States to punish their delinquencies. But after the militia had thus actually entered into the service of the Union, their character changed from State to National militia; and the authority of the General Government over such detachments became exclusive.

In a subsequent case,[1] which came up on a writ of error on a judgment of the highest court in the State of New York, where the decision had been against this power of the President over the militia, his claim was unanimously sustained by the Supreme Court. The power confided to the President was, indeed, considered of a very high and delicate nature, but one which could not be executed without corresponding responsibility.

1 12 *Wheat.* 19.

It is, nevertheless, limited in its terms, and confined to cases of actual invasion or imminent danger; and upon the question whether the President was the sole and exclusive judge of the existence of the exigency, or whether it was one which every officer to whom his order was addressed might decide for himself, the court was of opinion that the authority to decide belonged exclusively to the President, and that his decision was conclusive upon all other persons. This construction was held necessarily to result from the nature of the power given by the Constitution, and from the manifest object contemplated by the Act of Congress. The power itself is to be exercised on sudden emergencies, and under circumstances which may vitally affect the existence of the Union, and a prompt and unhesitating obedience is indispensable to the attainment of the object. The service is a military service, and the command of a military nature; and in such cases, every delay and obstacle to an efficient and immediate compliance, necessarily tends to put in jeopardy the public interests. While subordinate officers or soldiers are pausing to consider whether they ought to obey, or are scrupulously weighing the evidence of the facts on which the Commander-in-chief exercises the right to demand their services, the hostile enterprise may be accomplished without the means of resistance. If the power of regulating the militia, and of commanding its services in times of insurrection and invasion, be, as has been alleged, natural incidents to the duty of superintending the common defence, and watching over the internal peace of the Union, then must this power be so construed, with respect to its exercise, as not to defeat the important ends in view. If the Governor of a

State, or other superior officer, has a right to contest the orders of the President, upon his own doubts as to the existence of the exigency, it must be equally the right of every inferior officer, and of every private sentinel; and every act of any person in furtherance of such orders would render him liable in a civil suit, in which his defence must finally rest upon his ability to establish, by competent proof, the facts upon which the exigency was said to have arisen. Such a course would obviously be subversive of all discipline, and expose the best-intentioned officers to the chances of a ruinous litigation; and, in many instances, the evidence on which the President may have decided might not constitute technical proof, or its disclosure might reveal important secrets of state, which the public interests, and even safety, might require to remain concealed.

This power, therefore, "to provide for calling forth the militia to execute the laws, suppress insurrections, and repel invasions," confided to Congress by the Constitution, is carried into effect by the law which provides that, when any such exigency exists, the militia of the States may be "called forth" by the Chief Magistrate of the Union, who, by the Constitution, is Commander-in-chief of the militia when in the actual service of the United States, whose duty it is "to take care that the laws be faithfully executed," and whose responsibility for an honest discharge of his official obligations is secured by the highest sanctions. He is necessarily to judge, in the first instance, and is bound to act according to his belief of the facts. If he decide to call forth the militia, and his requisitions, which are *orders*, for this purpose, are in conformity with the provisions of the law, it would seem to follow, as a necessary consequence, that every subordinate officer is bound to obey them. Whenever the law gives to the President a discretionary power, to be exercised by him upon his own opinion of certain facts, it is a sound rule of construction, that the statute constitutes him the sole and exclusive judge of the existence of those facts, and it is not a valid objection that such power may be abused; for there is no power that is not susceptible of abuse. The remedy for this, and all other official misconduct, is to be found in the Constitution itself. In a free government the danger must be remote, since, in addition to the high qualifications which the Chief Magistrate must be presumed to possess, the frequency of elections, and the watchfulness of the National Representatives, carry with them all the checks that can be useful to guard against usurpation or tyranny.

It has, however, been objected, that even admitting the judgment of the President to be conclusive as to the existence of the exigency, still, it is necessary that it should appear that the particular exigency *in fact* existed; and the same principles were alleged to be applicable to the delegation and exercise of this power intrusted to the President for great political purposes, as are applied to the humblest agent of the Government, acting under the most narrow and special authority. But when the President exercises an authority confided to him by law, the presumption is, that it is exercised in pursuance of the law. Every public officer, indeed, is presumed to act in obedience to his duty, until the contrary be shown; and *à fortiori*, that presumption ought to be favorably applied to the Chief Magistrate. Nor can the non-existence of the exigency be averred and shown by the delinquent party; for if it could be averred, it would be traversable, and, of course, might be passed upon by a jury; and thus the legality of the order would depend, not on the judgment of the President, but upon the finding of those facts upon the proof submitted to the jury. It must, therefore, be sufficient if the President determine the exigency to exist, and all other persons must be bound by his decision.

V. *The power of raising money by taxation and loans* being the main sinew of that which is to be exerted in the national defence, is therefore properly arranged in the same class, especially as this object is specified in the Constitution as one of the purposes of vesting it in Congress. The support of the national forces, the expense of raising troops, of building and equipping fleets, and all the other expenditures in anywise connected with military and naval plans and operations, are not, however, the only objects to which the jurisdiction of Congress, with respect to revenue, extends. The terms by which the power is conferred, embrace a provision for the support of the civil establishments of the United States, the payment of the national debt, and, in general, for all those objects for which "the general welfare" requires the disbursement of money from the national treasury. The necessity of vesting this power in the Federal Government seems to be too obvious to require elucidation. Money is, indeed, the vital principle of the body politic. It is that which sustains its life and motion, and enables it to perform its most essential functions. No Government, therefore, can be supported without possessing the means within itself, independently of the concurrence of others, of procuring a regular and adequate supply of revenue, so far as the resources at its command will permit. There must, of necessity, then, be interwoven in the texture of every Government a power of taxation in some shape or other. In the Government of the United States, it is coextensive with the purposes of the Constitution. Congress is accordingly invested with power "to lay and collect taxes, duties, imposts, and excises, to pay the debts, and provide for the common defence and general welfare;"[1] and it has also a distinct power "to borrow money on the credit of the United States."[2]

It was originally urged as an objection to the Constitution, and it is still occasionally contended, that the latter branch of the former of these clauses amounts, in terms, to an authority to exercise every power which may be alleged to be necessary for the "*general* welfare." But this construction was promptly refuted by the authors of "The Federalist:" "Had no other enumeration or definition of the powers of Congress," say they, "been found in the Constitution, there might have been some color for this interpretation, though it would then have been difficult to have found a reason for so awkward a form of describing an authority to legislate in all possible cases." It is evident that the expressions in question must be taken in connection with the preceding branch of the clause, and were intended merely as a specification of the objects for which taxes are to be laid, and not to convey a distinct and independent power to provide for "the general welfare."[3]

1 Const. U. S., Art. I. Sect. VIII. 1.

2 *Ibid.*

3 "The Federalist," No. 41, by Mr. Madison.

The power of taxation is, moreover, limited, by requiring that "capitation and other direct taxes shall be apportioned among the several States according to their respective numbers, as ascertained by the census, and determined by the rule for the apportionment of Representatives in Congress." It is qualified, also, by a provision that "all duties, imposts, and excises shall be equal throughout the United States;" and it is further restricted by a prohibition upon Congress to "lay any tax or duties on articles exported from the United States." The Constitution does not define or select subjects for exclusive taxation by the Federal Government; although, in some instances, an interference must have been foreseen from the exercise of a concurrent power with the States. But it was thought better that a particular State should sustain this inconvenience, than that the National necessities should fail of supply; and it was manifestly intended that Congress should possess full power, subject to the restrictions and exceptions I have mentioned, over every species of taxable property.[1] But the adoption of the Constitution of the United States did not operate as a repeal of the

1 Where a company incorporated by the State of New York, *of which all the stockholders were residents*, were owners of vessels employed in the transportation of passengers and freight between the port of New York and that of San Francisco, in California, and between the latter and different parts of the Territory of Oregon, all of which vessels were ocean steamships, and duly registered in New York, and remained in California no longer than was necessary to land their passengers and freight, and prepare for the next voyage, it was held by the Supreme Court of the United States, that these vessels are not liable to assessment and taxation, under the laws of California, and authorities of San Francisco. 17 *Howard*, 596.

revenue laws of a State, before Congress passed an Act for the collection of duties.[1]

The term "taxes" is general, and was made use of in the Constitution to confer a plenary authority in all cases of taxation to which the powers vested in the Union extend. The most familiar general division of taxes is into *direct* and *indirect;* and although the Constitution designates only the former species, it necessarily implies the existence of the latter. The general term, then, includes,

1*st.* Direct taxes, which are, properly, capitation taxes, and taxes upon land; although a direct tax might be laid on other subjects, such as generally pervade all parts of the Union.

2*d.* Duties, imposts, and excises; and,

3*d.* All other taxes of an indirect operation.

A *direct tax* operates and takes effect independently of consumption or expenditure; while *indirect* taxes affect expense or consumption; and the revenue arising from them is dependent thereupon. This distinction between the different species of taxes is of practical importance, arising from the different modes in which they are levied; direct taxes being required to be "apportioned among the several States according to the respective numbers of their inhabitants;" while indirect taxes, not admitting of such apportionment, are directed to be "uniform throughout the United States."[2]

Whether direct or indirect taxation were most consistent with the interests of the country, and the genius of its government, was a point much discussed when

[1] *Har. & McHen.* 480.

[2] Const. U. S., Art. I. Sect. IX.; *Ibid.* Art. I. Sect. IX. 4.

the Federal Constitution was under the consideration of the State Conventions; and even among those who admitted the necessity of surrendering to the National Government sources of revenue sufficient to discharge its debts, and adequate to its support, there were some who were jealous of the powers conferred on it for those purposes, and wished to reserve all objects of internal taxation to the States, yielding to the United States the power merely of imposing duties on imported articles. But this discrimination, it was urged, would violate that fundamental maxim of good sense and sound policy, which holds that every power should be proportionate to its object; and that the General Government would still be left in such dependence on the several States as would be inconsistent with its proper vigor and efficiency. Commercial imports alone were shown to be unequal to the existing necessities and future exigencies of the Union; and as the latter did not admit of calculation or limitation, it was evident that the power of providing for them ought also to be unconfined, especially as, in the usual course of public affairs, the necessities of a nation, in every stage of its progress, are generally found to be at least equal to its resources.

Whether the present financial condition of this country may not form an exception in its favor, it would, perhaps, be premature to decide, notwithstanding the favorable indications of later years; and as the power in question was, at all events, vested in the Federal Government, the only practical importance of the distinction between direct and indirect taxation, consists in the different modes in which they are respectively to be levied. Direct taxes are required, as we have seen, to be apportioned among the States according to their respective numbers, while indirect taxes, not admitting of this apportionment, are to be uniform throughout the United States. Thus, if Congress should think proper to raise a sum of money by direct taxation, the *quota* of each State must be fixed according to the census, and in conformity to the rule of apportionment prescribed by the Constitution. If indirect taxation be resorted to, the same duty must be imposed on the article liable to it, whether its quantity or consumption be greater or less in the respective States.

The Judicial construction given to the powers of Congress relative to taxation has generally turned on this distinction. By an Act passed in 1794, a duty was laid upon carriages for the conveyance of persons; and the question arose whether it were a *direct* tax, within the meaning of the Constitution. If it were not a direct tax, it was admitted to be rightly laid; but if it were a direct tax, it was not constitutionally imposed; because, in that case, it should have been laid according to the representative numbers of the several States. The Circuit Court for Virginia, where the question arose, was divided in opinion; but on appeal to the Supreme Court, it was decided that the tax in question was *not* a direct tax, and had, therefore, been levied according to the Constitution. It was observed, on this occasion, that the Constitution contemplated no taxes as direct taxes but such as could be laid in proportion to the census; and that the rule of apportionment could not apply to the tax on carriages; nor could such a tax be laid by that rule, without great inequality and injustice; and the argument by which this inequality and injustice were shown was conclusive against the contrary construction.[1] But although duties must be uniform, and direct taxes apportioned according to numbers, yet the provision of the Constitution with respect to the latter does not restrict the power of Congress to impose taxes on the inhabitants of the States only, but extends equally to all places over which the Federal Government has jurisdiction; and applies to the District of Columbia, and to the *Territories*, which are not represented in Congress.[2] The power of Congress to exercise exclusive legislation, *in all cases whatsoever*, over the District of Columbia, includes the power of taxing its inhabitants. But Congress are not absolutely to exercise that power, though they may, in their discretion, extend a tax to all the Territories of the United States, as well as to the States. A direct tax, if laid at all, must be laid according to the census; and, therefore, Congress has no authority to exempt any State from its due share of the burden; and although they are not under the same necessity of extending a tax to the unrepresented District, set apart for the seat of the National Government, nor to the National Ter-

1 3 *Dall.* 171. An Act of Congress laying duties on stamped paper, &c., which enacted that certain deeds and writings should not be given in evidence in any Court, until stamped as required by the Act, was held to be constitutional. 1 *Virg. Cas.* 128. But a tax imposed by a State law on stock issued for loans made to the United States is unconstitutional. 2 *Peters*, 449. See also 3 *Har. & McHen.* 169; 4 *Ham.* 107; 5 *Ibid.* 14; 4 *N. H.* 565, 572; 5 *Hayw.* 246; 2 *Overt.* 215; 2 *Hawks*, 207; 1 *Yerg.* 452; 9 *Ibid.* 490. The charter of a bank is a *franchise* which is not taxable as such, if a price has been paid for it, and accepted by the Legislature. But the corporate property of the bank is separate from the franchise, and may be taxed, unless there is a special agreement to the contrary. 3 *Howard*, 133.

2 5 *Wheat.* 317.

ritories, yet, if the tax be actually extended to them, the same constitutional rule of apportionment must be applied in levying it. This construction allowing a discretion in Congress as to the imposition of taxes upon the inhabitants of these Territories, must, at all events, be admitted to be the most convenient, as the expense of collecting a tax in some of them might exceed its amount. Nor can this departure from the rule which holds representation and taxation to be inseparable, be considered very material or important with respect to those settlements which are still in their infancy, though rapidly advancing to manhood, and looking forward with perfect confidence to complete equality as soon as they attain the requisite maturity. As it relates to the District of Columbia, the construction in question can hardly be regarded as impugning the great principle alluded to, inasmuch as its inhabitants have voluntarily relinquished the right of representation, and adopted the whole body of Congress as its legitimate Government.

There is nothing, however, in the exclusive power of legislation vested in Congress over the District of Columbia, which necessarily confines the operation of laws made in virtue of that power, to the limits of the District. The power in question being conferred by the Constitution, carries with it all those incidental powers which are necessary to its complete and effectual execution. Congress, when legislating for this District, is still the Legislature of the Union, and its Acts, in relation to it, are laws of the United States.[1]

A question, however, of much greater interest and

1 6 *Wheat.* 424.

importance has arisen, in regard to this power of taxation, which, of late years, has been much discussed in our public councils, and has hardly yet ceased to agitate a portion of the Union. I refer to the authority of Congress to impose duties on articles of foreign importation for the encouragement and protection of domestic manufactures; and to the proceedings which call in question and deny the constitutional existence of any such authority in Congress, and denounce its exercise as usurpation. The constitutional validity of those Acts of Congress which impose duties on importations, with that end in view, has never been presented for adjudication in the Federal Courts, but a Legislative construction in favor of the right of Congress to pass them was adopted and acted upon at the earliest period of the existence and operation of the Federal Government. Of late years, however, a controversy has arisen on the subject, which at one time threatened the peace and integrity of the Union; and which, though suspended, can by no means be considered as definitively settled. Some examination, therefore, of its merits may be useful, if not necessary.

Although Congress has the express and exclusive power "to lay and collect duties, imposts, and excises, to pay the debts, and provide for the common defence and general welfare of the United States,"[1] yet it is denied that these words confer authority to lay duties and imposts for any other purposes than those of discharging the national debts, supporting the civil and military establishments of the Government, and of carrying into effect the powers specifically enumerated, and

[1] Const. U. S., Art. I. Sect. VIII.

vested by the Constitution in Congress; thus excluding from all share of meaning the last member of the clause, which specifies the "general welfare" as one of the objects for which this branch of taxation was wholly given up to the National Government. And while some contend that there is no express authority granted to Congress to lay duties on foreign commodities, in order to favor or protect similar productions and fabrics of our own growth or manufacture—nor any power, express or implied, to encourage domestic industry by any means whatsoever; and that no such authority or power arises from intendment, as necessary to carry into effect any of the enumerated powers; others allege that this authority, if it exist at all, can only be constitutionally exercised indirectly, as resulting incidentally from the power to regulate commerce with foreign nations; and that imposts beyond what may be requisite to provide a revenue to meet the necessary and ordinary expenditures of the Government, can only be imposed to the extent required to countervail the commercial restrictions of other countries.

It will be perceived, in the first place, that this exposition of the power in question denies, in effect, any operation whatever to that branch of the clause in the Constitution by which it is supposed to be conferred; and thus adopts the opposite extreme to that latitude of construction which would give to the expressions relative to providing for the "general welfare," a meaning more extensive than any other part of the Constitution, and invest Congress with a general power of legislation. It is, however "awkward," a sound rule of construction, and admitted to be universal in its application, that the different parts of the same instrument are to be so expounded as to give effect to the whole, and to every portion susceptible of meaning. It is not to be presumed that the words in question were introduced without some object; they are not, therefore, to be excluded from all share in the interpretation of the clause, unless incapable of bearing any signification in connection with those with which they are conjoined. But the specific ends embraced by these general terms cannot certainly be supposed to be comprised among those more definite objects, subsequently enumerated in another and separate clause in the same article of the Constitution; and it must, therefore, be intended that other objects were meant to be accomplished by means of the taxing power, than the payment of the "public debt," and providing for the "common defence;" and that those further objects comprehend everything to which the "general welfare" requires the power to be applied, as the direct means of effecting the end proposed.

A different view was, indeed, taken of this clause of the Constitution by the authors of "The Federalist;"[1] and that high authority has been quoted in support of a very different interpretation. In answering the objection urged against the general expressions with which the clause concludes, as conferring a distinct and substantive power "to provide for the common defence and general welfare of the United States," the authors of "The Federalist" did not advert to the circumstance that those expressions are used merely as a general and summary designation of the purpose for which taxes were to be laid, independently of the objects subse-

[1] No. 41, by Mr. Madison.

quently specified; but in refuting the objection, they seem to adopt, in part, the construction of their adversaries, and admit that the words in question confer a substantive and independent power, distinct from the power of taxation; and they meet the argument drawn from these terms, against this extensive and sweeping operation of the power, by alleging that it was restricted by the subsequent enumeration of the specific powers of Congress in the same section. It has since, however, been judicially decided, and is even admitted by those, who, nevertheless, seek to avail themselves of this authority, that these words do not invest Congress with any power whatsoever distinct from the power of taxation, but that they merely refer to the purposes for which that power may be exercised. So far, moreover, from affording support to the argument against the power of Congress to encourage manufactures, two of the authors of "The Federalist,"[1] soon after the organization of the Government, officially asserted that power to be exclusively vested in Congress, which body, they contended, was bound to exercise it. They derived it, indeed, from the power to regulate commerce; but the acknowledged construction of the clause conferring the power of taxation, referring to the exercise of that power, as the means or instrument of providing for the general welfare, affords an ampler basis for the right; and in order to establish it on this broader and more solid foundation, it becomes necessary to show that the "general welfare" is, in fact, promoted by

[1] Mr. Hamilton, as Secretary of the Treasury, in his celebrated Report on Domestic Manufactures; and Mr. Madison, as a member of the House of Representatives, in his support of the Bill for their encouragement.

imposing duties on foreign commodities to such an amount as will foster our home manufactures.

This is clearly a question of national policy and legislation, involving facts and opinions not cognizable, from their nature, in the Judicial tribunals, but depending for their determination upon a sound exercise of legislative discretion. Their decision must of necessity belong to the National Legislature; for the States cannot afford the protection in the mode contemplated, inasmuch as they are prohibited from laying any duties on imports, except such as may be necessary for executing their own health and inspection laws, and have no power whatsoever to regulate commerce. Whatever, therefore, may be the opinions of the most enlightened men as to the policy of protecting domestic manufactures, or, in other words, as to the question whether the "general welfare" is promoted by the imposition of duties on imports with that view, those opinions must necessarily be founded on facts and principles of political economy, concerning which none but the National Legislature can, for any practical purpose, authoritatively decide. The necessity of vesting in Congress the power of determining such a question, may be illustrated by analogy from the power of the President to judge of the existence of the exigency upon which his power of calling forth the militia is made to depend. Without such authority, we have seen that both the existence of the exigency and the legality of the proceedings would turn, not on his knowledge or belief of the one, or his judgment on the other, but upon the verdict of a jury as to the facts, and the judgment of the Court on the legal questions they might present. So with respect to the power now under consideration;

unless Congress have authority to decide on the circumstances upon which the exercise of their legislative discretion depends, both facts and principles of a complicated character, concerning which great conflict of opinions exists, would be subject to Judicial examination, and a construction given to the Constitution, not merely by the judgment of the Court on the question whether Congress is authorized "to lay duties to provide for the general welfare," but upon the opinion of the Jury whether "the general welfare" was, upon sound principles of public policy, in fact promoted by protective duties.

With regard to the existing laws imposing duties on imported articles, the objection, so far as founded on the nature of the objects to which the revenue thus produced is applied, loses much of its force, from the circumstance that these laws were passed before the extinction of the public debt, for the payment of which, as well as to the support of the national institutions, the proceeds of those duties were intended to be applied. Whether they have, in fact, been so applied, or to what purposes the surplus arising from them has been, from time to time, appropriated, are questions wholly independent of the constitutional validity of laws merely authorizing such duties to be collected. When collected, and paid into the National Treasury, they are mingled with the general mass of funds, and are at the disposal of Congress; and as, by the Constitution, "no money can be drawn from the treasury but in pursuance of appropriations made by law,"[1] the question as to the constitutionality of the objects to

1 Const. U. S., Art. I. Sect. IX. 7.

which any part of the public revenues may be applied can never arise, until a law be proposed or enacted for their specific appropriation.

It has been, moreover, objected, that the existing laws, imposing duties on imports, are *unequal* in their operation, and therefore contrary to that provision of the Constitution which requires all duties to be "*uniform* throughout the United States." But the uniformity required is plainly in the imposition, and not in the operation of the duties; and whatever may be the fact as to the inequality of their operation, it is equally plain that it never can be controlled by the Legislature, but must always be regulated by the consumption of the article; for all indirect taxes, except imposts on articles of absolute necessity, may be said to be voluntary in their operation; as the amount paid by any individual must always depend on his spontaneous purchase of the article.

In the late war with Mexico, the port of San Francisco was conquered by the arms of the United States, in 1846, and shortly afterwards they had military possession of the whole of California. Early in 1847, the President of the United States, as Commander-in-chief of the army and navy, authorized the military and naval commanders of the United States forces in California, in the exercise of the belligerent rights of conquest, to form a military government for the conquered territory, with power to impose duties on imposts and tonnage, for the support of the army which had the conquest in possession. This was done, and tonnage and import duties were levied under a war-tariff, established by the civil Government for that purpose, until official notice was received that a treaty of peace had been concluded with Mexico — by which Upper California was ceded to the United States. Upon receiving this intelligence, the Governor directed that imports and tonnage duties should thereafter be levied in conformity with such paid in other parts of the United States under the Acts of Congress; and for the purpose of collecting them, he appointed a Collector for the port of San Francisco.

A suit was brought against the Collector to recover from him the amount of certain duties paid by the plaintiffs between the 3d of February, 1848,—the date of the treaty of peace,—and the 13th of November, 1849, when the Collector appointed by the President entered upon the duties of his office — upon the ground that they had been illegally exacted. The Supreme Court of the United States decided that these duties were legally demanded and collected by the civil Governor, both during the war, and after the ratification of the treaty of peace, until the revenue laws of the United States were extended by Congress to California.[1]

VI. *The power of borrowing money on the credit of the United States* is conferred on the National Government in general terms; but as the public credit of the Union must depend on the sources of revenue placed at its command, this power must have been intended to be exercised in anticipation of the national resources, and must, consequently, be subject to the same restrictions as to its objects, to which the power of taxation is limited and confined.

When the present Constitution was adopted, the United States were indebted to foreign nations for the

[1] 16 *Howard*, 164.

expenses of our revolutionary war; and many of our own citizens had large claims either upon the Confederacy, or upon its separate members, for services and supplies during that eventful contest. To liquidate and consolidate those debts, discharge a part of them, and secure the remainder, were measures necessary to the preservation of the public faith and credit, and the maintenance of the public interests, both at home and abroad. But to have resorted to taxation, in order immediately to accomplish these objects, would, had it even been practicable, have proved injurious to the nation, and ruinous to private individuals. It was foreseen that many of the public creditors would be satisfied with the assumption or recognition by the new Government of the principal, and the payment of the interest of the public debts. Under the power conferred on Congress to borrow money, it was enabled to make the necessary provisions for combining the whole expenses of the war, whether incurred by the Confederacy or the States, in one general amount, and funding it as one consolidated debt. The sources of revenue placed at the disposal of the Federal Government have since enabled it to discharge, not only the whole of this debt, but that, also, which occurred in the last war with Great Britain. But in case of future exigencies, or a failure of the usual supplies of revenue, similar means are at its command for continuing its operations, maintaining its existence, and vindicating its honor.

LECTURE VIII.

ON THE POWERS VESTED IN THE FEDERAL GOVERNMENT FOR REGULATING INTERCOURSE WITH FOREIGN NATIONS.

The powers vested in the General Government for regulating foreign intercourse, consist,

First. Of the powers to make treaties, and to send and receive Ambassadors, and other public Ministers, and Consuls.

Secondly. Of the power to define and punish piracies and felonies committed on the high seas, and other offences against the law of nations; and,

Thirdly. Of the power of regulating foreign commerce; including a power to prohibit, after a certain period, now elapsed, the importation of slaves.

This class of powers forms an obvious and essential branch of Federal administration; for if the United States are one nation in any respect, they are most clearly so in respect to other nations.

I. *The powers to make treaties, and to send and receive Ambassadors and other public Ministers, and Consuls*, are essential attributes of national sovereignty, and of that international equality which the interests of every sovereignty require it to preserve. Both powers were possessed by Congress under the Confederation, but not to the extent to which they are now enjoyed; for then the former power was embarrassed by an exception, under which treaties might be substantially frustrated by regulations of the States, and the latter did not comprehend "other public ministers and consuls."

As treaties with France and Holland, and especially the treaty of peace with Great Britain, existed when the Constitution was adopted, it became necessary to vary its terms in regard to treaties, from those relative to the laws of the United States; the declaration it contains in respect to the supremacy of the latter operating only in future, while in reference to the former the terms are, "all treaties made, *or which shall be made*, under the authority of the United States, shall be the supreme law of the land." These terms were intended to apply equally to previously existing treaties, as well as to those made subsequently to the Constitution; and it has, accordingly, been adjudged, by the Supreme Court, that they effectually repeal so much of the State laws and Constitutions as are repugnant to them.[1]

More general and extensive terms, also, are used in vesting the power with respect to treaties, than in conferring that relative to laws; and, while the latter is laid under several restrictions, there are none imposed on the exercise of the former, notwithstanding it is committed to the President and Senate, in exclusion of the House of Representatives, and is executed through the instrumentality of agents delegated for the purpose. And although the President and Senate are thus invested with this high and exclusive control over all those subjects of negotiation with foreign powers, which, in their consequences, may affect important domestic in-

1 3 *Dall.* 199.

terests, yet it would have been impossible to have defined a power of this nature, and, therefore, general terms only were used. These general expressions, however, ought strictly to be confined to their legitimate signification; and in order to ascertain whether the execution of the treaty-making power can be supported in any given case, those principles of the Constitution, from which the power proceeds, should carefully be applied to it. The power must, indeed, be construed in subordination to the Constitution; and however, in its operation, it may qualify, it cannot supersede or interfere with, any other of its fundamental provisions, nor can it ever be so interpreted as to destroy other powers granted by that instrument. A treaty to change the organization of the Government, or annihilate its sovereignty, or overturn its Republican form, or to deprive it of any of its constitutional powers, would be void; because it would defeat the will of the people, which it was designed to fulfil.

A treaty, in its general sense, is a compact entered into with a foreign power, and extends to all matters which are usually the subject of compact between independent nations. It is, in its nature, a *contract*, and not a Legislative act; and does not, according to general usage, effect of itself the objects intended to be accomplished by it, but requires to be carried into execution by some subsequent act of sovereign power by the contracting parties, especially in cases where it is meant to operate within the territories of either of them. With us, however, a different principle is established, in certain cases. It has been settled by the Supreme Court,[1] that, inasmuch as the Constitution declares a

[1] 2 *Peters*, 314.

treaty to be the law of the land, it is to be regarded in Courts of Justice as equivalent to an act of the Legislature, whenever it operates of itself without requiring the aid of any legislative provision. But when the terms of any treaty stipulation import an *executory* contract, it addresses itself to the political, and not to the Judicial, department for execution, and Congress must pass a law in execution of the compact, before it becomes a rule for the Courts. The Constitution does not expressly declare whether treaties are to be held superior to the Acts of Congress, or whether the laws are to be deemed coequal with, or superior to treaties; but the representation it holds forth to foreign powers, is that the President, by and with the advice and consent of the Senate, may bind the nation in all legitimate contracts; and if preëxisting laws, contrary to a treaty, could only be abrogated by Congress, this representation would be fallacious. It would subject the public faith to just imputation and reproach, and destroy all confidence in the national engagements. The immediate operation of a treaty must, therefore, be to overrule all existing laws incompatible with its stipulations.

Nor is this inconsistent with the power of Congress to pass subsequent laws, qualifying, altering, or wholly annulling a treaty; for such an authority, in certain cases, is supported on grounds wholly independent of the treaty-making power. For, as Congress possesses the sole right of declaring war, and as the alteration or abrogation of a treaty tends to produce it, the power in question may be regarded as an incident to that of declaring war. The exercise of such a right may be rendered necessary to the public welfare and safety, by measures of the party with whom the treaty was made, contrary to its spirit, or in open violation of its letter; and on such grounds alone can this right be reconciled either with the provisions of the Constitution, or the principles of public law. A memorable instance has occurred in our history of the annulment of a treaty by the act of the injured party. In the year 1798, Congress declared that the treaties with France were no longer obligatory on the United States, as they had been repeatedly violated by the French Government, and our just claims for reparation disregarded. Nevertheless, all treaties, as soon as ratified by competent authority, become of absolute efficacy, and, as long as they continue in force, are binding upon the whole nation. If a treaty require the payment of money to carry it into effect, and the money can only be raised or appropriated by an Act of the Legislature, it is morally obligatory upon the legislative power to pass the requisite law; and its refusal to do so would amount to a breach of the public faith, and afford just cause of war. That department of the Government which is intrusted with the power of making treaties may bind the national faith at its discretion; for the treaty-making power must be coextensive with the national exigencies, and necessarily involves in it every branch of the national sovereignty, of which the operation may be necessary to give effect to negotiations and compacts with foreign nations. If a nation have conferred on its Executive department, without reserve, the right of treating and contracting with other sovereignties, it is considered as having invested it with all the power necessary to make a valid contract, because that department is the organ of the Government for the purpose, and its contracts are made by the deputed will of the nation. The fundamental laws of the State may withhold from it the power of alienating the public domain, or other property belonging to it; but if there be no express provision of that kind, the inference is that it has confided to the department, charged with the duty and the power of making treaties, a discretion commensurate with all the great interests of the nation.[1]

The concurrence of each branch of the Legislative power, we have seen, is necessary to a declaration of war, while the President, with the advice and consent of the Senate alone, may conclude a treaty of peace. Now a power to make treaties necessarily implies a power to settle the terms on which they shall be concluded; and foreign States could not deal safely with the Government on any other presumption. That branch of the Government which is intrusted thus largely and generally with authority to make valid treaties of peace, can, of course, bind the nation by the alienation of part of its territory; and this, according to an approved writer on the law of nations,[2] is equally the case, whether that territory be already in the occupation of the enemy, or remain in possession of the nation, or whether the property be public or private. In a case decided in the Supreme Court of the United States, it was admitted that individual rights acquired by war, and vested rights of the citizen, might be sacrificed by treaty for national purposes.[3]

1 *Vattel's* Law of Nations, b. 1, ch. 21, § 2; 3 *Dall.* 199; *Grotius's* Law of War and Peace, b. 3, ch. 20, § 7.

2 *Ibid.* b. 4, ch. 2, § 11, 12.

3 1 *Cranch*, 103.

And in another case, it was held to be a clear principle of national law, that private rights might be surrendered by treaty to secure the public safety, but the Government would be bound to make compensation and indemnity to the individual whose rights had thus been sacrificed.

The conclusion of a treaty of commerce and navigation with Great Britain, in 1794, gave rise to much public discussion as to the nature and extent of the treaty-making power. A resolution was passed by the House of Representatives, requiring the President to lay before them a copy of his instructions to the Minister who conducted the negotiation, with the correspondence and other documents, relative to the treaty, excepting such papers as any existing negotiations might render it improper to disclose. The illustrious individual who then held the office of President, returned for answer, "that, in his opinion, the power of making treaties was exclusively vested in the President, by and with the advice and consent of the Senate, provided *two thirds of the Senators present* concurred in the ratification; and that any treaty so made and ratified, on being duly promulgated, became the law of the land. It was thus," he added, "that the treaty-making power had been understood by foreign nations; and that in all treaties made with them, we had declared, and they had believed, that, when so ratified, they became obligatory on the nation." In this construction of the Constitution, every former House of Representatives had acquiesced, and until that time not a doubt or suspicion had appeared, to his knowledge, that it was held not to be the true construction; and he concluded by observing that "it was perfectly clear to his understanding, that the consent of the House of Representatives was not necessary to the validity of a treaty. As the treaty in question exhibited in itself all the objects requiring Legislative provision, upon which the papers called for could throw no light, and that, as it was essential to the due administration of the Government that the boundaries fixed by the Constitution between the different departments should be preserved, a just regard to the Constitution, and to the duties of his office, forbade a compliance with their request."

The principles thus laid down by General Washington were so far acquiesced in by the House, that they passed a resolution, disclaiming the power to interfere in making treaties; but asserting the right of the House of Representatives, whenever stipulations are made on subjects committed by the Constitution to Congress, to deliberate on the expediency of carrying them into effect; and subsequently it was declared, by a small majority, to be expedient to pass the laws necessary for carrying the treaty into effect. From that time the question remained undisturbed until the conclusion of a convention with Great Britain, in 1815, when the House of Representatives, after much debate, passed a bill specifically enacting, on a particular subject, the same provisions which were contained as stipulations in the treaty. This dangerous innovation on the treaty-making power was warmly opposed by a minority in the House, and disagreed to by the Senate; but, after several conferences between them, the affair terminated in a compromise, which it is difficult to reconcile with a sound construction of the Constitution. The law passed on the occasion briefly declares that so much of any Act as imposes a duty on tonnage, contrary to the provisions of the convention with Great Britain, should, *from the date of that instrument*, and during its continuance, be of no force or effect; thus setting a precedent which may produce future difficulty in our national legislation, though the Judicial tribunals would probably regard such a law as a work of supererogation, or a mere nullity, and, from its retroactive operation, at variance with the spirit of the Constitution.

Treaties of every kind, when made by competent authority, are not only to be observed with the most scrupulous good faith, but are to receive a fair and liberal interpretation. Their meaning is to be ascertained by the same rules of construction and course of reasoning as are applied to the interpretation of private contracts; and according to the most authoritative writers of International Law, if a treaty should be in fact violated by one of the parties, either by proceedings incompatible with its nature, or by an intentional breach of any of its articles, it rests with the injured party alone, to pronounce it broken. The treaty, in such cases, is not absolutely *void*, but *voidable* at the election of the injured party. If he chooses not to come to a rupture, the treaty remains obligatory. He may waive or remit the infraction, or demand a just satisfaction.

But the violation of one article of a treaty is a violation of the whole; for all its articles are dependent on each other; and the breach of a single article may, at the election of the injured party, overthrow the whole treaty. This consequence, however, may be, and usually is, prevented by an express provision in the treaty itself, that if one article be broken, the others shall nevertheless continue in force; and in this case, the

Legislative power could not annul the treaty on the ground of the breach. The nullification of a treaty by the Legislature of one of the parties, under the circumstances which render such an act justifiable, or its termination by war, does not, however, divest rights of property acquired under it.[1] Nor do treaties become, *ipso facto*, extinguished by war. Those articles which stipulate for a permanent arrangement of territorial, or other national rights, are, at most, suspended during the war, and revive at the restoration of peace, unless waived by the parties, or new or repugnant arrangements are made in a new treaty.

At a very early period of modern history, the principal European States made provision, by treaty, for the mutual surrender of fugitives from justice; such practice has been continued to the present time. The Constitution of the United States provides that "a person charged in any State with treason, felony, or other crime, who shall flee from justice, and be found in another State, shall, on demand of the Executive authority of the State from which he fled, be delivered up to be removed to the State having jurisdiction of the crime.[2] A similar provision is contained in many of our treaties with foreign powers. But, independently of any such stipulation, the most eminent and approved writers upon public law declare that every State is bound to deny an asylum to criminals, and upon application and due examination of the case, to surrender the fugitive to the foreign State where the crime was committed.[3] A difficulty, in the absence of posi-

[1] 8 *Wheat.* 492. [2] Const. U. S., Art. IV. Sect. II. 2.

[3] *Grotius, Lex.* P. & B. l. 2, ch. 21; *Burlamaqui*, P. 4, ch. 3; *Rutherforth's Institutes*, P. 2, ch. 9; *Vattel's* Law of Nations, b. 2, ch. 6.

tive *agreement*, arises in drawing the line between the class of offences to which the usage of nations applies, and that in which it does not. But it seems to be understood in practice to apply only to crimes of great atrocity, such as are punishable by the State in which the fugitive has sought refuge; and not to include political offences. This principle is adopted in an Act of the Legislature of New York, which authorizes the Governor, in his discretion, on requisition from a foreign Government, to surrender up fugitives charged with murder, forgery, larceny, or other crimes punishable by the laws of that State with death, or imprisonment in the State prison, provided the evidence of criminality be sufficient by the State laws to detain the party for trial on a like charge.[1] Such a provision was all that was requisite, and all that the Legislature could make; for the Judicial power can do no more than cause the fugitive to be arrested and detained, until opportunity be afforded for his surrender by the Supreme Executive power of the Union. And, in order to give effect to the treaty stipulations upon the subject between the United States and foreign Governments, an Act was passed by Congress for that purpose, prescribing the mode in which the *extradition* of the accused party is to be made.[2]

As the Constitution confers absolutely upon the Gov-

[1] In the case of *Holmes and Gennison*, 14 *Peters*, 540, four of the Justices of the Supreme Court expressed the opinion that the Governor of a State had no power to deliver up to a foreign Government, a person charged with having committed a crime in the territory of that Government; but no judgment was given in that case,—the Court being equally divided in opinion, on the question of jurisdiction.

[2] Passed August 12, 1808.

ernment of the United States, the powers of making war, and of making treaties, it follows that it possesses the power of acquiring territory, either by conquest or by treaty.[1]

The supplementary power of sending, receiving, and dismissing Ambassadors, and other public Ministers, and Consuls, results as a necessary incident to the leading part in the treaty-making power assigned to the President. The power of *dismissing* a foreign Minister was first exercised by President Washington, who broke off all intercourse with Citizen Genet, and demanded his recall by the French Government, in consequence of his insolent assumption of authority to commission private vessels of war, equip them in our ports, and erect consular tribunals, with admiralty jurisdiction within our territory. The only instance of the kind that has since occurred, was that of the British Minister, Mr. Francis Jackson, who, in consequence of his disrespectful conduct, and the insulting tone of his correspondence with the Government, was dismissed by President Madison.[2]

[1] 1 *Peters*, 542.

[2] This gentleman had previously obtained some notoriety by his belligerent diplomacy at Copenhagen; and his conduct on his extraordinary mission to this country, in relation to the attack of a British line-of-battle ship upon the frigate Chesapeake, fully vindicated the *nom de guerre* he earned by a similar attack, though upon a much larger scale, which he had promoted upon the former occasion. It was supposed here, that he had been selected for this mission by Mr. Canning, the British Secretary for foreign affairs, in consequence of his exploit in the Baltic; but a better motive was found in England for the choice, in the private friendship existing between the Secretary and the Envoy, arising from the gratitude of Mr. Canning to his friend's father, the Rev. Dr. Cyril Jackson, Dean of Christ Church,

A foreign Consul is a public agent clothed with authority only for commercial purposes. He is not usually considered as a diplomatic agent of his sovereign, intrusted, by virtue of his office, with authority to represent him in his negotiations with foreign States, or to vindicate his prerogatives. He cannot, without the special authority of his Government, interpose a claim in the Prize Courts, for the violation of the neutral territory of his Sovereign.[1] But he has a right, by virtue of his office, to interpose a claim in a Court of Admiralty, for the restitution of property belonging to the subjects of his country, without a special authority from those for whose benefit he acts; although, in the absence of such authority, he has no right to receive, in his natural character, the proceeds of property libelled, and transferred to the registry of the Courts.[2] And, though allowed to interpose a claim for subjects unknown, of his nation, he cannot demand actual restitution of the property, without proof of the individual proprietary interest.[3]

Notwithstanding the ordinary character of a Consul is confined to commercial agency, it has been the practice, both of our own Government and those of Europe,

Oxford, under whose tuition he had been placed at the University. Be that as it may, the son behaved, in this country, as unlike as possible to what it may be presumed would have been the conduct and manners of the father, had he been in his son's situation, judging from the character of the former as given by the author of "The Pursuits of Literature," and by Mr. Ward, in his novel of "De Vere."

1 3 *Wheat*, 435; 4 *Cond. Rep.* 286.

2 6 *Wheat.* 152; 5 *Cond. Rep.* 45.

3 10 *Wheat.* 66; 6 *Cond. Rep.* 30.

particularly with respect to the Barbary powers, and certain Eastern nations, to invest Consuls with diplomatic functions, not merely on special occasions, but as permanent duties of their office, in those peculiar situations.

II. *The power to define and punish piracies and felonies committed on the high seas, and offences against the Law of Nations*, is substantively and separately vested in Congress; although, as to the former of these objects, it seems unavoidably incident to the power of regulating foreign commerce, and, as to the latter, to be implied from the authority to declare war and make treaties.

The power to *define*, as well as *punish*, seems rather applicable to felonies, and offences against the Law of Nations, than to piracies, as piracy is well defined by that code; and by the "high seas," is understood not only the ocean out of sight of land, but waters on the sea-coast beyond the boundary of low-water mark.

1. *Piracy*, according to the most approved writers on international law, consists in *robbery*, or a forcible depredation upon the high seas without lawful authority.[1] But felonies, either on the ocean or on waters on the coast beyond low-water mark, and offences against the Law of Nations, are by no means completely ascertained and defined by any code recognized by the common consent of nations; so that, with respect to these offences, there was a peculiar fitness in granting to Congress the power to define as well as to punish. But in executing the power in regard

[1] *Cicero, in Verres.* 1 *Inst.* 113; *Bynkershoeck*, Q. & P. lib. 1; *Rutherforth's Inst.* b. 2; *Cro. Eliz.* 685; 3 *Woodern's Lect.* 429.

to piracy, it was not necessary for Congress to insert in the statute a definition of the crime in terms; it was enough to refer for its definition to the Law of Nations, as it is there defined with reasonable certainty, and sufficient precision, and does not depend on the particular provisions of any municipal code either for its definition or its punishment.[1]

The Act of Congress referring to the Law of Nations for a definition of the crime of piracy, was a constitutional exercise of the power to define, as well as punish it; as Congress may define by using a term of known and determinate meaning, as well as by an express enumeration of the particulars included in that term. In law, and in logic, that is deemed certain, which, by necessary reference, is made so; and the Law of Nations has described the crime of Piracy with reasonable certainty.

Congress has a right to pass laws to punish pirates though they may be foreigners, and have committed no particular offence against the United States; and in executing this power, it has declared, in conformity with the Law of Nations, that the punishment of piracy shall be death. The Act of Congress, which declares certain offences to be piracy which are not so by the Law of Nations, was intended to punish them as offences against the United States, and not as offences against the human race;[2] and such an offence, committed by a person not a citizen of the United States, on board of a vessel belonging exclusively to subjects of a foreign State, is not piracy under the

[1] Act of March 3, 1819; 5 *Wheat.* 153; *Ibid.* 163, *note.*

[2] Act of May 15, 1820; 3 *Wheat.* 610.

statute, nor punishable in the Federal Courts. The offence, in such cases, must be left to be punished by the nation under whose flag the vessel sails, and whose particular jurisdiction extends to all on board; for it is a clear and settled principle, that the jurisdiction of every nation extends to its own citizens, on board of its own public and private vessels, at sea.[1] But murder and robbery committed on the high seas by persons on board of a vessel not at the time belonging to any foreign power, but in possession of a crew acting in defiance of all law, and acknowledging obedience to no Government, is within the Act of Congress, and punishable in the Courts of the United States; for although the statute does not apply to offences committed against the particular sovereignty of a foreign power, and on board of a vessel belonging at the time, in fact as well as of right, to a subject of a foreign State, and in virtue of such propriety subject to his control, yet it does extend to all offences committed against all nations, by persons who, by common consent, are amenable to the laws of all nations.[2]

In pursuance of this principle, the moment a vessel assumes a piratical character, she loses all claim to national character, and the crew, whether citizens or foreigners, are equally punishable under the statute, for acts which it declares to be piracy. The laws of the United States declare those acts piracy in one of their own citizens, which would be merely belligerent acts if committed on a foreigner; and a citizen of the United States who offends against the Government, or

[1] *Rutherf. Inst.* b. 2, ch. 9.

[2] 5 *Wheat.* 144; 4 *Cond. Rep.* 619; Laws U. S. 1820, § 3.

his fellow-citizens, under color of a foreign commission, is punishable in the same manner as if he had no commission. The acts of an alien, under the sanction of a national commission may be hostile, and his Government may be responsible for them, but they are not regarded as piratical; and this rule extends to the Barbary powers, who are now regarded, by the Law of Nations, as lawful powers, and not as they formerly deserved to be, *pirates*.

2. *Felony*, when committed on the high seas, amounts in effect to piracy, and has, to a considerable extent, been so declared by Congress, who, in pursuance of the authority vested in them by the Constitution, have enacted that any person, on the high seas, or in any open roadstead or bay where the sea ebbs and flows, committing the crime of robbery in and upon any vessel, or its crew or lading, shall be adjudged a *pirate;* and further, that "if any person concerned in any piratical cruise or enterprise, or being of the crew or ship's company of any piratical ship or vessel, shall land and commit robbery on shore, such person shall be adjudged a *pirate;*" in which last respect, the statute seems to be merely declaratory of the Law of Nations.[1]

The power to define and punish piracy and felonies on the high seas is exclusive in its nature; but it has been doubted whether the power to punish other offences against international law ought not to be considered as exclusively vested in Congress, on the ground that the Law of Nations forms a part of the Common Law of every State in the Union, and that violations

[1] *Douglass*, 615.

of it may be committed on land as well as at sea. The jurisdiction of the several States is certainly superseded in regard to those offences against international law which are committed at sea; but it does not seem to follow, as a necessary consequence, that it is also superseded in regard to those committed on shore. These offences are of various kinds, and the power to define and punish them is, with great propriety, given to Congress, as it prevents difficulties which might arise from the doubt of a concurrent jurisdiction of them by the States; and, so far as they have been defined by Congress, they may be said to arise under the Constitution and laws of the United States, and to be finally, if not exclusively, cognizable under the Federal authority.

But there are some such offences not enumerated in the Acts of Congress; and if the doctrine be sound, that the criminal jurisdiction of the Union is confined to cases expressly provided for by Congress, either those violations of international law, of which the punishment remains unprovided for by Congress, must go unpunished, or the State Court must entertain jurisdiction of them. The United States being alone responsible to foreign nations for all that affects their mutual intercourse, it rests with the National Government to declare what shall constitute offences against the law regulating that intercourse, and to prescribe suitable punishments for their commission. But if cases arise for which no provision has been made by Congress, both the National and State Governments, within the spheres of their respective jurisdictions, are thrown upon those general principles, which, being enforced by other nations, those nations have a right to require to be applied in their favor.

The offences falling more immediately under the cognizance of the law of nations are, besides piracy, *violations of safe-conducts, and infringements of the rights of Ambassadors and other public Ministers.*

3. A safe-conduct or *passport* contains a pledge of the public faith that it shall be duly respected, and the observance of this duty is essential to the character of the Government which grants it. In furtherance of the general sanction of public law, Congress has provided that persons violating a safe-conduct or passport granted by the Government of the United States, shall, on conviction, be subjected to fine and imprisonment.[1] The same punishment is inflicted upon persons offering violence to Ambassadors or other public Ministers, or being concerned in prosecuting or arresting them;[2] and the process whereby their persons, or those of their domestics, may be imprisoned, or their goods seized or attached, is declared void. The policy of these laws regards such proceedings against foreign Ministers as highly injurious to a free and liberal communication between different Governments, and mischievous in their consequences to any nation. They tend, most certainly, to provoke the resentment of the Sovereign whom the Envoy represents, and to bring upon the country the calamity of war; and, therefore, every civilized nation has an equal interest in upholding the privileges of their representatives abroad, and punishing the breaches of them by its own citizens.

III. *The power of regulating foreign commerce* is intimately connected with the power of concluding treaties, especially those of commerce and navigation,

[1] Act of April 30, 1790, § 27. [2] *Ibid.* §§ 25, 26.

and is, with equal propriety, submitted to the National Government.

The oppressed and degraded state of commerce before the adoption of the Federal Constitution, and the injury it sustained from the impotent and disconnected efforts of the several States to counteract the restrictions imposed on it by foreign nations with a view to their own interests, contributed more, perhaps, to the introduction of our present system of Government, than any other of the numerous evils proceeding from the feebleness of the Confederation. The former Congress, indeed, possessed the power of making commercial treaties, but its inability to enforce them rendered that power, in a great degree, useless; and all who were capable of estimating the influence of commerce on national prosperity, perceived the necessity of giving the control over this important subject to the General Government. It is not, therefore, matter of surprise, that the grant should be as extensive as the mischiefs that had been experienced; and it is equally apparent that to construe the grant so as to impair its efficacy, would tend to defeat an object in the attainment of which the American people felt that deep interest which arose from a strong and just conviction that the whole commerce of the nation should be regulated by Congress. From its very nature, this power must be considered as exclusive; for if the several States had retained the right of regulating their own commerce, each of them, as experience had indicated, would probably have pursued a different system; mutual jealousies, rivalries, restrictions, and prohibitions would have ensued, which a common superior alone could prevent or cure, and, at the same time, command that confidence of foreign nations, which is necessary to the negotiation of commercial treaties.

But the nature and extent of this power has been fully and ably discussed, and satisfactorily settled by the Supreme Court of the United States, especially in a case which drew in question, and overruled the constitutionality of the laws of New York, vesting in certain individuals the exclusive right of steam navigation upon its waters.[1] On that occasion, it was held, that the general power to regulate commerce was not restricted merely to the buying and selling or exchanging commodities, but included the navigation of vessels, and commercial intercourse in all its branches, and extended to all vessels, by whatsoever force propelled, and to whatever purpose appropriated. It was observed by the venerable and lamented Chief Justice Marshall, in delivering the opinion of the Court, that, if commerce did not include navigation, the Government of the Union had no direct power over that subject, and could make no law prescribing the requisites to constitute American vessels, or require them to be navigated by American seamen; yet this power had been exercised from the beginning of the Government, with the universal consent of the States and of the Union, and had been as universally understood to be a commercial regulation. The word *commerce*, indeed, must have been understood to comprehend *navigation* when the Constitution was adopted, as the power over both was one of the primary objects for which the

[1] 19 *Wheat.* 446. Having been consulted by the late Mr. Gibbons before he determined to try the validity of this grant, it may not be improper to subjoin the opinion given on that occasion. *Vide* Appendix F.

Constitution was formed; and in that comprehensive sense is the term used in the Constitution. It is a rule of construction universally acknowledged, that the exceptions from a power mark its extent; for it would be absurd as well as useless to except from a power granted, that which the words of the grant could never comprehend. If, therefore, the Constitution contains plain exceptions from the power over navigation — plain inhibitions against the exercise of that power in a particular way — it is evident that the power to which they apply must have been intended to have been granted.[1]

The power to regulate commerce, thus understood, is held to extend to every species of commercial intercourse between the United States and foreign nations, and among the States; and although the expressions relative to the States were not intended to comprehend that commerce which is completely internal, and carried on between individuals in a State, or different parts of the same State, without extending to, or affecting other States, yet, in regulating commerce with foreign nations, the power of Congress does not stop at the jurisdictional lines of the several States.[2] It would be a very useless power if it could not pass those limits.

1 The Acts of Congress require that every vessel shall be *registered* by the Collector of the District in which is the port nearest to the place where the owner or owners reside. The name of this port must be painted on her stern in large letters; and every bill of sale of her must be recorded in the office where she is registered. 17 *Howard*, 596.

2 But under this power, Congress cannot interfere with the ferries of a State, except so far as they are used for carrying on the coasting-trade; nor with navigation on canals constructed by a State, or upon inland lakes and rivers. 3 *Cowen*, 713.

The commerce of the United States with foreign nations is the commerce of the whole Union, and every district has a right to participate in it. The deep streams which penetrate our country in every direction, and pass through the interior of almost every State in the Union, furnish the means of exercising this right. If Congress have the power to regulate, that power must be exercised wherever the subject exists. If it exist within the States—if a foreign voyage may commence or terminate at a port within a State—then the power of Congress may be exercised within a State.

The power to prescribe the rule by which commerce is to be governed, like all other powers vested in Congress, is complete in itself, and may be exercised to its utmost extent, without any limitations but such as are prescribed in the Constitution. The restrictions on the powers of Congress are there plainly expressed, and not one of them affects the power in question. If, then, as has always been understood, the sovereignty of Congress, though limited to specific objects, be, nevertheless, plenary as to those objects, the power over commerce with foreign nations, and among the several States, is as absolutely vested in the Government of the Union, as it would be in the Government of any single State, if the Union did not exist, and the State Constitution had contained the same restrictions on the exercise of the Legislative power as are found in the Constitution of the United States. The wisdom and the discretion of Congress; the identity of its members with the people; and their dependence on their constituents, are in this instance, as in that of declaring war, and many others, the sole restraints upon which the community have relied to secure them from the abuse of the power they have granted; and such are the securities upon which the people must often, of necessity, rely in all representative Governments.

From these considerations, the power of Congress was held to comprehend navigation within the limits of every State in the Union, so far as that navigation may be in any manner connected with "commerce with foreign nations, or among the several States, or with the Indian tribes;" for the power of controlling navigation is incident, as we have seen, to the power to regulate commerce, and, consequently, the power of Congress over vessels employed in navigation is coextensive with that expressly vested in it over their cargoes.[1]

This power to regulate commerce, including thus the regulation of navigation, as not confined to acts done on the water. It extends to acts done on land which interfere with, obstruct, or prevent commerce or navigation; and any offence of this character, though committed on land, may be punished by Congress, under its general authority to make all laws necessary and proper to execute its expressly-delegated powers. A larceny, therefore, of goods belonging to a ship in distress, committed on a beach above high-water mark, is held to be punishable in the Courts of the United States.[2]

Although this extensive power, like many other of the powers formerly exercised by the several States, is now transferred to the Government of the Union, and no part of it thus exclusively vested in Congress, can be exercised by a State, yet the State Governments

[1] 9 *Wheat.* 1. [2] 5 *Howard*, 504.

constitute an important part of our system, and have retained a concurrent power of legislation over many subjects of Federal jurisdiction. The power of taxation, for instance, is indispensable to their existence, and is a power which in its own nature is capable of residing in, and of being exercised by, different authorities at the same time. But the power of Congress to lay and collect taxes and duties for the purposes of the Union, does not, as we have seen, necessarily interfere with the power of the States to impose taxes for State objects; nor is the exercise of that power by the States an exercise of any portion of the power granted to the United States. In imposing taxes for State purposes, the State Legislatures are not exercising a power vested in them even concurrently with Congress; for Congress is not empowered to levy taxes for objects within the exclusive province of the States. Each Government, therefore, when it respectively exercises its proper power of taxation, does not exercise the power of the other. But when a State proceeds to regulate commerce with foreign nations, or among the several States, it exercises the identical power which is granted to the Union, and does the very thing that Congress is authorized to do. The sole question, then, is whether the States can exercise the power of regulating commerce *concurrently with the United States.*

It was insisted, in the case referred to, that the States possessed such concurrent power, and the party maintaining the proposition relied on the restriction in the Federal Constitution, which prohibits the States from laying duties on imports or exports. It was alleged, very truly, that limitations of a power furnish a strong argument in favor of its existence, and that the prohibition in this case proved that the power to which it related might have been exercised had it not been expressly forbidden; and hence it was inferred that any commercial regulation, not expressly prohibited, to which the power of the State was originally competent, might still be made by its Legislature.

It was admitted, indeed, on the other hand, that the restriction in question proved that the States might have imposed duties on imports and exports, had they not been expressly prohibited; but it was denied that it followed, as a consequence from that concession, that a State may regulate commerce. The levying of duties on imports and exports was held to be a branch of the *taxing* power, and entirely distinct from the power to regulate commerce. The latter power is enumerated in the Constitution subsequently to the former, and each is substantively and independently conferred on Congress. The power of imposing duties on imports is classed with the power of levying taxes; but the power of levying taxes conferred on Congress, although it abridges the subjects of State taxation, can never be considered as abridging the right of the States relative to taxation itself; and they might, consequently, have exercised it by levying duties on imports and exports, had not the Constitution forbidden them. This prohibition, then, is an exception from the acknowledged power of the States to levy taxes, and not from the questionable power to regulate commerce. So, also, the exception in the Constitution, with regard to duties on tonnage, is considered as a restriction on the power of taxation, not on that to regulate commerce; and, like the former prohibition, presupposes the existence of that which it restrains, and not of that which it does not purport to restrain.

Neither are the State inspection laws regarded as commercial regulations, although they may have a remote and important influence on commerce, and are certainly recognized in the Constitution as proceeding from the exercise of a power remaining in the States. But these, together with quarantine regulations, and health laws of every description, as well as laws regulating the internal commerce of a State, and those which relate to canals, turnpike roads, and ferries, are component parts of that immense mass of legislation which embraces every thing within the territory of a State not surrendered to the General Government, and which, being of a local character, can be more advantageously regulated by the States themselves. No direct general power being given over these subjects to Congress, they consequently remain subject to State legislation; and if the Legislative power of the Union reaches them at all, it is for national purposes, and must then be either where the power is expressly given for a special purpose, or where it is clearly incidental to some power expressly given to the National Government. A State has the same undeniable and unlimited jurisdiction over all persons and things within its territorial limits, as any foreign nation, when that jurisdiction is not surrendered or restrained by the Federal Constitution.[1] The laws of the United States regulating the transportation of passengers in vessels arriving from foreign ports, are obviously regulations of

[1] The soil under the navigable waters of East New Jersey belongs to the State, and not to the riparian proprietors. The Supreme Court so decided in 16 *Peters*, 367; and the principle was held to cover a case where land has been reclaimed from the water under an Act of the State Legislature. 15 *Howard*, 426.

commerce, as they only affect, through the power over navigation, passengers *on their voyage*, and until they have landed; after that, and when they have ceased to be passengers, the Acts of Congress, applying to them only as such, and as such only professing to legislate in regard to them, have then performed their office, and can with no propriety of language be said to *come into conflict* with the laws of a State requiring the master of every vessel arriving therein from abroad to make a report in writing of the names, ages, and last legal settlement of his passengers; for such law does not assume *to regulate commerce;*[1] its operation begins only where the laws of Congress end, and is not even on the same subject; for although the persons on whom it operates are the same, yet, having ceased to be passengers, they no longer stand in the only relation in which the laws of Congress either professed or intended to act upon them.

The laws enacted in some of the States, prohibiting or regulating the sale of intoxicating liquors within their limits, are held not to interfere with the trade in ardent spirits while the article remains a part of foreign commerce, and is in the hands of the importer for sale, in the cask or vessel in which the laws of Congress authorize it to be imported. The State laws in question act altogether upon the retail or domestic traffic within their respective borders,—upon the article after it has passed the line of foreign commerce, and become a part of the general mass of property in the State. Such laws may discourage imports by diminishing the price which ardent spirits would bring; but no State is

[1] 11 *Peters*, 103.

bound to furnish a market for any article of merchandise which Congress authorizes to be imported, or to abstain from enacting a law which it may deem necessary to guard the health or morals of its citizens,—notwithstanding such law may discourage importation, or diminish the profits of the importer, or lessen the revenue of the General Government.[1]

It is obvious, therefore, that the Government of the Union, in the exercise of its express powers, may use means which may also be employed by a State in the exercise of its acknowledged powers. If Congress, for instance, license vessels to sail from one port to another in the same State, the act is supposed to be necessarily incidental to the power expressly granted to regulate commerce with foreign nations and among the States, and implies no claim of a direct power to regulate the purely internal commerce of a State, or to act directly on its system of domestic police. So, if a State, in passing laws on subjects acknowledged to be within its control, and, with a view to those subjects, adopt a measure of the same character with one which Congress may adopt, the State does not derive its authority from the *residuum* which it retains of the particular power granted to the Union, but from some other power which remains with the State, and may be executed by the same means used for the execution of the power by Congress. All experience shows that the same measure or measures, scarcely distinguishable from each other, may flow from distinct powers; but this does not prove that the powers are identical; and although the means used in their execution may sometimes ap-

[1] 5 *Howard*, 504.

proach each other so nearly as to be confounded, there are other situations in which they are sufficiently distinct to establish their individuality.

In our complex system, presenting the rare and difficult scheme of a Federal Government, supreme over the whole of its members, but possessing only certain enumerated powers, and of numerous State Governments, retaining and exercising all power not delegated to the Federal head, contests respecting power must necessarily arise. Measures taken respectively by the Governments of the Union and of the States, in the execution of their acknowledged powers, must often be of the same description, and may sometimes interfere. But this does not prove that the one is, in fact, exercising, or has a right to exercise, the powers of the other. The States may sometimes enact laws, the validity of which may depend on their not interfering with, or being contrary to, an Act of Congress, passed in pursuance of its constitutional powers; in all such cases, the inquiry is, whether the State law has, in its application, come into collision with the Act of Congress; and should an actual collision be found to have taken place, it would be immaterial whether the former were passed by the State in virtue of its concurrent power with Congress, or in virtue of a distinct and independent power relating to a different subject; in either case, the Act of the State Legislature, and the right or privilege conferred by it, must yield to rights and privileges derived from the Act of Congress. It was therefore held, in the case referred to, that a license under the Acts of Congress, for regulating the coasting trade, is not merely intended to confer a national character on vessels engaging in it, but gives to them permission to carry on that trade; and as the power of Congress to regulate commerce extends to navigation carried on in vessels exclusively employed in the transportation of passengers, whether those vessels be propelled by steam, or by the instrumentality of wind and sails—on waters wholly within a State, but which may be approached by the ocean—a case of actual collision was presented between the exclusive privilege conferred by the State law on the one side, and the authority to carry on the coasting trade derived, on the other, from the Act of Congress; and in so far as this interference extended, the State law was declared to be void, as repugnant to the Federal Constitution.

In a subsequent case, it was laid down by the same authority, that, as the power to regulate commerce thus reaches the interior of a State, and may there be exercised, it must be capable of authorizing *the sale* of those articles which it introduces, because its efficacy would not be complete if it ceased to operate at the point where the continuance of its operation is indispensable to its value. The power to allow importation would, indeed, be nugatory, if unaccompanied with the power to authorize the sale of the thing imported; for sale is the object of importation, and an essential ingredient of that commercial intercourse of which importation constitutes a part, and is as indispensable to the existence of that intercourse as importation itself. The right of sale, as well as the right to import, was, therefore, considered as involved in the power to regulate commerce; and it was accordingly held that Congress had a right, not only to authorize importation, but to authorize the importer to sell. An Act of the Legislature of Maryland, requiring all wholesale importers and sellers of foreign goods to obtain a license from that State, and to pay a sum of money on receiving it, was consequently adjudged to be void, as repugnant not only to that provision of the Federal Constitution which declares that "no State shall, without the consent of Congress, lay any impost or duty on imports or exports," but to that also which invests Congress with power "to regulate commerce."[1] The principles laid down on this occasion apply equally to importations from another State, as, in both cases, the powers remaining in the States, when so exercised as to come in conflict with those vested in Congress, that which is not *supreme* must yield to that which is. This great universal truth is inseparable from the nature of things; and the Constitution has applied it to the often interfering powers of the General and State Governments, as a vital principle of perpetual operation, so long as the power to regulate commerce is admitted to be exclusive. It has been so considered by every department of the Government, and by all classes of citizens in every quarter of the Union, ever since the adoption of the Federal Constitution. It was, indeed, to effect this transfer of power that the Constitution was established. This was the primary and avowed motive for assembling the Convention of 1787. The exclusive grant of this power to the National Govern-

[1] 9 *Wheat.* 1. But the Pennsylvania Statutes, imposing a duty on *retailers* of foreign merchandise, have been held by the Supreme Court of that State, not to be repugnant to the Constitution of the United States. 1 *Serg. & Raw.* 405. See also 2 *McCord*, 495; 14 *Wend.* 87; 1 *Dev. & Bar.* 19. So also of a tax imposed on all persons trading in foreign and domestic goods, within the State, whether the capital employed be owned there or elsewhere. 4 *Ham.* 107.

ment was essential to impart to our shipping engaged in foreign commerce its nationality and protection; and the surrender of this power became, in several of the States, the most formidable obstacle to the ratification of the new Constitution. The State of New York, where the opposition was the strongest, possessed the finest harbor on the coast; the fertility of its yet uncultivated western territory was already known; the rapid increase of its population had been confidently anticipated; the tide of immigration had begun to flow in upon it; and the consequent accession of wealth and power afforded the most seductive objects to gratify the ambition of its statesmen and politicians. These causes, indeed, combined to delay and render doubtful its adoption of the Federal Constitution, until it was rendered certain, by the assent of nine of the thirteen members of the Confederation, that the new Government would go into immediate operation among the States which had already acceded to it; and that the recusant States would thereby be deprived of the benefits both of the former Confederacy and of the new compact by which it was superseded.

A controversy, however, has of late years arisen, and still exists, between the supporters of the National jurisdiction and the advocates of "State Rights," with regard to the constitutionality of laws for the improvement of the Rivers and Harbors of the United States, under the power vested in Congress "to regulate commerce," or any other power granted to the General Government. On the one hand, it is maintained "that the great object of the Constitution was to *nationalize* the commerce and navigable waters of the Union by uniting them under a common authority, to be uniformly exercised, and that it therefore expressly prohibited the several States from interfering in any way with that authority. To those who assert that the States possess merely a concurrent authority which they may lawfully exercise upon the subject, until it be superseded by the paramount power of the Federal Government, it has been deemed sufficient to answer that the authority of the Union, at any rate, becomes supreme when exercised. Again, that at the time of forming the Federal Constitution, the common right of all the citizens of all the States to navigate the Mississippi and the Great Lakes was emphatically declared to be a "RIGHT OF THE UNION," as contradistinguished from the right of any separate State; and it is now claimed that this sacred and fundamental *right* is accompanied by a duty equally sacred and fundamental; that the States surrendered to the Union all revenue derived from commerce, and thus parted with the very means of facilitating the business which produced that revenue; that they parted, too, with the control of those navigable waters which furnish the channels of that commerce; that the States could never have intended to deliver themselves up to the care of the Federal Government, stripped of the means of securing the first elements of their prosperity, and thus manacled and fettered—without an equivalent; and the only equivalent which the case admitted was the substitution of the Federal Government for the exercise of the powers, and the performance of those correlative duties which the exigencies of the Confederacy forbade to the States; that, in the very nature of things, the Federal Government took the place, and received the powers—and, thereby, assumed the duties, of the States respec-

tively—*which they could not separately exercise consistently with the peace and prosperity of the whole; and that this was the great compromise of the Constitution.*"[1]

On the other hand, it is contended "that the Government of the United States is not a UNION, but a 'CONFEDERACY'; in other words, that the People of the United States are not a Nation, but merely a League of States absolutely sovereign; that the Nation acts, on a grand scale, only as a common attorney for those Sovereign States, each of which may judge of the extent of the powers granted—which are strictly limited and must be strictly construed; that the Tribunals expressly provided by the Constitution have no authority to decide upon the extent of such limitation, but that the President—especially if elected by the party holding these doctrines—has full power to narrow the exercise of the powers by Congress to suit his own peculiar tenets." It is somewhat difficult to define or comprehend the doctrines of this class of politicians, but they seem to be these: That the power to regulate commerce is merely the abstract power to regulate the duties to be imposed upon it, and prohibit the States from imposing such duties; that if the power exists at all to afford any physical facilities, it is limited to high-water mark; that Rivers cannot be improved above the ports of entry established by Congress; that a River *cannot* be *improved* if lying wholly within a State;

[1] *Vide* the Address of the Convention of Delegates from eighteen of the States, assembled at Chicago, in July, 1847, drawn up by that distinguished jurist and statesman, the late JOHN C. SPENCER, who attended as a Delegate from New York,—and their Memorial presented to Congress at its next session.

that it is not enough for a River to separate two States, but it must adjoin or pass through three, at least; that Harbors constructed by the General Government, must be harbors for shelter and not for commerce; that if it be lawful to deepen navigable waters, it is not lawful to place in them piers or any similar structures, as that would encroach upon the territorial jurisdiction of a State, and trespass on its sovereignty; that it is not lawful to remove obstructions in navigable waters, but that it is lawful to erect beacons on those obstructions, although at a cost greater than the expense of removal."

On grounds such in substance as these, bills for the improvement of certain Rivers and Harbors have been vetoed by several of our Presidents; and on the last occasion, a public meeting was held in the city of New York, which was addressed by Samuel B. Ruggles, Esq., an eminent member of the Bar, with great force and eloquence. He observed that the "masterly exposition" made by Mr. Spencer at Chicago, of the right and duty of Congress to improve the Rivers and Harbors of the Union, was "not only one of the most valuable state-papers ever produced in this country," and conclusive upon the immediate subject, but that it demonstrated besides, "the utter fallacy, folly, and unconstitutionality of a plan of State tonnage duties" which had been proposed by the opponents of the improvements contemplated by the Bills in question. A Bill had been introduced into the House of Representatives, giving the consent of Congress to certain local tonnage duties to be levied by the States, and was referred to the Committee of Commerce, of which Mr. Washington Hunt, afterwards Governor of New York, was Chairman. The Report he presented to the House condemned the plan in the strongest terms. It took a broad and comprehensive view of the commerce, foreign and domestic, of the United States, and insisted upon the just right of every portion of the Union to be fairly protected in its enjoyment; it placed upon a proper national basis, the duty which the Federal Government had for a long time neglected, and reprobated the *veto* interposed by the President to the Harbor Bill passed by both Houses of Congress. The Resolutions by which the Report was accompanied were passed by large majorities, although the votes of two thirds of the House of Representatives were not obtained to pass the Harbor Bill, notwithstanding the objections of the President. Nor was any such bill passed by Congress until the accession of Mr. Fillmore to the Presidency.[1]

Although the power to regulate commerce includes, as we have seen, navigation, and pilot-laws are regulations of navigation, and, therefore, of commerce, within the grant to Congress, yet it does not preclude the States from passing laws to regulate the pilotage. The power in question includes various subjects, upon some of which there should be a uniform rule, and upon others, different rules in different localities. The power in the former class, is exclusively in Congress; but not in the latter.[2]

Under this power to regulate commerce, Congress can exclude, either partially or wholly, any subject falling within the legitimate sphere of commercial regulation.[3] Nor is this doctrine inconsistent with those

[1] *Vide* "A Defence of the Rights and Duties of the American Union to improve its Navigable Waters," by Samuel B. Ruggles, Esq., New York, 1852.

[2] 12 *Howard*, 299.

[3] 9 *Ibid.* 560.

maintained by the Supreme Court in the case of Fox *v.* The State of Ohio,[1] where it was held that the power conferred on Congress "to provide for the punishment of counterfeiting the securities and current coins of the United States," does not prevent a State from passing a law to punish the offence of *circulating* such counterfeit coins.

The power of prohibiting the importation of slaves into the United States, after a certain period had elapsed, and of imposing a duty on their importation during the intermediate period, is virtually included in the power to regulate commerce, as the exception which postponed its exercise arose from an express restriction of the general power, and in construing the Constitution as to grants of power to the United States and the restrictions upon the States, the Supreme Court has always held that an exception of any particular case, presupposes that those which are not excepted, are included within the grant or prohibition; and has laid it down as a general rule, that where no exception is made in terms, none will be made by implication or construction.[2]

The words of the Constitution vesting this power are, "The migration or importation" (not of *slaves*, for that word is not to be found in the Constitution, but) "of such persons as any of the States now existing shall think proper to admit, shall not be prohibited prior to the year 1808." It is by no means difficult to account either for the existence of this restriction, or for the terms in which it is expressed; and although it is

1 5 *Howard*, 433.
2 12 *Peters*, 419, 657; 6 *Wheat.* 264; 9 *Ibid.* 206.

certainly to be wished that the power in question had been free from it, yet it ought to be remembered that a great point was gained in favor of humanity by fixing a period for the termination of this barbarous traffic. Before the time arrived, the interdiction was prospectively enacted by Congress, and it took effect in time to afford an example to civilized Europe of abolishing a species of commerce which had been the opprobrium of modern policy. This interdiction was followed up by denouncing the *foreign* slave-trade as piracy, and rendering it punishable with death when pursued by our own citizens; and, by the treaty with Great Britain of 1815, we have stipulated to coöperate with her, by means of our navy, to suppress it more effectually. But still the blot remains: for, though the toleration granted by the Constitution was confined to the States "then existing," yet Congress has refused to imitate the example of their predecessors under the Confederation, who prohibited slavery in the Territories ceded by the elder States for the common benefit, by a similar restriction upon the new States created in them; it has abstained from suppressing the domestic slave-trade, or "the *migration* of such persons as any of the States then existing should think proper to admit," which was not exempted from the power of regulating commerce among the States for any longer period than the foreign slave-trade was tolerated as an exception to the power of regulating commerce with foreign nations. Nor has it listened to the numerous petitions for abolishing slavery and the slave-trade in the Territories under its exclusive jurisdiction, and especially in the District of Columbia, the seat of the National Government, the residence of the representatives of foreign sovereigns, and the resort of strangers and visitors from all quarters of the globe.

The founders of the Republic seem, universally, to have regarded slavery as an evil; and under the Confederation, provided, in the Ordinance of 1787 for the government of the Territory of the United States, Northwest of the River Ohio, against the introduction and existence of slavery therein.

The original author of this celebrated measure was Mr. Jefferson. As chairman of a committee appointed to prepare a plan for the government of this newly acquired Territory, he reported to Congress an Ordinance for that purpose in 1784. As it came from his hands, it contained the prohibition against the introduction of slavery; but the clause was stricken out in Congress, at the instance of the three Southern States present, because it was unaccompanied by any provision for the recovery of fugitive slaves; and the Ordinance was passed without any attempt to reinstate the clause. The next year, this prohibitory clause, with some modification, was moved by Mr. Rufus King, then of Massachusetts, and was referred, as a proposition to a Committee, but was not then acted upon.[1] Upon its revision, in 1787, the Ordinance was adopted as it now stands, and it may well be considered as a Southern measure, not only from the source whence it sprang, but from the circumstance that three of the six members who composed the Committee were from slave-holding States—two of them, including the Chairman, from Virginia,[2]—and it was finally passed by the votes

[1] See Journ. Cong. 1784–1785.

[2] The authorship of the Ordinance of 1787, has been claimed for Mr. Nathan Dane, of Massachusetts; but that gentleman did not

of the eight States present, and received the individual vote of every member present, except one from New York.[1] By the same vote the Ordinance of 1784 was repeated.[2]

The evil as it existed in the individual States, was not considered beyond cure. In several of them, systems of gradual emancipation were adopted at an early day; and for some years a remedy, slow but sure, was silently operating in those slave States which bounded upon those from which slavery was excluded. It was supposed that the former would be compelled to abandon slave labor, from its inability to compete successfully with the labor of freemen. But the introduction of the cotton-plant into the Southern States, and its cultivation as an article of profitable commerce, increased the demand for laborers of African birth or descent, who, by their physical constitution, were supposed to be the best adapted, if not alone able, to bear the exposure incident to that species of cultivation. The foreign slave-trade was soon to be abolished, and the subsequent supply could then only be afforded by those States in which slavery still existed. The demand thus created operated as a temptation to retain slavery where the labor of slaves was no longer necessary, for the mere purpose of furnishing, through their natural increase, an article of commerce with those States where their labor continued to be, or had become profitable.

enter Congress until nearly two years after 1784, and although a member of the committee of 1787, he was not its Chairman.

1 Mr. Yates, afterwards Chief Justice of the Supreme Court of that State.

2 See Journ. Cong. July 11, 12, 13, 1787.

The acquisition of Louisiana brought with it an additional number of slaves; and as its population increased, and its agriculture extended, a new market opened for them. When the Missouri Territory, which had been set off from Louisiana, organized itself as a State, in 1829, and sought admission into the Union, as a slave State, it did not gain it until after a severe struggle. The opposers of the measure endeavored to apply to it the provision of the Ordinance of 1787, the authorship of which had been ascribed to Mr. Jefferson, whose authority they quoted in support of their arguments. As one of the Revisers of the Laws of Virginia, soon after the Revolution, that eminent statesman and philanthropist proposed to emancipate all slaves born subsequently to the adoption of the revised statutes, but that they should continue with their parents to a certain age, and then be brought up at the public expense, until the females should have attained the age of eighteen years, and the males, twenty-one; "*when they should be colonized to such place as the circumstances of the time should render most proper, to declare them an independent people, and extend to them our alliance and protection, till they have acquired strength.*"[1] Thus foreshadowing, with a remarkable coincidence, the scheme since so beneficially carried out by the American Colonization Society.[2]

1 Notes on Virginia, Query, XIV. page 203, Pennington & Gould's edit., N. Y., 1801.

2 Amongst the objections that Mr. Jefferson supposed would be made to his project, he anticipated the question, "Why not retain, and incorporate the blacks into the State?" To this he emphatically replied: "Deep-rooted prejudices entertained by the whites; ten thousand recollections by the blacks of the injuries they have sustained; new provocations; the real distinctions that nature has made,

The opposition to the admission of Missouri into the Union as a State, terminated, as is well known, in the compromise that no other slave State should be admitted beyond the parallel of 36° 30′ of North latitude; and thus was an agitation which, for a while, interrupted the harmony, and threatened the integrity of the Union, quieted for a season. When the Floridas were acquired, and had passed from the condition of a Territory into that of a State, no question of this kind could arise, as it lay below the line reserved to freedom. But upon the subsequent acquisition of the extensive territories ceded by Mexico, another and more violent agitation of the same questions which, on the former occasions, disturbed the peace of the Union, again arose, and were again ended in a compromise which included

and many other circumstances, will divide us into parties, and produce convulsions which will probably end but in the extermination of one or the other race. *Ibid.* p. 204.

In 1803, another Virginian of equal celebrity, *John Randolph, of Roanoke*, as Chairman of a Committee of the House of Representatives, to whom was referred a memorial from Indiana, praying for a temporary suspension of the anti-slavery clause of the Ordinance of 1787, reported against it as follows: "That the rapid population of the State of Ohio sufficiently evinces that the labor of the slave is not necessary to promote the growth and settlement of colonies in that region; that this labor,—demonstrably the dearest of any,—can only be employed to advantage in the cultivation of products more valuable than any known to that quarter of the United States; and the Committee deem it highly dangerous and inexpedient to impair a provision wisely calculated to promote the happiness and prosperity of the Northwestern Country, *and to give strength and security to that extensive frontier.* In the salutary operation of this sagacious and benevolent restraint, it is believed that the inhabitants of Indiana will, at no very distant day, find ample remuneration for a temporary privation of labor and emigration." *Journ. H. of Rep.* 1803.

further and more stringent provisions for the surrender of "fugitives from labor," or slaves escaping from their Southern Masters, and taking refuge in the free States.

A provision for this purpose was one of the *compromises* of the Constitution; and from the phraseology of the clause containing it, it would seem to have been intended to throw the duty of surrendering the fugitive upon the State into which he might escape; and, consequently, to impose upon the Courts and Magistrates of that State, the obligation of giving effect to the provision by their official interposition.[1] But, as we have seen, the duty of executing the laws of the Union, by those Courts and officers, was held to be optional with them, and no State had passed a law to render it otherwise. From these circumstances, probably, Congress was induced, notwithstanding the prevalence of the opinion just mentioned, and not until some few years after the adoption of the Federal Constitution, to pass the Act of 1793, relative to fugitives from labor, as well as from justice.

The constitutionality of this Act, though strenuously questioned, has been eventually affirmed by the Supreme Court of the United States, in all its leading provisions,—except that which confers authority upon State Magistrates.[2] The Judges, however, were not unanimous in their general view of this clause of the Constitution; and the question may again be brought in review before the Court in relation to the new Act upon the subject passed in 1850, as that Act presents new matter for consideration; and from the contrariety

[1] See Const. U. S., Art. IV. Sect. II. 3.

[2] 16 *Peters*, 539.

of the views taken by the Judges in regard to the former Act, as well as from circumstances since transpired in some of the States, it is, indeed, desirable that the subject should be deliberately reconsidered.[1]

[1] An occasion for such a review will probably be afforded in consequence of a recent decision of one of the State Courts, which it may be safely presumed will not be acquiesced in, but carried up to the Supreme Court of the United States. A person charged with having participated in the forcible rescue of a fugitive slave was brought up on a *Habeas Corpus* before one of the Judges of the Supreme Court of Wisconsin, and discharged. The opinion delivered by the Judge is very long and elaborate. The chief points made are that the article in the Constitution on which the law of 1850, for the reclamation of fugitive slaves rests, was merely a compact by the contracting parties to the Constitution, by which the free States were to be bound to provide legislation under due course of law, and after examination of facts, for the return of such persons, but that no power was conferred upon Congress to legislate upon the matter, and that it is the duty of the States to provide such legislation. The fact that Congress has not power to punish State officers for refusing to provide such legislation, is a proof that the matter remains in form of a compact. That it is clear that Congress cannot constitutionally act upon this subject; while it is also clear that the States cannot pass laws discharging fugitives from service. All such laws must be void. That the Constitution contemplates an examination into the claims of the claimant of the fugitive, to be made where he is, by presumption, free, while the Act of 1850 makes the decision or warrant of a Judge or Commissioner a judgment in fact, without trial or examination. That, in order to ascertain to whom "such service or labor is due," examination and inquiry must be made. If services or labor, is due, the fugitive must be given up; but the fact must be ascertained. There is an issue of fact to be tried. The suit to try this fact is not a suit in Equity or Admiralty, and must be at Common Law; hence a trial by Jury is demanded properly. The Act of 1850 is unconstitutional, in that it violates the principles which forbid that persons shall be deprived of liberty without "due process of law." The summary proceedings under this Act of 1850 clearly violate this

This Act of 1850, together with others passed at the same time, formed a new compromise. It adopts the same parallel of latitude for the exclusion of slavery, extending through the additional territory acquired from

provision. He refers at length to the varying sentiments of the Court in the case of Prigg *v.* Pennsylvania, and thinks that, in view of the doubts thrown around that case by the United States Judges themselves, they ought to review their decision. The case having been carried up to the Supreme Court of the State, this opinion was sustained and affirmed mainly on two grounds: the insufficiency of the commitment, and the unconstitutionality of the Fugitive Slave Act in delegating to Commissioners the power to hear and determine in cases arising under this Act. One of the Judges, who concurred with his brethren in holding that the party was properly discharged from arrest, and that the writ of *Habeas Corpus* was rightly granted, dissented from the view taken of the unconstitutionality of the Fugitive Slave Act.

The Court, in giving its opinion, insisted upon the fallacy in the argument that the proceedings under the Fugitive Slave law are analogous to those by which the fugitive from justice is delivered up.

The fugitive from justice is delivered to an agent appointed by the Governor of the State where the offence is alleged to have been committed, without any adjudication upon the question of his guilt or innocence; in other words, he is delivered to the officer of the law, and is in the custody of the law for the purpose of being taken to the State where alone he can be tried for the alleged offence. But the case is very different with the alleged fugitive from labor. There is an adjudication before the Commissioner, that he owes service or labor, and that he has escaped. By force of the Act of Congress under consideration, the record made in the State from which he is said to have escaped, is conclusive evidence that his status is that of a slave.

The Commissioner is obliged, if his identity is proved, so to adjudge, and the certificate, which is given to the claimant, is given because the Commissioner has so adjudged.

But the Court regarded this power given to the Commissioner to send the alleged fugitive from labor back to the State from which he is alleged to have escaped, *as a condemned slave*, to be unconstitutional,

Mexico. It withdraws from the State Courts and Magistrates all jurisdiction in regard to fugitives from labor, vesting it, exclusively, in the Courts and officers of the United States; and gives greater facilities for the recovery of the fugitive, and heavy penalties for interference with its execution. Thus, again, was agitation calmed, and peace restored, as it was supposed, permanently. But that hope has proved delusive. At the first session of the thirty-third Congress, an Act passed for organizing the Territorial Governments of Nebraska and Kansas, portions of the former Province of Louisiana, but lying north of the parallel of 36° 30′, and nearly uninhabited, except by roving bands of Indians.

This Act, which repeals the prohibition of slavery beyond that parallel, and thus opens to it those extensive regions, has given rise to greater and more determined opposition, and more violent and serious agitation than was manifested on any former occasion. A remedy, however, may, in this case, be afforded by the projected settlement of these Territories by free

because judgment is entered against him without "due process of law," and without his rights being determined by a jury. A State under its general and admitted power to define and punish offences against its own peace and policy, may repel from its borders an unacceptable population, whether paupers, criminals, *fugitive, or liberated slaves;* and consequently may punish her citizens, and others who thwart this policy, by harboring, secreting, or in any way assisting such fugitives. 15 *Howard*, 13. In this case, it was held by Taney, Chief Justice, that not only are the States not prohibited from legislating respecting the surrender of fugitive slaves, but, on the contrary, that it is enjoined upon them as a duty to protect and support the owner when he is endeavoring to obtain possession of his property found within their respective limits.

immigrants. Such, indeed, would probably have been their character, without any attempt to secure that result, and notwithstanding the efforts to counteract the design by the immediate introduction of slaves. Nor do the authors of the repeal seem to have contemplated any other event; but to have advocated and sustained their measure with the view of establishing it as a "*principle,*" and applying it, as a precedent, to future acquisitions of territory. Unfortunately, their designs have been forwarded, rather than impeded, by the very interference intended to defeat them. But, however impotent must ever prove the rash and untoward attempts of those claiming to be the exclusive friends and infallible advocates of emancipation, who, with the blindness of ignorance and fanaticism, denounce all who refuse to coöperate in their impracticable schemes, henceforth, the influence of these zealots, increased as it has been by the equally rash proceedings of fanatics of another character, and in another quarter, will be merged in a more general and enlightened opposition to the measures in question. And may we not hope that the latent patriotism of their authors and abettors will deter them from persevering in their reckless course, at the risk of severing the Union, and the sacrifice of their own usefulness; or, if this should fail, may we not still hope that the natural influence of benevolence, mildness, and Christian charity and moderation will advance in geometrical progression, until the foul blot upon the national escutcheon be obliterated, rather by the hand of Providence, than by any effort of our own.

Deus hæc fortasse benigna,
Reducit in sedem vice.

LECTURE IX.

ON THE POWERS VESTED IN THE FEDERAL GOVERNMENT FOR MAINTAINING HARMONY AMONG THE STATES.

The authority vested in the General Government *to provide for the maintenance of harmony and proper intercourse among the States*, comprises the third class of powers enumerated in the Constitution. Under this head might, with propriety, be included the particular restraints on the authority of the States, and certain powers vested in the Judicial department; but the former are reserved for a distinct head of consideration, and the latter have already been reviewed in our examination of the structure and organization of the Government.

The remaining powers comprehended in this description are,

First. To regulate commerce among the several States, and with the Indian tribes.

Second. To establish post-offices and post-roads.

Third. To coin money, and regulate the value thereof, and of foreign coin; to fix the standard of weights and measures.

Fourth. To provide for the punishment of counterfeiting the securities and current coin of the United States.

Fifth. To prescribe by general laws the manner in

which the public acts, records, and Judicial proceedings of one State shall be proved, and the effect they shall have in another.

Sixth. To establish a uniform rule on the subject of naturalization throughout the United States.

Seventh. To establish uniform laws on the subject of bankruptcies.

I. *The power to regulate commerce among the States* had been clearly pointed out, by experience under the Confederation, to be essential to the General Government. Without this supplemental provision, indeed, the primary and indispensable power of regulating foreign commerce would have been incomplete and ineffectual, if not altogether nugatory. A very material object of the power was to secure those States which import and export through other States from unjust contributions levied on them by the latter. It was foreseen that, if the several States were left at liberty to regulate their mutual commerce, means would be discovered or devised to load articles of produce and merchandise, in their transit, with duties that would eventually fall on the growers or manufacturers of the one, and the consumers of the other. Such practices had prevailed, and it was justly apprehended that their continuance would nourish increasing animosities, and not improbably terminate in serious interruptions of the public tranquillity.

In the important case referred to in the last Lecture,[1] the whole doctrine relative to the construction of this part of the Constitution was largely and deliberately discussed, and definitively and satisfactorily settled. It

[1] Gibbons *v.* Ogden.

was declared on that occasion, that the power to regulate commerce among the States did not extend to that commerce which is completely internal; and that, comprehensive as are the terms in which it is conferred, the power in question is, nevertheless, restricted to that commerce which concerns more States than one. Those terms would hardly have been selected to indicate the completely interior traffic of a State, because they are not apt terms for that purpose; and the enumeration of the particular classes of commerce to which the power was to extend would not have been made, had the intention been to extend the power to commerce of every description. The specification itself presupposes something not specified, and from the language and subject of the clause, it would seem that the exclusively internal commerce of a State is not comprehended. The genius and character of the whole Government, indeed, evince that its action is to be applied to all the external concerns of the nation, and to those internal concerns which affect the States generally, but not to those which are completely within a particular State, which do not affect other States, and with which it is not necessary to interfere for the purpose of executing any of the general powers of the Federal Government.

The completely internal commerce, therefore, of every State is reserved for the State itself. But as the power of Congress in regulating foreign commerce does not stop at the jurisdictional lines of the States, and would be a very useless power if it did not pass those limits, it is, if possible clearer, that the power to regulate commerce among the States is not limited by State boundaries. For not only do waters communicating with the ocean penetrate into the interior of the country, and pass in their course through several States, but in many cases—in the signal instance of the Western Lakes—there are waters in and upon the boundaries of several States, which are not navigable to the sea for the purposes of foreign commerce, while they furnish means of commercial intercourse between those States, and, consequently, afford occasions to Congress for the exercise of the power in question. This power must be exercised wherever the subject exists, and if the means of commercial intercourse among the States exist within a State—if a coasting voyage may commence or terminate within a State—then the power of Congress to regulate commerce among the several States may be exercised *within a State*.

The States either join each other, in which case they are separated by a mathematical line, or they are remote from each other, in which case other States lie between them. How, then, it has been asked, is commercial intercourse between them to be conducted? A trading expedition between two adjoining States cannot commence and terminate beyond the limits of either; and if the trading intercourse be between two States remote from each other, it must commence in one, terminate in another, and pass through at least a third. Commerce among the States must of necessity, then, be commerce within a State. In the regulation of the trade with the Indian tribes, the action of the law, especially when the Constitution was made, was chiefly within a State; and in this case, as well as in regard to commerce among the States, the power of Congress is coextensive with the subject on which it acts. It cannot, in either case, be stopped at the external boundary of a State, but must enter the limits, and be exercised within the territorial jurisdiction of all the States. The grant of Congress, however, to regulate commerce on the navigable waters of the several States, contains no cession of territory, or of public or private property; the States may regulate the use of fisheries within their territorial limits, though upon navigable waters, provided their free use for the purposes of navigation and commerce be not interrupted.[1]

The power of Congress to regulate commerce among the States, extends to the regulation of navigation, and to the coasting trade, and fisheries within, as well as without any State,[2] wherever they are connected with the commercial intercourse with any other State, or with foreign nations. It extends also to the regulation and government of seamen; to conferring privileges upon vessels engaged in the coasting trade; and to the navigation of vessels engaged solely in carrying passengers, as well as to those engaged in traffic, whether propelled by steam or otherwise.

The principles laid down in another case, also referred to in my last Lecture, where an Act of a Legislature requiring importers and venders of foreign goods

[1] 4 *Wash. Cir. Rep.* 371. A State, under its general and admitted power to define and punish offences against its own peace and policy, may repel from its borders an unacceptable population, whether paupers, criminals, fugitives, or liberated slaves, and, consequently, may punish its citizens, or others who thwart this policy, by harboring, secreting, or in any way assisting such persons; and it is no objection to such legislation that the offender is liable to punishment under the law of Congress, for the same acts, when injurious to the owner of a fugitive slave. 14 *Howard*, 13.

[2] See note, p. 258.

to pay for a license from a State Government in order to entitle them to pursue that branch of mercantile business, were declared repugnant to the Constitution were held to apply equally to a similar interference with importations from one State into another. In that case, although the power of the State to regulate its purely internal commerce, and to establish its own police to control and promote that trade and intercourse, and to guard the public health and safety, was held to be sacred; yet it was by no means admitted that these, or any other acknowledged State powers, could, consistently with the Federal Constitution, be so used as to obstruct or defeat the power of Congress to regulate commerce in any of its branches. But it was again explicitly declared that, whenever the powers remaining in the States are so exercised as to come into conflict with those vested in Congress, the former must yield to what the Constitution has ordained to be *the supreme law of the land.*[1] Nevertheless, if measures undoubtedly within the powers of the States do not come into actual collision with those of the General Government, the Federal Courts can take no cognizance of them or their effects.[2]

[1] The Statutes of New York and Massachusetts, imposing taxes upon alien passengers arriving at their ports, have been declared by the Supreme Court to be contrary to the Constitution and laws of the United States, and therefore null and void. 6 *Howard*, 283. But a State has a right to tax its own citizens for the prosecution of any particular business or profession within the State. 8 *Howard*, 93. Nor is a State law, imposing a tax upon inheritance and successions to property, by foreigners, not domiciliated therein, repugnant to the Constitution of the United States. *Ibid.* 490.

[2] 2 *Peters*, 250.

With respect to *commerce with the Indian tribes*, we are to adopt the same broad interpretation of the power of Congress. Under the Confederation, this power was restrained to Indians *not members of any of the States;* and was not to violate or infringe the Legislative right of any State within its own limits. But what description of Indians were to be deemed *members of a State*, was a question of perplexity and contention in the Federal councils, and was never settled; and how the trade with the Indians *not members of a State*, yet residing within its Legislative jurisdiction, could be regulated by Congress without intruding upon the right of internal legislation, seems to have been considered incomprehensible by that compact. The power in question was, therefore, very properly, unfettered by the new Constitution from limitations which rendered the former provision so obscuré and contradictory. As it now stands, it is applicable to all the Indian *tribes;* and it is immaterial whether they continue within the boundaries of a State, or inhabit a part of one of the *Territories*, or roam at large through regions over which the United States have no jurisdiction; the trade with them is, in all its forms, subject exclusively to the regulation of Congress. By the wisdom and benevolence of this provision, the Indians are no longer distracted by the discordant regulations of different sovereignties, but are taught to trust to one supreme head, whose justice they should ever have as much reason to respect, as cause to fear its power.

The relation of the aborigines to the Government of the United States is marked by peculiar and cardinal distinctions. The Indian territory is admitted to compose a part of the Federal domain; in all our maps, geographical treatises, histories, and laws, it is so considered: in all our intercourse with foreign nations; in our commercial regulations; in any attempt at intercourse between the Indians and foreign powers, they are considered as within the jurisdictional limits of the United States, subject to many of those restraints which are imposed on our own citizens. They acknowledge themselves in their treaties to be under the protection of the Federal Government; they admit that it shall have the sole and exclusive right of regulating the trade with them, and managing all their affairs as it may think proper. In the particular instance of the Cherokees, they were allowed by a treaty, which preceded the present Constitution, "to send a deputy of their choice, whenever they saw fit, *to Congress;*" and, under the unsettled construction of the Articles of Confederation, treaties were made with some tribes by the State of New York, by which they ceded all their unsettled lands within that State, taking back a limited grant to themselves, in which they admit their dependence on that State.

As to those tribes which reside within the acknowledged boundaries of the Union, we have seen that they are not deemed *foreign nations* within the meaning of the Constitution, but are considered as *domestic, dependent nations;* they occupy a territory to which we assert a title which must take effect when their right of occupancy ceases; and, in the mean time, they are in a state of pupilage to the Federal Government. They and their country are considered by foreign nations, as well as ourselves, as being so completely under the sovereignty and dominion of the United States that any attempt to acquire their lands, or form a political connection with them, would be considered as a hostile invasion of our territory. They are distinguished in the Constitution, by an appropriate name, from foreign nations, as well as from the several States of the Union; and the objects to which the power now under consideration may be directed, are divided into distinct classes corresponding with that distinction. A brief reference to the origin of these discriminations will explain the principles on which they are founded, and enable us to determine with greater accuracy the nature and character of the subsisting relations between the United States and the Indian tribes.

When the great maritime powers of Europe visited and discovered different parts of this continent at nearly the same time, the principle adopted for deciding their respective rights was, "that discovery gave title to the Government by whose subjects or by whose authority it was made, against all other European Governments, which title might be consummated by possession."[1] The admission of this principle gave to the nation making a discovery, as an inevitable consequence, the sole right of acquiring the soil and of making settlements upon it; and while the principle itself was, as to them, an exclusive one, and shut out the right of competition among those who agreed to it, it could not annul the previously acquired rights of those who had never adopted or acknowledged it. It regulated the right given by discovery among the European claimants, but could not affect the rights of those already in possession, either as original occupants, or as occupants by virtue

[1] 8 *Wheat.* 573.

of a discovery beyond the memory of man. It gave an exclusive right to purchase, but did not found that right on a denial of the right of the occupant to sell.

The relation between the Europeans and the natives was determined in each case by the particular Government which asserted, and could maintain, this preemptive privilege in the particular place. The United States succeeded to all the claims of Great Britain, both territorial and political; but no attempt, so far as is known, has been hitherto made to enlarge them. So far as they existed merely in theory, or were, in their nature, exclusive only of the claims of other civilized nations, they still retain their original character, and continue dormant. But so far as they have been practically exerted, they exist in fact; they are well understood by both parties; have been asserted by the one and admitted by the other. When the war of the Revolution commenced, so far from advancing a claim to their lands, or asserting any right of dominion over their persons, Congress resolved "that the securing and preserving the friendship of the Indian nations was a subject of the utmost moment." Commissioners were appointed "to treat with the Indians, in the name and on the behalf of the United Colonies, in order to preserve their peace and friendship;" and the most strenuous exertions were made to procure those articles on which Indian friendships were supposed to depend; and, in short, every thing was done to promote trade and avoid hostilities with them.

The general law of European sovereigns, respecting their claims in America, limited the intercourse of individuals, in a great degree, to the particular potentate whose ultimate right of domain was acknowledged by the others. The consequence was, that their supplies were derived chiefly from that nation, and their trade confined to it. Goods indispensable to their comfort, in the shape of presents, were received from the same hand; and, what was of still more importance, the strong arm of Government was interposed to restrain the disorderly and licentious from intrusions into their country, encroachments on their lands, and from those acts of violence which were often attended by reciprocal bloodshed and slaughter. The Indians perceived, in this protection, only what was beneficial to themselves. It involved, practically, no claim upon their lands; no dominion over their persons; but merely bound them to the British Crown before the Revolution, and to the United States afterwards, as dependent allies, claiming the protection of a powerful friend and neighbor, and receiving the advantages of that protection, without involving a surrender of their national character.

From the commencement of the Government, Congress has, from time to time, passed laws to regulate trade and intercourse with the Indian tribes, which treat them as *nations*, respect their rights, and manifest a firm purpose to afford that protection to them which treaties stipulate. All these Acts, and especially the law now in force, obviously consider the several Indian nations as distinct political communities, having territorial boundaries, within which their authority is exclusive. The treaties and laws of the United States contemplate the Indian territory as completely separated from that of the States, and provides that all intercourse with them shall be carried on exclusively by the Government of the United States; while the powers to regulate commerce, declare war, make peace, and conclude treaties, comprises all that is required for regulating our intercourse with the Indian tribes.

II. *The power to establish post-offices and post-roads* is necessarily connected with the regulation of commerce and the promotion of the general welfare. A regular system of free and speedy communication is not only of vital importance to the mercantile interests of the country, but, on a more enlarged view of the subject, must be admitted to be of great general benefit. In time of peace, it facilitates and promotes commercial intercourse, tends to keep the people informed of their political interests, assists the measures of Government and the private communications between individuals. In war, the rapid transmission of intelligence by means of the public mails, and the greater facility of transferring bodies of troops, and transporting military stores, by means of good and substantial roads, are advantages as evident as they are desirable.

If the establishment of post-offices and post-roads should in practice be productive of no revenue to the public, the expense would be properly chargeable on the general funds of the Union, and the proceeds of taxation in the common forms be justly applied to defray it. If, however, as has proved to be the case, the post-office establishment should continue to yield a revenue, which, in common with the other funds of the Union, is applicable only to the purposes of the General Government, it is obvious that no State should be permitted to interfere by establishing a post-office department of its own. The power, therefore, vested in Congress is exclusive, so far as relates to the conveyance of letters, and other articles transmissible by post. In regard to post-roads, it would be unnecessary, and therefore unwarrantable, in Congress, to make another road where a sufficient one already exists; while, on the other hand, no State has power to deny or obstruct the passage of the mails, the marching of troops, or the transportation of the property of the United States over its public roads.

The power of Congress in relation to the subject was brought into operation soon after the adoption of the Constitution, and various provisions respecting it have since, at different times, been enacted, all founded on the principle of its being exclusive, so far as it respects the establishment of post-roads, and the conveyance of letters and other articles by post. Under this power, in conjunction with the powers of Congress to raise money to provide for the general welfare, and to pass all laws necessary and proper to carry into execution the other powers vested in the General Government, Congress has from time to time set apart funds *for internal improvements*, in the several States, by means of roads and canals. This power has been exercised for a long series of years; and although often questioned and denied, is vindicated by precedent. The practice has been to allow to the new States, on their admission into the Union, a certain proportion of the proceeds arising from the sale of the public lands therein, to be laid out in the construction of roads and canals within those States, or leading thereto. In the year 1806, Congress authorized a road to be opened from Nashville, in Tennessee, to Natchez, in the then Mississippi Territory, without asking the consent of the State of Tennessee; and in 1809, the President was authorized to cause the canal De Carondelet, leading from the Lake Ponchartrain to the city of New Orleans, to be extended to the River Mississippi. The bill authorizing the former of these works was objected to by Mr. Jefferson, but was, upon reconsideration, passed, notwithstanding his objections, by the constitutional majority of two thirds of the members present in both houses of Congress; while the bill authorizing the latter was not objected to, though passed under the same administration, from the circumstance, it may be presumed, that the improvement it contemplated was wholly within a *Territory* of the United States.

The *Cumberland* Road, upon which so much has been said in and out of Congress, and so much public money has been expended, was first authorized by an Act of Congress, passed also in 1806, and was constructed under a covenant with the State of Ohio, that a portion of the proceeds of the public lands lying within that State should be applied to the opening of roads leading to it, with the consent of the States through which the road might pass. But the expenditures upon it having exceeded the proceeds of the lands appropriated for its construction, President Madison, in 1816, objected to a bill appropriating a fund, of which a portion would have been available for continuing it, on the ground that the Constitution did not extend to making roads and canals, and improving water-courses through the different States; and that the assent of those States could not confer the power. Afterward, in 1822, President Monroe objected to a bill appropriating money for repairing the Cumberland Road, and establishing gates and tolls upon it, on similar grounds; and in both instances the bills were eventually lost.

On these and other similar occasions, there was, however, a decided difference of opinion between the majority of Congress and the President. Mr. Jefferson, in 1806, Mr. Madison, in 1816, and Mr. Monroe in 1822, denied any such power in Congress as these bills assumed to exist; or that it could be vested in that body, either by the consent of the States to the works proposed, or in any other mode than an amendment of the Federal Constitution. On the other hand, it appears that Congress claims the power to lay out, construct, and improve post-roads and military roads, at all events with the assent of the States through which they pass, as well as to cut canals for promoting internal commerce, and the more safe and economical transportation of military stores in time of war, leaving, in all these cases, the jurisdictional right over the soil in the respective States. By an Act passed in 1824, with the assent of Mr. Monroe, the necessary surveys, plans, and estimates were directed to be made of such roads and canals as the President might deem of material importance in a commercial or military point of view, or necessary for the transportation of the public mail, and appropriated a sum of money for the purpose.

The younger President Adams, in his inaugural address in 1825, alluded to this question; and his opinion seemed to be in favor of the right, as well as the policy, of a liberal application of the national resources to the internal improvement of the country. He intimated that speculative scruples on the subject would probably be solved by the practical blessings resulting from the application of the power. But in the year 1836, this subject was again discussed in Congress, and a bill passed both houses, appropriating a sum of money for a subscription to the stock of a turnpike road, exclusively within the State of Kentucky, but leading from Maysville, in the interior of that State, to the River Ohio. This bill was returned by President Jackson, and, on the question of its passage, notwithstanding the objections of the President, was finally lost in the House of Representatives, in which it had originated. In his annual message at the commencement of the session, the President had adverted to the difficulties which had before attended appropriations for purposes of internal improvement, and expressed a hope that some plan might be devised to attain its benefits in a satisfactory manner. He observed, that the mode adopted on former occasions had been deprecated by many as an infraction of the Constitution, while it had been viewed by others as inexpedient, and that all felt that it had been employed at the expense of harmony in the public councils. Upon returning the bill relative to the Maysville Road, he referred to the sentiments he had expressed at the opening of the session, and proceeded to consider the constitutional power of the General Government to construct or promote works of internal improvement, as then presenting itself, in two points of view; first, as bearing on the sovereignty of the States within whose limits the execution was contemplated, if jurisdiction of the territory they occupy were claimed as necessary to their preservation and use; the second, as asserting the simple right to appropriate money from the National Treasury in aid of such works when undertaken by State authority, surrendering the claim of jurisdiction on the part of the United States.[1]

In the first view, he regarded the question of power as an open one, which could be decided without the

[1] *Vide ante*, p. 287.

embarrassments attending the other, arising from the practice of the Government. To the extent contemplated by this first view of the power, he asserted that, although frequently and strenuously attempted, it had never been attained in a single instance. The Government, he insisted, did not possess it; and he therefore declared that *no* bill admitting it would receive his official sanction. But in the other view of the power, he considered the question differently situated, and remarked, that the ground taken at an early period of the Government was, that whenever money raised by the general authority was proposed to be applied to a particular measure, a question arose whether that measure was within the enumerated authorities vested in Congress. If it were, the money requisite might be applied to it. If it were not, no such application could be made. In all cases, he averred, in which the power to apply money had, in fact, been exercised by the General Government, such grants had always been professedly under the control of the general principle, that the works thus aided should be of a general, not local; of a National, not of a State character. This distinction he considered sufficiently definite and imperative to forbid his approbation of a bill of the character of that in question, which he was not able to view in any other light than as a measure purely local. As to the *principle*, indeed, he was indubitably right, but he was wrong in its application; for, most assuredly, a road terminating on the very river which forms the great line of communication between the Western and the Atlantic States, must be considered of infinitely more importance in its general and National, than in its local and State character. The true rule on the subject, which seems to have been forgotten or disregarded on this occasion, had been laid down by Chief Justice Marshall long before, and is this: "That the action of the General Government should be applied to all the external concerns of the nation, and to those internal concerns which affect the States generally, but not to those which are completely within a particular State, which do not affect other States, and with which it is not necessary to interfere for the purpose of executing any of the general powers of the Government."[1]

III. *The powers to coin money, to regulate its value, and that of foreign coins, and to fix the standard of weights and measures*, were possessed by the old Congress, with the exception of that relating to foreign coins. The new Constitution, therefore, supplied a material omission in the Articles of Confederation, by which the power of Congress was restrained to coin *struck* by its own authority, or that of the respective States. It must be obvious that the proposed uniformity in the value of the current coin might be destroyed by subjecting the foreign coin to the different regulations of the several States. The power with respect to the *coin*, both domestic and foreign, is rendered *exclusive*, by a subsequent provision of the Constitution, prohibiting the individual States from its exercise. And the power of fixing the standard of weights and measures seems also proper to be exclusively exercised by Congress; but until it shall legislate on the subject, each State, it is presumed, retains the right of adopting and regulating its own standard.

Nor does the power relative to the *coin*, prohibit the

[1] 10 *Wheat.* 446.

States, as we have seen, from enacting laws to punish the circulating of false coins. The offences of counterfeiting or debasing the coin, are entirely distinct. The former is a crime directly against the Government, by which individuals may be affected; the latter is a private wrong, by which Government may be reached remotely, if at all. This distinction is recognized in the criminal law of England, where counterfeiting coin is made high treason,—whether it be uttered or not,—but those who barely utter false money, are guilty neither of treason, nor *misprision* of treason.[1] Congress, nevertheless, under the power to regulate the value of foreign coins, can protect the creature and object of that power, and the Act passed for the punishment of persons bringing into the United States, with intent to pass, any false, forged, or counterfeited coins, or knowingly utter the same, was warranted by the Constitution.[2]

IV. *The power of providing for the punishment of counterfeiting the public securities and current coin of the United States* is incidental to the foregoing powers relative to the coin, and in itself seems to purport the exclusion of State power, as it is an appropriate means for carrying into effect other delegated powers not antecedently existing in the States. It appears, nevertheless, by the Acts of Congress relative to this subject, that cognizance of such cases may, under certain circumstances, be concurrently exercised by the State Courts. The Judiciary Act of 1789, vested, as we have seen, in the Federal Courts, exclusive jurisdiction of all offences cognizable under the authority of the United States, unless where their laws should otherwise direct.[3]

[1] 5 *Howard*, 410. [2] 9 *Ibid.* 560.

[3] 9 *Wheat.* 26; 11 *Johns. Rep.* 549.

The States, therefore, could not exercise a concurrent jurisdiction in those cases without coming into direct collision with the laws of Congress. But by a *proviso* in a subsequent Act concerning counterfeiters of the current coins of the United States, Congress has declared that the jurisdiction of the Federal Courts, in certain specified cases, should not be exclusive; so that the concurrent jurisdiction of the State Courts is restored, so far as it can be exercised under State authority. There are, besides, other Acts of Congress which permit jurisdiction over the offences described in them to be exercised by the State Courts under the same condition, and in all these cases where the jurisdiction of the State Courts is made concurrent with that of the Federal Courts, the sentences of the one, whether of acquittal or conviction, are a bar to the prosecution in the other, for the same offence.

V. *The power to prescribe by general laws the manner in which the public acts, records, and Judicial proceedings of each State shall be proved, and the effect they shall have in other States*, is referred to this class by the authors of "The Federalist." It is an evident and valuable improvement on the provision relating to the same subject in the Articles of Confederation, of which the meaning was so indeterminate as to render it of little practical importance. The power, as it now stands, has been found, as was intended, to be a convenient instrument of justice, and particularly beneficial on the borders of contiguous States, where persons and effects liable to Judicial process may be suddenly and secretly withdrawn to a foreign jurisdiction.

The clause in the Constitution which vests this power in Congress, previously declares that "full faith and credit shall be given in each State to the public Acts, Records, and Judicial proceedings of every other State." And the Act passed by Congress in execution of this power, prescribes the manner of authenticating such acts, records, and proceedings; and declares that, when so authenticated, they "shall have such faith and credit given to them in every Court within the United States, as they have by law or usage in the Courts of the State from whence they are taken."[1]

Under the clause of the Constitution, and this Legislative provision for giving it effect, if a judgment have the effect of record evidence, or, in other words, be *conclusive* evidence, *i. e.* admitting neither of impeachment nor contradiction in the Courts of the State in which it was rendered, it has the same effect in the Courts of all the other States.[2] And the Supreme Court of the United States, in so ruling, declared that the Common Law gives to a judgment of the Courts of one State the effect of *primâ facie* evidence, *i. e.* evidence open to impeachment, explanation, or contradiction, in the Courts of every other State; but that the Constitution contemplates a power in Congress to give a *conclusive* effect to such judgments, which power it has exercised by rendering a judgment *conclusive* when the Courts of the particular State would pronounce the same decision.[3] And in a recent case, it was declared that the clause in question cannot, by any just construction of its words, be held to embrace an alleged error in a decree of a State Court, asserted to be in collision with a prior decision of the same case.[4]

1 Const. U. S., Art. IV. Sect. I.

2 Laws U. S. 1790, ch. 38.

3 7 *Cranch*, 481.

4 3 *Wheat.* 234.

Nor did Congress intend by this Act to declare that a judgment rendered in one State, against the person of a citizen of another, who had not been served with process, or voluntarily made defence, should have such faith and credit in every other State, as it had in the Courts of the State in which it was rendered.[1]

VI. The power "*to establish a uniform system of naturalization*," which was the next we proposed to examine, is necessarily exclusive; especially as it is provided, in a subsequent part of the Constitution, that "the citizens of each State shall be entitled to all the privileges and immunities of citizens in the several States."[2]

The dissimilarity of the rules of naturalization which existed in the different States, had given rise, under the Confederation, to some intricate and delicate questions, from the ambiguous terms of the article in relation to the subject. To put an end to all such questions in future, the new Constitution authorized the General Government to establish a uniform rule throughout the United States. There is, indeed, no express prohibition of State legislation in regard to it; but if each State retained the power of naturalization, while the citizens of each State were entitled to the privileges of citizens in the several States, any one State might impose on all the others such persons as citizens whom it might think proper to admit. In one State, a short residence, with a slight declaration of allegiance, as was the case under the first Constitution of Pennsylvania, might confer the right of citizenship; in another, higher qualifications, as was, in fact, generally the case, might be

1 14 *Peters*, 481.

2 2 *Wheat.* 259; 5 *Ibid.* 49; 4 *Const.* 111.

required; and an *alien*, desirous of eluding the latter, might, by complying with the former, become a citizen of a State in opposition to its own regulations; and thus the laws of one State might become paramount in a matter of vital consequence to another. Hence the importance of rendering this power exclusive. That it is, indeed, so vested in Congress, was considered incontrovertible by the Supreme Court of the United States, in a case in which the decision depended on that point;[1] and it was declared, subsequently, to have been so held on the ground of a *direct repugnancy or incompatibility* in the exercise of a similar power by the States.[2]

No definition of the character of a citizen is contained in the Constitution of the United States. The term is used with a plain indication that its meaning must have been generally understood, by reference to that system of national jurisprudence which, as I had occasion to observe in a former Lecture, is justly regarded as *the means or instrument* of exercising the jurisdiction conferred by the Constitution. At the time of its adoption, the citizens of the several States collectively constituted the citizens of the United States. They were either *native citizens*, or those born within the States, or *naturalized citizens*, or persons born elsewhere, but who, upon assuming the allegiance, became entitled to the privileges of native citizens. All who were resident citizens at the time of the Declaration of Independence, and deliberately yielded to that measure an express or implied assent, became parties to it, and are considered as natives, their social tie being coeval with the nation itself.

[1] 2 *Wheat.* 269; 2 *Dall.* 370. [2] 5 *Wheat.* 49.

And by the Constitution of the United States, it is declared, as we have seen, that "the citizens of each State shall be entitled to all the privileges and immunities of citizens in the several States."[1] But a limited, not a full operation has been given to these words. It has been held in some of the States, that they do not mean the right of election, of being elected, or holding office; but merely that the citizens of all the States shall have the peculiar advantage of acquiring and holding real, as well as personal property, and that such property shall be protected and secured by the laws of the State, in the same manner as is the property of its own citizens, and shall not be liable to any taxes or burdens to which the property of the citizens of the State is subject.[2] It seems, moreover, that no person can be deemed a citizen of a State, under the Article of the Federal Constitution, who is not entitled, on the terms prescribed by the institutions of the State, to all the rights and privileges conferred by those institutions upon the highest classes of society. Thus, free negroes and mulattoes are held not to be such citizens as were contemplated by the Article in question, inasmuch as, before the adoption of the Constitution of the United States, each State had a right to make citizens of such persons as it pleased, but as the Constitution does not authorize any but "WHITE" persons to become citizens of the United States, it creates a presumption that no State had made citizens of persons of any other color; and this presumption will stand until repelled by positive testimony.[3]

[1] Const. U. S., Art. IV. Sect. II. 2.

[2] 3 *Har. & McHen.* 554; 2 *Munf.* 396.

[3] 1 *Litt.* 33; 1 *Bailey,* 215; 10 *Conn.* 340.

A citizen of the United States, however, residing in any State of the Union, is a citizen of that State.[1] A temporary absence will not divest a person of the character of a citizen of the State to which he may belong. There must be a removal with an intention of laying aside that character, and he must actually join himself to some other community.[2]

A corporation aggregate is not a citizen.[3] A corporation created by the laws of one State, and composed entirely of its own citizens, is not entitled, under this Article of the Constitution, to all the privileges and immunities of citizens of every other State. Such a construction would deprive a State of all control

[1] 3 *Peters*, 128; 1 *Wallace*, 51; 2 *Binn.* 120; 3 *Ibid.* 75; 3 *Cranch*, 97; 4 *Ibid.* 209, 321; 7 *Ibid.* 603; 1 *Wheat.* 197; 2 *Ibid.* 259; 3 *Ibid.* 1, 563, 589; 4 *Ibid.* 453, 575; 7 *Ibid.* 535, 545; 9 *Ibid.* 354, 489; 10 *Ibid.* 181; 11 *Ibid.* 332; 1 *Johns. Cas.* 29; 2 *Ibid.* 399; 3 *Ibid.* 109; 6 *Ibid.* 360; 4 *Johns. Rep.* 20, 75; *Ibid.* 313, 707; 6 *Ibid.* 332; 7 *Ibid.* 214; 9 *Ibid.* 303; 11 *Ibid.* 418; 1 *Const. Rep.* 61, 111; 1 *Desauss.* 449; 3 *Ibid.* 106; 4 *Ibid.* 330; 2 *Leigh*, 109; 2 *Dall.* 133; 4 *Ibid.* 353; 1 *Peters*, 343; 3 *Ibid.* 121, 156, 160, 164, 242; 4 *Ibid.* 393; 6 *Ibid.* 102; 7 *Ibid.* 413; *Bee*, 25; *Harp. Eq. Rep.* 5; 1 *Mass.* 256; 2 *Ibid.* 179, note; *Ibid.* 226, note; *Ibid.* 236; 7 *Ibid.* 523; 9 *Ibid.* 363, 377; 12 *Ibid.* 143; 15 *Ibid.* 354; *Kirby*, 407; 1 *Hayw.* 338, 485; 2 *Ibid.* 37, 104; 1 *N. & M.* 292; 2 *Ibid.* 293, 400; 2 *Dev.* 249; 3 *Ibid.* 191, 196; 4 *Mason*, 208; 1 *Brock*, 466; 1 *Har. & Gill.* 280; 1 *McCord*, 187; 4 *Ibid.* 552; 2 *Bing.* 20; *Ibid.* 150; 6 *Monr.* 260; 7 *Ibid.* 143; 3 *Call.* 122; 5 *Ibid.* 364; 6 *Ibid.* 60; 4 *Wend.* 507; 7 *Ibid.* 333, 367; 10 *Ibid.* 9, 379; 12 *Ibid.* 342; 13 *Ibid.* 458, 546; 9 *Hard.* 61; *Martin & Yerg.* 248; *McCord, Chan.* 352, 370; 1 *Litt.* 149; 3 *Ibid.* 375; 4 *Har. & McHen.* 409; 3 *Stew.* 60; 5 *Manf.* 117, 160; 1 *Bald.* 216; 1 *Rep. Const. Ct.* 411; 4 *Conn.* 44; 4 *Bibb*, 90; 3 *Serg. & Rawle*, 29; 1 *Greenl.* 196; 3 *Ibid.* 455; *Charlt.* 285; 1 *Miles*, 82; 5 *Day*, 169; 2 *Pick.* 394; 13 *Ibid.* 345; 2 *Rand.* 276; 4 *Ibid.* 204.

[2] 2 *Munf.* 397; 3 *Wash. C. C.* 546; 1 *Litt.* 265; 3 *Marsh.* 549.

[3] 5 *Cranch*, 86.

over the extent of corporate franchises proper to be granted within its limits. But, by the comity of nations, a corporation created by one Government, may make a contract within the domain of another; and such contract will be enforced in the foreign tribunals.[1] The Courts of the United States will, therefore, presume that a State has adopted the comity of nations towards other States as part of its jurisprudence.[2]

It has been admitted, both in the English Courts and our own,[3] that all persons born within the Colonies while subject to the Crown of Great Britain, were natural-born subjects; but it was held, as a necessary consequence, that this character was changed by the separation of the Colonies from the parent State, and the acknowledgment of their independence. The rule, however, as to the point of time at which Americans born before the separation ceased to be British subjects, differs in this country and in England. The rule established by the English Courts adopts the date of the treaty of peace in 1783; whilst ours have fixed upon that of the Declaration of Independence. But in the application of the rule to different cases, some difference of opinion may arise. The settled doctrine in this country is, that a person born here, who left the Colonies before the Declaration of Independence, and never returned, become thereby an alien; and, as a general rule, the character in which Americans born before the Revolution are to be regarded, depends on the situation of the party, and the election made by him, at the Declaration of Independence, according to our rule, and at

1 5 *Cranch*, 86. 2 *Ibid.*

3 3 *Peters*, 128, and cases above cited with it.

the treaty of peace, according to the English. Difficulties, however, have occurred where rights have accrued between these dates. But, if the right of election be admitted at all, it must be determined by what took place during the Revolution, and between the Declaration of Independence and the treaty of peace.

The Declaration of Independence did not operate so completely to separate the United States from Great Britain, as to subject all the British *ante-nati* to the disability of alienage; their rights continued until the acknowledgment of our independence by Great Britain.[1] The concessions made by the British Crown in the treaty of 1783, amounted to a formal renunciation of all claim to the allegiance of the citizens of the United States; but the question, Who were citizens at that period? was necessarily left to depend on the laws of the respective States, who, previously to the Federal Constitution had, in their sovereign capacities, acted authoritatively of the subject. The allegiance formerly due to the Sovereign of Great Britain, was transferred by the Revolution to the several States; and the treaty of peace left their citizens in the situation it found them,—neither making those citizens who, by the laws of any State, had been declared citizens, nor releasing from their allegiance any who had become, and were claimed as citizens.[2]

Persons born in this country who left it before the Declaration of Independence, and never returned, are aliens. So those born here before that event and remaining during infancy in a place in this country occu-

[1] 2 *Halst.* 305; 6 *Call.* 60.

[2] 4 *Cranch*, 209; 2 *Cond. Rep.* 86.

pied by the British troops, and before attaining their majority, were carried by loyalist parents to England, and never returned to the United States, must be considered aliens. If such a person were born after the Declaration of Independence, and before the British troops took possession of the place of his residence, and those adjacent, infancy would have incapacitated him from making any election for himself, and his election and character would follow those of his father, subject, however, to the right of disaffirmance within a reasonable period after the termination of his minority.[1] But the provisions of the treaty of peace protect such persons, holding lands in the United States, from the disability of alienage in regard to descents and sales.[2]

It is a doctrine of the English law that natural-born subjects owe an allegiance which is intrinsic and perpetual, and which cannot be diverted by any act of their own. But it has been made a question, frequently and earnestly debated, whether this doctrine of perpetual allegiance applies, in its full extent to the United States.[3] The best writers on public law[4] have treated this subject rather loosely, but seem, generally, to favor the right of the citizen to emigrate and abandon his native country, unless there be some positive restraint by law, or he is, at the time, in possession of some public trust, or his country be in distress, or at war, and in need of his services. The principle de-

1 3 *Peters*, 99.

2 *Ibid.* 242; 9 *Ibid.* 642.

3 7 *Wheat.* 348; 3 *Binn.* 85; *Peters's Adm. Cas.* 61; 3 *Peters*, 121, 160; 2 *Johns. Cas.* 407; 2 *Cranch*, 120; 2 *Munf.* 393; 4 *Hall's* Am. Law Journ. 361; 9 *Mass.* 461.

4 *Grotius*, b. 2, ch. 5; *Puffend.* b. 8, ch. 11; *Vattell*, b. 1, ch. 19.

clared in some of our State Constitutions, that the citizens have a natural right to emigrate, goes far towards a renunciation of the English law, as repugnant to the natural liberty of mankind—provided *emigration* is intended in those cases to be used as synonymous with *expatriation.* But the allegiance of our citizens is due, not merely nor principally to the local Government of the State in which they reside, but primarily and chiefly to the United States, which Government alone affords them national protection, and imparts to them their national character; and the doctrine of final and absolute expatriation, though frequently discussed in our Courts, remains yet to be settled, and requires to be defined with precision, and subjected to certain established limitations, before it can be admitted into our jurisprudence, or laid down broadly as a wise and salutary rule of national policy.

It is not, however, applied by the English Courts to the American *ante-nati;* as is manifest from a case decided some years since in the Court of the King's Bench,[1] in which the treaty of peace was considered as a release from their allegiance of all British subjects who remained in this country. The British doctrine, therefore, is that the American *ante-nati*, by remaining in this country after the peace, lost their character as British subjects; and our doctrine is, that by withdrawing from this country they lost, or perhaps, more properly speaking, they never acquired the character of American citizens.

All persons born out of the allegiance and jurisdiction of the United States are termed *aliens.* There

[1] 2 *Barn. & Cress.* 779.

are, however, some exceptions to this rule derived from the ancient English law; as in the case of the children of public ministers born abroad, for their parents owed not even a local allegiance to the foreign power. So, also, in every case, the children born abroad of English parents were considered as natives of England if the father went and continued abroad in the character of an Englishman. By the existing law of the United States relative to naturalization, it is declared that the children of persons who were or had been citizens of the United States *at the time of passing the Act*, should, though born out of the United States, be considered as citizens; but that the right of citizenship should not descend to persons whose fathers had never resided within the United States. This statute does not extend to the children of persons who left the country before the Declaration of Independence, and not being prospective in its operation, the benefit of it narrows rapidly by lapse of time, and the period will soon arrive when there will be no statutory regulation in favor of children born abroad of American parents; and, unless one be made in season, they will be driven to resort for aid to the dormant and doubtful principles of the Common Law.

Aliens coming to this country with the intention of making it their permanent residence, have many inducements to become citizens. They are incapable, until naturalized, of holding a stable interest in land in many of the States; or of holding any civil office; or of voting at elections; or of taking any active share in the administration of the Federal or State Governments. A convenient and easy mode (perhaps too easy and convenient) has been provided by Congress for removing the disabilities of alienage; and the terms on which every alien, being *a free white person*, can obtain the qualifications and privileges of a natural-born citizen, are prescribed in the several Acts of Congress on the subject.[1] But an alien *enemy* cannot be permitted to make the declaration required by law preparatory to naturalization.[2] And the provision of this Act, which excludes from citizenship aliens whose country shall at the time of the application be at war with the United States, extends to the supplementary Act, authorizing the naturalization of the widow and children of persons who, having pursued the directions of the original Act, died before they became naturalized. Consequently, the minor son of an alien who had made report of himself conformably to the Act, but died before he had resided long enough to be entitled to naturalization, is held not to be admissible to the rights of citizenship,—the country from which he emigrated being, at the time of the son's application, at war with the United States.[3]

The right of aliens to the privileges of naturalization are, by these laws relating to the subject, submitted to the decision of any Court of Record within the United

[1] Laws of U. S. 1802, ch. xviii.; 1813, ch. clxxxiv.; 1816, ch. xxxii.

[2] 1 *Gall.* 11, *contrà;* 2 *Binn.* 218.

[3] 5 *Binn.* 371. See also *Peters's C. C.* 106, 457, 466; 1 *Dall.* 69; 1 *Gallis.* 366, 563; 2 *Ibid.* 105; 1 *Wash. C. C.* 484; 1 *Johns. Cas.* 206; 10 *Johns. Rep.* 69, 117, 183; 11 *Ibid.* 418; 6 *Cranch*, 176; 7 *Ibid.* 428; 9 *Ibid.* 180; 1 *Johns. Ch. Cas.* 399; 2 *Ibid.* 588; 1 *Blackf.* 255; 6 *Litt.* 226; *Paine*, 68; 1 *Wheat.* 46; *Ibid.* 128, *note*; 10 *Wend.* 379; 13 *Ibid.* 524; 16 *Ibid.* 617, 625; 4 *Peters*, 406; 1 *McCord*, 187; 1 *Ibid. Ch.* 370; 1 *Hill*, 141; 2 *Car. Law Rep.* 112; 1 *Cowen*, 89; 4 *Rand.* 585.

States; and a person duly naturalized (which he may be after a residence of five years) becomes entitled to all the privileges and immunities of a natural-born citizen, except that a residence of seven years is required by the Constitution to enable him to hold a seat in the House of Representatives, of nine years to hold a seat in the Senate, and that he remains always ineligible to the offices of President of the United States and Governor in several of the States. The policy of these laws has been strongly doubted by some of our wisest and best statesmen and native politicians, and every year's experience tends amply to confirm those doubts. For a short period, during the administration of the elder Adams, the term of residence prescribed by law to entitle an alien to naturalization was fourteen years. But the passing of that law was one of the most powerful causes of the expulsion of Mr. Adams and the Federal party from the administration of the General Government; and however some of his successors may have regretted its repeal, they have been too well convinced of the difficulty of recalling a popular concession to attempt its reënactment. There are two improvements, however, that seem equally practicable and desirable, and would go far to remedy the existing evils of the system; the one is, to render, by an amendment of the Constitution, the naturalized citizen incapable of holding any office of trust or profit; the second, to vest, by an amendment of the statutes, the jurisdiction in cases of naturalization, exclusively in the Federal Courts.

VII. *The power of Congress "to establish uniform laws on the subject of bankruptcies"* is intimately connected with the regulation of commerce; and there are peculiar reasons why the National Government should be intrusted with this power, arising from the importance of preserving uniformity and equality of rights among the citizens of all the States, and of maintaining commerce, credit, and intercourse with foreign nations. It has been found necessary, in Governments which authorize personal arrests and imprisonment for debt, to interpose and provide relief for the debtor in cases of inevitable misfortune; and this has been particularly the case in regard to insolvent merchants, who are frequently tempted, if not obliged, by the habits, pursuits, and enterprising nature of trade, to give and receive credit, and encounter extraordinary hazards; and, besides relieving the debtor, bankrupt and insolvent laws are intended to secure the application of his effects to the payment of his debts. *Bankruptcy*, in the English law, has by long and settled usage received an appropriate meaning; and has been considered applicable to unfortunate or fraudulent *traders*, who do certain acts affording evidence of their *inability* to pay their debts, or of their intention to *avoid* it. But the line of partition between bankrupt and insolvent laws is not so distinctly marked as to enable laymen, or even lawmen to determine with positive precision what belongs exclusively to the one or to the other; and it is the more difficult to discriminate between them, because bankrupt laws may, and frequently do, contain regulations which are generally found in insolvent laws; and in insolvent laws, some that are common in a bankrupt law. And although bankrupt laws are generally and properly confined to the trading classes, who are most exposed to pecuniary vicissitudes, yet, as misfortune and poverty may also overtake those who pursue other occupations, the latter ought not to be excluded from the humane protection of the State Legislatures. Nor, indeed, should the former, or their creditors, be left without the means of relief, in case Congress does not in its discretion think proper to exercise the power vested in them in relation to bankruptcy. This power of Congress has, accordingly, been held not to exclude the right of the States to legislate on the same subject, except where the power has been already executed by a subsisting law of Congress with which the State law would conflict.[1]

Whenever, indeed, the terms in which a power is granted by the Constitution, or the nature and character of the power itself, require that it should be exercised exclusively by Congress, the subject, as we have already seen, is as completely taken away from the State as if its Legislature had been expressly forbidden to act on it. But the power now in question is held not to be of this description; and a State has a right, consistently with the provision in the Federal Constitution, to pass bankrupt and insolvent laws, *provided they do not impair the obligation of contracts*, and there be no Act of Congress in force with which the State laws would come into collision. Nor is the right of a State to pass bankrupt laws extinguished by the enactment of a uniform law by the Legislature of the Union; but is only suspended while the law of Congress exists, and so far only as the State law might be found to

[1] 4 *Wheat.* 122; 12 *Ibid.* 213. It was originally held by Mr. Justice Washington in the Circuit Court of the United States for Pennsylvania, that the exercise by a State of the power to pass a bankrupt law, was prohibited by the grant of the power of Congress to pass *uniform* bankrupt laws. 5 *Wash. C. C.* 313.

conflict with it. While the Act of Congress remains in force, the power of the State continues over such cases which the Act of Congress does not embrace. Hence the power of passing insolvent laws, not coming within the technical description of bankrupt laws, is always in force; and from the expiration or repeal of a bankrupt law of Congress, the ability of the State to exercise its concurrent power in regard to bankruptcy, qualified as I have mentioned, immediately revives.

The Legislature of the Union, then, possesses the power of enacting bankrupt laws, and those of the States of passing insolvent laws;[1] and a State has, moreover, authority to pass a bankrupt law when no Act of Congress exists on the subject with which the State law might conflict; but no State bankrupt or insolvent law is permitted to impair the obligation of contracts. There is this further limitation upon the power of the several States to pass either bankrupt or insolvent laws—that they cannot, in the exercise of that power, act upon the rights of citizens of other States; and hence the greater necessity of investing Congress with power to establish a uniform system of bankruptcy throughout the Union; as a discharge under a State law would be no bar to a suit by a citizen of another State in the Courts either of the United States, or any other State than that in which the discharge was obtained. It only operates upon contracts made within the State; between its own citizens or

[1] Mr. Justice Story, however, observes, in reference to the case of Sturges v. Crowninshield, that "no distinction was ever practically, or even theoretically, attempted to be made between bankruptcies and insolvencies." *Comm. 1106.*

suitors subject to State powers.[1] And it is a principle of universal law, that the municipal law of the State is the law of the contract made and to be executed within the State, and that it travels with it, wheresoever the parties to it may be found; unless it refer to the law of some other country, or be immoral, or contrary to the policy of the country where it is sought to be enforced; and, consequently, the discharge of the contract, or of the party where the contract was made, is a discharge everywhere. But a discharge under a State law is no bar to a suit on a contract *not existing when the law was passed;* as the exercise of the power remaining in the States to pass bankrupt and insolvent laws does not, in the sense of the Federal Constitution, impair the obligation of *posterior contracts*, but only of those made *antecedently to the law*.[2]

Upon the question of the constitutionality of the insolvent law of New York, passed in 1811, the principles of construction are thus summed up by C. J. Marshall: "The intention of the instrument must prevail. This intention must be collected from its words; its words must be understood in that sense in which they are generally used by those for whom the instrument was intended; and its provisions are neither to be restricted into insignificance, nor extended to objects not comprehended in them, nor contemplated by its framers."

Acts of Congress, which have been pronounced constitutional, secure to the United States priority in

[1] 12 *Wheat.* 213.

[2] The validity of a State insolvent law cannot now be considered as an open question. 17 *Howard*, 157.

payment of debts due to them over all other creditors, in all cases of insolvency and bankruptcy. But they do not extend to cases where the debtor has not made an assignment of his whole property.[1]

The first bankrupt law passed by Congress pursued strictly the power vested in that body, and was in its terms confined to merchants and traders. It was but a few years in operation, and was suffered to expire by its own limitation. Nor was any attempt made for a long time to revive the system; and when afterwards the effort was made, it was for some years unsuccessful; nor was the last Act on the subject ever renewed.

The obstacles to its revival were such as to repress every hope of renewing the experiment until a material change is wrought in public opinion. These objections were, in the first place, the difficulty of defining, to the satisfaction of all parts of the Union, the precise class of debtors who could, consistently with the constitutional jurisdiction of Congress, be made subjects of a bankrupt law. It seemed, on all these occasions, to be taken for granted that the power of Congress extended no further than to bankruptcy in its technical and limited sense, by which its operation is restricted to *merchants and traders.* But the more general, and, perhaps, more substantial objection, was the expense, delay, and litigation which had been found to attend its proceedings; and the still more grievous abuses and frauds to which the system leads, however great the vigilance and integrity of those to whom its administration is committed. It was observed by the Chancellor and the

[1] 3 *Cranch*, 73; 2 *Wheat.* 396. See also Acts of Congress, August 4, 1790, May 2, 1792, March 3, 1797.

Judges of the Supreme Court of New York, in a report made to the Legislature of that State, by whom their opinions had been requested as to the expediency of the insolvent laws, that, "judging from their former experience, and from observation in the course of their Judicial duties, they were of opinion that it was a source of fraud and perjury. They were apprehensive," they stated, "that the evil was incurable, and arose principally from the infirmity inherent in such a system." With respect to the *infirmities* of the English system of bankruptcy, which are the growth of more than two centuries, during which it has been constantly under the view of Parliament, and maturing by the wisdom of a succession of distinguished Judges, the late Lord Eldon, one of the ablest ministers and soundest lawyers of modern times, after his appointment as Chancellor, took the earliest opportunity to express his indignation at the frauds which had been committed under cover of that system, and emphatically remarked, that "the abuse of the bankrupt law was a disgrace to the country."

In the face of such testimony, thus derived from men of the greatest learning and experience in the practice and administration of the law both in England and in this country, the friends and advocates of the bankrupt system have persevered, and by straining the constitutional point, and inducing Congress, on the last occasion, to adopt a latitude of construction which had not been thought of on any of the former occasions, eventually procured the passage of an Act which, under the title of a Bankrupt Law, embraced provisions peculiar to insolvent laws, rendering it the voluntary refuge of the debtor, and extending its benefits to every description of persons owing debts, with the exception of those created in consequence of a defalcation as a public officer, or as an executor, administrator, guardian, or trustee, or while acting in any other fiduciary capacity. It moreover subjected merchants, traders, bankers, factors, brokers, and underwriters to be declared bankrupt on the petition of their creditors, and proof of their having committed an act of bankruptcy. And this measure prevailed more from the atrophy under which commercial enterprise and credit had labored for the few preceding years, than from real conviction of its consistency either with the provisions of the Constitution, or the rules of sound policy. It was, indeed, considered as a temporary expedient, to be abandoned when it had performed its office, and the causes which produced it had ceased to operate; and it has, accordingly, been since repealed. None of the States have enacted bankrupt laws, technically so called. Most of them, however, have permanent insolvent laws; but, inasmuch as they cannot discharge the debtor from the obligation of his contract, and imprisonment for debt has been abolished in most of the States, the operation of those laws is, in effect, confined to the person of the debtor in the States where that relic of a barbarous age is still preserved,

> "And where he cannot be discharged,
> Till nature tire with its own weight, and then
> Is he but more undone to be at liberty."

LECTURE X.

ON THE POWERS VESTED IN THE FEDERAL GOVERNMENT RELATIVE TO CERTAIN MISCELLANEOUS OBJECTS OF GENERAL UTILITY.

THE first to be enumerated in this class is the power "*to promote the progress of science and the useful arts, by securing, for limited times, to authors and inventors, the exclusive right to their writings and discoveries.*"[1]

The claims of authors and inventors are so congenial to our notions of natural justice, and accord so harmoniously with the ultimate objects of society in establishing the rights of property, that, at first sight, it seems strange that the existence of this right should ever have been made a question. It was so, however, in the great case of literary property which arose in England. It was, nevertheless, finally settled, by a solemn judgment of the House of Lords, that, although such right had existed at Common Law, yet that the statute passed in the reign of Queen Anne for securing copyrights had limited the right, which had before been perpetual, to a term of years. But those Judges, whose opinions were overruled by this reversal of an almost unanimous opinion of the Court of King's Bench,[2] and who, reasoning upon different principles,

[1] Const. U. S., Art. I. Sect. VIII. 8.

[2] This celebrated case is reported in 4 *Burrow*, 2303, under the

arrived at a different result, were perplexed by the indefinite nature of the right, and embarrassed by the consequences of admitting it. On the one hand, to

title of Miller *v.* Taylor, which was the cause decided in the Court of King's Bench, all the Judges, excepting Mr. Justice Yates, agreeing that an author had the sole right of printing and publishing his work in perpetuity by the Common Law, and that such right is in nowise impeached by the statute of Anne. A writ of error was afterward brought, but the plaintiff in error suffered himself to be *non-prossed;* and the Court of Chancery granted an injunction in 1770. In 1774, the case of Donaldson *v.* Becket brought the question on appeal before the House of Lords. The Lords Commissioners of the Great Seal had granted an injunction against violating a copyright *at Common Law;* and when the appeal from that decree was brought up to the Lords, the Judges were directed to deliver their opinions upon the following questions, viz: —

1. Whether, at Common Law, an author had the sole right of *first* printing and publishing his book for sale; and might bring an action against any person who printed, published, and sold the same without his consent?

2. If the author had such right originally, did the law take it away upon his printing and publishing his work for sale; and might any person afterward reprint and sell it for his own benefit against the will of the author?

3. If such action would have laid at Common Law, is it taken away by the statute of Anne? And is an author by that statute precluded from every remedy, except on the foundation of said statute, and on the terms and conditions prescribed thereby?

4. Whether the author of any literary composition, and his assigns, had the sole right of printing and publishing the same in perpetuity by the Common Law?

5. Whether this right is in any way impeached, restrained, or taken away by the statute?

Upon the first question, the Judges were eight to three in the affirmative; on the second, seven to four; on the third, six to five in the negative; so that the general result was, "that an author had the sole right in perpetuity at Common Law, and that such right was in nowise impeached by the statute." It was known that Lord Mansdeprive men of genius of the right to the profits of invention was discouraging literature and the useful arts, and throwing impediments in the way of science and learning. On the other hand, an unlimited right to the exclusive enjoyment of the fruits of genius and discovery, though for a time it might stimulate both, yet, in its consequences, would levy a perpetual tax on posterity, and check the progress of invention itself.

The full result of admitting an exclusive and perpetual right of property in the produce of intellectual labor was not, and could not be fully known or estimated; but that it would operate as a bar to the advancement of human knowledge, and powerfully retard the progress of society, was clear to demonstration. Yet, to deny to inventors the fair profits derivable from their talents and exertions, seemed to be at variance with every idea of natural justice and every dictate of liberal policy. It was, in effect, to deny to genius its appropriate reward, and to withhold from the powers of intellect one of the strongest stimulants to their exertion. From a balanced consideration, therefore, of both sides of this important question, the statute of Anne, limiting the rights of authors and inventors, in their writings and discoveries, to a term

field adhered to the opinion delivered by him in the Court of King's Bench; and therefore concurred with the eight upon the first question; and with the seven upon the second; and with the five on the third. But, it being unusual for a peer to support his own judgment on an appeal, he gave no opinion; and the Lord Chancellor (Apsley) seconding Lord Camden's, his predecessor's, motion "to reverse," the decree of the Court of Chancery was *reversed*. So that the decision of the Peers was, in effect, that the right was perpetual at Common Law, but reduced by the statute to a term of years.

of years, was regarded as a compromise, by which the claims of the inventor were acknowledged, his rights defined and protected, and his reward secured; while a public interest was effectually created, and a barrier against injurious consequences erected for the benefit of posterity.

Hence may be collected both the origin and the policy of the Act of Parliament. With this statute before them, and with a full knowledge of the principles and policy on which it was founded, the several States ceded to Congress "a power to promote the progress of science and the useful arts, by securing to authors and inventors the exclusive right to their writings and discoveries." The English law had limited the right *to a term of years.* The power ceded by our Constitution was to secure it "*for limited times;*" the former restricting the right to a definite period; the latter adopting the same principle, but leaving the *quantum* of interest to the discretion of the National Legislature. In execution of this power, several Acts have been passed by Congress, and are now in force, defining the limits for which the exclusive rights of authors and inventors to their writings and discoveries shall be enjoyed, and securing such enjoyment for different periods in different cases, by penalties and other appropriate remedies against those who violate the right.[1]

The object, therefore, of this provision of the Constitution, and of the laws enacted in virtue of it, is twofold: first, to secure to inventors and to authors a

[1] The first of these Acts, passed in 1790, instead of sanctioning a preëxisting perpetual right in an author, *created* the right, and secured it for a limited time. 8 *Peters*, 591.

reward for their labors; and, secondly, to secure to the public the benefit of their works, by bringing the property in them into the common stock, after the expiration of the times limited for the exclusive privilege; and it is manifest that this double object can only be effected by such a construction of the Constitution as will leave to Congress the *exclusive power* of legislation on the subject. Prior to the adoption of the Federal Constitution, Legislative Acts in favor of valuable discoveries and improvements had been passed in several of the States; but their efficacy being confined to the limits of those States, the privileges thus secured were of little value; and, whatever they were worth, all these State enactments ceased as soon as the Federal Constitution was adopted. For greater caution, however, it was provided, in one of the first Acts of the National Legislature, that the applicant for the benefit of the protection of Congress should surrender his right under the State law, and that his obtaining a patent under the laws of the United States should be evidence of such surrender.

An important and protracted controversy, nevertheless, arose in the State of New York as to the nature and extent of the power in question, which occupied, at different times, the attention both of the Legislature and Courts for several years before it was happily set at rest by the Supreme Court of the United States — not by an express construction of this particular power, but by a series of decisions upon analogous cases involving similar principles, and bearing in one case on the subject itself. I refer to the case of *Livingston and Van Ingen*, in which the question arose as to the validity of the grant made by the Legislature of New

York to certain individuals, of the exclusive right of navigating its waters with boats propelled by means of fire or steam.

Before the adoption of the Federal Constitution, an Act was passed by the Legislature of that State granting and securing to one John Fitch "the sole right and advantage of employing the STEAMBOAT *by him lately invented*," and investing him and his representatives "with the exclusive right and privilege of navigating all kinds of boats, propelled by the force of fire or steam, within all the waters within the territory and jurisdiction of" the State of New York, "for the term of twenty years" from the passing of that Act, in March, 1789. In March, 1798, nearly ten years subsequent to the ratification of the Federal Constitution, and after Congress had passed that Act, in execution of the power under discussion, which contains the provisions requiring the surrender by applicants under it of the State rights before granted to them, another Act was passed by the Legislature of the same State, of which the preamble sets forth, "that Robert R. Livingston had represented that he was *possessed* of a mode of applying the steam-engine to propel a boat on new and advantageous principles; but that he was deterred from carrying it into effect by the uncertainty and hazard of a very expensive experiment, unless he could be assured of an exclusive advantage from it *should it be found successful;*" and that "he was also deterred from the enterprise by the existence of the previous Act in favor of Fitch, who was stated to be dead, or to have withdrawn from this State *without having made any attempt to execute the plan* for which he had obtained the exclusive privilege," whereby it was alleged to have been justly forfeited; it was "therefore enacted that privileges similar to those granted to John Fitch" should be extended to Mr. Livingston and his representatives, for the term of twenty years, upon condition that he should, within one year, build a boat to be propelled by fire or steam, "the mean rate of whose progress should not be less than four miles an hour; and that he should at no time omit, for the space of one year, to have a boat," of a certain burden and construction, "plying between the cities of New York and Albany."

These conditions not having been performed within the period specified, the time for fulfilling them was repeatedly enlarged by successive Acts of the Legislature for the purpose. One of these, passed after the former ones had expired, *revived* the privileges granted by them in favor of Robert R. Livingston and *Robert Fulton*. In the year 1807, the proof required of performance of the first condition of the grant was duly exhibited, and a boat propelled by steam, at the rate of more than four miles an hour, began to "ply between the cities of New York and Albany," in pursuance of the second. Other boats were subsequently built by the grantees of the State, and after they had continued for some years in successful operation, rival boats, propelled in the same manner, were established, in defiance of the State grant, both on the Hudson River and on Lake Champlain, by persons denying its validity. Application for redress was speedily made by Messrs. Livingston and Fulton to the State Courts of New York, and the question presented was, whether the grant made to them by the Legislature was not absolutely void, as made in contravention of the powers of Congress to promote the progress of science and the arts, and to regulate commerce. It was decided in the Court of Chancery that the State grant was void on the ground alleged; but on an appeal to the Court of Errors and Appeals, that decision was overruled, and it was declared by this tribunal of the last resort in the State, that the grant was not absolutely void, on two distinct grounds, viz: that, considering Messrs. Livingston and Fulton as *inventors*, the State had a *concurrent* power with Congress to reward them as such, by the grant of exclusive privileges to be exercised within its jurisdiction; and, secondly, that, considering them merely as the *possessors and importers* of a foreign invention, the State had an *independent* power to reward them for the introduction of such invention into beneficial use upon its waters — a power not ceded to Congress at all. It was observed, however, by one of the Judges, that "if the opposite party could have shown a right by *patent from the United States*, as inventors, they must have prevailed, and the State law would have given way to the superior power of Congress." For it must be borne in mind that the opponents of Messrs. Livingston and Fulton claimed no right or title whatsoever, either under a patent or coasting license; and, for aught that appeared, their mode of applying the steam-engine in the navigation of their boats might be, as in fact it was, the same which had been introduced by the grantees of the State.[1]

After notice of an appeal, on the part of their adversaries, to the Supreme Court of the United States, Messrs. Livingston and Fulton offered terms of com-

[1] 9 *Johns. Rep.* 557.

promise which were too advantageous to be refused by the other side, and, consequently, these questions were not then carried up to the Federal Court; and in the subsequent case,[1] referred to in a former Lecture, the question respecting the nature and effect of the power to promote the progress of science and the arts, did not arise. That case turned wholly upon the collision between the exclusive privilege granted by the State Legislature and the power of Congress to regulate commerce; and the State laws were declared to be void, merely from their repugnance to the exercise of that power by the Federal Government. The leading principles, however, of that decision, as well as much of the reasoning in the case relative to the licenses required by the State of Maryland from importers of foreign goods, apply with equal force to the power now under discussion; and although the invalidity of the State grant has thus been established, and the question relative to the nature and operation of a patent from the United States can never arise with respect to that grant, yet it may become material in other controversies, and, from its general importance, deserves examination. With all due deference to the opinion of "the highest Court in the State" of New York, I shall endeavor to show the obvious meaning of the Constitution to be, that Congress shall secure "the exclusive rights of authors and inventors to their respective writings and discoveries," by the exercise of an *exclusive* power of legislation.

In a confederated Government, extending, like ours, over many independent sovereignties, it seems difficult

[1] 10 *Wheat.* 446.

to conceive in what manner the right in question can possibly be secured, except by vesting such exclusive power in a paramount authority; and the necessity of such a power to the attainment of the end was an adequate reason for vesting it in the Supreme Legislature of the Union. The power under consideration comes under that class of cases enumerated in the thirty-second number of "The Federalist,"[1] to which the exercise of a similar power in the States would be repugnant and contradictory. The example which the learned and eloquent author of that paper selected to illustrate his reasoning, involved a contradiction by direct implication, *from the force of the terms.* It was an example taken from the power of Congress to establish a uniform system of naturalization; and it was argued that such power must necessarily be exclusive, because, if each State had power to prescribe a distinct rule, the rule of Congress could not be uniform. In the present case, the power given is necessarily exclusive, both from the *terms* and the *nature* of the grant. The words are, that "Congress shall have power to secure the exclusive rights of authors and inventors, *for limited times.*" Now, if a State have a concurrent power with Congress over the subject, it must be a power arising from the unceded portion of its sovereignty, and, consequently, a power to grant *without limit of time.* But how could Congress secure to the inventor, *for a limited period*, the enjoyment of that which the State might grant to another *forever?* It was said, on the occasion referred to, in the Court of Errors, by one of its most eminent judges, "that if an

[1] By Mr. Hamilton.

author or inventor, instead of resorting to the Act of Congress, should apply to the State Legislature for an exclusive right to his production, there is nothing to prevent the State from granting such exclusive privilege, provided it be confined in its exercise to the particular jurisdiction." But, with all due submission, if this opinion be correct, one of two things must follow: either that Congress may secure to an inventor or author an exclusive right in his discovery or writing, and the State secure to another, either as author or *possessor* of the same invention, the exclusive right to use it within its own jurisdiction; or that Congress cannot secure such a right to the *inventor* after the State has secured it to the *possessor.* In the former conclusion this consequence seems to be involved: that Congress may grant an exclusive right to one person to the use of a certain thing *throughout the Union;* and that the individual States may grant an exclusive right to another person to use the same thing within the limits of a particular district; or, in other words, that over the same subject, and within the same jurisdiction, two coördinate powers may grant exclusive privileges to different persons. The other branch of the dilemma supposes the State to derogate, by an assumption of power, from the express terms of its grant to the Federal Government, and actually to exercise an exclusive power to secure *exclusive* privileges, in direct contradiction to the terms of the power ceded to Congress. Nor does it obviate this repugnancy to say that, when these separate powers come into direct conflict, the grant of the State must yield to "the supreme law of the land," because the repugnancy is, from the nature of the subjeet, different from that arising under the power to regulate commerce, and is directly deducible from the propositions themselves, and not from any casual effects or consequences arising from the accidental collision of concurrent or of independent powers.

The power now in question is, moreover, exclusive, *from the nature of the grant;* because, if each State have a concurrent power, its exercise would defeat the twofold object for which the Federal Constitution intended to provide. That object, we have seen, was to secure to the public the benefit and transmission of invention, as well as to secure to genius a reward for its productions and discoveries. But if the individual States have a concurrent power with Congress, neither branch of this object can be secured by the latter; for, in regard to the former branch, if Congress prescribe fourteen years as the limit of exclusive rights, and render them common at the expiration of that period, each State might fix a different period, or might secure a right of property to authors and inventors in perpetuity. Nor could the latter branch of the object be secured by Congress if the States could exercise a concurrent power; because each State might, upon that supposition, reduce the term of exclusive enjoyment to a *minimum*, or declare, at once, the fruits and industry of genius to be common property.

The arguments against the exclusive nature of this power of Congress, drawn from the nature and effect of a patent in merely securing, as was alleged, a title or right of property, without conferring a right of sale or of use; and the objection deduced from the right of legislation retained by the States in regard to their purely internal trade and intercourse, and their police, health, and inspection laws,[1] have, in effect, been met and refuted by the Supreme Court, in their opinions declaring that a coasting license not only ascertains the national character and ownership of a vessel, but confers a right of navigation; that a right to import goods involves the right to sell them; and that, whenever those rights come into collision with State laws, passed in virtue either of a concurrent or of an independent right of legislation, on these, or any other subjects, and the exercise of the Federal and State authorities are found repugnant or irreconcilable to each other, the State law must yield to the superior power of Congress. So a patent or a copyright not only ascertains the title of the patentee or author, but confers the same paramount right of using, and vending to others to use, their respective discoveries and writings.

In applying, however, the reasoning of Chief Justice Marshall to the case of a patent or copyright, it is, perhaps, necessary to remark that the property which an author may have in his writings appears to be somewhat different from that which an inventor may have in his discoveries. The former has no beneficial use or property whatever in his writings, independently of that which may be derived from the sale of them. The latter may, though in a very restricted sense, use his invention for purposes of profit; to both, however, a right of sale is indispensable, but more manifestly so in the first case than in the last. Every other subject of property may be partially enjoyed, though the right

[1] *Vide* a pamphlet entitled "A Vindication of the Laws of New York, granting exclusive privileges to Robert R. Livingston and Robert Fulton," by Cadwallader D. Colden, Esq., Albany, 1818.

of sale be restricted or forbidden; but the right of property of authors and inventors is so essentially connected with the right of sale, that the inhibition of that right annihilates the whole subject. The right of sale, in these instances, therefore, is an elementary principle in the very idea of property. Separate it from the rest, and the complex legal notion of property is destroyed; the *value*—the thing intended to be secured, is lost to it. All human laws proceed upon the assumption of value as implicitly involved in the idea of property; and as new discoveries in science, and new improvements in the arts, give rise to new modifications of property, the first thing that attracts the attention of the Legislature to any subject as being capable of appropriation or exclusive ownership is its VALUE. Accordingly, we find that the laws passed by Congress[1] in virtue of the constitutional power now in question, secure to an author or his assignee "the sole right and liberty of printing, reprinting, publishing, and *vending*" his work; and to a patentee, "the full and exclusive right and liberty of making, constructing, using, and *vending* to others to be used," his invention or discovery within the several times limited for the enjoyment of their respective privileges.

How far the exercise of this right of property is liable to be controlled and regulated by the municipal laws of the several States, depends in a great measure on the principles recognized and established in the two cases to which I have so often referred, as decided in the Supreme Court of the United States. In the prior case,[2] decided in the Court of Errors of the State of

[1] Laws U. S. 1 Cong. 2 Sess. ch. xv.; 2 Cong. 2 Sess. ch. xi.

[2] 9 *Johns. Rep.* 507.

New York, it was held that the Legislature of a State may prohibit the use of any particular invention, as noxious to the health, injurious to the morals, or in any respect prejudicial to the welfare of its citizens. But, in addition to the qualifications which this assertion must receive from the doctrine of the Supreme Court, it seems to me that the Government of the Union must possess exclusively the power of determining whether an invention for which a patent is sought be useful or pernicious; or, in other words, whether it be one for which a patent ought to be granted. The object of the constitutional power of Congress is the promotion of the "*useful* arts;" an invention useless or pernicious would not be a proper object for its exercise; but should a patent for such an invention have unadvisedly issued, there can be no doubt that the Federal authority might repeal the patent, and interdict the use of the noxious discovery. If a thing in itself pernicious be patented, the patentee could recover no damages for the violation of his right, as his patent would confer no right of property upon him. If it be useful in itself, but the art or manufacture to which it relates be injurious, in its exercise, to the public health, the patent would afford no protection for the nuisance, because private interests must yield to the public good, and not because the Federal power is superseded or controlled by the State law. So, if the author of an immoral or libellous book prosecute for the invasion of his copyright, he could receive no indemnity; and if prosecuted for his offence against the State law, in issuing such a publication, the authority of the United States would not protect him, as, in the one case, his copyright would invest him with no right of property, and, in the other, would convey no right to use his property to the injury of others. Nor would the patentee of a newly-invented vehicle, any more than the owner of a post-coach conveying the mail of the United States, be entitled to pass over a State turnpike-road without paying the toll, nor a patented steamboat permitted to ply on a ferry established by State authority, without being subjected to the accustomed ferriage, or to the penalties provided in cases of such violation of the particular right to the ferry, any more than that or any other vessel would be exempted from them by a coasting license. Restrictions of this nature are general in their operation. They are *not confined to the patentee*, and in no sense do they derogate from the exclusive power of Congress in relation to the promotion of science and the useful arts. But a construction of the Constitution admitting that the States, in the exercise of an absolute discretion, may prohibit the introduction or use of any particular invention for which a patent had been regularly obtained, would render the power in question completely nugatory, and the States would retain substantially the very power they had nominally parted with.

This power of securing to authors and inventors a right of beneficial ownership in their writings and discoveries, has been surrendered to Congress, and any encouragement to invention, invitation to the introduction of improvements, or attempt to promote the progress of literature, science, and the arts, which interferes with, or prevents the exercise of that power, is an assumption of authority fairly, and on good consideration, yielded to the General Government. The several States, nevertheless, retain all other means of securing rewards to genius, of promoting learning and science, of encouraging new discoveries, and inviting improvements in the arts, except the power thus ceded to the Union. And although an individual State can neither secure to an inventor an exclusive property in his invention, nor, for any known and used improvement, grant exclusive privileges in the use of anything that may become the subject of a patent, yet it may promote the progress of learning, encourage new discoveries in science, and invite the introduction of new improvements in all the liberal and useful arts, in any other way that human ingenuity can devise, or good policy may dictate, and which does not interfere with the exercise of the power vested for the same purposes in Congress. And the reason of the difference is simply this: that all the other modes of effecting those objects may, without danger of being defeated by the clashing laws of coördinate Legislatures, be safely committed to the several States, while the simple mode of securing the right of property must be possessed by the supreme Federal authority alone; for, in the peculiar condition and circumstances of the country, that end cannot otherwise be effected.

II. The power vested in Congress "*to exercise exclusive legislation, in all cases whatsoever, over such District, not exceeding ten miles square, as may, by cession of particular States, and the acceptance of Congress, become the seat of the Government of the United States; and to exercise like authority over all places purchased by the consent of the Legislatures of the States in which the same shall be situated, for the erection of forts, magazines, arsenals, dockyards, and other needful buildings.*"

This power was granted to Congress from a conviction of the indispensable necessity of investing that body with complete supremacy and control at the seat of the National Government. Without the possession of such a power, the Federal authority might be insulted, and its proceedings interrupted with impunity; and the dependence of the functionaries of the General Government on one of the States for protection in the exercise of their duties, might subject the national councils to the imputation of partiality, and be productive of an influence equally dishonorable to the Government, and dissatisfactory to the other members of the Union. This consideration was of greater weight, as the public archives liable to destruction would accumulate, and the gradual multiplication of public improvements at the permanent residence of the National Government would, it was thought, create so many additional obstacles to its removal, and still further abridge its necessary independence. The necessity of a like authority over the forts, arsenals, and dockyards, and their appendages, established by the Federal Government, was supposed to be not less evident. The public money expended on such establishments, and the public property deposited in them, require their exemption from the local authority of the State where they are situated. Nor would it be proper that places on which the security of the entire Union may depend, should be in any degree dependent on a particular member; and all objections and scruples were obviated by requiring the concurrence of the States concerned in every such establishment.

The cessions of territory contemplated by the Constitution were duly made by the States of Maryland

and Virginia, whereby Congress was enabled to execute this power by establishing, under its own jurisdiction, a permanent seat for the National Government. This territory was erected into a "District," under the exclusive jurisdiction of Congress, by the name of the "District of Columbia." The City of "WASHINGTON" was built, and the necessary edifices for the accommodation of all the different branches of the Federal Government were erected on the banks of the Potomac, in conformity with a favorite wish of General Washington, and almost in sight of the place of his residence in life, and his repose in death. The seat of Government was removed thence at the commencement of the present century. Municipal corporations were created by Congress for managing the local concerns of the "Federal city," and of the cities of Georgetown and Alexandria,[1] situated within the "ten miles square," ceded by the respective States within whose limits they had been previously included. Laws have, from time to time, been passed by Congress for the government of the District of Columbia, and local courts established, as we have seen, for the administration of justice within its limits. But the Acts of Congress adopted the laws of Maryland and Virginia as the laws of the several portions of the District ceded by those States respectively, with such alterations only as were rendered necessary by the change of jurisdiction.[2] Nor were the separation of the territory and the transfer of the jurisdiction permitted to affect existing contracts between individuals.[3]

[1] The city of Alexandria has since been receded to the State of Virginia.

[2] 1 *Cranch*, 252. [3] 6 *Ibid.* 192.

Although the inhabitants of the District of Columbia, by its separation from Maryland and Virginia, ceased to be citizens of those respective States, yet, as citizens of the United States, they are entitled to the benefit of all commercial and political treaties with foreign powers, and to the protection of the Union at home, as well as abroad.[1] And notwithstanding the power of Congress to exercise exclusive legislation over this Federal territory includes the power of taxing its inhabitants, they do not in any manner participate in the election of members of the House of Representatives. I have already had occasion to explain upon what principles this anomaly in the Constitution has been justified;[2] and it may now be added, that the adequate provisions for their local government, and the advantages derived from the residence of the General Government, are deemed by the inhabitants themselves sufficient to counterbalance their political disabilities; that no public inconvenience has been experienced from their existence; and that the circumstance was known before the cession of the territory, and when the inhabitants voluntarily established their residence within it.

III. The next power falling within this miscellaneous class is the power of Congress "*to declare the punishment of treason*" *against the United States.*

It is a general principle, that every Government contains within itself the means and capacity for its own preservation. Had the express enumeration, therefore, of this power been omitted in the Constitution, it could not have been intended that the Federal Government was to depend upon the individual States to protect it

[1] 2 *Cranch*, 243. [2] 5 *Wheat.* 324.

from treason and conspiracies; yet, to have left the power of self-defence to inference or argument, would have been unwise and unsafe. As the crime of treason against the United States was one which might be committed, the United States themselves might, without this express authority, have punished its perpetrators; but as artificial and constructive treasons had been frequently made engines of oppression by tyrannical governments, and, during the prevalence of vindictive factions, by such as were comparatively free, it was deemed expedient to insert in the Constitution a definition of the crime, to prescribe the proof necessary for conviction, and to restrain Congress, in punishing it, from extending the consequences of guilt beyond the person of its author.

Treason against the United States is, accordingly, declared to "consist only in levying war against them, or in adhering to their enemies, giving them aid and comfort."[1] The term "levying war" is of technical signification, and is adopted from the English statute of treasons, and receives the same construction with us which has been given to it in England; and the "war," included in the term, embraces internal rebellion, as well as hostilities from without. A conspiracy to subvert by force the Government of the United States, violently to dismember the Union, to *coerce* the repeal of a general law, or to revolutionize a Territorial Government by force, if carried into effect, by imbodying and assembling an armed force in a military posture, is an *overt act* of levying war; and not only those who bear arms, but those who perform the various essential

[1] Const. U. S., Art. III. Sect. III.

parts which must be assigned to different persons for the purpose of prosecuting the war, are guilty of the crime.[1] But a mere conspiracy for any such purpose, unaccompanied by any *overt act*, is not treason; and to constitute a "levying of war," there must be an assemblage of persons, with intent to effect by force a treasonable purpose.[2] The mere enlistment of men for the purpose is not sufficient. Nor is it necessary, on the other hand, that an individual should appear in arms against his country to constitute the guilt of treason. If war be actually levied, that is, if a body of men be actually assembled in arms for the purpose of effecting by force a treasonable design, all those who perform any part in the conspiracy, however minute, or however remote themselves from the scene of action, if actually leagued in the general enterprise, are considered as traitors. Similar acts committed against the Government or laws of a particular State are punishable according to the law of that State, but adhering to a foreign nation at war with the United States, and affording it aid in the prosecution of hostilities, is treason against the United States, and not against the particular State of which the party is a citizen.[3]

The Constitution further declares, that "no person shall be convicted of treason unless on the testimony of two witnesses to the same *overt act*, or on confession in open court." A confession out of Court, although before a magistrate, is not sufficient;[4] but after the treason is proved by two witnesses, such confession may be given in evidence by way of corroboration.

[1] 4 *Cranch*, 470. [2] 4 *Ibid.* 75–126. [3] 11 *Johns. Rep.* 553.
[4] Fries's Case, in U. S. Cir. Ct. for Pennsylvania.

The testimony of the two witnesses must be to the *same overt act*, and not, as in England, to two different *overt acts* of the *same treason.* The restriction on Congress with respect to the punishment is, that "no attainder of treason shall work corruption of blood or forfeiture, except during the life of the person attainted." *Corruption of blood*, in common with many better things, we derive again from the Common Law. It signifies that an attainted person can neither inherit land from his ancestors, retain that of which he is in possession, nor transmit it to his heirs; and that he is, moreover, incapable of transmitting a title derived by descent through him, even from a remote ancestor. This is visiting the sins of the fathers upon the children with a vengeance, as it is not confined to the third and fourth generations, but extends to a man's latest posterity. The doctrine is founded upon a legal fiction; and is equally at variance with the liberal principles of modern times, and the very elements of justice. And in carrying this power into execution, Congress has humanely stopped short of their constitutional authority; for, in affixing the punishment of death to the crime of treason, it has declared, that "no conviction or judgment shall work corruption of blood, *or any forfeiture of estate;*" thus acting upon a construction of the Constitution which assumes a discretion in omitting the latter as a part of the punishment of treason, even during the life of the offender himself.

IV. The fourth power of a miscellaneous nature vested in Congress is that of "*admitting new States into the Union.*"

The Constitution of the United States treats the admission of new States into the Union as a political question, and has placed it in the hands of Congress. The exercise of this power, therefore, by the Courts, would be entirely inconsistent with any existing legislation of Congress on the subject.[1]

No provision of this kind was made in the Articles of Confederation, and great inconvenience, and much assumption of power, were the necessary consequences. With great propriety and advantage, therefore, the new Constitution supplied this defect. But the power was not granted without restriction; for "no new State" can "be formed or erected within the jurisdiction of any other State; nor can any State be formed by the junction of two or more States, without the consent of the Legislatures of the States concerned, as well as of Congress."[2] These precautions, which prevent either the partition of a large State, or the junction of small ones, without their consent, were necessary to allay the jealousies existing on the subject, both in the more powerful and in the weaker members of the Confederacy.

Upon the purchase of Louisiana by the United States, some doubt was entertained whether the power of the General Government to admit new States into the Union extended to territories not comprised within the boundaries of the United States at the adoption of the Constitution. This question, although never presented in a form for Judicial decision, was, however, decided in the affirmative by large majorities of both houses of Congress, on the several occasions of admitting different parts of that province into the Union, as the separate States of Louisiana, Mississippi, Missouri, and Arkansas; which Acts were severally approved by

[1] 6 *Howard*, 1.

[2] Const. U. S., Art. IV. Sect. III. 1.

successive Chief Magistrates of the Union. It must therefore be considered as practically settled, and it would savor too much of the spirit of controversy, and betray too much self-confidence, to offer, at this time of day, any argument in support of the negative side of that question, and to assert that such a measure required not only the consent of the inhabitants of the territory, but an amendment of the Constitution to render it valid. All doubt, indeed, seems long since to have subsided, and public opinion has sustained the Government in this exercise of the power in question, on the ground of constitutional right, as strongly as it has been declared in favor of its policy.

V. The power "*to dispose of and make all needful regulations respecting the territory or other property belonging to the United States*," is the next one comprehended in this class.[1]

It was requisite that this power should be vested in Congress, by considerations similar to those upon which rests the propriety of its possessing the power next preceding it; and it is accompanied by a condition, not only proper in itself, but which was probably rendered absolutely necessary by the jealousies and controversies that existed concerning the Western territory, and which provides that "nothing in the Constitution shall be so construed as to prejudice any claims of the United States, or of any particular State."[2]

The authority thus restricted, is adapted to all the territorial rights of the Federal Government, beyond the limits of any of the States; but is not applicable, it seems, to a fortress which has never been actually

1 Const. U. S., Art. IV. Sect. III. 2. 2 *Ibid.*

ceded to the United States; nor to any land occupied by the General Government for any similar purpose, with the tacit consent of the State, although the title to the soil may have been conveyed to the United States. It is under this power that Congress claims authority to legislate for the *Territories*, erected in provinces, acquired, like Louisiana and the Floridas, since the adoption of the Federal Constitution. But if the Federal Government possessed authority to purchase them, there seems no necessity for resting the right of legislation in regard to them on such narrow and insufficient grounds, for the power of governing a territory is the inevitable consequence of the right to acquire and hold it.

The formation of civil government in Upper California at the time of its conquest, was the lawful exercise of a belligerent right. It was the existing Government when the Province was ceded to the United States, and did not cease, as a matter of course, or as a consequence of the restoration of peace; and was rightfully continued after peace was made, and until Congress established a Territorial Government there, under its constitutional power to dispose of and make all needful rules and regulations respecting the territory and other property belonging to the United States.[1]

VI. The *guarantee* by the " *United States to every State in the Union of a Republican form of Government; to protect each of them against invasion; and on application of the Legislature, or of the Executive, when the Legislature cannot be convened, against domestic vio-*

[1] 16 *Howard*, 164.

lence," may also be classed among the miscellaneous powers of the Federal Government, as it gives to it a right of interference to effect the objects of the guarantee.[1]

Governments of dissimilar principles and forms have been found less adapted to a Federal coalition of any sort, than those of a kindred nature. In a Confederacy founded on Republican principles, and composed of Republican members, the paramount superintending Government created by it ought certainly to possess the authority to defend the whole system against innovation; and the more intimate the union, the greater the interests of its members in the separate institutions of each other, and the more imperative the right to insist that the respective forms of government under which the general compact was entered into should be substantially maintained. But a right implies a remedy, and nowhere else could an effectual remedy be found in such a case than where it is actually deposited by the Constitution. The mere stipulation, without the power to enforce its observance, would be of little value; hence the term "*guarantee*" indicates that the United States are authorized to oppose, and, if possible, prevent every State in the Union from abandoning the Republican form of Government. But the authority extends no further; and it presumes the preëxistence of Governments of the form guaranteed. So long, therefore, as the Republican forms existing at the time the Constitution was adopted are continued by the States, they are guaranteed by the Federal Government, and the Federal Constitution imposes no other

[1] Const. U. S., Art. IV. Sect. IV.

restriction upon the alteration of the respective State Constitutions than that they shall not vary from the Republican form. Whenever a State may choose to substitute another Republican Government in place of that previously existing, it has a right so to do, and is equally entitled to claim for it the benefit of a Federal guarantee.

Protection against invasion is due from every society to the members composing it, and the latitude of the expressions used in the Constitution secures each State, not only from foreign hostility, but against the ambitious or vindictive enterprise of its more powerful neighbors. The protection against domestic violence is added with equal policy and propriety, as it affords the means of enforcing the guarantee before provided for, whenever a faction or minority in a State endeavors by violence to subvert the Republican form of its Constitution. It is by no means, however, confined to that particular case, nor that particular object, but extends to protection against the acts even of a majority of the people of a State, when directed to any object of unconstitutional violence. For, although it may at the first view appear inconsistent with the Republican theory either that the minority will have the power, or that a majority have not the right to subvert the Government, yet mere speculative reasoning must in these cases, as in all others, be qualified by the lessons of practice and experience.

Unlawful combinations for purposes of violence may be formed by a majority of persons in a State, especially in a slave-holding State, as well as by a majority of a county, or other subdivision of a State; and if the authority of the State is bound in the latter case to protect the local magistracy, the Government of the Union is equally bound in the former to protect the State authority. Besides, there are certain parts of the State Constitutions which are so interwoven with the Federal compact, that a violent assault cannot be made on the one without injury to the other. The power in question, however, can only be exercised when the blow is directed against the State Constitution and authority, or when it *incidentally* or *indirectly* affects the Government of the United States. Where the violence is *immediately* directed against the Federal authority, the General Government is invested with power to suppress it, independently of any requisition of the State Government. But insurrections against the State Governments will rarely require Federal interposition, unless the number of those concerned in them bears some proportion to the friends of the State Constitution; and it will then be much better that the violence should be suppressed by the superintending power, than that even a majority in a State should be left to maintain its cause by a bloody and obstinate contest. The existence itself of the right of the General Government to interpose will, however, generally prevent the necessity of exercising the power; and in cases where it may be doubtful on which side justice lies, no better umpire could be desired in a State quarrel than the representative authority of the Union, which would be free from the influence of local interests, and from participation in local or pe sonal animosities.

VII. The power of Congress to "*propose amendments to the Constitution, and call conventions for the purpose*," is the last to be referred to in this class of the Federal powers.[1]

That useful alterations would be suggested by experience, could not but have been foreseen by the framers of the Constitution. It was requisite, therefore, that a mode for introducing amendments should be provided; and that which was adopted guards equally against that extreme facility which would render the Constitution too mutable, and the extreme difficulty which might perpetuate its faults. The article in question provides that "Congress, whenever two thirds of both houses shall deem it necessary, shall propose amendments to the Constitution; or, on the application of two thirds of the Legislatures of the several States, shall call a Convention for proposing amendments, which, in either case, shall be valid to all intents and purposes, as part of the Constitution, when ratified by the Legislatures of three fourths of the States, or by Conventions in three fourths thereof, as the one or the other mode of ratification may be proposed by Congress; *provided* "that no amendment, which may be made prior to the year 1808, shall in any manner affect" the previous provisions respecting the importation of slaves, and the proportional imposition of capitation and other direct taxes; "and that no State, without its consent, shall be deprived of its equal suffrage in the Senate."

Thus the General and State Governments are equally enabled to originate amendments, as their necessity is pointed out by experience; and I have already had occasion to remark that those proposed or adopted since the ratification of the Constitution, were few in

[1] Const. U. S., Art. V.

number. They consist only of three: first, that which declares "that the Judicial power of the United States shall not be construed to extend to any suit in law or equity commenced or prosecuted against one of the United States by citizens of another State, or by citizens or subjects of any foreign State;[1] second, that which changed the mode of balloting for President and Vice-President by the Electors;[2] and, third, an amendment ordaining that, "if any citizen of the United States shall accept, claim, receive, or retain any title of nobility or honor; or shall, without the consent of Congress, accept or retain any present, pension, office, or emolument of any kind whatever, from any emperor, king, prince, or foreign power, such person shall cease to be a citizen of the United States, and shall be incapable of holding any office of trust or profit under them, or either of them."[3]

The previous and more numerous amendments were proposed by some of the States as conditions of their accession to the Constitution. They all operate as general restrictions upon the powers of Congress, and are, for the most part, affirmative either of the inalienable rights of individuals, or of the civil and political rights and privileges substituted in their stead, as explained in our review of the fundamental principles of the Government; and they were manifestly adopted from superabundant caution, inasmuch as those rights were already sufficiently guarded by the State Constitutions and bills of rights. The following, however, may be enumerated as exceptions, viz: —

1st. That which prohibits Congress from making any

1 Amend. Const. U. S., XI. 2 *Ibid.* XII. 3 *Ibid.* XIII.

law respecting a religious establishment, prohibiting the free exercise of religious worship, or abridging the freedom of speech or of the press.[1]

2d. That "the enumeration in the Constitution of certain rights shall not be construed to deny or disparage others retained by the people."[2] And,

3d. That "the powers not delegated to the United States by the Constitution, nor prohibited by it to the States, are reserved to the States respectively, or to the People."[3]

The second of these amendments was intended to prevent any perverse or ingenious misapplication of the maxim that "an affirmation in particular cases implies a negation in all others." The one last specified is merely an affirmation of a necessary rule for the interpretation of the Constitution; which, being an instrument of limited and enumerated powers, what is not conferred by it is withheld, and retained by the State Governments, if vested in them by their Constitutions, and if not so vested, remains with the People, as a part of their residuary sovereignty. This amendment, however, does not confine the Federal Government to the exercise of *express* powers; for *implied* powers must necessarily have been admitted, unless the Constitution had descended to the regulation of the minutest details of legislation. It is a general principle, that all bodies politic possess all the powers incident to a corporate capacity, without any express declaration to that effect; and one of those defects of the Confederation which led to its abolition, was its prohibiting Congress from the exercise of any power "not *expressly* delegated."

1 Amends. Const. U. S. I. 2 *Ibid.* IX. 3 *Ibid.* X.

It could never, therefore, have been intended by the amendment in question to abridge any of the powers granted under the new Constitution, whether express or implied, direct or incidental. Its manifest and sole design was to exclude any interpretation by which *other powers* should be assumed beyond those granted. All the powers granted by the Constitution, whether express or implied, direct or incidental, are left by the amendment in their original state, while all powers "not *delegated*" (not all powers "not *expressly* delegated") and not prohibited are reserved.

In these, and all the other restrictions on the Legislative powers of the Union, the two great objects were *to secure the rights of the People, and to preserve the Federal system.*

LECTURE XI.

OF THE CONSTITUTIONAL RESTRICTIONS UPON THE POWERS OF THE SEVERAL STATES.

THE fifth class of provisions in favor of the Federal authority consists of restrictions on the powers of the several States. These may be distinguished by their character as *two* sorts: the *first* comprehending those limitations which are *absolute ;* and the *second,* such as are *qualified.*

I. The former prohibit any State from entering into any treaty of alliance or confederation; from granting letters of marque and reprisal; from coining money, emitting bills of credit, or making any thing but gold or silver coin a tender in payment of debts; from passing any bill of attainder, *ex post facto* law, or law impairing the obligation of contracts; and from granting any title of nobility.[1]

1*st.* The prohibition against treaties, alliances, and confederations was contained in the articles of the former union of the States, and copied in the new Constitution. It rests upon the consideration that if every State were at liberty to enter into treaties, alliances, and confederacies with foreign States, or with other members of the Union, the power confided to the

[1] Const. U. S., Art. I. Sect. x. 1.

National Government in regard to the former would be rendered nugatory, while the Constitution itself might be subverted by the exercise of such a power among the States.

The prohibition of letters of marque and reprisal was also a part of the old system, and adopted, but with some extension, in the new. According to the former, they might be granted by the States, after a declaration of war by Congress; under the latter, they must be obtained, as well during the war as previously to its declaration, from the General Government. This alteration is fully justified by the advantages of uniformity, in all points relating to foreign powers; and by the necessity of an immediate responsibility to the nation, in all matters in which the nation itself is responsible to others. Moreover, were it otherwise, it would be in the power of a single State to involve the whole Union in war, at its pleasure; and although the issuing of letters of marque is not always designed as a preliminary or provocative to war, yet, in its essence, it is a measure of hostile retaliation for unredressed grievances, real or supposed, and is most generally succeeded by open hostilities.

2d. The prohibition of the States to coin money was necessary to give complete effect to the power of the Union in relation to the current coin, and arose from a consideration of the danger and facility of circulating base or spurious coins, where the coins are various in value and denomination, and issued by several independent and irresponsible authorities. Under the Confederation, it was left in the hands of the States as a concurrent right, with an exception in favor of the exclusive right of Congress to regulate the alloy and the value. In this particular, these two provisions have been found to be an improvement on the old; for while the alloy and the value depended on the General Government, a right of coinage in the individual States could have no other effect than to multiply expensive mints, and diversify the forms and weights of the coins in circulation. The latter measure was found to defeat the purposes for which the power was originally submitted to the Federal authority; and so far as the former might prevent the easy remittance of gold and silver to the central mint for recoinage, the end can be as well attained by local mints established by the General Government in particular States. But the general substitution of a paper medium for a metallic currency obviates the objection entirely, and gives, therefore, greater importance to the extension of the prohibition to "*bills of credit.*"

The loss which this country had sustained between the war of the Revolution and the adoption of the Federal Constitution, from the fatal effects of paper money on public and private confidence, on the industry and morals of the people, the national reputation, and the character of Republicanism itself, could be redeemed in no other way than by the voluntary surrender by the several States of the power which had been rendered the instrument of such profligate and destructive mischief. In addition to these considerations, the same reasons which evince the necessity of denying to the individual States the power of regulating the coin, apply with equal force to inhibit them from substituting a paper medium in its place. Were every State at liberty to regulate the value of its metallic currency, there would be as many different currencies as States;

and thus the commercial intercourse between them would be embarrassed and impeded; retrospective alterations of the value of its coin might be made by any State, in fraud not only of its own citizens, and those of other States, but of foreigners, which would not merely interrupt the harmony among the States, and engender animosities between them, but discredit and compromise the Union with foreign nations, by the indiscretion or profligacy of a single State. Nor are these mischiefs less incident to a power in the States to emit bills of credit than to coin money; and the power to make anything but gold or silver coin a tender in payment of debts is withdrawn from the States, on the same principle as that of issuing a paper currency.

This restriction upon the power of the States has received a construction of the utmost importance, both to their individual rights and the authority of the Federal Government. It has been ruled by the Supreme Court, that although the term "bills of credit," in its enlarged, and, perhaps, in its literal sense, may comprehend any instrument by which a State engages to pay money at a future day, thereby including a certificate given for money borrowed, yet that the language of the Constitution, and the mischief intended to be prevented, equally limit its interpretation. The word "emit," it was observed, is never employed in describing those contracts by which a State binds itself to pay money at a future day, for services actually received, or money borrowed for immediate use. Nor are instruments executed for such purposes denominated in common language "bills of credit." To *emit bills of credit* conveys to the mind the idea of issuing paper, redeemable at a future day, in anticipation of the public resources, and intended to circulate as money.[1] This is the sense, indeed, in which the terms have always been understood, and in which they were interpreted by the Court. The Constitution, moreover, considers the emission of bills of credit, and the enactment of tender laws, as distinct operations, which may be separately performed, independently of each other. Both acts are forbidden; and to affirm, as has been done in some of the States,[2] that bills of credit may be emitted, if not made a legal tender, is, in effect, to expunge that distinct and independent prohibition, and to read the Constitution as if that branch of the clause had been omitted. But there is too much reason to fear that such an expedient has since been resorted to, or, rather, that a successful attempt has been made to elude this wholesome restriction.

The Legislature of Kentucky, in the year 1820, passed an Act establishing a bank, and constituting the president and directors a corporation, with a capital consisting of all moneys paid into the treasury of the State for the sale of its vacant lands, and other property. The bank was authorized to receive money on deposit, to make loans, and issue promissory notes; and was the exclusive property of the State. In relation to this bank, thus constituted, with such a capital, and so owned, it was held that its notes thus issued were not bills of credit within the meaning of the Constitution.[3] It was admitted, indeed, that to constitute *a bill of credit* within the purview of the prohibition, it must be issued by a State, on the faith of a State, and designed

1 4 *Peters*, 431. 2 8 *Ibid.* 40. 3 11 *Ibid.* 257.

to circulate as money; that the paper which it issues must circulate on the credit of the State, and be so received and used in the ordinary business of life; that the persons issuing it must have power to bind the State; they must act as agents, and, of course, not incur any personal responsibility, nor impart as individuals any credit to the paper. These were admitted to be the leading characteristics of a bill of credit, and yet the notes issued by this "Bank of the Commonwealth of Kentucky"—for such, moreover, was its title—were held not to be *bills* of credit within the meaning of the Federal Constitution. Before we assent to this conclusion, let us bring the question to the test merely of the characteristics specified by the Court. These shall serve as interrogatories, to which answers will be drawn from its own statement of the facts.

1*st.* Were the notes of this bank issued by the State?

Answer. The bank was established by the State; its capital consisted of the funds of the State, and it was authorized by the State to issue its notes.

2*d.* Did its paper circulate on the credit of the State?

Ans. Its issues were founded on its capital, which was the property of the State.

3*d.* Had the persons who issued its notes authority to bind the State?

Ans. The bank was the property of the State, who named or appointed its directors in the Act of incorporation.

4*th.* Did the directors or officers of the bank act as agents of the State, without incurring personal responsibility?

Ans. Of course. There was no other stockholder than the State; and they could not have acted on any other responsibility to the public than that of the State, as they were not made personally responsible as principals by the act of incorporation.

5th. Did the directors or officers of the bank impart any credit, as individuals, to the notes of the bank?

Ans. No other than is imparted by the signatures of the officers of every other bank. It is to the capital of the bank, and to the responsibility of the stockholders, that the public look for security, and not to the persons whose *official* signatures are affixed to its notes.

If there be any "other matter or thing" which may be put by way of general interrogatory, the answer is obvious: "*Qui facit per alium, facit per se.*" In short, if a State wishes to evade the Constitution and emit bills of credit, it has merely to incorporate its public officers, or other agents, as a bank, and thus render a prohibition intended to prevent a recurrence of those evils, which had been found from experience to attend the practice, a dead letter.[1]

3*d.* It is a principle of universal jurisprudence, that laws, civil or criminal, must be prospective, and cannot ordinarily have a retroactive effect. Bills of attainder, *ex post facto* laws, and laws impairing the obligation of contracts, are, therefore, contrary to the first principles of the social contract, and to every principle of sound legislation. The two former are expressly prohibited to

[1] The decision in this case was made *after the death* of Chief Justice Marshall, and the opinion of the Court delivered by Mr. Justice M'Lean; Mr. Justice Thompson concurring, and Mr. Justice Story *dissenting*. This decision was confirmed in a subsequent case. 13 *Howard*, 12.

Congress by the Federal Constitution, and to some of the State Legislatures, by declarations of rights prefixed to their Constitutions.[1] The framers of the Federal compact were, nevertheless, admonished by their own experience, of the necessity of additional bulwarks in favor of personal security and private rights; and the experience of their successors has shown that, in imposing these restrictions, the Convention maintained its character for strict integrity, high moral sense, and sound practical wisdom.

Bills of attainder are such special acts of the Legislature as inflict capital punishment upon persons whom they declare to be guilty of high offences, without trial or conviction in the ordinary course of Judicial proceedings. They have generally been confined to cases of treason, and have never been resorted to but in times of internal commotion and arbitrary misgovernment. If the bill inflict a milder punishment than death, it is called *a bill of pains and penalties;* but, in the sense of the Constitution, bills of attainder include bills of pains and penalties, as the former may affect the life of an individual, or may confiscate his property, or both.

[1] The Bill of Rights prefixed to the Constitution of New Hampshire declares that retrospective laws are injurious, oppressive, and unjust, and ought not to be made. Within the intent and meaning of this article, every statute which takes away or impairs vested rights acquired under existing laws, or creates a new obligation, imposes a new duty, or attaches a new disability in respect to transactions already past must be deemed retrospective. *Per* Story, J., 2 *Gallis*, 139. See also 5 *Yerg.* 320; 1 *Ibid.* 360; 7 *Johns. Rep.* 477; 18 *Ibid.* 138; 3 *Dall.* 381, 386; 2 *Root*, 350; 2 *Pick.* 165, 170, 172; 11 *Ibid.* 28; 9 *Mass.* 363; 3 *N. H.* 475; 5 *Monr.* 133; 7 *Johns. Rep.* 488; 2 *Peters*, 861; 8 *Ibid.* 110; 1 *Blackf.* 193, 196; 6 *Binn.* 271; 1 *J. J. Marsh*, 563; 3 *Cowen*, 347; *Harper*, 88; 2 *Gallis.* 105; 1 *Yerg.* 360.

Ex post facto laws are often supposed to signify all laws having a retroactive operation. Every *ex post facto* law must necessarily be retrospective, but every retrospective law is not an *ex post facto* law. The terms are not synonymous; and the technical meaning of the latter is confined to such as render criminal an act done before the law was passed, which was then innocent; or to such as aggravate the offence, or render it more criminal than it was when committed; or such as inflict a greater punishment than the law annexed to the crime when perpetrated; or such as alter the rules of evidence, and admit different or less testimony than was required at the time the offence was committed, to convict the offender. With more comprehensive brevity, these laws have been defined by Chief Justice Marshall as "those which render an act punishable in a manner in which it was not punishable when committed;" and this definition includes both laws inflicting personal or pecuniary penalties for acts before innocent, and laws passed after the commission of an *unlawful* act, which enhance its guilt or aggravate its punishment.

The Constitution of the United States does not prohibit the States from passing retrospective laws generally, but only *ex post facto* laws.[1] Hence the Supreme Court of the United States cannot pronounce an Act of a State Legislature void, merely because such Act divests *antecedent* vested rights of property.[2]

4th. A similar restriction with regard to bills of attainder and *ex post facto* laws is imposed by the Constitution on Congress, as well as upon the State Legislatures; but not with regard to *laws impairing the*

[1] 8 *Peters*, 110; 2 *Ibid.* 414; 1 *Bald.* 74.

[2] 11 *Peters*, 420.

obligation of contracts, which are also retrospective in their operation, and equally inconsistent with sound legislation, and the fundamental principles of the social compact.

The reason of this difference is obvious. By *contracts*, in the sense of the Constitution, we are to understand every *executed* agreement, whether between individuals, or between individuals and a State, by which a right is vested; and also every *executory* agreement which confers a right of action, or creates a binding obligation in relation to subjects of a valuable nature, which may be asserted in a court of justice; but it does not comprehend the political relations between a Government and its citizens. The power possessed by a State Legislature to which every thing not expressly reserved is granted, and the temptations to abuse that power, render express restrictions, if not absolutely necessary, at least prudent and useful; but the National Legislature has no power to interfere with contracts, except where it is expressly given to it. By the *obligation* of contracts, in the meaning and intendment of the Constitution, is understood not merely the *moral*, but the *legal* obligation. Nor is it an obligation arising from the universal law of civilized nations; but that which results from the laws of the State where the contract is made;[1] and in this sense, a system of bankruptcy impairs the obligation of contracts when it releases the party from the necessity of performing them; but Congress is expressly invested with this power in regard to bankruptcies, as an enumerated, and not as an implied power, and in no other form can it impair the obligation of a contract.

[1] 12 *Wheat.* 213.

This prohibition in regard to the States extensively and deeply affects their Legislative authority; and there is no part of the Federal Constitution that has given rise to more various and able discussions, or to more obstinate and protracted litigation. Contracts executed, as well as executory, are included in it; not only conveyances of land, public grants from a State to corporations or individuals, grants and charters in existence when the Federal Constitution was adopted, but even those existing before the Revolution; and contracts between the different States themselves.[1] But the clause in question does not extend to *a State law* enacted before the Constitution commenced its operation, though such law operate on rights of property vested before that time.[2] A compact between two States, or a grant from a State (which amounts to a contract) to individuals, is as much protected by it as a grant from one individual to another, and the State is as effectually inhibited from impairing its own contracts, or those to which it is a party, as it is from impairing the obligation of a contract between two individuals. And the rule for determining these questions in the Courts of the United States, is of an international character; and is not to be collected from the decisions of the Courts of either of the States who are parties to the compact.[3]

The clause under consideration was first brought into direct judicial discussion by an Act of the Legislature of Georgia, passed in the year 1795. This Act authorized the sale of a large tract of wild land, in what was

[1] 6 *Cranch*, 137; 9 *Ibid.* 52; 2 *Hayw.* 310, 374; 4 *Wheat.* 641, 651; 8 *Ibid.* 1; 4 *Gill & Johns.* 1.

[2] 5 *Wheat.* 420.

[3] 11 *Peters*, 22.

called the *Yazoo* country, and a grant was made in pursuance of the law, to a number of individuals, under the name of the "Georgia Company." But by an Act passed the next year, the Legislature declared its previous grant to be null and void, on the ground of fraud and corruption in obtaining it. One of the questions presented to the Supreme Court of the United States for decision arose upon a sale to a third person, by a grantee of the State under the first Act, and it was this: Whether the Legislature of Georgia had the constitutional power to repeal the former law, and avoid the sale made under its authority. The Court declared that, when a law in its nature imports a contract, and absolute rights have vested under it, its repeal could neither divest those rights, nor annihilate or impair the title thus acquired.[1] A party cannot pronounce his own deed invalid, whatever cause may be assigned to impeach it, although that party be the Legislature of a State. It was accordingly declared that an estate held under the Act of 1795, having passed into the hands of a *bonâ fide* purchaser for a valuable consideration, the State of Georgia was disabled by the Constitution from passing any law by which that estate could be legally impaired and rendered void.

The next case in which this prohibition was brought in review was from the State of New Jersey; on which occasion it was held that, where a State Legislature declared by law that certain lands to be purchased for the use of certain Indians should not be subject to taxation, such Act amounted to a contract, which could not

[1] 6 *Cranch*, 87.

be rescinded by a subsequent Legislature.[1] In this case the Colonial Legislature, in 1758, authorized a purchase of lands for the Delaware Indians, and made the stipulation mentioned. The Indians occupied the land in pursuance of the law until the year 1803, when it was sold under the authority of the Legislature. In 1804, the Legislature repealed the Act exempting the land from taxation; but the Act of 1758 was held to be a contract, and that of 1804 a breach of it, and it was accordingly declared void, under the Constitution of the United States; thereby at once confirming the former decision, and recognizing the principle alluded to in a former Lecture, that a change of Government does not affect the previously vested rights of property.

In a subsequent case from the State of Virginia, the same points again arose, and the Court went more largely into the consideration of this delicate and interesting constitutional doctrine, not only establishing the last-mentioned principle in regard to the effect of the Revolution on prior contracts, but at the same time declaring that a Legislative grant, competently made, vested an indefeasible and irrevocable title.[2]

There is, indeed, no authority which can support on principle the contrary position. The Legislature of a State cannot repeal statutes creating private corporations, or confirming to them property acquired under the faith of previous laws, and, by such repeal, vest it in others, without the consent or default of the corporators. Nor can rights legally vested in any corporation be controlled or destroyed by a subsequent statute, unless power for that purpose be expressly reserved to the

1 7 *Cranch*, 164. 2 9 *Ibid.* 43.

Legislature in the Act of incorporation.[1] This rule applies as well to implied as to express powers.[2] A contrary doctrine would be equally repugnant to the letter and spirit of the Constitution, and to the principles of natural justice. But the charter of any corporate body may be altered in its most essential features, by the Legislature granting it, if the alteration be agreed to by the corporators either before or after the Act making the alterations.[3]

Where the legal interest in literary or charitable institutions is vested by law in trustees in order to promote the objects for which they were incorporated, and donations made to them, they are considered within the protection of the Constitution; and it was in the great case of *Dartmouth College* that this inhibition

1 2 *Mass.* 146. 2 9 *Wend.* 351.

3 1 *Rawle*, 190; 1 *Monr.* 5. An apt illustration of the refined legal notion of property, to which this provision applies, is afforded in the right which the representative of a person deceased has to the disposition of the corpse in case of its removal. This right was drawn in question by proceedings instituted in the Supreme Court of New York for removing a cemetery and its contents; when the question was referred to Samuel B. Ruggles, Esq., already mentioned as an eminent member of the bar. In his "Report"— which was adopted by the Court — the "LAW OF BURIAL" is examined and discussed in a manner at once elaborate and lucid, and with equal learning and ingenuity. He thoroughly explores the grounds of both the Common and the Ecclesiastical Law of England relating to the subject; and points out, with great clearness and precision, the modifications they have received in this country from the Revolution, and consequent separation of Church and State. This remarkable document forms a complete, as well as a luminous and recondite treatise, of an original character and permanent value, upon a branch of national jurisprudence which its author may be said, indeed, to have created.

upon the States received the most elaborate discussion, and the most efficient and instructive application.[1] It was there decided that the charter granted by the British Crown to that institution in 1769, was a *contract* within the meaning of the Constitution, and protected by the clause in question. It was held that the College was a private charitable institution, not liable to Legislative control, and that a law of New Hampshire altering the charter in a material point, without the consent of the corporation, was a "law impairing the obligation" of the charter, and it was consequently declared to be unconstitutional and void. Chief Justice Marshall, in delivering the opinion of the Court, observed, "that Dartmouth College was a private eleemosynary institution, endowed with a capacity to take and hold property for objects unconnected with Government. Its funds were bestowed by individuals on the faith of the charter, and consisted entirely of private donations. The corporation was not invested with any portion of political power, nor did it, in fact, partake in any degree in the administration of civil government. It was instituted as a private corporation for general charity; and the charter was a contract to which the donors, the trustees, and the Crown were the original parties, and it was made on a valuable consideration for the security and disposition of property."

The legal interest in every literary and charitable institution is vested in trustees, to be asserted by them, and they claim or defend in behalf of the object to promote which the corporation was created and the donations made. Contracts of this kind are most rea-

[1] 4 *Wheat.* 518.

sonably considered within the purview and protection of the Constitution. The one in question remained unchanged by the Revolution, and the duties as well as the powers of the former Government devolved on the people of New Hampshire. But the law of that State transferred the whole power of governing the college from the trustees, under the charter, to the Executive of New Hampshire; and the will of the State was thereby substituted for the will of the donors, in every essential operation of the college. The charter was reorganized in such a manner as to convert a literary institution, moulded according to the will of its founders, into a machine entirely subservient to the will of the State. A proceeding thus subversive of the contract on the faith of which the donors invested their property was, consequently, held to be repugnant to the Constitution. This celebrated case, it has been well said,[1] "contains one of the most full and elaborate expositions of the constitutional sanctity of contracts anywhere to be met with; and has done more than any other single act proceeding from the authority of the United States to throw an impregnable barrier around all rights and franchises derived from the grant of Government, and to give solidity and inviolability to the literary, charitable, and commercial institutions of the country."[2]

In another case, in which this prohibitory clause of the Federal Constitution came again under discussion,

[1] 1 *Kent's Comm.* 389.

[2] The Supreme Court of North Carolina declared unconstitutional and void, an Act of the Legislature repealing a grant of land to the University of that State. 2 *Hayw.* 310; *Murphy*, 58. See also 2 *McCord*, 354.

it was observed by the Court that the objection to a law, on the ground of its impairing the obligation of contracts, did not depend *on the extent of the change effected by the law;* any deviation from the terms of the contract, by accelerating or postponing the period of performance, which the latter prescribes, imposing conditions not expressed in it, or dispensing with the performance of those which are, however minute or apparently immaterial or partial in their effect on the contract, impairs its obligation. Another material point decided on this occasion was, that *a compact between two States* was a contract within the constitutional prohibition.[1]

Another case, which led to a very extensive inquiry into the operation of this constitutional restriction, arose under an Insolvent Act of New York, passed in 1811. This law was retrospective, and discharged the debtor, upon his single petition and the surrender of his property, without the concurrence of any creditor, from all preëxisting debts, and from all liability and responsibility by reason of them. The Court on this occasion recognized the doctrine adverted to in a former Lecture, that until Congress exercise its power on the subject of bankruptcy, the individual States may pass bankrupt laws, provided they contain no provision violating the obligation of contracts. It was admitted that the States might discharge debtors from imprisonment, because imprisonment is *no part of the contract*, but only a means for coercing its performance. It was also admitted that a State may pass statutes of limitations, as they are termed, for these also relate only *to the remedy*,

[1] 8 *Wheat.* 1.

and not to the *obligation* of the contract; and it was stated that the insolvent laws of far the greater number of States only discharged the person of the debtor, and left the obligation in full force. But a law which discharged the debtor from his contract, and released him without payment, impaired, because it entirely discharged the obligation of the contract; for it is to be observed that there is an obvious distinction in the nature of things, between the *obligation* of a contract, and the *remedy* to enforce it. The latter may be modified as the wisdom of the Legislature may direct. But the Constitution intending to restore and preserve completely the public credit and confidence, established as a fundamental principle, that the former shall be inviolable.[1]

The case in which the above decision was made, had arisen in a Federal Court, and the contract existed when the State law was passed; but it was afterwards held that there was no difference when the suit is brought in a Court of a State, of which both parties are citizens, and in which the contract was made, and the discharge obtained, and where the parties continue to reside until the suit be brought.[2] A distinction, however, was taken in the Courts of New York and Massachusetts, between a contract made before, and one made after the passing of the State law.[3] The doctrine they maintained was this, that an insolvent Act in force when the contract was made, did not, in the sense of the Constitution, impair its obligation, because the parties to every contract have reference to

1 4 *Wheat.* 122. 2 6 *Ibid.* 131.

3 16 *Johns. Rep.* 233; 7 *Johns. Ch. Rep.* 297; 13 *Mass.* 1.

the existing laws of the country where it is made, and are presumed to make their contracts in reference to them. This distinction was supposed to be consistent with the decision of the Supreme Court of the United States. But in a subsequent case, where the discharge was under an insolvent law of a different State from that in which the contract was made, the Supreme Court went a step further, and held that a discharge under such a law existing when the debt was contracted, was equally within the principle before established.[1]

It remained, however, to be settled whether a State could constitutionally pass an insolvent law which should effectually discharge the debtor from a debt contracted after the passing of the Act, and within the State in which the law was passed. The general language of the Court on the last occasion, seemed to reach this case; but the facts on which the question then arose, did not cover the whole ground. The decision, therefore, was not authority to the extent mentioned; and it was subsequently ruled by a bare majority of the Court, and after much apparent hesitation, that a bankrupt or insolvent law of a State, discharging both the person of the debtor, and his future acquisitions of property, is not a law "impairing the obligation of contracts," *in respect to debts contracted within the State, subsequently to its enactment.*[2]

The venerable Chief Justice Marshall was among the minority of the Court, and delivered the reasons for their dissent. He admitted that none of the former decisions comprehended the question then presented,

1 4 *Wheat.* 209.

2 12 *Ibid.* 213.

and that, consequently, it was an open one. He also admitted that there was an essential difference in principle between laws which act on past or future contracts; and that while those of a former description could seldom be justified, those of the latter were proper subjects of ordinary Legislative discretion. A constitutional restriction, therefore, on the power to pass laws of the one class, might very well consist with entire Legislative freedom in regard to the other. Yet, when we consider the nature of the Union; that it was intended to make us, in a great measure, one people as to commercial objects; that so far as respects the intercommunication of individuals, the lines of separation between States are in many respects obliterated, it would be matter of surprise if, on the delicate subject of contracts actually formed, the interference of State legislation should not be greatly abridged, or entirely forbidden. In the nature of the existing provision, then, there seems to be nothing which should induce us to adopt the limited construction which had been given in that case to the prohibitory clause.

The former part of the section, comprehending the prohibition, enumerates the cases in which the action of the State Legislatures is absolutely and entirely forbidden; while the latter part specifies those in which the prohibitions are qualified. The former comprehends two classes of powers; those of the first class are political and general in their nature, consisting in the exercise of sovereignty without affecting the rights of individuals; while the second class comprehends those laws which operate upon individuals,—and includes, among others, "laws impairing the obligation of contracts." In all the cases embraced in both classes, whether the thing prohibited be the exercise of mere political legislation, or Legislative action upon individuals, the prohibition is complete and total. Legislation of every description on those subjects is, without any exception, comprehended and forbidden. A State is as entirely prohibited from passing laws impairing the obligation of contracts as from making treaties or coining money. So much of the prohibition as restrains the power of the State to punish offenders in criminal cases, and inhibits bills of attainder and *ex post facto* laws, is, in its very terms, confined to pre-existing cases. But that part of the clause which relates to the civil transactions of individuals is expressed in more general terms—in terms which comprehend, in their ordinary acceptation, cases which occur after, as well as before the passing of the Act. It forbids a State to make anything but gold or silver coin a tender in payment of debts, or to pass any law impairing the obligation of contracts. These prohibitions relate to kindred subjects; they contemplate Legislative interference with private rights, and restrain such interference. In construing that part of the clause which respects tender laws, a distinction has never been attempted between debts existing at the time the law was passed and those afterwards contracted. The prohibition in that case is total; and yet the difference in principle between making property a tender in payment of debts contracted after the passage of the Act, and discharging those debts without payment or by a surrender of property; in other words, between an *absolute* and a *contingent* right to tender in payment, is not clearly discernible. Nor is the difference in language so obvious as to denote plainly a difference of intention in the framers of the Constitution. The same train of reasoning which would confine the words relative to contracts to those contracts only which existed at the passage of the law, would go far in limiting those relative to a tender in payment of debts to such as previously existed; yet the distinction between these and such as were contracted subsequently to the law seems never before to have occurred to any expounder of the Constitution, and would unquestionably defeat the object of the clause.

A point of greater difficulty, and that upon which the decision of the question appears to have turned, was the nature of the original obligation of the contract made after the passage of such an insolvent law; whether it were unconditional to perform the very act stipulated; or whether a condition were implied that, in the event of insolvency, the contract should be satisfied by a surrender of property. It was admitted on all hands that the Constitution refers to, and preserves the *legal*, not the moral obligation of a contract; because obligations purely moral are not enforced by the agency of human laws; and the restraints imposed on the States by the Constitution are intended for objects which, if not restrained, would be the subject of State legislation. The principle insisted on by the Chief Justice was, that laws act *upon* a contract, and do not enter *into* it and become a stipulation of the parties. "Society," he observed, "affords a remedy for breaches of contract, and if that remedy has been applied, the claim to it is extinguished." The external action of law upon contracts, by administering the remedy for their breach, is the usual exercise of Legislative power; and an interference with those contracts, by introducing into them conditions not agreed to by the parties, would be a very unusual and extraordinary exercise of the power of legislation, and one not, certainly, to be gratuitously attributed to laws which do not profess to claim it.

If the law becomes part of the contract, change of place will not expunge the condition. A contract made in New York would be the same in any other State; and would still retain the stipulation originally introduced into it—that the debtor should be discharged by the surrender of his estate. It cannot be true that contracts are entered into in contemplation of the insolvency of parties to be bound by them. They are framed with the expectation that they will be literally performed. Insolvency, undoubtedly, is a casualty which may possibly occur, but it is never expected. In the ordinary course of human transactions, if its probability be even suspected, security is taken against it. But when it comes unlooked for, it would be entirely contrary to reason to consider it as a part of the contract. However, therefore, a law may act upon contracts, it does not enter into them and become a part of them. The effect of such a principle would be a mischievous abridgment of Legislative power over subjects within the proper jurisdiction of a State, by arresting its power to repeal or modify such laws with respect to existing contracts.

But it has been objected that "a contract, being a creature of civil society, derives its obligation from the law, which, although it may not enter into the agreement, still acts externally upon it, and determines how far the principle of coercion shall be applied to it; and this rule being universally understood, no individual can justly complain of its application to himself." This argument was illustrated by reference to the statutes to prevent frauds, which require certain contracts to be reduced to writing, in order to render them obligatory; to those against usury, which declare an usurious contract void from its origin; and to the statutes of limitations, which enable one party to prevent the other from enforcing the contract between them, after the expiration of a certain period from its breach or non-performance. But here the fallacy lies at the very foundation of the argument, as it assumes that the contract is the mere creature of civil society, and derives all its obligation from human legislation; that it is not the stipulation that the individual makes which binds him, but some declaration of the supreme power of the body politic to which he belongs; and that, though the original declaration to this effect be lost in remote antiquity, yet it must be presumed to be the origin of the obligation of contracts. It is, however, an objection of no considerable weight against the truth of this position, that no trace exists of any such enactment. As far back as human research extends, we find the Judicial power administering remedies to violated rights or broken contracts, and applying those remedies on the idea of a preëxisting obligation on every man to do that which he has promised to do; that the breach of this obligation is an injury for which the party has a just claim for compensation; and that society ought to afford him a remedy for that injury. We find, too, allusions to the modes of acquiring property; but from the earliest time, we find no allusion to any supposed act of the governing power as giving obligation to contracts. On the contrary, all the proceedings respecting them, of which we know anything, support the notion of a preëxisting obligation. which human laws merely enforce.

Upon this supposition, that the obligation of the contract is derived from the agreement of the parties, let us proceed to inquire *how far* laws act externally upon contracts, and in that way control their obligation. It was not denied that a law might have such an effect upon subsequent contracts; nor that it may be capable of discharging a debtor, under the circumstances and conditions prescribed in the statute, which was relied on in the case referred to. But as that was an effect neither contemplated nor intended by the parties, an Act of the Legislature can only have this operation when it has the full force of *law*. A law may determine the obligation of a contract on the happening of a contingency, because it *is* the law. But if it be *not* the law, it cannot have this effect; and when its existence or force as law is denied, they cannot either of them be proved by showing what are the *qualities* of a law. Law has been defined to be "a rule of civil conduct, prescribed by *the supreme power* in a state." In our system, the Legislature of a State is the supreme power in all cases in which its action is not restrained by the State Constitution or the Constitution of the United States. Where it is so restrained, the State Legislature ceases to be the supreme power, and its Acts are not law. It was, therefore, begging the question to say that, because contracts may be discharged by a law previously enacted, it was discharged in that case by the Act of the Legislature set up for the purpose; for the question returned, *Was that act* LAW? Was it consistent with, or repugnant to, the Constitution of the United States?

It was readily admitted that the whole subject of contracts was under the control of society, and that all the power of society over them resides in the State Legislatures, except in those special cases where restraint is imposed by the Federal Constitution. The extent of the restraint on the power to impair the obligation of contracts cannot, however, be ascertained by showing that the Legislature may prescribe the circumstances on which their original validity may be made to depend. If the Legislative will were that certain agreements should be in writing; that they should be sealed and attested by a given number of witnesses; that they should be recorded, or assume any prescribed form before they became obligatory, all these are regulations which society may rightfully make; and they do not come within the restriction of the Constitution, because they do not impair the obligation of the contract. The obligation must exist before it can be impaired; and a prohibition to impair it when made, does not imply an inability to prescribe those conditions which shall *create* its obligation. The statutes of frauds which have been enacted in the several States, and which are acknowledged to flow from the proper exercise of State sovereignty, prescribe regulations which must precede the obligation of the contract, and, consequently, cannot impair it. Acts of this description, therefore, are most clearly not within the prohibition. The Acts against usury are of the same character; they declare the contract to be void from the beginning, and deny that the instrument ever became a contract; they deny it all original obligation, and cannot, therefore, *impair* that which never came into existence. Statutes of limitation approach more nearly to the subject under consideration, but can never be identified with it; they defeat a contract once obligatory, but, as has been before observed, they relate only to the remedies furnished to enforce the contract, and their language is generally confined to the remedy; they do not purport to dispense with the performance of the contract, but proceed upon the presumption that a certain length of time, if unexplained by circumstances, affords reasonable evidence of its having been performed. In prescribing the proofs that shall be received in their Courts, and the effect of those proofs, the States exercise their acknowledged powers, as they also do in regulating the remedies and modes of proceeding in those Courts.[1]

It was, nevertheless, insisted that the right to regulate the remedy, and to modify the obligation of the contract, were the same; that obligation and remedy were identical and synonymous. But the answer given to this proposition seems to be conclusive. It was, "that the obligation and the remedy originate at different times." The obligation to perform is certainly coeval with the contract itself, and operates anterior to the time of performance; while the remedy acts upon a broken contract, and enforces a preëxisting obligation. The right to contract is the acknowledged attribute

[1] A repeal of the statutes of limitations is void so far as it respects claims already barred. 3 *N. H.* 473. See also 5 *Pick.* 65; 11 *Mass.* 396; 2 *Pick.* 284; 3 *Greenl.* 326. And statutes of limitations which do not allow a reasonable time after the passing thereof for commencing suits on existing causes of action, are unconstitutional. 8 *Mass.* 430; 2 *Greenl.* 294; 2 *Gallis.* 141; 4 *Wheat.* 207. See also 2 *Peters,* 290; 1 *Blackf.* 36; 1 *Car. Law Rep.* 385; 2 *Ibid.* 428; *Pick.* 1; 5 *Monro,* 98; 7 *Ibid.* 11; *Ibid.* 544–588; 4 *Litt.* 34–53; *Charlt.* 175.

of a free agent, and he may rightfully coerce performance from another free agent, who violates his faith. Contracts have, consequently, an intrinsic obligation. When men enter into societies, they can no longer exercise this original and natural right of coercion; it is surrendered for the means of coercion afforded by society. But the right to contract is not surrendered with the right to coerce performance. The former is still incidental to that degree of free agency which the laws of society leave to every individual, and the obligation of the contract is the necessary consequence of the right to make it. Laws regulate this right; and where it is not regulated, it is retained in its original extent. Obligation and remedy, then, are not identical; they originate at different times, and are derived from different sources.

But it was alleged that "the power of the State over the remedy might be used to the destruction of all beneficial results from the right;" and hence it was inferred that "the construction which maintains the inviolability of the obligation must be extended to the power of regulating the remedy." The difficulty, however, which this view of the subject presents, does not proceed from the identity or connection of right and remedy, but from the existence of distinct Governments, acting on kindred subjects. The Constitution of the United States contemplates restraint as to the obligation of contracts, not as to the application of the remedy. If this restraint affect a power which the Constitution did not mean to touch, it can only be when that power is used as an instrument of hostility to invade the inviolability of contracts, which is placed beyond its reach. A State may use many of its acknowledged powers in such a manner as to come into conflict with the provisions of the Federal Constitution; thus the powers over the domestic police, and the power to regulate its purely internal commerce, may, as we have already seen, be so exercised as to interfere with the regulation by Congress of commerce with foreign nations, or among the States. In such cases, as we have before observed, the power which is *supreme* must control that which is subordinate. This principle neither involves self-contradiction, nor denies the existence of the several powers in the respective Governments. So, if a State shall not merely modify or withhold a particular remedy, but shall apply it in such a manner as to extinguish the obligation without performance of a contract, it would be an abuse of power which could scarcely be misunderstood; but it would not prove that remedy could not be regulated without regulating obligation.

It was urged, however, as a conclusive argument against the existence of a distinct line of division between obligation and remedy, that "the same power which can withdraw the remedy against the *person* of the debtor, can also withdraw that against his *property*," and thus effectually defeat the obligation. "The Constitution," it was said, "did not deal with form, but with substance; and could not be presumed, if it designed to protect the obligation of contracts from State legislation, to have left it thus obviously exposed to destruction." The answer is, that the State law goes further, and annuls the obligation without affording the remedy which satisfies it; or, if its action on the remedy be such as palpably to impair the obligation of the contract, the very case arises which was supposed to be prohibited. If the law leaves the obligation untouched, but withholds the remedy, or affords one which is merely nominal, why, this is like all other cases of misgovernment, and leaves the debtor still liable to his creditors, should he, or his property, be found where the laws afford a remedy. But should it even be determined that such a law was a successful evasion of the Constitution, it would not follow that an Act which operates directly on the contract after it is made was not within the restriction imposed on the States. The validity of a law acting immediately upon the obligation is not proved by showing that the Constitution has provided no means for compelling the States to enforce the contract. The prohibition in question is, therefore, not incompatible with the fair exercise of that discretion which the State Legislatures possess, in common with all Governments, to regulate the remedies afforded by their own Courts.

It is impossible to look back to the history of the times when the august spectacle was exhibited of a whole people assembling by their representatives in order to unite thirteen independent sovereignties under one Government, so far as might be necessary for the purposes of union, without being sensible of the great importance which was attached to this article of the Constitution. The power of changing the relative situations of debtor and creditor, of interfering with contracts, a power which comes home to the business of every man, touches the interest of all classes, and controls the conduct of every individual in those things which he supposes proper for his own exclusive management, had been abused to such an excess by the State Legislatures as to break in upon the ordinary intercourse of society, and destroy all confidence between man and man. The mischief had become so great and so alarming, as not only to impede commercial intercourse and threaten the existence of public credit, but to injure the morals of the people, and destroy the sanctity of private faith. To guard against the recurrence of such evils was an object of deep interest with all the truly wise and virtuous men in the community, as well as in the Convention, and one of the most important benefits anticipated and realized from the reform of the Government.

The imposition of restraints on State legislation in regard to this delicate subject was thought necessary by all who took an honest, enlightened, and comprehensive view of the situation of the country, and the principle in question obtained an early admission into the various schemes of Government submitted to the Convention. In framing a national compact intended to be perpetual, the presumption is, that every important principle introduced into it was intended to be perpetual also; and, if expressed in terms which give it operation in all future time, the fair inference is, that it was intended so to operate. But, if the construction against which we have been contending be the true one, the Constitution will have imposed a restriction in words, which every State in the Union may elude at pleasure. The obligation of contracts in force at any given period is but of short duration, and if the inhibition be of retrospective laws only, a very short lapse of time would remove every subject on which the Act is forbidden by the Constitution to operate, and render this provision so far useless. Instead of introducing a great principle prohibiting all laws of this obnoxious character, the Constitution would only suspend their operation for a season, or only except preëxisting cases; an object which would hardly have been deemed of sufficient importance to have found a place in that instrument. Such a construction, moreover, would change the character of the provision, and convert an inhibition to pass laws impairing the obligation of contracts into an inhibition to pass retrospective laws. Had this been all that was intended by the Convention, it would probably have been expressed in those very words; the prohibition would have been against "*any retrospective law*," instead of the more general one against "any law impairing the obligation of contracts;" or, if the intention had been not to embrace all retrospective laws, but those only which related to contracts, the State Legislature would have been forbidden to pass "any retrospective law *impairing the obligation of contracts*," or "any law impairing the obligation of contracts *previously made*." For if the minds of the Convention, in framing this prohibition, had been directed not generally to the operation of laws upon the obligation of contracts, but particularly to their retrospective operation, it is scarcely conceivable, notwithstanding the imperfection of human language, that some words would not have been used to indicate that idea, and limit their intention. In instruments prepared on great consideration, and especially in those granting political power, general terms, comprehending a whole subject, are seldom employed to designate a particular or minute portion of it. The general language of this clause is such as might be suggested by a general intent to prohibit State legislation on the subject to which that language is applied — the obligation of contracts—not such as would be suggested by a particular intent to prohibit retrospective legislation. Besides, the laws which had effected all the mischief the Constitution intended to prevent, were prospective, as well as retrospective in their operation. They embraced future contracts as well as those previously made; from this circumstance, therefore, there is less reason for imputing to the Convention an intention not manifested by their language, and adopt a construction which would confine a restriction designed to guard against those mischiefs in future, to retrospective legislation.

Notwithstanding all this, the decision of the majority of the Supreme Court, in the case which gave rise to this discussion, was, as we have mentioned, in favor of the validity of a discharge under a State insolvent law, where the contract was made *between citizens of the State under the insolvent system of which the discharge had been obtained, and in whose Courts it had been pleaded.* But upon the question whether a discharge of a debtor, under a State insolvent law, would be valid against a creditor or citizen of another State, who had never voluntarily subjected himself to the State authority, otherwise than by the origin of his contract, one of the judges in the majority agreed with those in the minority on the former question, that the discharge was not available in an action brought by a citizen of another State, either in the Courts of the United States, or of any other State than that in which the discharge was obtained. So that the decision in favor of State insolvent laws impairing the obligation of *subsequent* contracts, is restricted to cases in which the contract was made within the State, and between citizens of the same State, or aliens, but is sought to be enforced in the Courts of that State in which the law was passed.[1]

[1] That a State law may be retrospective in its character, and devest private rights, without violating the Federal Constitution, unless it also impairs the obligation of contracts, was affirmed, more recently, by the Supreme Court of the United States, in a case brought up on appeal from the highest Court of Massachusetts. The Legislature of that State had granted to Harvard College the liberty and power of disposing of a ferry from Charlestown to Boston, and of receiving a rent for it. Afterward the Legislature incorporated a company to erect a bridge over Charles River, at the place where the ferry had been established, the company paying annually to the college a certain sum of money. The charter gave the company the right to take tolls for forty years, and afterward extended it to seventy. Before the forty years expired, the Legislature authorized the erection of another bridge, so near the first as injuriously to affect its tolls. The proprietors of the first bridge applied to the Massachusetts Court to restrain by injunction the construction of the second bridge; but the Court dismissed the bill, and the case was carried by appeal to the Supreme Court of the United States, on the ground that the first charter was a contract, and the grant of the second a violation of it. The decree of the Massachusetts Court was *affirmed;* and in giving its opinion, the Supreme Court observed, that "a uniform course of action, involving the right to the exercise of an important power by the State Government for half a century, and this almost without question, was not satisfactory evidence that the power was rightfully exercised." *Vide* 11 *Peters's Rep*. 257. On the other hand, an Act of the Legislature of Vermont, releasing the body of a debtor from imprisonment, and directing that the bond he had given for the prison-liberties should be discharged, was held to be void. 1 *Chip.* 257. See also 2 *Stew.* 30; 3 *Ibid.* 387; *Ibid.* 199; 2 *Fairf.* 118; 7 *Gill & Johns.* 7; 2 *Pennsyl.* 184; 1 *Rawle*, 181, 190; 1 *Monr.* 5; 1 *Blackf.* 220; 2 *Yerg.* 534; 7 *Johns. Rep.* 477; 17 *Ibid.* 195; 20 *Ibid.* 269; 1 *Wend.* 53; 13 *Ibid.* 325; 5 *Cowen*, 538; 7 *Ibid.* 349, 585; 4 *Wheat.* 659, 694; 6 *Ibid.* 593; 12 *Pick.* 184; 8 *Mass.* 468; 9 *Ibid.* 151, 360; 12 *Ibid.* 443; 15 *Ibid.* 197; 4 *Ham.* 457; 5 *Greenl.* 342;

If any part of a State law is unconstitutional, such part may, as we have seen, be disregarded, while full effect is given to the rest. The present Constitution did not commence its operation until the first Wednesday in March, 1789, and the prohibition against laws impairing the obligation of contracts, does not extend to a State law enacted before that day, and operating upon rights previously vested.

II. The other limitations on the State powers are those in which the prohibition is *qualified*, and restrict a State, *without the consent of Congress*, from laying "any imposts or duties on imports or exports, except what may be absolutely necessary" for executing its inspection laws; from laying any duty on tonnage; keeping troops or ships of war in time of peace; entering into any agreement or compact with another State, or with a foreign power, or from engaging in war, unless actually invaded, or in such imminent danger of invasion as will not admit of delay.

1st. The restraint on the power of the States as to imports and exports is enforced by all the arguments which prove the necessity of submitting the regulation of commerce to the General Government. From the vast inequality between the different States as to commercial advantages, few subjects were viewed with deeper interest, or excited greater irritation, than the manner in which the several States exercised, or seemed under the Confederation disposed to exercise, the power of laying duties on imports. From motives which were thought sufficient by the Convention, the general power of taxation, indispensably necessary as it was, and

Walk. 328; *Litt.* 326; 3 *Peters*, 280; 6 *Serg. & Rawle*, 322; 2 *Whart.* 395; 1 *Monr.* 24.

jealous as the States were of any encroachments upon it, was so far abridged as to forbid their touching imports or exports, with the single exception specified in the Constitution; and they were thus restrained from a general conviction that the interest of all would be promoted by placing the whole subject under the exclusive control of Congress.

In considering the power of Congress to regulate commerce, I referred to a decision of the Supreme Court, declaring unconstitutional an Act of a State Legislature requiring importers of foreign goods, and the vendors of the same at wholesale, to obtain a license from the State, and pay a sum of money for the same to the State Treasury.[1] This Act was also declared to be repugnant to the prohibition of the States from laying duties on exports and imports without the consent of Congress. An impost or duty on imports is a custom or tax levied upon articles brought into the country for sale or use; and is most usually secured before the importer is allowed to exercise his right of ownership over them, because evasions of the revenue laws can be prevented more certainly by executing them while the articles are in the custody of the Government. It would not, however, be less an impost on the articles if it were levied on them after they were landed. The policy, and consequent practice of levying or securing the duty before or on entering the port, does not limit the exercise of the power to that period; and, consequently, the prohibition on the States is not limited to that state of circumstances, unless the true meaning of the clause so confines it. If we resort

[1] 12 *Wheat.* 419.

either to technical authority or to common usage for the meaning of the term "imports," we find it signifies "the things imported," or the articles themselves, which are brought into the country. It is not in its literal sense confined to a duty levied while the article is entering the country, but extends to a tax levied after it has actually entered it. Again, if we look to the objects of the prohibition, we find that there is no difference, in effect, between the power to prohibit the sale of an article and a power to prohibit its introduction. The one is a necessary consequence of the other. No goods would be imported if none could be sold; nor can any object of any description be accomplished with equal certainty by laying a duty on the thing imported in the hands of the importer; and it is obvious that the same power which imposes a light duty might impose one amounting to a prohibition. The prohibition on the States to lay a duty on imports may, indeed, come in conflict with their acknowledged power to tax persons and property within their jurisdiction; and although this power, and the restriction of it, are easily distinguishable when they do not approach each other, yet they may approach so nearly as to perplex us in marking the distinction between them. The distinction, nevertheless, exists, and must be defined as the cases in which it exists arise. It was deemed sufficient, in the case referred to, to say generally, that when the importer has so dealt with the thing imported that it has become incorporated and mixed up with the mass of property in the country, it has, perhaps, lost its distinctive character as an import, and become subject to the taxing power of the State; but while it continues the property of the importer, and remains in his warehouse in the original form or package in which it was imported, a tax upon it is too plainly a duty on imports to escape this prohibition of the Constitution.

The general power of taxation is retained by the States, without being abridged by the grant of a similar power to the Government of the Union, and is to be concurrently exercised by both Governments, under their respective Constitutions; but, from the paramount authority of the General Government, the States are restrained, without any express prohibition, from any exercise of their taxing power, which, in its nature, is incompatible with, or repugnant to, the constitutional laws of the Union. As they have no power, by taxation or otherwise, to retard, impede, burden, or in any manner to control the operation of constitutional laws enacted by Congress to carry into execution any of the powers vested in the Federal Government, they cannot tax certificates issued by it for money borrowed on the credit of the United States,[1] nor the stock of a bank chartered by Congress; the latter is an instrument, and the former are incidents of a power essential to the fiscal operations of the Union.[2]

2d. The other *qualified* prohibitions have their origin in the same general policy which *absolutely* forbids any State from entering into any treaty, alliance, or confederation, and from granting letters of marque and reprisal; and they are supported by the same reasoning which establishes the propriety of confiding every thing relative to the power of declaring war to the exclusive direction and control of the General Government. Treaties of alliance, for purposes of peace or war, of

[1] 2 *Peters*, 449. [2] 4 *Wheat.* 316; 9 *Ibid.* 738.

external political dependence, or general commercial privileges; treaties of confederation for mutual government, political coöperation, or the exercise of political sovereignty, or for conferring internal political jurisdiction, are *absolutely* prohibited to the States. But compacts and agreements, which apply to the mere private rights of sovereignty, such as questions of boundary between a State and a foreign province, or another State; interests in land situate within their respective boundaries, and other internal regulations for the mutual accommodation of States bordering on each other, may be entered into by the respective States, *with the consent of Congress*. A total interdiction of such agreements or contracts might have been attended with permanent inconvenience, or public injury to the States; and the consent of Congress to their being entered into is required to guard against every infringement of the national rights, which might be involved in them. Hence it is that the rule of decision adopted by the Courts of the United States in questions that arise under a compact between States, is of an international character; and is not, as we have seen, to be collected from the decisions of the Courts of either State.[1]

As the maintenance of an army and navy by a State in time of peace might produce jealousies and alarm in neighboring States, and in foreign nations bordering on its territory, the States are prohibited from such establishments, unless with the consent of the General Government. But as a State may be so situated in time of war as to render a military force necessary to

[1] 11 *Peters*, 22. See also 8 *Wheat.* 1; 1 *Peters*, 457, 465; 4 *Bibb*, 54; 1 *Litt.* 367; 1 *Yeates*, 513; 3 *Ibid.* 440, 448; 2 *Pennsyl.* 49; *Cooke*, 130, 149; 1 *Overt*, 243.

resist an invasion, of which the danger may be too imminent to admit of delay in organizing it, the States have a right to raise troops, and fit out fleets for its own safety in time of war, without obtaining the consent of Congress.

Besides the express restrictions upon the powers of the several States, there are others arising by necessary implication from the supremacy of the Federal Government within the sphere of its proper jurisdiction, and which, from its paramount authority, restrain the State Governments: —

1. Where an exclusive power is expressly granted to Congress, there the State power ceases to operate, as in the grant of exclusive legislation over places ceded for forts and arsenals.[1]

2. Where there is a direct incompatibility in the exercise of a power by the States, which has been granted to the United States; as in the power to establish an uniform rule of naturalization, and the exercise of admiralty and maritime jurisdiction.[2]

3. Where the law of a State attempts to impede or control the lawful institutions or measures of the General Government; as to interfere with the judgments, process, or proceedings of the Courts or officers of the United States.[3]

In all these cases, the powers of the National Government are, as we have seen, exclusive, and the laws of the States conflicting with them, are absolutely void. But, as we have also seen: —

[1] 2 *Mason*, 69; 5 *Ibid.* 356; 5 *Wheat.* 317.

[2] 1 *Wheat.* 304; 2 *Ibid.* 269; 5 *Ibid.* 49.

[3] 2 *Cranch*, 397; 5 *Ibid.* 117; 7 *Ibid.* 279; 4 *Wheat.* 316; 6 *Ibid.* 598; 2 *Peters*, 449.

4. Where a power is granted to Congress, not in its nature exclusive, and a law passed in virtue of such power, comes in direct and manifest collision with a State law,—the former being paramount,—the latter must yield so far, and so far only, as the incompatibility extends; as in the cases of bankrupt laws, tax laws, and others in which, under the proper heads, it has been shown that the powers of the two Governments are concurrent, and the State law binding in the absence of any incompatible law of Congress.

The powers granted to Congress then are not exclusive of similar powers existing in the States, unless where the Constitution has in express terms given exclusive power to Congress, or the exercise is prohibited to the States, or there is a direct repugnancy or incompatibility in the exercise of it by the States.[1] An example of the first class we have found in the exclusive legislation of Congress, over places purchased by consent of a State Legislature for forts, arsenals, &c. Of the second class, besides the examples already adduced, is the prohibition of a State to coin money, or emit bills of credit; of the third, is the power of Congress to establish a uniform rule of naturalization, and the delegation of admiralty and maritime jurisdiction to the General Government: in all other classes of cases the States retain concurrent jurisdiction with Congress. We have seen, also, that although a mere grant of power, in affirmative terms, to Congress does not *per se*, transfer an exclusive sovereignty over such subjects, unless it be incompatible with the existence of a like power in the States, yet when the Legis-

[1] 4 *Wheat.* 122; 5 *Ibid.* 1, 49; 4 *Cond.* 109.

lature of the Union has exercised its powers on the given subject, the State power over that subject, which had before been concurrent, becomes, by such exercise, prohibited. And we have previously seen that in construing the Constitution of the United States, in regard to the restrictions on the powers of the States, as well as to the grants of power to the Union, the Supreme Court has ever held that an exception of any particular case, presupposes that those which are not excepted are included, and has laid it down as a general rule that, where no exception is made in terms, none will be made by implication or construction.[1]

[1] 12 *Peters*, 657; 6 *Wheat.* 264; 9 *Ibid.* 206; 12 *Ibid.* 419. See also Lecture VIII.

LECTURE XII.

ON THE PROVISIONS CONTAINED IN THE CONSTITUTION FOR GIVING EFFICACY TO THE FEDERAL POWERS.

The sixth, and last class of powers enumerated in the Constitution, consists of certain provisions by which efficiency is given to the rest. The first of these is the power "*to make all laws necessary and proper for carrying the foregoing powers into execution.*"[1]

I. It was remarked by the authors of "The Federalist," that "without the *substance* of this power, the whole Constitution would be a dead letter;" and, as few parts of that instrument had been assailed with more intemperance, they justly inferred that "it was the *form* only of the provision that was objected to, and they accordingly proceeded to consider" whether a better one could have been substituted. "There were four other methods," they observe, "which the Convention might have pursued; they might have copied the article of the Confederation which prohibited the exercise of any power not *expressly* delegated; they might have attempted a *positive* enumeration of the powers comprehended under the general terms *necessary and proper;* they might have attempted a *negative* enumeration of them, by specifying the powers ex-

[1] Const. U. S., Art. I. Sect. VIII. to XVIII.

cepted from the general definition; or they might have been altogether silent on the subject, and left these necessary and proper powers to construction and inference."[1]

Had the first method been adopted, it is evident that the new Congress, like their predecessors, would have been continually exposed to the alternative, either of construing the term "expressly" with so much rigor as to disarm the Government of all real authority, or with so much latitude as altogether to destroy the force of the restriction. It would be easy to show, were it necessary, that no important power delegated by the Articles of Confederation was or could have been executed by Congress, without recurring, more or less, to the doctrine of construction or implication. As the powers delegated under the new system were more extensive, the Government, which was to administer it, would have found itself still more frequently driven to the dilemma of doing nothing, or violating the Constitution, by exercising powers indispensably *necessary*, but not *expressly* granted.

Had the Convention made a *positive* enumeration of the powers necessary and proper for carrying the other powers into effect, it would have involved a complete digest of laws on every subject to which the Constitution relates; accommodated, too, not only to the existing state of things, but to all possible changes which futurity might produce. Had they attempted to enumerate the particular powers or means *not* necessary or proper for carrying the general powers into execution, the undertaking would have been no less chimerical,

[1] No. 144, by Mr. Hamilton.

and would, moreover, have been liable to this further objection, that every defect in the enumeration would have been equivalent to a positive grant of authority. If, to avoid this consequence, they had attempted a partial enumeration of exceptions, and described the residue by the general terms "necessary and proper," the enumeration must have comprehended only a few of the excepted cases, and those the least likely to be assumed or tolerated; because the enumeration would, of course, have selected such as would have been least necessary and proper, and therefore the unnecessary and improper powers included in the remainder would be less *forcibly* assumed than if no particular enumeration had been made.

Had the Constitution been silent on this subject, there can be no doubt that all the particular powers requisite, as means of executing the general powers, would have resulted to the Government by unavoidable implication. No axiom is more clearly established in law or reason, than that, wherever an end is required, the means are authorized; wherever a general power to do a thing is given, every particular power necessary for doing it is included. Had this last method, therefore, been pursued, every objection urged against this part of the Constitution would have remained, in all its plausibility, and the real inconvenience felt of not removing a pretext which might be used on critical occasions for drawing in question the essential powers of the Union. But, with the view of quieting the excessive jealousy which had been excited by this provision, an amendment of the Constitution was adopted, which, omitting the word "expressly" in the Articles of Confederation, simply declares that the powers "not delegated to the United States, nor prohibited to the States, are reserved to the States or to the People;" thus leaving the question, whether the particular power, which may become the subject of controversy, has been delegated to the one Government or the other, to depend upon a fair construction of the whole instrument.

The first occasion which called for an interpretation of this part of the Constitution, arose during the first Congress assembled under its authority. Alexander Hamilton, at that time Secretary of the Treasury, had recommended the institution of a National Bank, as of primary importance to the prosperous administration of the finances, and of the greatest utility in the operations connected with the support of public credit. The bill introduced into the House of Representatives for that purpose, was opposed, as unconstitutional. It was contended that the Federal Government was limited to the exercise of its enumerated powers, and that the power to incorporate a Bank was not one of them; that if such power was vested in the Government, that it must be an implied power, and that the power given to Congress to pass all laws necessary and proper to execute the specified powers, must be limited to means necessary to the end, and incident to the nature of the specified power. On the other side, it was urged that incidental as well as express powers necessarily belong to every Government; and that when a power was delegated to effect particular objects, all the known and usual means of effecting them followed, as incidental to it; and it was on this ground insisted that a Bank was a known and usual instrument which several of the enumerated powers of the Government required for their due execution.

After the bill had passed both Houses of Congress, the question touching its conformity to the Constitution was agitated with equal ability and ardor in the Executive cabinet. Mr. Jefferson, the Secretary of State, and Mr. Edmund Randolph, the Attorney-General, conceived that Congress had transcended its powers; but the Secretary of the Treasury maintained the opposite opinion, and was supported by General Knox, the Secretary at War. It was argued against the validity of the Act, that "the power to incorporate a Bank was not among the enumerated powers; and to take a single step beyond the boundaries specially drawn around the powers of Congress, would be to take possession of an undefined and undefinable field of power; that, though Congress were authorized to make all laws necessary and proper for carrying into execution the enumerated powers, they were confined to those means which were necessary, and not merely convenient. It meant those means without which the grant of the power would be nugatory; and if such a latitude of construction were allowed as to give to Congress any implied powers on the ground of convenience, it would swallow up all the enumerated powers, and reduce the whole list to one phrase."

To this it was replied, that "every power vested in a Government was, in its nature, sovereign, and gave a right to employ all the means fairly applicable to the attainment of the end of the power, and not specially precluded by specified exceptions, nor contrary to the essential ends of political society; and though the Government of the United States was one of limited and specified powers, it was sovereign with regard to its proper objects and declared purposes and trusts;

that it was incident to sovereign power to erect corporations, and, consequently, it was incident to the Government of the United States to erect one in relation to the objects intrusted to its management; that implied powers are as completely delegated as those which are expressed, and the power of erecting a corporation may as well be implied as any other instrument or means of carrying into execution any of the specified powers; that the exercise of the power in that case had a natural relation to the lawful ends of the Government, and it was incident to the sovereign power to regulate the currency, and to employ all the means which apply with the best advantage to that regulation; that the word *necessary* in the Constitution ought not to be confined to those means without which the grant of the power would be nugatory; that it often means no more than *needful*, *requisite*, *useful*, or *conducive to;* and that this was the sense in which the word was used in the Constitution. The relation between the measure and the end was the criterion of constitutionality, and not whether there was a greater or less degree of necessity or utility. The infinite variety, extent, and complexity of national exigencies, necessarily required great latitude of discretion in the selection and application of means; and the authority intrusted to Government ought and must be exercised on principles of liberal construction."

General Washington gave to these arguments a deliberate and profound consideration, which terminated in his conviction that the incorporation of a Bank was a measure authorized by the Constitution. The bill for that purpose accordingly received his approval and became a law.

The same question came before the Supreme Court of the United States, in 1819, in reference to the then existing Bank, which had been incorporated in 1816, and upon which the State of Maryland had subsequently imposed a tax; and although the question had twice been settled, so far as a Legislative Act could settle it, yet it was thought worthy of a renewed discussion in the Judicial department. The Chief Justice,[1] however, observed "that it could hardly be considered an open one, after the principle had been so early introduced and recognized by many successive Legislatures, and had acted upon the Judiciary as a law of undoubted obligation." He nevertheless admitted that it belonged to the Supreme Court alone to make a final decision, and that the question involved a consideration of the Constitution in its most interesting and vital parts.

It was, moreover, admitted that "the Government of the United States was one of enumerated powers; but, though limited in its powers, it was *supreme* within its sphere of action." There was nothing, however, in the Constitution which excluded incidental or implied powers. The Articles of Confederation, indeed, gave nothing to the United States but what was expressly granted; but the amendment to the new Constitution had dropped the word "expressly," and left the question whether a particular power was granted to depend, as we have seen, on a fair construction of the whole instrument. "No Constitution," he continued, "can contain an accurate detail of all the subdivisions of its powers, and of all the means by which they may be

[1] Marshall.

carried into execution. Its nature required that only the great outlines should be marked, and its important objects designated, and all the minor ingredients left to be deduced from the nature of those objects. The sword and the purse, all the external relations, and no inconsiderable portion of the industry of the nation, were intrusted to the General Government; and a Government intrusted with such ample powers, on the due execution of which the happiness and prosperity of the nation vitally depend, must also be intrusted with ample means for their execution; and unless the words imperiously require it, we ought not to adopt a construction which would impute to the framers of the Constitution, when granting great powers for the public good, the intention of impeding their exercise by withholding a choice of means."

"The powers given to the Government," he said, "imply the ordinary means of execution; and the Government, in all sound reasoning and fair interpretation, must have the choice of the means which it deems the most convenient and appropriate to the execution of the power. The power of creating a corporation, though appertaining to sovereignty, was held not to be a great substantive and independent power, but merely a means by which other objects are accomplished; in like manner as no seminary of learning is instituted in order to be incorporated, but the corporate charter is conferred to subserve the purposes of education. The power of creating a corporation, indeed, was never used for its own sake, but always for the purpose of effecting something else. It was nothing, therefore, but the ordinary means of attaining some public and useful end. But the Constitution had not left the right of Congress to employ the necessary means for the execution of its powers to general reasoning; it was expressly authorized to employ such means; and '*necessary means*,' in the sense of the Constitution, did not import an absolute physical necessity so strong that one thing could not exist without the other, but the term signified any means calculated to produce the end."

"The word *necessary*," it was observed, "admitted of all degrees of comparison. A thing might be *necessary*, or *very* necessary, or *absolutely and indispensably* necessary; to no mind would the same idea be conveyed by these several phrases;" and the remark was well illustrated by a reference to that article of the Constitution which prohibits a State from laying "imposts or duties on imports or exports, except what may be *absolutely necessary* for carrying into execution its inspection laws." It is impossible to compare this clause with that under consideration, without feeling a conviction that the Convention understood itself to change materially the meaning of the word "necessary," by prefixing to it the word "absolutely" in the one case, and to qualify its signification by dropping it in the other.

The word "necessary," then, like many others, is used in various senses; and in fixing its construction, the intention, the subject, the context, are all to be taken into view. The powers of the General Government were given for the welfare of the nation; they were intended to endure for ages, and to be adapted to the various exigencies of human affairs. To have prescribed the specific means by which the Government should, in all future time, execute its powers, would have changed entirely the character of the Constitution, and given it the properties of a legal code. It would have been an unwise attempt to provide by immutable rules for cases which, if foreseen at all, must have been perceived indistinctly, and which could have been better provided for as they occurred. To have declared that the best means should not be used, but those only without which the power given would be nugatory, would have deprived Congress of the capacity to avail itself of experience, or to exercise its reason and accommodate its legislation to circumstances.

If the end be legitimate, and within the scope of the Constitution, all means which are appropriate and plainly adapted to those ends, and which are not prohibited, are lawful; and a corporation was considered as a means not less usual, nor of higher dignity, nor more requiring a particular specification, than other means. A National Bank was deemed a convenient, useful, and essential instrument in the prosecution of the fiscal operations of the Government. It was clearly an appropriate measure; and while the Court declared it to be within its power, and its duty to maintain that an Act of Congress exceeding its constitutional power of legislation was not the law of the land, yet, if a law was not prohibited by the Constitution, and was really calculated to effect an object intrusted to the Government, it did not pretend to the power to inquire into the degree of its necessity, as that would be passing the line which circumscribes the Judicial power, and treading on Legislative ground.

The Court, therefore, decided that the law creating the Bank was made in pursuance of the Constitution, and that the branches of the National Bank, proceeding from the same stock, and conducing to the complete accomplishment of its objects, were equally consistent with the Constitution.[1] It was afterward led, in some degree, to review this decision, and, in a subsequent case, admitted that Congress could not create a corporation for its own sake or for private purposes.[2] It was observed on this occasion, that the opinion in the former case was founded on and sustained by the idea that the Bank was an instrument which was "necessary and proper for carrying into effect the powers" vested in the Government. It was created for national purposes only, though it was undoubtedly capable of transacting private as well as public business; and while it was the great instrument by which the fiscal operations of the Government were effected, it was also engaged in trading with individuals for its own advantage. It could not, on any rational calculation, effect its object unless it were endowed with the faculty of dealing in money, which, indeed, was necessary to render the Bank competent to fulfil the purposes of the Government, and was, therefore, constitutionally and rightfully ingrafted on the institution.

The Acts of Congress[3] giving to the United States a priority in the payment of debts over other creditors, are held, as we have seen, to be constitutional and valid, as founded on this authority of Congress to make all laws necessary and proper to carry into effect the powers vested by the Constitution in the General Government. That Government is to pay the debts of the Union; and is authorized to use the means most eligible to effect that object. If this claim of priority

1 4 *Wheat.* 316. 2 9 *Ibid.* 860.

3 Passed August 4, 1790, May 2, 1792, March 3, 1797.

interferes with the right of a State respecting the dignity of debts, and defeats the measures it would otherwise be entitled to adopt to secure them, it is a necessary consequence of the supremacy of the laws of the Union on all subjects to which the Legislative power of Congress extends.[1] From the construction given by the Supreme Court to the fifth section of the Act of 1797, the following points are clearly established, viz:—

1. That no lien is created by the statute.

2. That the priority established can never attach while the debtor continues the owner, and in possession of the property, although he may be unable to pay his debts.

3. That no evidence can be received of the insolvency of the debtor until he has been divested of the property in one of the modes stated in the section.

4. Whenever the debtor is thus divested of his property, the person who becomes invested with the title is thereby made a trustee for the United States, and is bound to pay their debt first, out of the proceeds of the bankrupt's or insolvent's property.

The priority of the United States attaches as well with respect to debts owing, but not yet payable, as to those already payable, where death or insolvency takes place. This construction is consistent with the language and reason of the Act, and required by the public policy which led to its passage.[2]

The right of priority of payment of debts due to the Government, is a prerogative of the British Crown, well known to the Common Law. It is founded, not

[1] 2 *Cranch*, 358; 1 *Cond.* 420.

[2] 6 *Peters*, 29.

so much upon any personal advantage to the Sovereign, as upon motives of public policy, in order to secure an adequate revenue to sustain the public burdens, and discharge the public debts. The claim of the United States, however, does not stand upon any sovereign prerogative, but is exclusively founded upon their own statutes. The same policy which governed in the case of the royal prerogative may, nevertheless, be clearly traced in these statutes; and as that policy has mainly reference to the public good, there is no reason for giving them a strict and narrow interpretation. Like all other statutes of this nature, they should receive a fair and liberal construction, according to the just import of the terms.

II. The next provision for giving effect to the powers of the Federal Constitution is that requiring *the Senators and Representatives in Congress, and the members of the State Legislatures, and all Executive and Judicial officers, both of the United States and of the several States, to be bound by oath or affirmation to support the Constitution of the United States.*

The election of the President and Senate depends, in all cases, on the Legislatures of the several States; and the election of members of the House of Representatives depended in the first instance, and still, in fact, depends on the same authority, and will probably always be conducted by the officers, and according to the laws of the States. In order, therefore, to insure the stability, and, as far as possible, the perpetuity of the Federal Government, it was necessary to provide a sanction similar to that relied on for the continuance of the State Governments, and to obtain, by an appeal to the consciences of individuals, an equal security in both cases. This dependence on the action of the State Governments for the organization of the Executive and Legislative branches of the National Government, and especially for the appointment of electors of President and Vice-President, and the election of Senators, has been used as an argument in support of the right of a State, in virtue of its sovereign power, *to secede from the Union.* But were it even true that the Legislative powers of the Union would be suspended if all the States, or a majority of them, were to refuse to elect Senators, yet, if any one State should refuse, Congress would not, on that account, be the less capable of performing all its functions. The same reasoning would apply to any number of States less than a majority of the whole; and the argument founded on this delinquency proves rather the subordination of the parts to the whole than the complete independence of any one of them. The framers of the Constitution were unable to make any provision which should protect it against a general combination of the States or of the People for its destruction, and, conscious of this inability, they did not make the attempt. But they were able to provide against the operation of measures adopted in any one State, the tendency of which might be to arrest the execution of the laws of the Union; and this they have done.

To this it may be added, that they provided against a dissolution of the Union, and against any direct or indirect attempts on the part of a State to withdraw from the Union, not only by this provision requiring all officers, civil and military, of the State Governments to take an oath to support the Federal Constitution, but by creating distinct Executive and Judicial departments, and by adopting various other provisions, operating immediately and individually upon the People of the several States. Thus the Constitution exacts no pledge from *the States* to maintain its inviolability, but makes its preservation depend on *individual* obligation and duty. It permits no man to sit in the Legislature of a State who is not first sworn to support the Constitution of the United States. From the obligation of this oath no State power can discharge them. All the members of all the State Legislatures are as religiously bound to support the Federal Constitution as they are to support their own State Constitution, and as solemnly sworn to do so as the members of Congress. No member of a State Legislature can refuse to proceed at the appointed time to elect Senators in Congress, or to provide for the choice of Electors of President and Vice-President, any more than the members of the Senate of the United States can refuse, when the appointed time arrives, to meet the members of the other House to witness the counting of the votes given by the Electors for those officers, and ascertain who are chosen. In either case, the duty binds with equal strength the conscience of the individual, and is imposed on every member by an oath in the same words. It cannot, therefore, be a matter of discretion with the States whether they will continue the Government or break it up, by refusing to elect Senators and appoint Electors. Nor can the members of their Legislatures neglect or evade those duties, when the times arrive for their performance, without such a violation of their oaths and duties as would destroy any other Government.

III. Among the provisions for giving efficacy to the

Federal *Legislative* powers may be included those specially vested in the *Executive* and *Judicial* departments, and especially the provision extending the jurisdiction of the Federal Courts to all cases arising under the Constitution of the United States. But these powers have already been subjected to particular examination in our review of the structure and organization of the Government, and do not, perhaps, require any further elucidation. It may, however, be as well here to observe, that the provision last specified in effect creates in the Supreme Court of the United States a COMMON ARBITER in all cases of collision between the power and authority of the Union and of the several States. Such collisions, we have seen, have already taken place, in times, too, of no extraordinary commotion, and have hitherto been happily adjusted. "But a Constitution," said its great Judicial oracle,[1] "is framed for ages to come, and designed to approach immortality as nearly as human institutions can attain to it. Its course cannot always be tranquil; experience as well as reason teaches us that it is exposed to storms and tempests." The same lesson had been taught to its framers under the Confederation, and had confirmed the suggestions of their own experience, and induced them to devise a new form of Government for themselves and their posterity. They accordingly provided it, as far as its nature would permit, with the means of self-preservation from the perils it was destined to encounter. They well understood that no Government should be so defective in its organization as not to contain within itself the means of securing the execution of its own laws

[1] Chief Justice Marshall.

against other dangers than those of ordinary occurrence. They were aware that courts of justice were the means most usually employed; and under the full pressure of the evils which had arisen from the want of such a power under the Confederation, they created in the new system a distinct and independent Judicial department; they conferred on it the power of construing the Constitution and laws of the Union, in the last resort, in all cases, and of preserving them from all violation from any quarter, so far as Judicial decisions could preserve them; and they conferred on the Chief Executive Magistrate the powers necessary to carry into effect the judgments and decrees of the Courts, either directly in the Constitution itself, or indirectly, by vesting in the Legislative department authority to do so.

IV. The next provision for giving effect to the powers of the General Government is the declaration that the "*Constitution, and the laws of the United States which shall be made in pursuance thereof, and all treaties made, or which shall be made, under the authority of the United States, shall be the supreme law of the land; and the judges in every State shall be bound thereby, any thing in the Constitution and laws of any State to the contrary notwithstanding.*"[1]

Without this provision, the Constitution would have been evidently and radically defective. To be fully sensible of this, we need only suppose, with the authors of "The Federalist,"[2] that the supremacy of the State Constitutions had been left complete by a saving clause in their favor. In the first place, as those Constitutions invested the State Legislatures with absolute

[1] Const. U. S., Art. VI. Sect. II.

[2] No. 44.

sovereignty in all cases, not excepted by the Articles of Confederation, all the authorities contained in the present Constitution, so far as they exceed those enumerated in the Confederation, would have been annulled, and the new Congress would have been reduced to the same impotent condition as their predecessors, which it was the avowed and leading design of the Convention in this particular to amend. In the next place, as the Constitutions of some of the States did not expressly and fully recognize the powers even of the former Confederacy, an express saving of such Constitutions would in those States have brought in question every power contained in the new Federal Constitution. In the third place, as the Constitutions of the States differ much from each other, it might have happened that a treaty, or national law of great importance to the States, would interfere with some, and not with others, of the State Constitutions, and would, consequently, have been valid in some States, and not in others. In the last place, there would have been exhibited a system (such as some modern theorists and political visionaries have conceived the Federal Constitution to be) founded on an inversion of the fundamental principles of all Government, in which the authority of the whole society would be subordinate to that of the parts, the head under the direction of each of the members.

But the provision in question marks the characteristic distinctions between the Government of the Union and the Governments of the States; and when the Constitution or laws of a State have been deemed repugnant to, or incompatible with, the Federal Constitution, with laws made in pursuance of it, or with treaties negotiated under its authority, the validity of the former has been inquired into and decided upon in a variety of cases; and in every instance where the repugnance existed, such State Constitutions or laws, or such parts of them as were incompatible with the former, have been, as we have seen, judicially abrogated and annulled. In the important case of the Bank of the United States, referred to in the last Lecture,[1] it was declared that the law of Maryland imposing a tax on the Bank was unconstitutional and void, on the ground that the State Governments have no right to tax any of the constitutional means employed by the Government of the Union to execute its constitutional powers; nor, by taxation or otherwise, to retard, impede, burden, or in any manner control the operation of constitutional laws enacted by Congress, to carry into effect the powers vested in the National Government.

It was contended, on that occasion, on behalf of the State authority, that the powers of the General Government were delegated by the State Governments, and that the Federal authority must be exercised in subordination to the States, who alone possessed supreme dominion. But the impossibility of sustaining such a proposition was fully and clearly demonstrated. It was admitted, indeed, that the Convention that framed the Constitution was elected by the State Legislatures; but that instrument, when it came from the hands of the Convention, was a mere proposal, without actual obligation, or any pretension to it. It was reported to the then existing Congress, to "be submitted to a Convention of delegates to be chosen in each State by the

[1] 4 *Wheat.* 316.

People thereof, under the recommendation of its Legislature, for their assent and ratification." This mode of proceeding was adopted, and the proposed Constitution was accordingly submitted to the People, who acted upon it in the only manner in which they can act effectually and wisely on such subjects, by assembling in Conventions. They assembled *in their respective States*, not merely from convenience, but from necessity. There existed no authority under the Confederation, as now exists under the Constitution, for calling a General Convention; and if such authority had existed, that mode would not have been the proper one, in a case where the People were, in effect, to pass upon virtual amendments and partial abrogations of their State Constitutions. They assembled and acted, therefore, in their several States, the People of each State thus exercising a separate and independent voice in the adoption of the Federal Constitution. But the measure they adopted did not on that account cease to be the act of the People themselves, or become the measure of the State Governments.

From these State Conventions, then, the Constitution of the United States owes its whole authority. The instrument submitted to them purports on the face of it to proceed from "the People of the *United States*," to be "ordained and established" in their name; and is declared to be thus ordained and established "in order to form a more perfect union, to establish justice, insure domestic tranquillity, and secure the blessings of liberty to them and their posterity." Now, if the People of the United States had never before acquired a common character, they assumed it then. The preamble to the Federal Constitution, containing these declarations, is an essential and necessary part of that instrument; and it not only enumerates the objects for which it was formed, but designates the parties by whom, and by whose authority alone, it was "ordained and established." The assent of the States in their sovereign capacities is implied, if not expressed, in calling their Conventions, and thus submitting the new scheme of Government to the People. But the People of each State were at perfect liberty to accept or reject it, and their act was final. The Constitution required not the affirmance of the State Governments, nor could it be negatived by their act; but, when ratified by the People, it became of perfect obligation, and bound the States.

It has, to be sure, been said that the People had already surrendered all their powers to the State Governments, and had nothing more to give. But the question whether the People may resume and modify the powers granted by them to the State or General Governments for their own benefit, does not, surely, remain to be settled in this country. The same sovereign powers which had separately established the State Governments, united with each other in forming a paramount sovereignty, and establishing a Supreme Government. For this purpose each yielded a portion of its individual sovereignty, and modified its State Constitution, by rendering it subordinate to the Federal power. Their authority to do this cannot for a moment be seriously doubted. Much more, indeed, might the legitimacy of the Federal Government have been questioned, had it been erected by the States to operate upon the individual citizens of the several States. The powers delegated to the State Governments were to be exercised by themselves, not by a distinct and independent sovereignty erected by them. To the formation of a league such as the Confederation, the State Governments were certainly competent. But when, "in order to form *a more perfect union*," and change that league into an effective Government, clothed with high sovereign powers for national objects, and acting directly on the People as individuals, the necessity of referring it to the People themselves, and deriving its powers immediately from them, was universally felt and acknowledged; and the Article of the Constitution which provides, as one of the modes for its amendment, *a Convention of the People of the United States*, is conclusive as to the real character of the instrument, and the sense in which it must have been understood.

The Government of the Union, then, is emphatically and truly a Government of *the People*. In form and substance, it emanates from them; its powers are granted by them, and are to be exercised directly on them as individuals, and for their common benefit; and can be abrogated only by their consent. This Government, however, is acknowledged by all to be a Government of enumerated powers. The principle that it can only exercise the powers granted to it is admitted on all hands; but questions respecting the extent of the powers actually granted to it are, as we have seen, perpetually arising, and will probably continue to arise, as long as the system shall exist. In discussing these questions, the conflicting powers of the General and State Governments must be brought into view; and the supremacy of their respective laws, when in opposition to each other, must be settled by that power in the Federal Constitution which was created, among other purposes, for this one expressly. Though limited in its powers, it would seem to result necessarily, from the nature of the General Government, that it should be supreme within its sphere of action. It is the Government of all; its powers are delegated by all; it represents all; and it acts for all, and upon all. Though any one State may be willing to control its operations, no other State is willing that other States should control them. The *Nation*, on those subjects upon which it can act at all, must necessarily bind its component parts. But the question is not left to mere reason, the People have in express terms decided it, by adopting the clause now under discussion, in conjunction with that requiring the oath to support the Federal Constitution to be taken by every State, as well as Federal officer. And yet we have witnessed an attempt on the part of one of the States, not merely to assert and vindicate its own supremacy, in cases of collision with the authority of the Union, and to reject the control and jurisdiction of the SUPREME ARBITER on all constitutional questions, but by its own act to repudiate and *nullify* an Act of Congress, which it took upon itself to pronounce to be contrary to the Constitution, and insisted that its decision was final. This monstrous claim it is even pretended to reconcile with the doctrines of the Federal Constitution itself, founding it principally on the amendment which declares that "the powers not delegated to the United States, nor prohibited to the States, are reserved to the States respectively, or to the People," and thereby assuming that the power exercised by Congress in passing the law in question was not delegated to the General Government, and that the power claimed by the State was not prohibited to it by the Federal Constitution, which were no other than the very points in controversy.

It was, moreover, asserted that any State had the right to arrest the execution of an Act of Congress, until three fourths of the States should approve it; and, in the mean time, to resist all attempts to enforce it. The equally untenable position was also contended for, that a State, at its pleasure, had a right to secede peaceably, and separate permanently from the Union, without necessarily producing a revolution in the Government. And these extravagant claims were sought to be justified by the doctrines put forth in the celebrated Virginia Resolutions of 1798,[1] and especially by some expressions in those of Kentucky in 1799—erroneously, as it seems, attributed to Mr. Jefferson.

These Resolutions, as is well known, were called forth by the enactment of the Alien and Sedition Laws by Congress; and it is equally well known that Mr. Madison, although not then a member of the Virginia Legislature, was the author not only of the Resolutions of 1798, but of the Report by which they were introduced. Upon being appealed to, upon the occasion now in question, by several of his correspondents, he vindicated those documents from the construction given to them in favor of *nullification*, and referred to a letter of Mr. Jefferson's to prove the Resolutions of the Legislature of Kentucky, in which that word occurs,

1 These famous Resolutions were reported by *John Taylor, of Caroline*; but Mr. Madison was always reputed to be their author; and in a letter to Mr. James Robertson, written in March, 1831, he distinctly avows the authorship, both of the Resolutions and the Report. See "Select Correspondence of Mr. Madison."

were not drawn up by him, although that gentleman was the author of those adopted by it the year previous, "which do not," however, as he says, "contain this, or any equivalent word."[1]

From a "Memorandum on Nullification," written by the survivor of those venerable and illustrious statesmen, in the eighty-sixth and last year of his life, thus proving at once, both his solicitude upon the subject and the undiminished vigor of his mind in treating it, Mr. Madison observes that "although the Legislature of Virginia, at a late session, declared almost unanimously,[2] that South Carolina was not supported in her doctrine of nullification by the Resolutions of 1798, it appears that those Resolutions are still appealed to as expressly or constructively favoring the doctrine. And what," he asks, "is the text in the proceedings of Virginia which this spurious doctrine of nullification claims for its patronage?" "It is found," he adds, "in the third of the Resolutions of 1798.[3] Now, is there

[1] In a letter of May 31, 1830, to J. C. Cabell, Mr. Madison vindicates both Mr. Jefferson and Mr. Monroe from any participation in the Kentucky Resolutions of 1799, and refers to a letter to W. C. Nicholas, in the 3d vol. of Mr. Jefferson's Correspondence, page 429, to prove it.

[2] Alluding to the Resolutions to that effect, passed by the Legislature, in 1835.

[3] The third of these Resolutions is as follows: "That this Assembly doth explicitly and peremptorily declare, that it views the powers of the Federal Government as resulting from the compact, to which the States are parties, as limited by the plain sense of the instrument constituting that compact; and that in case of a deliberate, palpable, and dangerous exercise of other powers not granted by the said compact, the States who are the parties thereto, have the right, and are in duty bound to interpose for arresting the progress of the evil, and

anything here," he demands, "from which a *single* State can infer a right to arrest or annul an act of the General Government, which it may deem unconstitutional? So far from it," he declares, "that the obvious and proper inference precludes such a right. In a word," he adds, "the nullifying claims, if reduced to practice, instead of being the conservative principle of the Constitution, would necessarily, and it may be said, obviously, be a deadly poison."

"The true question, therefore," as he concludes, "is whether there be a *Constitutional* right in a single State to nullify a law of the United States?" He then proceeds to remark on "the absurdity of such a claim, in its naked suicidal form, and "turns to it as modified by South Carolina, into a right in every State to resist within itself the execution of a Federal law, deemed by it to be unconstitutional, and to demand a Convention of the States, to decide the question of constitutionality, the annulment of the law to continue in the mean time, and to be permanent, unless three fourths of the States concur in overruling the annulment."

"Thus," he continues, "during the temporary nullification of the law, the results would be the same as those proceeding from an unqualified nullification, and the result of a Convention might be that seven out of twenty-four States might make the temporary results permanent.

"It follows, that any State which could obtain the concurrence of six others, might abrogate any law of the United States whatever, and give to the Constitu-

for maintaining within their respective limits the authorities, rights, and liberties appertaining to them."

tion, constructively, any shape they pleased, in opposition to the construction and will of the other seventeen.[1] Every feature of the Constitution might thus be successively changed; and after a scene of unexampled confusion and distraction, what had been unanimously agreed to as a whole, would not, as a whole, be agreed to by any single party."

But these heresies were promptly met and ably refuted by the proclamation issued on the occasion by the President of the United States.[2] This admirable document, which confers more durable and honorable fame on the name of General Jackson than even the victory of New Orleans, exhibits the true doctrines of the Constitution in strict conformity with those principles of construction which I have endeavored to explain and enforce. In language becoming the dignity and responsibility of his station, the Chief Magistrate of the Union reminds the individuals concerned in these proceedings of their paramount obligations as citizens of the United States, and warns them of the treasonable tendency of their acts; and upon his subsequent reference of the subject to the National Legislature, he recommended the adoption of such measures as were necessary to enforce the laws of the Union, and suppress the opposition to their execution, devised by evil councils and authorized in an evil hour, by the State of South Carolina. The Act required was passed;

[1] This was written when the number of States was twenty-four. Their number being now thirty-one, the corresponding proportions would be eight to twenty-three, to produce the same results.

[2] This celebrated state paper is well known to have been the production of the late Edward Livingston, then Secretary of State. *Vide* Appendix E.

and thus has every department of the Government concurred in the declaration approved and sanctioned by a vast majority of the People, that the Government of the United States is *supreme* within its limited jurisdiction, and that its laws in pursuance of the Constitution form the *supreme law* of the land, "anything in the Constitution and laws of any State to the contrary notwithstanding;" and that the existence and effect of a collision between them must be decided by the general head, and not by any of the members of the Union.

V. The last provision contained in the Constitution for giving efficacy to its powers is that by which effect and operation were given to the system by declaring that "*the ratifications of the conventions of nine States should be sufficient for its establishment between the States so ratifying the same.*"[1]

The express authority of the People alone could give validity to the Constitution; and to have required the unanimous ratification of the People of the several States would have subjected the essential interests of the whole to the caprice or corruption of the smallest majority in any one State. But a question of a very delicate nature arose with respect to this article when the Constitution was proposed for adoption — a question similar in its character to the one which has just been discussed. It was asked by the objectors to the Federal system, upon what principle it was that the Confederation, which stood in the solemn form of a compact between the States, could be superseded without *unanimous consent;* and it was thereupon suggested

1 Const. U. S., Art. VII.

by Mr. Madison, in one of the numbers of "The Federalist,"[1] that an answer might be found without searching beyond the principles of the former compact itself. It had been noted among its defects, that in many of the States it had received no higher sanction than a mere Legislative ratification. The principle of reciprocity, therefore, seemed to require that its obligation on the other States in which it had been ratified by the People in their Conventions should be reduced to the same standard. A compact between independent sovereigns, founded, as was the Confederation, upon acts of Legislative authority, could pretend to no higher validity than a league or treaty between the parties; and it is the established doctrine that all the articles of a treaty are mutual conditions; a breach of any one article is a breach of the whole; and a breach committed by any of the parties absolves the others, and authorizes them, if they choose, to pronounce the compact violated, and at an end.

Had it been necessary to appeal to these principles as a justification for dispensing with the consent of particular States to a dissolution of the compact then existing, it would by no means have been difficult to confront the objecting parties with multiplied and important infractions of the Articles of Confederation. But a more direct answer was given to them by recurring to the absolute necessity of the case, to the great principle of self-preservation, to the transcendent law of God and nature, which declares the safety and happiness of society to be the objects which all political institutions should aim to accomplish, and for which

[1] No. 43.

they may all be sacrificed; and from what is known of the state of public affairs at that portentous crisis, we cannot doubt that this answer was felt to be conclusive.

It is, however, well worthy of observation, that it was not pretended on this occasion that any of the States could withdraw even from the Confederation, considered merely as a treaty of alliance, at its mere will and pleasure; nor absolve itself at its own discretion from its perpetual obligation, except in cases of the extreme urgency of self-preservation, or of the breach or violation of the compact by some other of the parties, of which the several parties, from the very nature of the Confederation, as a treaty between independent sovereigns, were themselves the judges. It has, nevertheless, been contended, as we have already had occasion to lament, that a State has a right, under the present Constitution, independently of the natural right of self-preservation, and resistance to intolerable oppression, to secede, at its own will and discretion, from the Union. But if the Federal Constitution be a Government owing protection to individuals and entitled to their obedience, whether formed by the People of the United States in the aggregate, or by the same People as citizens of the respective States, no State authority can dissolve the relations subsisting between that Government and the individuals subjected, in either mode, to its authority. From the very nature of those relations, nothing can dissolve them but REVOLUTION; and there can, therefore, be no such thing as *secession* without *revolution.* The Constitution establishes a union between the *People* of the several States, intended to be *perpetual.* It contains numerous provisions founded on that supposition, and among them, one for its own amendment; none for its abandonment. It declares that new States may be admitted into the Union, but not that old States may withdraw from it. The Union is not, like the Confederation, reducible even to a perpetual alliance between the States, much less to a temporary one; but it is an association of the People of the several States in one mass, under a permanent and paramount constitution of Government, operating upon them as individuals, created and assented to by that power in each State which alone had authority to abrogate its particular Constitution, or so far to modify it as to surrender powers to the General Government which had previously been delegated to the State Governments. *No State, therefore, can undo what the People have done*, nor absolve its citizens from their obligations to obey the laws of the Union. It cannot divest them of their paramount rights as citizens of the United States; nor can the members of the State Legislatures renounce their own oaths to support the Federal Constitution as the supreme law of the land; neither can any Convention of the People of any State, any more than the People themselves, collectively or individually, dispense with their obligations, or dissolve their allegiance to the United States, unless they respectively possess the constitutional power of settling for themselves the construction of this supreme law in all doubtful cases.

The practical result of this great question turns, then, on this single point. It has not as yet been seriously pretended that each individual may judge for himself, and determine in his own case, the nature and extent of his obligations as a member of the Union. But if the State within whose local jurisdiction he may happen to reside, may judge for him, or for itself, in a case of an alleged violation of the Federal Constitution, and finally decide and execute their respective decisions by their own powers, the inference follows that, being *sovereign*, there is no power to control the decision of the State, and its own judgment on its own contract must be conclusive. But this doctrine is founded in mere theory and assumption; and is refuted, not only by plain and express constitutional provisions, but by the very nature of the compact. It has been shown most conclusively, in the legislative halls,[1] as well as in the judicial tribunals of the Union, that the Government of the United States possesses, in its appropriate departments, the authority of final decision on all these questions of power, both by *necessary implication* and *express grant*.

If the Constitution be, indeed, a Government existing over all the States, operating upon individuals, and not a mere treaty of alliance, it must, upon general principles, possess the authority in question, as it is, in fact, an authority naturally belonging to all *Governments*. And although the Constitution establishes a Government of limited powers, yet, as it extends equally over all the States, it follows, independently of the express declaration to that effect, that to the extent of those powers it must necessarily be supreme; while, from the nature of the powers granted, that Government must be *National* in its character, as well as *Federal* in its principles of organization. The inference, then, appears to be irresistible, that the Govern-

1 *Vide* the speeches of Mr. Webster on this subject in the Senate of the United States.

ment, thus created by the whole, for the whole, and extending over the whole, must possess an authority superior to that of the particular Governments of any of its parts. As the Government of the Union, it has a Legislative power of its own, and a Judicial power coextensive with the Legislative power. To hold, therefore, that these are not supreme, but subordinate in authority to the Legislative and Judicial powers of a State, is equally repugnant to common sense, to sound reasoning, and established principles. The Legislative, Executive, and Judicial departments of the Union must each necessarily judge of the extent of their own powers, as often as it is called on to exercise them; and that independently of State control, or they could not act at all. Without any express declaration, therefore, to that effect in the Constitution, the whole question is necessarily decided by those provisions which create a Legislative, an Executive, and a Judicial power; for if the powers exist in a Government intended for the Union, the inevitable consequence is, that the acts of the Federal Legislature and the decisions of the Federal Judiciary must be binding over the whole Union, and on each of its federative parts. From the nature of the case, then, and as an inference wholly unavoidable, the laws of Congress and the decisions of the Federal Courts must be of higher authority than those of the States.

But the Constitution, as we have already seen, has not left this point without full and explicit provision. For if the express grant to Congress of distinct and substantive power to make all laws necessary and proper for carrying into execution all other powers vested in the Government of the United States, mean anything, it means that Congress may determine what is necessary and proper for that purpose; and if Congress may judge of what is requisite for the execution of those powers, it must of necessity judge of their extent, as well as interpret them. With regard to the Judicial power, the Constitution is still more explicit and emphatic. If any case arise depending on the construction of the Federal Constitution, the Judicial power of the Union, we have seen, extends to it, in whatsoever Court it may originate. Of all such cases the Supreme Court of the Union has appellate jurisdiction, and its judgments are final and conclusive. Nothing more effectual could have been done for subjecting all constitutional questions, whenever and wherever they may arise, to the ultimate decision of the Supreme Court than has actually been accomplished by this salutary provision of the Constitution. Congress was saved by it from the necessity of any supervision of the State laws; and while the whole sphere of State legislation was thus left untouched, an adequate security was obtained against any infringement of the constitutional power of the General Government.

It is clear, then, that the Constitution, by express grant, as well as by necessary implication, has rendered the Government of the United States, in its several departments, the judge of its own powers; and that the Supreme Court, in order to preserve uniformity in the interpretation and administration of the laws of the Union, must be the ultimate tribunal to decide in the last resort upon them, in all cases of a constitutional nature which arise in a suit at law or equity, either in the Federal or State Courts. The early legislation of Congress, the Judiciary Act of 1789, and the whole course of Judicial decisions since that period, concur in proving that there is, in fact and in truth, *a supreme law*, and a final interpreter of the Constitution, created by the Constitution itself, to the exclusion of the authority and jurisdiction of the several States. A State, therefore, having no power to interpret the Constitution finally for itself, cannot secede from the Union without adopting a proceeding essentially *revolutionary* in its character; and every attempt by a State to abrogate or *nullify* a law of Congress is not only a usurpation of the powers of the National Government, but of the rights of the other States; for if the States, as such, have equal rights in matters concerning the whole, then for one State to set up its judgment against that of the others, and to insist on executing its own judgment by force, is a manifest usurpation upon the rights of all the rest; and if that be revolutionary which arrests the Legislative, Executive, and Judicial powers of the General Government in their course, dispenses with existing oaths, dissolves the obligations of allegiance to the supreme authority of the Union, and elevates another power in its place, then are *nullification* and secession, in character and principle, equally revolutionary.[1]

[1] In a letter to Mr. Edward Everett, written in August, 1830, and published shortly afterwards in the North American Review, Mr. Madison expresses his opinion on this subject as follows: —

"Between these different constitutional Governments, — the one operating on all the States, the others operating separately in each, with the aggregate powers of Government divided between them, it could not escape attention that controversies would arise concerning the boundaries of jurisdiction. That to have left a final decision, in such cases, to each of the States, could not fail to make the Constitution and laws of the United States different in different States, was

I have now completed the proposed examination of the *powers* vested in the General Government, as well as of its fundamental principles and *organization*. And I trust it has abundantly and satisfactorily appeared, 1. That all the powers requisite to secure the objects of National Union are vested in the Federal Government, while those only which are not essential to that object are reserved to the States, or to the People. 2. That this National Government, though limited in its powers to national objects, is *supreme* in the exercise of those powers, whether exclusive or concurrent, express or implied; and that, whenever any of these powers come into collision with the concurrent or independent powers of the States, the State authority, which is subordinate, must yield to that of the nation, which is supreme. 3. That this Constitution, the laws

obvious, and not less obvious that this diversity of independent decisions, must altogether distract the Government of the Union, and speedily put an end to the Union itself. To have made the decision under the authority of the individual States coördinate in all cases with decisions under the authority of the United States, would unavoidably produce collisions incompatible with the peace of society. To have referred every clashing decision under the two authorities, for a final decision, to the States as parties to the Constitution, would be attended with delays, with inconveniences, and expenses, amounting to a prohibition of the expedient. To have trusted to negotiation for adjustment of disputes between the Government of the United States and the State Governments, as between independent and separate sovereignties, would have lost sight altogether of a Constitution and Government of the Union, and opened a direct road, from a failure of that resort, to the *ultima ratio* between nations wholly independent of and alien to each other. Although the issue of negotiation might sometimes avoid this extremity, how often would it happen, among so many States, that an unaccommodating spirit in some would render that resource unavailing."

made in pursuance of it, and treaties made under the authority of the United States, whether before or after the adoption of the Federal Constitution, are the *supreme law of the land*, and that both from the nature of the case, and the provisions of the Constitution, the National Legislature must judge of and interpret the supreme law, as often as it exercises its Legislative functions; that the Chief Executive Magistrate of the Union, in like manner, possesses the right of judging of the nature and extent of his political authority; and that, in all cases assuming the character of a suit in law or equity, the supreme Judicial tribunal of the Union is the final interpreter of the Constitution. 4. That no State authority has power to dissolve the relations between the Government of the United States and the People of the several States, and that, consequently, no State has a right to secede from the Union, except under such circumstances as would justify a revolution; and that an attempt by any State to abrogate or annul an Act of the National Legislature is a direct usurpation of the powers of the General Government, an infringement of the rights of all the other States, and a violation of the paramount obligation of its members to support and obey the Federal Constitution.

In this exposition, it has, I trust, been rendered also manifest, that unless such were the nature and principles of that Constitution, it would never have accomplished, as it has most effectually and happily, the great ends for which it was ordained, nor delivered the People of this country from the evils they had experienced under the Confederation. I trust, too, that, in reviewing this system of Government in its practical operation and results, you will have perceived that we have abundant cause of gratitude to Heaven, not only for defending us from those former evils which must necessarily have increased under a mere alliance between the States, but for bestowing on us, in their stead, those blessings of liberty, law, order, peace, and prosperity, which, under Providence, the present Constitution has secured to the present generation and promises to posterity. And, finally, I trust, most confidently, that you will not hesitate to join with me in earnest and devout prayer to the Supreme Ruler of the Universe that our National Government, as established by this Constitution, and the happiness hitherto enjoyed under it, may stand as fast and endure as long as the vast continent over which it seems destined to extend its influence or its sway.

ALTHOUGH but one of the uses contemplated by the foregoing work is that of a text-book for Colleges, Academies, and other public schools, the following questions are appended the better to accommodate it to that purpose.

QUESTIONS ON THE FEDERAL CONSTITUTION.

INTRODUCTORY.

1. By what body, and by what authority, was the Constitution of the United States framed?

2. For what objects is it declared to be established?

3. To whose assent was it submitted, and by whom was it ratified?

4. Upon what fundamental principle is it grounded?

5. Among what *Departments* are the powers of government it grants distributed?

6. Upon what principle is the distribution made?

7. To what extent is the principle of *representation* applied, and in what manner modified or restricted?

8. Under what modifications does the Constitution adopt or recognize the English Common Law?

9. Whence are its principles immediately derived by the Constitution, and in what cases are they applicable under it?

10. What natural rights are secured by the Constitution to the citizens of the United States?

11. To what extent are those rights surrendered, and for what objects?

12. What are the civil rights and privileges secured by the Constitution to the People and the States in lieu of the security and advantages afforded by the Federal Government?

13. What character does the Constitution impart to the States, and what relation does it establish between them and the Federal Government?

14. What does it declare to be the *supreme law of the land?*

15. What are the principal points of view under which the Federal Constitution is to be considered?

1. WITH REGARD TO THE ORGANIZATION OF THE GOVERNMENT.

1. What is the first general point of view in which the Constitution is to be considered?

2. Among what separate *Departments* are the powers of the Federal Government distributed?

1st. *The Legislative Power.*

1. In whom is the Legislative Power vested?

2. Of what separate bodies does Congress consist?

3. Upon what principle or rule of representation, is each of them respectively founded?

4. At what times, and place, and how often is Congress required to assemble?

5. When and how may it adjourn?

6. For how long a time can one house adjourn without the other?

7. In cases of disagreement between them, by whom may they be adjourned?

8. When must Congress of necessity adjourn.

9. What peculiar benefit is secured by the Constitution in regard to the assembling and adjournment of Congress?

10. Of whom are the members of the House of representatives composed?

11. What qualifications are required in the electors of members of the House of Representatives?

12. What are the qualifications requisite in its members?

13. In what manner, and by what rule are Representatives apportioned among the States?

14. What is the provision in case the States neglect or refuse to pass laws for holding elections of Representatives?

15. What powers are separately vested in the House of Representatives?

16. How is the Senate organized?

17. Whom do the Senators represent?

18. Do they vote, by States or individually?

19. Into how many *classes* are the Senators divided, in what manner, and for what purpose?

20. What separate powers are vested in the Senate?

21. In what manner is the Court of Impeachment organized?

22. Of whom does it consist besides the Senators?

23. What is required of the members of the Court before proceeding to the trial of an Impeachment?

24. Who presides when the President of the United States is to be tried?

25. The concurrence of what proportion of the members of the Court is requisite to a conviction upon an impeachment?

2d. The Executive Power.

1. In whom is the Executive Power vested by the Constitution?

2. What are the qualifications required in the President?

3. By whom, and in what manner, is he chosen?

4. By whom, and in what manner, are the Electors chosen?

5. What qualifications are required in the Electors?

6. When and where are they directed to meet?

7. How are they to be organized, and proceed to vote?

8. How are vacancies in their number to be supplied?

9. What duties are they to perform after giving their votes?

10. When, where, and by whom is the general result to be declared?

11. What proportion of Electoral votes is necessary to a choice?

12. How and when is the election to be determined when no person has such majority?

13. In what manner are the votes of the Representatives taken in that case?

14. What number of Representatives, from what proportion of States, constitute a *quorum* for the purpose of such election?

15. In cases where no choice is made before the time to which the action of the House is limited, who is to act as President?

16. How is the Vice-President chosen?

17. How is he chosen in case of not receiving a majority of the Electoral votes?

18. What proportion of Senators constitute a *quorum* for the purpose?

19. What qualifications are required in the Vice-President?

20. What were the reasons for creating the office?

21. For what term are the President and Vice-President elected?

22. What is the effect of the law declaring the day on which that term shall commence?

23. In what cases, and for what period is the Vice-President to execute the office of President?

24. Enumerate the powers and duties of the President.

25. In what cases, and in what form, is the qualified negative of the President upon the Acts and Resolutions of Congress to be exercised?

26. What is its effect when interposed?

27. What proportion of each House is requisite to pass such Act or Resolution, notwithstanding the objections of the President?

28. What was the *primary* inducement for conferring this power upon the President?

29. What the *secondary*?

30. Whence the propriety of investing him with his military powers?

31. Why is he invested with the power of granting reprieves and pardons?

32. Under whose authority and direction are international affairs and negotiations with foreign powers conducted?

33. What number of the Senators is necessary to concur in advising and consenting to Treaties?

34. What number is required to advise and consent to nominations to office made by the President?

35. What duties are required of him in relation to Congress?

36. What powers and duties has he in relation to foreign ambassadors and other public ministers?

37. What in reference to officers of the United States?

38. What provision is made for executing the office of President, in cases of vacancies in the offices of both President and Vice-President?

3d. *The Judicial Power.*

1. How is the *Judicial Power* of the United States vested by the Constitution?

2. How are the Judges appointed?

3. Upon what *tenure* do they hold their offices?

4. What provision does the Constitution make for their support?

5. What precautions does it adopt to secure their responsibility?

6. To what cases does the Judicial Power of the United States extend?

7. Whence the propriety of vesting this jurisdiction in the Courts of the United States?

8. What was the design of the Constitution in separating the Judicial Power from the other Departments, and of the precautions for maintaining its independence?

9. Among what Courts has the Federal jurisdiction been distributed?

10. By what power was the SUPREME COURT created, and how is it organized?

11. From what authority is its organization derived?

12. In what cases has it *exclusive* jurisdiction?

13. In what cases has it *original*, but not *exclusive* jurisdiction?

14. In what cases has it *appellate* jurisdiction?

15. What authority has it over the subordinate Courts of the United States?

16. What *subordinate Courts* have been established by law?

17. In what manner are the CIRCUIT COURTS of the United States organized?

18. In what cases have they *original and exclusive* jurisdiction?

19. In what cases is their jurisdiction *concurrent*, and with what other Courts?

20. In what cases have they appellate jurisdiction?

21. How far, and in what sense, are they *Inferior* Courts?

22. From what power is the organization and authority of the DISTRICT COURTS derived?

23. How are they organized?

24. In what cases is their jurisdiction *original* and *exclusive*?

25. In what cases is it *concurrent*, and with what Courts?

26. What power has a District Judge in cases where parties have not reasonable time to apply to the Circuit Court?

27. By what authority were the COURTS OF THE TERRITORIES OF THE UNITED STATES created?

28. How are they organized in the respective *Territories*?

29. What jurisdiction is vested in them respectively?

30. In what cases arising under the laws of the United States have the *State Courts and Magistrates* jurisdiction, vested in them by Congress?

II. POWERS VESTED IN THE FEDERAL GOVERNMENT, AND RESTRAINTS IMPOSED UPON THE STATES.

1. To what classes may the powers conferred on the Federal Government be reduced?

2. Enumerate the powers relating to.

1st. Security from foreign danger.

3. In whom is *The power of declaring war* vested by the Constitution?

4. Is this power *exclusive* or *concurrent?*

5. In whom is the power of agreeing to *truces* and treaties of peace vested by the Constitution?

6. What powers derived from, involved in, or subservient to that of declaring war, are vested in Congress?

7. Why is the power of *raising money by taxation or loans* included in this class?

8. How is this power limited?

9. What taxes are included under this general term?

10. What are *direct taxes?*

11. How do they operate and take effect?

12. How are direct taxes to be levied?

13. What is affected by *indirect taxes?*

14. How are they to be levied?

2d. Powers for regulating intercourse with foreign nations.

1. Enumerate the powers vested in the Federal Government for regulating foreign intercourse.

2. In whom are the powers *to make treaties*, and *to send and receive ambassadors and other public ministers*, vested?

3. What is the nature of a treaty?

4. When are treaties to be regarded by the Courts of Justice as equivalent to laws?

5. What is the effect of a treaty upon the Acts of Congress?

6. From what other power does that of sending and receiving ambassadors, and other public ministers, and consuls result as a necessary incident?

7. What other power does the latter include by implication?

8. Why is *the power to define and punish piracies and felonies committed on the high seas, and offences against the law of nations*, vested in Congress?

9. Define Piracy.

10. What does Felony, when committed on the high seas, in effect amount to?

11. Is this power *exclusively* vested in Congress?

12. What other offences besides piracy fall more immediately under the cognizance of the law of nations?

13. Why was the power *to regulate foreign commerce* submitted to the Federal Government?

14. What is its nature and extent?

15. What else does it comprehend?

16. What was temporarily excepted from its exercise?

17. When did that exception cease to operate?

3d. Powers for maintaining harmony among the States.

1. Besides the *particular restraints* upon the States, and certain powers vested in the Judiciary, enumerate the remaining powers comprehended under this head.

2. How far does the power to *regulate commerce among the States* extend?

3. What particular objects does it comprehend?

4. What interpretation has been given to the power with respect to *commerce with the Indian tribes?*

5. In what character and relation are they regarded by the Constitution and laws of the United States?

6. With what is the power *to establish Post-offices and Post-roads* necessarily connected?

7. Mention some of the benefits derived from it.

8. How far is it *exclusive?*

9. What implied powers have been exercised as incidental to it?

10. What rule has been laid down in relation to the exercise of incidental and implied powers?

11. What is the extent or limitations of the *powers to coin money, to regulate its value, and that of foreign coins?*

12. What is the extent or limitation of the power *to fix the standard of weights and measures?*

13. To what other powers is that of *providing for the punishment of counterfeiting the public securities, and current coin of the United States*, incidental?

14. How far is it *exclusive?*

15. What is the nature and advantage of the power *to prescribe by general laws the manner in which the public acts, records, and judicial proceedings of each State shall be proved, and the effect they shall have in other States?*

16. What faith and credit are those of each State entitled to in the Courts of the United States?

17. What effect have they as evidence in different cases?

18. Under what circumstances are they admitted as *primâ facie* evidence?

19. Under what circumstances, as *conclusive* evidence?

20. What is meant by *primâ facie* evidence?

21. What is the nature and extent of the power *to establish a uniform system of naturalization?*

22. To what rights are the citizens of each State entitled in all the others?

23. Upon what ground is the power of naturalization held to be *exclusive* in the Federal Government?

24. Who were entitled to the privileges of *citizens of the United States*, at the time of the Declaration of Independence?

25. What difference is there in the rules upon this subject in the United States and Great Britain?

26. What is the difference between the two Governments as to the doctrine of allegiance?

27. What is the term applied to persons born out of the United States?

28. What exceptions are they in the application of the term?

29. What is the existing law of the United States relative to naturalization?

30. What inducements have *aliens* coming to reside in this country to become citizens?

31. What reasons were they for investing Congress with the power *to establish uniform laws on the subject of bankruptcies?*

32. Define the term "bankruptcy."

33. How far is this power *exclusive?*

4th. Miscellaneous objects of general utility.

1. What is the object of the power *to promote the progress of science and the useful arts?*

2. What construction is given to the Constitution to effect that object?

3. What reasons were they for vesting in Congress *exclusive legislation over the seat of Government, forts, magazines, arsenals, dockyards, and other needful buildings of the United States?*

4. Where was the seat of the Federal Government established?

5. What extent of territory was granted for that purpose, and by which of the States?

6. In what body is the power of legislation over that *District* vested?

7. What cities are comprehended within it?

8. How are those cities organized and governed?

9. Upon what ground is the power *to declare the punishment of treason against the United States* vested in Congress?

10. In what does treason against the United States consist?

11. What testimony is requisite to a conviction of treason?

12. What restriction is there upon the power of Congress with respect to the punishment of treason?

13. What power has Congress as to *admitting new States into the Union*, and how is it restricted?

14. What new States have been admitted since the adoption of the Constitution?

15. Of what territory were they severally composed?

16. From what considerations was the power *to dispose of and make all needful regulations respecting the territory or other property belonging to the United States* vested in Congress?

17. How is this power restricted?

18. What do the United States *guarantee* to the several States?

19. What power or duties result from this provision?

20. In what cases may the power be exercised?

21. What power has Congress with respect to *amendments to the Constitution?*

22. In what modes may this power be exercised?

23. What are the restrictions upon this power?

24. What is the general character of the amendments proposed by some of the States as conditions of their accession to the Constitution?

25. Which of them only may be regarded as necessary?

26. What is the effect of these amendments, or of any of them?

27. What were their chief objects?

5th. Restrictions upon the States.

1. How may *the restrictions upon the powers of the several States* be distinguished by their character.

2. Specify those which are *absolute*, and the grounds and policy of each in succession.

3. In what manner are the other restrictions on the State powers *qualified?*

4. Enumerate them, with the grounds on which they respectively rest.

6th. Provisions for giving efficacy to the Federal powers.

1. What provisions are contained in the Constitution, *for giving efficacy to the Federal powers?*

2. Whence the necessity of vesting Congress with authority *to make all laws necessary and proper for carrying those powers into execution?*

3. What construction has been given to the terms "necessary and proper?"

4. Whence the necessity or propriety of requiring the Legislative, Executive, and Judicial officers, both of the United States, and of the several States *to be bound by oath to support the Constitution of the United States?*

5. What other provisions already considered may be included among those already specified upon this subject?

6. Whence the necessity and effect of declaring and specifying what shall be considered *the Supreme Law of the land,* and enumerating the persons *bound thereby?*

7. Why was the ratification of the Constitution by the People of the several States required?

8. In what manner was the Constitution adopted?

9. What number of States was required for carrying it into operation, and by how many was it ratified previously to its going into effect?

10. What were the reasons for requiring it so to be ratified, adopted, and carried into effect?

APPENDIX.

A, p. 11.

DECLARATION OF INDEPENDENCE.

In Congress, July 4, 1776.

WHEN, in the course of human events, it becomes necessary for one people to dissolve the political bands which have connected them with another, and to assume, among the powers of the earth, the separate and equal station to which the laws of nature and of nature's God entitle them, a decent respect to the opinions of mankind requires that they should declare the causes which impel them to the separation.

We hold these truths to be self-evident: that all men are created equal; that they are endowed by their Creator with certain unalienable rights; that among these are life, liberty, and the pursuit of happiness; that to secure these rights, governments are instituted among men, deriving their just powers from the consent of the governed; that whenever any form of government becomes destructive of these ends, it is the right of the people to alter or to abolish it, and to institute a new government, laying its foundation on such principles, and organizing its powers in such form, as to them shall seem most likely to effect their safety and happiness. Prudence, indeed, will dictate that governments long established should not be changed for light and transient causes; and, accordingly, all experience hath shown that mankind are more disposed to suffer, while evils are sufferable, than to right themselves by abolishing the forms to which they are accustomed. But when a long train of abuses and usurpations, pursuing invariably the same object, evinces a design to reduce them under absolute despotism, it is their right, it is their duty, to throw off such government, and to provide new guards for their future security. Such has been the patient sufferance of these colonies, and such is now the necessity which constrains them to alter their former systems of government. The history of the present King of Great Britain is a history of repeated injuries and usurpations, all having in direct object the establishment of an absolute tyranny over these States. To prove this, let facts be submitted to a candid world.

He has refused his assent to laws the most wholesome and necessary for the public good.

He has forbidden his governors to pass laws of immediate and pressing importance, unless suspended in their operation till his assent should be obtained; and when so suspended, he has utterly neglected to attend to them.

He has refused to pass other laws for the accommodation of large districts of people, unless those people would relinquish the right of representation in the Legislature; a right inestimable to them, and formidable to tyrants only.

He has called together legislative bodies at places unusual, uncomfortable, and distant from the depository of their public records, for the sole purpose of fatiguing them into compliance with his measures.

He has dissolved representative houses repeatedly, for opposing, with manly firmness, his invasions on the rights of the people.

He has refused for a long time, after such dissolutions, to cause others to be elected; whereby the legislative powers, incapable of annihilation, have returned to the people at large for their exercise; the state remaining, in the mean time, exposed to all the dangers of invasion from without, and convulsions within.

He has endeavored to prevent the population of these States; for that purpose obstructing the laws for naturalization of foreigners; refusing to pass others to encourage their migrations hither, and raising the conditions of new appropriations of lands.

He has obstructed the administration of justice, by refusing his assent to laws for establishing judiciary powers.

He has made judges dependent on his will alone for the tenure of their offices, and the amount and payment of their salaries.

He has erected a multitude of new offices, and sent hither swarms of officers, to harass our people and eat out their substance.

He has kept among us, in times of peace, standing armies, without the consent of our legislatures.

He has affected to render the military independent of, and superior to, the civil power.

He has combined with others to subject us to a jurisdiction foreign to our Constitution, and unacknowledged by our laws; giving his assent to their acts of pretended legislation:

For quartering large bodies of armed troops among us:

For protecting them, by a mock trial, from punishment for any murders which they should commit on the inhabitants of these States:

For cutting off our trade with all parts of the world:

For imposing taxes on us without our consent:

For depriving us, in many cases, of the benefits of trial by jury:

For transporting us beyond seas to be tried for pretended offences:

For abolishing the free system of English laws in a neighboring province, establishing therein an arbitrary government, and enlarging its boundaries, so as to render it at once an example and fit instrument for introducing the same absolute rule into these colonies:

For taking away our charters, abolishing our most valuable laws, and altering fundamentally the forms of our governments:

For suspending our own legislatures, and declaring themselves invested with power to legislate for us in all cases whatsoever.

He has abdicated government here, by declaring us out of his protection, and waging war against us.

He has plundered our seas, ravaged our coasts, burned our towns, and destroyed the lives of our people.

He is, at this time, transporting large armies of foreign mercenaries to complete the works of death, desolation, and tyranny, already begun with circumstances of cruelty and perfidy scarcely paralleled in the most barbarous ages, and totally unworthy the head of a civilized nation.

He has constrained our fellow-citizens, taken captive on the high seas, to bear arms against their country, to become the executioners of their friends and brethren, or to fall themselves by their hands.

He has excited domestic insurrections among us, and has endeavored to bring on the inhabitants of our frontiers the merciless Indian savages, whose known rule of warfare is an undistinguished destruction of all ages, sexes, and conditions.

In every stage of these oppressions, we have petitioned for redress in the most humble terms: our repeated petitions have been answered only by repeated injury. A prince whose character is thus marked by every act which may define a tyrant, is unfit to be the ruler of a free people.

Nor have we been wanting in attentions to our British brethren. We have warned them, from time to time, of attempts by their Legislature to extend an unwarrantable jurisdiction over us. We have reminded them of the circumstances of our emigration and settlement here. We have appealed to their native justice and magnanimity, and we have conjured them, by the ties of our common kindred, to disavow these usurpations, which would inevitably interrupt our connections and correspondence. They, too, have been deaf to the voice of justice and of consanguinity. We must, therefore, acquiesce in the necessity which denounces our separation, and hold them, as we hold the rest of mankind, enemies in war, in peace friends.

WE, therefore, the representatives of the United States of America, in General Congress assembled, appealing to the Supreme Judge of the world for the rectitude of our intentions, do, in the name, and by authority of the good people of these colonies, solemnly publish and declare, that these United Colonies are, and of right ought to be, FREE and INDEPENDENT STATES; that they are absolved from all allegiance to the British crown, and that all political connection between them and the State of Great Britain is, and ought to be, totally dissolved; and that, as free and independent States, they have full power to levy war, conclude peace, contract alliances, establish commerce, and to do all other acts and things which independent States may of right do. And for the support of this declaration, with a firm reliance on the protection of Divine Providence, we mutually pledge to each other our lives, our fortunes, and our sacred honor.

JOHN HANCOCK.

New Hampshire.	Josiah Bartlett, William Whipple, Matthew Thornton.
Massachusetts Bay.	Samuel Adams, John Adams, Robert Treat Paine, Elbridge Gerry.
Rhode Island, &c.	Stephen Hopkins, William Ellery.
Connecticut.	Roger Sherman, Samuel Huntington, William Williams, Oliver Wolcott.

New York.	William Floyd, Philip Livingston, Francis Lewis, Lewis Morris.
New Jersey.	Richard Stockton, John Witherspoon, Francis Hopkinson, John Hart, Abraham Clark.
Pennsylvania.	Robert Morris, Benjamin Rush, Benjamin Franklin, John Morton, George Clymer, James Smith, George Taylor, James Wilson, George Ross.
Delaware.	Cæsar Rodney, George Read, Thomas M'Kean.
Maryland.	Samuel Chase, William Paca, Thomas Stone, Charles Carroll, of Carrollton.
Virginia.	George Wythe, Richard Henry Lee, Thomas Jefferson, Benjamin Harrison, Thomas Nelson, Jun., Francis Lightfoot Lee, Carter Braxton.
North Carolina.	William Hooper, Joseph Hewes, John Penn.
South Carolina.	Edward Rutledge, Thomas Heyward, Jun., Thomas Lynch, Jun., Arthur Middleton.
Georgia.	Button Gwinnett, Lyman Hall, George Walton.

B, p. 13.

ARTICLES OF CONFEDERATION AND PERPETUAL UNION

Between the States of New Hampshire, Massachusetts Bay, Rhode Island and Providence Plantations, Connecticut, New York, New Jersey, Pennsylvania, Delaware, Maryland, Virginia, North Carolina, South Carolina, and Georgia.

In Congress, July 8, 1778.

Article I. The style of this Confederacy shall be, "*The United States of America.*"

Art. II. Each State retains its sovereignty, freedom, and independence, and every power, jurisdiction, and right which is not by this confederation expressly delegated to the United States in Congress assembled.

Art. III. The said States hereby severally enter into a firm league of friendship with each other, for their common defence, the security of their liberties, and their mutual and general welfare, binding themselves to assist each other against all force offered to, or attacks made upon them, or any of them, on account of religion, sovereignty, trade, or any other pretence whatever.

Art. IV. § 1. The better to secure and perpetuate mutual friendship and intercourse among the people of the different States in this Union, the free inhabitants of each of these States, paupers, vagabonds, and fugitives from justice excepted, shall be entitled to all privileges and immunities of free citizens in the several States; and the people of each State shall have free ingress and regress to and from any other State, and shall enjoy therein all the privileges of trade and commerce, subject to the same duties, impositions, and restrictions as the inhabitants thereof respectively; provided that such restrictions shall not extend so far as to prevent the removal of property imported into any State to any other State of which the owner is an inhabitant; provided, also, that no imposition, duties, or restriction shall be laid by any State on the property of the United States, or either of them.

§ 2. If any person guilty of or charged with treason, felony, or other high misdemeanor in any State, shall flee from justice, and be found in any of the United States, he shall, upon the demand of the Governor or Executive power of the State from which he fled, be delivered up and removed to the State having jurisdiction of his offence.

§ 3. Full faith and credit shall be given in each of these States to the records, acts, and Judicial proceedings of the courts and magistrates of every other State.

Art. V. § 1. For the more convenient management of the general interests of the United States, delegates shall be annually appointed, in such manner as the Legislature of each State shall direct, to meet in Congress on the first Monday in November in every year, with a power reserved to each State to recall its delegates, or any of them, at any time within the year, and to send others in their stead for the remainder of the year.

§ 2. No State shall be represented in Congress by less than two, nor by more than seven members; and no person shall be capable of being a delegate for more than three years, in any term of six years; nor shall any person, being a delegate, be capable of holding any office under the United States, for which he, or another for his benefit, receives any salary, fees, or emolument of any kind.

§ 3. Each State shall maintain its own delegates in a meeting of the States, and while they act as members of the committee of these States.

§ 4. In determining questions in the United States in Congress assembled, each State shall have one vote.

§ 5. Freedom of speech and debate in Congress shall not be impeached or questioned in any Court or place out of Congress, and the members of Congress shall be protected in their persons from arrests and imprisonments during the time of their going to and from, and attendance on Congress, except for treason, felony, or breach of the peace.

Art. VI. § 1. No State, without the consent of the United States in Congress assembled, shall send any embassy to or receive any embassy from, or enter into any conference, agreement, alliance, or treaty with any king, prince, or State, nor shall any person holding any office of profit or trust under the United States, or any of them, accept of any present, emolument, office, or title of any kind whatever, from any king, prince, or foreign State; nor shall the United States in Congress assembled, or any of them, grant any title of nobility.

§ 2. No two or more States shall enter into any treaty, confederation, or alliance whatever between them, without the consent of the United States in Congress assembled, specifying accurately the purposes for which the same is to be entered into, and how long it shall continue.

§ 3. No State shall lay any imposts or duties which may interfere with any stipulations in treaties, entered into by the United States in Congress assembled, with any king, prince, or State, in pursuance of any treaties already proposed by Congress to the courts of France and Spain.

§ 4. No vessels of war shall be kept up in time of peace by any State, except such number only as shall be deemed necessary by the United States, in Congress assembled, for the defence of such State, or its trade; nor shall any body of forces be kept up by any State in time of peace, except such number only as, in the judgment of the United States in Congress assembled, shall be deemed requisite to garrison the forts necessary for the defence of such State; but every State shall always keep up a well-regulated and disciplined militia, sufficiently armed and accoutred, and shall provide, and constantly have ready for use, in public stores, a due number of fieldpieces and tents, and a proper quantity of arms, ammunition, and camp equipage.

§ 5. No State shall engage in any war, without the consent of the United States in Congress assembled, unless such State be actually invaded by enemies, or shall have received certain advice of a resolution being formed by some nation of Indians to invade such State, and the danger is so imminent as not to admit of delay till the United States in Congress assembled can be consulted; nor shall any State grant commissions to any ships or vessels of war, nor letters of marque or reprisal, except it be after a declaration of war by the United States in Congress assembled; and then only against the kingdom or State, and the subjects thereof, against which war has been so declared, and under such regulations as shall be established by the United States in Congress assembled, unless such State be infested by pirates; in which case vessels of war may be fitted out for that occasion, and kept so long as the danger shall continue, or until the United States in Congress assembled shall determine otherwise.

Art. VII. When land-forces are raised by any State for the common defence, all officers of or under the rank of colonel shall be appointed by the Legislature of each State respectively by whom such forces shall be raised, or in such manner as such State shall direct, and all vacancies shall be filled up by the State which first made the appointment.

Art. VIII. All charges of war, and all other expenses that shall be incurred for the common defence or general welfare, and allowed by the United States in Congress assembled, shall be defrayed out of a common treasury, which shall be supplied by the several States, in proportion to the value of all land within each State, granted to or surveyed for any person, as such land, and the buildings and improvements thereon, shall be estimated, according to such mode as the United States in Congress assembled shall, from time to time, direct and appoint. The taxes for paying that proportion shall be laid and levied by the authority and direction of the Legislatures of the several States within the time agreed upon by the United States in Congress assembled.

Art. IX. § 1. The United States in Congress assembled shall have the sole and exclusive right and power of determining on peace and war, except in the cases mentioned in the sixth article; of sending and receiving ambassadors; entering into treaties and alliances, provided that no treaty of commerce shall be made whereby the Legislative power of the respective States shall be restrained from imposing such imposts and duties on foreigners as their own people are subjected to, or from prohibiting the exportation or importation of any species of goods or commodities whatsoever; of establishing rules for deciding in all cases what captures on land or water shall be legal, and in what manner prizes taken by land or naval forces in the service of the United States shall be divided or appropriated; of granting letters of marque and reprisal in times of peace; appointing courts for the trial of piracies and felonies committed on the high seas; and establishing courts for receiving and determining finally appeals in all cases of capture: provided that no member of Congress shall be appointed a judge of any of the said courts.

§ 2. The United States in Congress assembled shall also be the last resort on appeal in all disputes and differences now subsisting, or that hereafter may arise between two or more States concerning boundary, jurisdiction, or any other cause whatever; which authority shall always be exercised in the manner following: Whenever the Legislative or Executive authority, or lawful agent of any State in controversy with another, shall present a petition to Congress, stating the matter in question, and praying for a hearing, notice thereof shall be given by order of Congress to the Legislative or Executive authority of the other State in controversy, and a day assigned for the appearance of the parties by their lawful agents, who shall then be directed to appoint by joint consent commissioners or judges to constitute a Court for hearing and determining the matter in question; but if they cannot agree, Congress shall name three persons out of each of the United States, and from the list of such persons each party shall alternately strike out one, the petitioners beginning, until the number shall be reduced to thirteen; and from that number not less than seven, nor more than nine names, as Congress shall direct, shall, in the presence of Congress, be drawn out by lot; and the persons whose names shall be so drawn, or any five of them, shall be commissioners or judges, to hear and finally determine the controversy, so always as that a major part of the judges who shall hear the cause shall agree in the determination; and if either party shall neglect to attend at the day appointed, without showing reasons which Congress shall judge sufficient, or, being present, shall refuse to strike, the Congress shall proceed to nominate three persons out of each State, and the secretary of Congress shall strike in behalf of such party absent or refusing; and the judgment and sentence of the court, to be appointed in the manner before prescribed, shall be final and conclusive; and if any of the parties shall refuse to submit to the authority of such court, or to appear or defend their claim or cause, the court shall, nevertheless, proceed to pronounce sentence or judgment, which shall in like manner be final and decisive; the judgment or sentence and other proceedings being in either case transmitted to Congress, and lodged among the Acts of Congress, for the security of the parties concerned: provided that every commissioner, before he sits in judgment, shall take an oath, to be administered by one of the judges of the Supreme or Superior Court of the State where the cause shall be tried, "well and truly to hear and determine the matter in question, according to the best of his judgment, without favor, affection, or hope of reward." Provided, also, that no State shall be deprived of territory for the benefit of the United States.

§ 3. All controversies concerning the private right of soil claimed under different grants of two or more States, whose jurisdictions, as they may respect such lands, and the States which passed such grants, are adjusted, the said grants, or either of them, being, at the same time, claimed to have originated antecedent to such settlement of jurisdiction, shall, on the petition of either party to the Congress of the United States, be finally determined, as near as may be, in the same manner as is before prescribed for deciding disputes respecting territorial jurisdiction between different States.

§ 4. The United States in Congress assembled shall also have the sole and exclusive right and power of regulating the alloy and value of coin struck by their own authority, or by that of the respective States; fixing the standard of weights and measures throughout the United States; regulating the trade and managing all affairs with the Indians, not members of any of the States; provided that the Legislative right of any State within its own limits be not infringed or violated; establishing and regulating post-offices from one State to another, throughout all the United States, and exacting such postage on the papers passing through the same as may be requisite to defray the expenses of the said office; appointing all officers of the land-forces in the service of the United States, excepting regimental officers; appointing all the officers of the naval forces, and commissioning all officers whatever in the service of the United States; making rules for the government and regulation of the said land and naval forces, and directing their operations.

§ 5. The United States in Congress assembled shall have authority to appoint a committee, to sit in the recess of Congress, to be denominated *A Committee of the States*, and to consist of one delegate from each State; and to appoint such other committees and civil officers as may be necessary for managing the general affairs of the United States under their direction; to appoint one of their number to preside, provided that no person be allowed to serve in the office of President more than one year in any term of three years; to ascertain the necessary sums of money to be raised for the service of the United States, and to appropriate and apply the same for defraying the public expenses; to borrow money or emit bills on the credit of the United States, transmitting every half year to the respective States an account of the sums of money so borrowed or emitted; to build and equip a navy; to agree upon the number of land-forces, and to make requisitions from each State for its quota, in proportion to the number of white inhabitants in such State, which requisition shall be binding; and thereupon the Legislature of each State shall appoint the regimental officers, raise the men, and clothe, arm, and equip them in a soldierlike manner, at the expense of the United States; and the officers and men so clothed, armed, and equipped, shall march to the place appointed, and within the time agreed on by the United States in Congress assembled; but if the United States in Congress assembled shall, on consideration of circumstances, judge proper that any State should not raise men, or should raise a smaller number than its quota, and that any other State should raise a greater number of men than the quota thereof, such extra number shall be raised, officered, clothed, armed, and equipped in the same manner as the quota of such State, unless the Legislature of such State shall judge that such extra number cannot be safely spared out of the same, in which case they shall raise, officer, clothe, arm, and equip as many of such extra number as they judge can be safely spared; and the officers and men so clothed, armed, and equipped, shall march to the place appointed, and within the time agreed on by the United States in Congress assembled.

§ 6. The United States in Congress assembled shall never engage in a war, nor grant letters of marque and reprisal in time of peace, nor enter into any treaties or alliances, nor coin money, nor regulate the value thereof, nor ascertain the sums and expenses necessary for the defence and welfare of the United States, or any of them, nor emit bills, nor borrow money on the credit of the United States, nor appropriate money, nor agree upon the number of vessels of war to be built or purchased, or the number of land or sea forces to be raised, nor appoint a commander-in-chief of the army or navy, unless nine States assent to the same; nor shall a question on any other point, except for adjourning from day to day, be determined, unless by the votes of a majority of the United States in Congress assembled.

§ 7. The Congress of the United States shall have power to adjourn to any time within the year, and to any place within the United States, so that no period of adjournment be for a longer duration than the space of six months, and shall publish the journal of their proceedings monthly, except such parts thereof relating to treaties, alliances, or military operations, as in their judgment require secrecy; and the yeas and nays of the delegates of each State on any question shall be entered on the journal, when it is desired by any delegate; and the delegates of a State, or any of them, at his or their request, shall be furnished with a transcript of the said journal, except such parts as are above excepted, to lay before the Legislatures of the several States.

Art. X. The Committee of the States, or any nine of them, shall be authorized to execute, in the recess of Congress, such of the powers of Congress as the United States in Congress assembled, by the consent of nine States, shall from time to time think expedient to vest them with; provided that no power be delegated to the said committee, for the exercise of which, by the Articles of Confederation, the voice of nine States, in the Congress of the United States assembled, is requisite.

Art. XI. Canada, acceding to this Confederation, and joining in the measures of the United States, shall be admitted into, and entitled to all the advantages of this Union; but no other colony shall be admitted into the same, unless such admission be agreed to by nine States.

Art. XII. All bills of credit emitted, moneys borrowed, and debts contracted by, or under the authority of Congress, before the assembling of the United States, in pursuance of the present confederation, shall be deemed and considered as a charge against the United States, for payment and satisfaction whereof the said United States and the public faith are hereby solemnly pledged.

Art. XIII. Every State shall abide by the determinations of the United States in Congress assembled, on all questions which by this confederation are submitted to them. And the articles of this confederation shall be inviolably observed by every State, and the Union shall be perpetual; nor shall any alteration at any time hereafter be made in any of them, unless such alteration be agreed to in a Congress of the United States, and be afterward confirmed by the Legislatures of every State.

AND WHEREAS it hath pleased the great Governor of the world to incline the hearts of the Legislatures we respectively represent in Congress to approve of, and to authorize us to ratify the said Articles of Confederation and perpetual Union, KNOW YE, that we, the undersigned delegates, by virtue of the power and authority to us given for that purpose, do, by these presents, in the name and in behalf of our respective constituents, fully and entirely ratify and confirm each and every of the said Articles of Confederation and perpetual Union, and all and singular the matters and things therein contained. And we do further solemnly plight and engage the faith of our respective constituents, that they shall abide by the determinations of the United States in Congress assembled, on all questions which by the said Confederation are submitted to them; and that the articles thereof shall be inviolably observed by the States we respectively represent, and that the Union shall be perpetual. IN WITNESS whereof, we have hereunto set our hands in Congress.

Done at Philadelphia, in the State of Pennsylvania, the 9th day of July, in the year of our Lord 1778, and in the third year of the Independence of America.

New Hampshire.	Josiah Bartlett, John Wentworth, Jun.
Massachusetts Bay.	John Hancock, Samuel Adams, Elbridge Gerry, Francis Dana, James Lovell, Samuel Holten.

Rhode Island, &c.	William Ellery, Henry Marchant, John Collins.
Connecticut.	Roger Sherman, Samuel Huntington, Oliver Wolcott, Titus Hosmer, Andrew Adams.
New York.	James Duane, Francis Lewis, William Duer, Gouverneur Morris.
New Jersey.	John Witherspoon, Nathaniel Scudder.
Pennsylvania.	Robert Morris, Daniel Roberdeau, Jonathan Bayard Smith, William Clingan, Joseph Reed.
Delaware.	Thomas M'Kean, John Dickinson, Nicholas Vandyke.
Maryland.	John Hanson, Daniel Carrol.
Virginia.	Richard Henry Lee, John Banister, Thomas Adams, John Harvey, Francis Lightfoot Lee.
North Carolina.	John Penn, Cornelius Harnett, John Williams.
South Carolina.	Henry Laurens, William Henry Drayton, John Matthews, Richard Hutson, Thomas Heyward, Jun.
Georgia.	John Walton, Edward Telfair, Edward Longworthy.

C, p. 21.

CONSTITUTION OF THE UNITED STATES.

The Constitution framed for the United States of America, by a Convention of Deputies from the States of New Hampshire, Massachusetts, Connecticut, New York, New Jersey, Pennsylvania, Delaware, Maryland, Virginia, North Carolina, South Carolina, and Georgia, at a Session begun May 25, *and ended September* 17, 1787.

We, the people of the United States, in order to form a more perfect Union, establish justice, insure domestic tranquillity, provide for the common defence, promote the general welfare, and secure the blessings of liberty to ourselves and our posterity, do ordain and establish this Constitution for the United States of America.

ARTICLE I.

SECTION I.

All Legislative powers herein granted shall be vested in a Congress of the United States, which shall consist of a Senate and House of Representatives.

SECTION II.

1. The House of Representatives shall be composed of members chosen every second year, by the people of the several States; and the electors in each State shall have the qualifications requisite for electors of the most numerous branch of the State Legislature.

2. No person shall be a Representative who shall not have attained to the age of twenty-five years, and been seven years a citizen of the United States, and who shall not, when elected, be an inhabitant of that State in which he shall be chosen.

3. Representatives and direct taxes shall be apportioned among the several States which may be included within this Union, according to their respective numbers, which shall be determined by adding to the whole number of free persons, including those bound to service for a term of years, and ex-

cluding Indians not taxed, three fifths of all other persons. The actual enumeration shall be made within three years after the first meeting of the Congress of the United States; and, within every subsequent term of ten years, in such manner as they shall by law direct. The number of Representatives shall not exceed one for every thirty thousand; but each State shall have at least one Representative; and, until such enumeration shall be made, the State of New Hampshire shall be entitled to choose three; Massachusetts, eight; Rhode Island and Providence Plantations, one; Connecticut, five; New York, six; New Jersey, four; Pennsylvania, eight; Delaware, one; Maryland, six; Virginia, ten; North Carolina, five; South Carolina, five; and Georgia, three.

4. When vacancies happen in the representation from any State, the executive authority thereof shall issue writs of election to fill such vacancies.

5. The House of Representatives shall choose their speaker and other officers, and shall have the sole power of impeachment.

SECTION III.

1. The Senate of the United States shall be composed of two Senators from each State, chosen by the Legislature thereof, for six years; and each Senator shall have one vote.

2. Immediately after they shall be assembled, in consequence of the first election, they shall be divided, as equally as may be, into three classes. The seats of the Senators of the first class shall be vacated at the expiration of the second year; of the second class, at the expiration of the fourth year; and of the third class, at the expiration of the sixth year; so that one third may be chosen every second year. And if vacancies happen, by resignation or otherwise, during the recess of the Legislature of any State, the Executive thereof may make temporary appointments until the next meeting of the Legislature, which shall then fill such vacancies.

3. No person shall be a Senator who shall not have attained

to the age of thirty years, and been nine years a citizen of the United States, and who shall not, when elected, be an inhabitant of that State for which he shall be chosen.

4. The Vice-President of the United States shall be President of the Senate, but shall have no vote unless they be equally divided.

5. The Senate shall choose their other officers, and also a President *pro-tempore* in the absence of the Vice-President, or when he shall exercise the office of President of the United States.

6. The Senate shall have the sole power to try all impeachments. When sitting for that purpose, they shall be on oath or affirmation. When the President of the United States is tried, the Chief Justice shall preside; and no person shall be convicted without the concurrence of two thirds of the members present.

7. Judgment, in cases of impeachment, shall not extend further than to removal from office, and disqualification to hold and enjoy any office of honor, trust, or profit under the United States. But the party convicted shall, nevertheless, be liable and subject to indictment, trial, judgment, and punishment, according to law.

SECTION IV.

1. The times, places, and manner of holding elections for Senators and Representatives shall be prescribed in each State by the Legislature thereof; but the Congress may, at any time, by law, make or alter such regulations, except as to the places of choosing Senators.

2. The Congress shall assemble at least once in every year; and such meeting shall be on the first Monday in December, unless they shall, by law, appoint a different day.

SECTION V.

1. Each House shall be the judge of the elections, returns, and qualifications of its own members; and a majority of each

shall constitute a quorum to do business; but a smaller number may adjourn from day to day, and may be authorized to compel the attendance of absent members, in such manner and under such penalties as each House may provide.

2. Each House may determine the rules of its proceedings; punish its members for disorderly behaviour; and, with the concurrence of two thirds, expel a member.

3. Each House shall keep a journal of its proceedings, and from time to time publish the same, excepting such parts as may in their judgment require secrecy; and the yeas and nays of the members of either House on any question shall, at the desire of one fifth of those present, be entered on the journal.

4. Neither House, during the session of Congress, shall, without the consent of the other, adjourn for more than three days, nor to any other place than that in which the two Houses shall be sitting.

SECTION VI.

1. The Senators and Representatives shall receive a compensation for their services, to be ascertained by law, and paid out of the treasury of the United States. They shall, in all cases except treason, felony, and breach of the peace, be privileged from arrest during their attendance at the session of their respective Houses, and in going to and returning from the same: for any speech or debate in either House, they shall not be questioned in any other place.

2. No Senator or Representative shall, during the time for which he was elected, be appointed to any civil office, under the authority of the United States, which shall have been created, or the emoluments whereof shall have been increased, during such time; and no person holding any office under the United States shall be a member of either house during his continuance in office.

SECTION VII.

1. All bills for raising revenue shall originate in the House

of Representatives; but the Senate may propose or concur with amendments, as on other bills.

2. Every bill which shall have passed the House of Representatives and the Senate shall, before it become a law, be presented to the President of the United States. If he approve it, he shall sign it; but if not, he shall return it, with his objections, to that House in which it shall have originated, who shall enter the objections at large on their journal, and proceed to reconsider it. If, after such reconsideration, two thirds of that House shall agree to pass the bill, it shall be sent, together with the objections, to the other House, by which it shall likewise be reconsidered; and, if approved by two thirds of that House, it shall become a law. But in all such cases the votes of both Houses shall be determined by yeas and nays; and the names of the persons voting for and against the bill shall be entered on the journal of each House respectively. If any bill shall not be returned by the President within ten days (Sundays excepted) after it shall have been presented to him, the same shall be a law, in like manner as if he had signed it, unless the Congress, by their adjournment, prevent its return; in which case it shall not be a law.

3. Every order, resolution, or vote to which the concurrence of the Senate and House of Representatives may be necessary, (except on a question of adjournment,) shall be presented to the President of the United States, and, before the same shall take effect, shall be approved by him, or being disapproved by him, shall be re-passed by two thirds of the Senate and House of Representatives, according to the rules and limitations prescribed in the case of a bill.

SECTION VIII.

The Congress shall have power,

1. To lay and collect taxes, duties, imposts, and excises to pay the debts and provide for the common defence and general welfare of the United States; but all duties, imposts, and excises shall be uniform throughout the United States:

2. To borrow money on the credit of the United States:

3. To regulate commerce with foreign nations, and among the several States, and with the Indian tribes:

4. To establish a uniform rule of naturalization, and uniform laws on the subject of bankruptcies throughout the United States:

5. To coin money, regulate the value thereof, and of foreign coin, and fix the standard of weights and measures:

6. To provide for the punishment of counterfeiting the securities and current coin of the United States:

7. To establish post-offices and post-roads:

8. To promote the progress of science and useful arts, by securing, for limited times, to authors and inventors, the exclusive right to their respective writings and discoveries:

9. To constitute tribunals inferior to the Supreme Court:

10. To define and punish piracies and felonies committed on the high seas, and offences against the law of nations:

11. To declare war, grant letters of marque and reprisal, and make rules concerning captures on land and water:

12. To raise and support armies; but no appropriation of money for that use shall be for a longer term than two years:

13. To provide and maintain a navy:

14. To make rules for the government and regulation of the land and naval forces:

15. To provide for calling forth the militia to execute the laws of the Union, suppress insurrections, and repel invasions:

16. To provide for organizing, arming, and disciplining the militia, and for governing such part of them as may be employed in the service of the United States, reserving to the States respectively the appointment of the officers, and the authority of training the militia according to the discipline prescribed by Congress.

17. To exercise exclusive legislation, in all cases whatsoever, over such District (not exceeding ten miles square) as may, by cession of particular States, and the acceptance of Congress, become the seat of the government of the United States; and

to exercise like authority over all places purchased by the consent of the Legislature of the State in which the same shall be, for the erection of forts, magazines, arsenals, dockyards, and other needful buildings; and,

18. To make all laws which shall be necessary and proper for carrying into execution the foregoing powers, and all other powers vested by this Constitution in the Government of the United States, or in any department or officer thereof.

SECTION IX.

1. The migration or importation of such persons as any of the States now existing shall think proper to admit, shall not be prohibited by the Congress prior to the year one thousand eight hundred and eight; but a tax or duty may be imposed on such importation, not exceeding ten dollars for each person.

2. The privilege of the writ of *habeas corpus* shall not be suspended, unless when, in cases of rebellion or invasion, the public safety may require it.

3. No bill of attainder or *ex post facto* law shall be passed.

4. No capitation or other direct tax shall be laid, unless in proportion to the census or enumeration hereinbefore directed to be taken.

5. No tax or duty shall be laid on articles exported from any State.

6. No preference shall be given by any regulation of commerce or revenue to the ports of one State over those of another; nor shall vessels bound to, or from one State, be obliged to enter, clear, or pay duties in another.

7. No money shall be drawn from the treasury but in consequence of appropriations made by law; and a regular statement and account of the receipts and expenditures of all public money shall be published from time to time.

8. No title of nobility shall be granted by the United States; and no person holding any office of profit or trust under them shall, without the consent of the Congress, accept of any pres-

ent emolument, office, or title of any kind whatever, from any king, prince, or foreign State.

SECTION X.

1. No State shall enter into any treaty, alliance, or confederation; grant letters of marque and reprisal; coin money; emit bills of credit; make any thing but gold and silver coin a tender in payment of debts; pass any bill of attainder, *ex post facto* law, or law impairing the obligation of contracts; or grant any title of nobility.

2. No State shall, without the consent of the Congress, lay any imposts or duties on imports or exports, except what may be absolutely necessary for executing its inspection laws; and the net produce of all duties and imposts, laid by any State on imports or exports, shall be for the use of the treasury of the United States; and all such laws shall be subject to the revision and control of the Congress.

3. No State shall, without the consent of Congress, lay any duty of tonnage, keep troops or ships of war in time of peace, enter into any agreement or compact with another State, or with a foreign power, or engage in war, unless actually invaded or in such imminent danger as will not admit of delay.

ARTICLE II.

SECTION I.

1. The Executive power shall be vested in a President of the United States of America. He shall hold his office during the term of four years, and together with the Vice-President, chosen for the same term, be elected as follows:

2. Each State shall appoint, in such manner as the Legislature thereof may direct, a number of Electors, equal to the whole number of Senators and Representatives to which the State may be entitled in the Congress; but no Senator or Representative, or person holding any office of trust or profit under the United States, shall be appointed an elector.

3. The Electors shall meet in their respective States, and vote by ballot for two persons, of whom one at least shall not be an inhabitant of the same State with themselves. And they shall make a list of all the persons voted for, and of the number of votes for each; which list they shall sign and certify, and transmit sealed to the seat of the Government of the United States, directed to the President of the Senate. The President of the Senate shall, in the presence of the Senate and House of Representatives, open all the certificates, and the votes shall then be counted. The person having the greatest number of votes shall be the President, if such number be a majority of the whole number of Electors appointed; and if there be more than one who have such majority, and have an equal number of votes, then the House of Representatives shall immediately choose by ballot one of them for President; and if no person have a majority, then from the five highest on the list the said House shall in like manner choose the President. But in choosing the President, the votes shall be taken by States, the representation from each State having one vote; a quorum for this purpose shall consist of a member or members from two thirds of the States, and a majority of all the States shall be necessary to a choice. In every case, after the choice of the President, the person having the greatest number of votes of the Electors shall be the Vice-President. But if there should remain two or more who have equal votes, the Senate shall choose from them by ballot, the Vice-President.

4. The Congress may determine the time of choosing the Electors, and the day on which they shall give their votes; which day shall be the same throughout the United States.

5. No person, except a natural-born citizen, or a citizen of the United States at the time of the adoption of this Constitution, shall be eligible to the office of President; neither shall any person be eligible to that office who shall not have attained to the age of thirty-five years, and been fourteen years a resident within the United States.

6. In case of the removal of the President from office, or of his death, resignation, or inability to discharge the powers and duties of the said office, the same shall devolve on the Vice-President; and the Congress may by law provide for the case of removal, death, resignation, or inability, both of the President and Vice-President, declaring what officer shall then act as President, and such officer shall act accordingly, until the disability be removed, or a President shall be elected.

7. The President shall, at stated times, receive for his services a compensation, which shall neither be increased nor diminished during the period for which he shall have been elected, and he shall not receive within that period any other emolument from the United States, or any of them.

8. Before he enter on the execution of his office, he shall take the following oath or affirmation: —

"I do solemnly swear (or affirm) that I will faithfully execute the office of President of the United States; and will, to the best of my ability, preserve, protect, and defend the Constitution of the United States."

SECTION II.

1. The President shall be Commander-in-Chief of the army and navy of the United States, and of the militia of the several States when called into the actual service of the United States; he may require the opinion, in writing, of the principal officer in each of the Executive departments, upon any subject relating to the duties of their respective offices, and he shall have power to grant reprieves and pardons for offences against the United States, except in cases of impeachment.

2. He shall have power, by and with the advice and consent of the Senate, to make treaties, provided two thirds of the Senators present concur; and he shall nominate, and by and with the advice and consent of the Senate, shall appoint ambassadors, other public ministers, and consuls, judges of the Supreme Court, and all other officers of the United States

whose appointments are not herein otherwise provided for, and which shall be established by law; but the Congress may by law vest the appointment of such inferior officers as they think proper in the President alone, in the courts of law, or in the heads of departments.

3. The President shall have power to fill up all vacancies that may happen during the recess of the Senate, by granting commissions which shall expire at the end of their next session.

SECTION III.

He shall, from time to time, give to the Congress information of the State of the Union, and recommend to their consideration such measures as he shall judge necessary and expedient; he may, on extraordinary occasions, convene both Houses, or either of them, and, in case of disagreement between them with respect to the time of adjournment, he may adjourn them to such time as he shall think proper; he shall receive ambassadors and other public ministers; he shall take care that the laws be faithfully executed, and shall commission all the officers of the United States.

SECTION IV.

The President, Vice-President, and all civil officers of the United States, shall be removed from office on impeachment for, and conviction of treason, bribery, or other high crimes and misdemeanors.

ARTICLE III.

SECTION I.

The Judicial power of the United States shall be vested in one Supreme Court, and in such inferior courts as the Congress may, from time to time, ordain and establish. The judges, both of the supreme and inferior courts, shall hold their offices during good behaviour, and shall, at stated times, receive for their services a compensation which shall not be diminished during their continuance in office.

SECTION II.

1. The Judicial power shall extend to all cases in law and equity arising under this Constitution, the laws of the United States, and treaties made, or which shall be made, under their authority; to all cases affecting ambassadors; other public ministers, and consuls; to all cases of admiralty and maritime jurisdiction; to controversies to which the United States shall be a party; to controversies between two or more States; between a State and citizens of another State; between citizens of different States; between citizens of the same State claiming lands under grants of different States; and between a State, or the citizens thereof and foreign States, citizens, or subjects.

2. In all cases affecting ambassadors, other public ministers, and consuls, and those in which a State shall be a party, the Supreme Court shall have original jurisdiction. In all the other cases before mentioned, the Supreme Court shall have appellate jurisdiction, both as to law and fact, with such exceptions, and under such regulations, as the Congress shall make.

3. The trial of all crimes, except in cases of impeachment, shall be by jury, and such trial shall be held in the State where the said crimes shall have been committed; but when not committed within any State, the trial shall be at such place or places as the Congress may by law have directed.

SECTION III.

1. Treason against the United States shall consist only in levying war against them, or in adhering to their enemies, giving them aid and comfort. No person shall be convicted of treason unless on the testimony of two witnesses to the same overt act, or on confession in open court.

2. The Congress shall have power to declare the punishment of treason; but no attainder of treason shall work corruption of blood or forfeiture, except during the life of the person attainted.

ARTICLE IV.

SECTION I.

Full faith and credit shall be given, in each State, to the public acts, records, and judicial proceedings of every other State. And the Congress may, by general laws, prescribe the manner in which such acts, records, and proceedings shall be proved, and the effect thereof.

SECTION II.

1. The citizens of each State shall be entitled to all privileges and immunities of citizens in the several States.

2. A person charged in any State with treason, felony, or other crime, who shall flee from justice and be found in another State, shall, on demand of the Executive authority of the State from which he fled, be delivered up, to be removed to the State having jurisdiction of the crime.

3. No person, held to service or labor in one State under the laws thereof, escaping into another, shall, in consequence of any law or regulation therein, be discharged from such service or labor; but shall be delivered up on claim of the party to whom such service or labor may be due.

SECTION III.

1. New States may be admitted by the Congress into this Union; but no new State shall be formed or erected within the jurisdiction of any other State; nor any State be formed by the junction of two or more States, or parts of States, without the consent of the Legislatures of the States concerned, as well as of the Congress.

2. The Congress shall have power to dispose of and make all needful rules and regulations respecting the territory or other property belonging to the United States; and nothing in this Constitution shall be so construed as to prejudice any claims of the United States, or of any particular State.

SECTION IV.

The United States shall guarantee to every State in this Union a republican form of government, and shall protect each of them against invasion; and on application of the Legislature, or of the Executive, (when the Legislature cannot be convened,) against domestic violence.

ARTICLE V.

The Congress, whenever two thirds of both Houses shall deem it necessary, shall propose amendments to this Constitution, or, on the application of the Legislatures of two thirds of the several States, shall call a convention for proposing amendments; which, in either case, shall be valid to all intents and purposes, as part of this Constitution, when ratified by the Legislatures of three fourths of the several States, or by conventions in three fourths thereof, as the one or the other mode of ratification may be proposed by the Congress: Provided that no amendment which may be made prior to the year one thousand eight hundred and eight, shall in any manner affect the first and fourth clauses in the ninth section of the first article; and that no State, without its consent, shall be deprived of its equal suffrage in the Senate.

ARTICLE VI.

1. All debts contracted, and engagements entered into before the adoption of this Constitution, shall be as valid against the United States under this Constitution as under the Confederation.

2. This Constitution, and the laws of the United States which shall be made in pursuance thereof, and all treaties made, or which shall be made, under the authority of the United States, shall be the supreme law of the land, and the judges in every State shall be bound thereby, anything in the Constitution or laws of any State to the contrary notwithstanding.

3. The Senators and Representatives before mentioned, and the members of the several State Legislatures, and all Executive and Judicial officers, both of the United States and of the several States, shall be bound, by oath or affirmation, to support this Constitution; but no religious test shall ever be required as a qualification to any office or public trust under the United States.

ARTICLE VII.

The ratification of the conventions of nine States shall be sufficient for the establishment of this Constitution between the States so ratifying the same.

Done in Convention by the unanimous consent of the States present, the seventeenth day of September, in the year of our Lord one thousand seven hundred and eighty-seven, and of the independence of the United States of America the twelfth. In witness whereof, we have hereunto subscribed our names.

GEORGE WASHINGTON, *President,*
and Deputy from Virginia.

New Hampshire.	John Langdon, Nicholas Gilman.
Massachusetts.	Nathaniel Gorham, Rufus King.
Connecticut.	William Samuel Johnson, Roger Sherman.
New York.	Alexander Hamilton.
New Jersey.	William Livingston, David Brearley, William Paterson, Jonathan Dayton.
Pennsylvania.	Benjamin Franklin, Thomas Mifflin, Robert Morris, George Clymer, Thomas Fitzsimmons, Jared Ingersol, James Wilson, Gouverneur Morris.

Delaware.	George Read, Gunning Bedford, Jun., John Dickinson, Richard Bassett, Jacob Broom.
Maryland.	James M'Henry, Daniel of St. Thomas Jenifer, Daniel Carroll.
Virginia.	John Blair, James Madison, Jun.
North Carolina.	William Blount, Richard Dobbs Spaight, Hugh Williamson.
South Carolina.	John Rutledge, Charles Cotesworth Pinckney, Charles Pinckney, Pierce Butler.
Georgia.	William Few, Abraham Baldwin.
Attest,	WILLIAM JACKSON, *Secretary*.

AMENDMENTS.

The following Articles in addition to, and amendment of, the Constitution of the United States, having been ratified by the Legislatures of nine States, are equally obligatory with the Constitution itself.

I. CONGRESS shall make no law respecting an establishment of religion, or prohibiting the free exercise thereof, or abridging the freedom of speech or of the press; or the right of the people peaceably to assemble, and to petition the Government for a redress of grievances.

II. A well-regulated militia being necessary to the security of a free State, the right of the people to keep and bear arms shall not be infringed.

III. No soldier shall, in time of peace, be quartered in any house, without the consent of the owner; nor in time of war, but in a manner to be prescribed by law.

IV. The right of the people to be secure in their persons, houses, papers, and effects, against unreasonable searches and seizures, shall not be violated; and no warrants shall issue, but upon probable cause, supported by oath or affirmation, and particularly describing the place to be searched, and the persons or things to be seized.

V. No person shall be held to answer for a capital or otherwise infamous crime, unless on a presentment or indictment of a grand-jury, except in cases arising in the land or naval forces, or in the militia, when in actual service, in time of war, or public danger; nor shall any person be subject, for the same offence, to be twice put in jeopardy of life or limb; nor shall be compelled, in any criminal case, to be witness against himself; nor be deprived of life, liberty, or property, without due process of law; nor shall private property be taken for public use, without just compensation.

VI. In all criminal prosecutions, the accused shall enjoy the right to a speedy and public trial, by an impartial jury, of the State and district wherein the crime shall have been committed; which district shall have been previously ascertained by law; and to be informed of the nature and cause of the accusation; to be confronted with the witnesses against him; to have compulsory process for obtaining witnesses in his favor; and to have the assistance of counsel for his defence.

VII. In suits at common law, where the value in controversy shall exceed twenty dollars, the right of trial by jury shall be preserved; and no fact tried by a jury shall be otherwise reexamined in any court of the United States than according to the rules of the common law.

VIII. Excessive bail shall not be required; nor excessive fines imposed; nor cruel and unusual punishments inflicted.

IX. The enumeration in the Constitution of certain rights shall not be construed to deny or disparage others retained by the people.

X. The powers not delegated to the United States by the Constitution, nor prohibited by it to the States, are reserved to the States respectively, or to the people.

XI. The Judicial power of the United States shall not be construed to extend to any suit in law or equity commenced or prosecuted against one of the United States by citizens of another State, or by citizens or subjects of any foreign State.

XII. § 1. The Electors shall meet in their respective States, and vote by ballot for President and Vice-President, one of whom, at least, shalt not be an inhabitant of the same State with themselves; they shall name in their ballots the person voted for as President, and in distinct ballots the person voted for as Vice-President; and they shall make distinct lists of all persons voted for as President, and of all persons voted for as Vice-President, and of the number of votes for each, which list they shall sign and certify, and transmit sealed to the Government of the United States, directed to the President of the Senate; the President of the Senate shall, in the presence of the Senate and House of Representatives, open all the certificates, and the votes shall then be counted; the person having the greatest number of votes for President shall be the President, if such number be a majority of the whole number of Electors appointed; and if no person have such majority, then from the persons having the highest numbers not exceeding three on the list of those voted for as President, the House of Representatives shall choose immediately, by ballot, the President. But, in choosing the President, the votes shall be taken by States, the representation from each State having one vote; a quorum for this purpose shall consist of a member or members from two thirds of the States, and a majority of all the States shall be necessary to a choice. And if the House of Representatives shall not choose a President whenever the right of choice shall devolve upon them, before the fourth day of March next following, then the Vice-President shall act as President, as in the case of the death or other constitutional disability of the President. § 2. The person having the greatest number of votes as Vice-President shall be Vice-President, if such number be a majority of the whole number of Electors appointed; and if no person have a majority, then from the two highest numbers on the list the Senate shall choose the Vice-President; a quorum for the purpose shall consist of two thirds of the whole number of Senators, and a majority of the whole number shall be necessary to a choice. § 3. But no person constitutionally ineligible to the office of President shall be eligible to that of Vice-President of the United States.

D, p. v.

WILLIAM DUER[1] TO JAMES MADISON.

New York, June 23, 1788.

DEAR SIR,

As it is probable you may not hear by this post from our mutual friend, Colonel Hamilton, I take the liberty of giving you a short sketch of our political prospects in this quarter on the great question of the Constitution. My information is from Colonel Laurance,[2] who left Poughkeepsie on Saturday.

A considerable majority of the Convention are undoubtedly Anti-Federal; or, in other words, wish for amendments previous to the adoption of the Government. A few of the leaders (among which I think I may, without scruple, class the Governor)[3] would, if they could find support, go further, and hazard every thing rather than agree to any system which tended to a consolidation of our Government. Of this, however, I have at present no apprehensions, many of their party having avowed themselves friends to the Union. With respect to amendments, as far as I can understand the party in opposition, they cannot agree among themselves. It is therefore possible that this circumstance may create a division in favor of the Federalists.

[1] Formerly a member of the Continental Congress, and then Secretary to the Treasury-board of the United States.

[2] John Laurance, Judge-Advocate General in the revolutionary army, and afterwards a Senator in Congress from New York.

[3] George Clinton.

As to the rejection of the Constitution, there is not the least probability of it. The great points of discussion will probably be, whether they will adjourn without coming to any decision, or whether they will adopt it conditionally, or follow the example of Massachusetts and South Carolina.

The conduct of your Convention will influence, in a great degree, ours. If you adjourn without doing any thing, we shall do the same; but, if you do not, there is still some hope that we may adopt, with proposed amendments: for, as to the second point, the inconsistency of it will, I think, be too apparent after a decision to command a majority. While I am writing, a gentleman has favored me with a copy of a letter from an intelligent bystander,[1] who has attended the debates of the Convention; I therefore inclose it, as a more faithful history than I can give.

I am, with sentiments of the most profound esteem,
Your obedient, humble servant,
WILLIAM DUER.

JAMES KENT[2] TO ROBERT TROUP.[3]

Poughkeepsie, Friday, June 20, 1788.

DEAR SIR,

I had the pleasure of receiving your letter by Mr. Harison,[4] and in compliance with your desire, I shall shortly state to you the proceedings of the Convention hitherto.

They met on Tuesday in pretty full house, and elected Governor Clinton president, and appointed by ballot Duane, Morris, Lansing,[5] Jones,[6] and Hening, a committee for reporting rules for

[1] James Kent.

[2] The late Chancellor, who had lately commenced the practice of the law at Poughkeepsie, where the State Convention was sitting.

[3] Afterwards District Judge of the United States for New York.

[4] Afterwards United States District Attorney for New York.

[5] Afterwards Chancellor of the State.

[6] An eminent lawyer, afterwards Recorder of the city of New York, and subsequently Comptroller of the State Treasury.

the regulation of the Convention. On Wednesday, the rules were adopted, the Constitution read, and a motion made by Mr. Lansing, and agreed to, that they would on the next day resolve themselves into a committee of the whole for the purpose of discussing the Constitution. On Thursday, which was yesterday, the house resolved itself into a committee, Mr. Oouthout, of Albany, chairman. Chancellor Livingston[1] rose and called our attention to a fine introductory speech of one hour's length. He mentioned the importance of the occasion, and the peculiar felicity of this country, which had it in its power to originate and establish its government from reason and choice, while on the Eastern Continent, their governments and the reforms of them were the children of force. He then pointed out the necessity of *Union*, particularly in this State, from its local situation, which rendered it peculiarly vulnerable, not only to foreigners, but to its neighbors. He stated that a Union was to be expected only from the old Confederation, or from the government now under their consideration. He then demonstrated the radical defects of the Confederation; that its principle was bad, in legislating for States in their political capacity, as its constitutional demands could only be coerced by arms; that it was equally defective *in form*, as the Congress was a single body, too small and too liable to faction, from its being a single body, to be intrusted with Legislative power, and too numerous to be intrusted with Executive authority. The Chancellor, on this head, only gave a summary of the arguments of *Publius*[2] when treating on the defects of the Confederation; but the summary was neither so perfect nor so instructive, by a vast difference, as the original. It was not, however, to be expected in a short address. He concluded that survey by entreating the House to divest themselves of prejudice and warmth, to examine the plan submitted with the utmost coolness and candor, to consider themselves as citizens assembled to

[1] Robert R. Livingston, afterwards United States Minister to the French Republic during the Presidency of Mr. Jefferson.

[2] The signature adopted by the authors of "The Federalist."

consult for the general good, and not as State officers, who might be opposed, in that capacity, to every determination of their authority. He concluded his speech by a motion which, with some amendments, was agreed to by the House, that they would discuss the Constitution by paragraphs, and any amendments which might be proposed in the course of the debate, without taking the question as to any paragraphs, or as to any amendments which might be offered, until the whole Constitution was discussed. This, sir, is a sketch of the proceedings of the Convention to this day. We expect they will this morning enter on the subject by paragraphs. I imagine they will be some time engaged in the discussion, probably three weeks. As to the result, I can only say I look forward to it with anxious uncertainty. I do not abandon hope. I think the opposition discover great embarrassment. I believe they do not know what to do. Some of them, I am told, have said they will not vote against it. The decision in New Hampshire and Virginia, we are flattering ourselves, will be favorable; and that they will give energy to the debate on one side in our Convention, and confusion, if not absolute despair, to the other side. I hope you and our friends in New York will give us the earliest information from those States.

In giving you the heads of the Chancellor's speech, I believe I am not mistaken. He spoke rather low, and there was so much noise, and the bar so much crowded, that I confess I lost at least one third of the speech, though I trust not the general course of reasoning. What I regretted more, I lost some of his figures, for which he is peculiarly eminent. I shall take the liberty to trespass on your patience by every opportunity, as I trust your curiosity will excuse me.

I am, &c., &c., JAMES KENT.

P. S. I am directed by Mr. Benson,[1] to request you will communicate this information to Colonel Duer.

[1] The late Judge Egbert Benson.

WILLIAM DUER TO JAMES MADISON.

1788.

MY DEAR SIR,

Our mutual friend, Hamilton,[1] has communicated to me, in confidence, the substance of your letter on the political prospects in Pennsylvania and Virginia. I learn with extreme regret the division of the Federalists in the former State, and the malignant perseverance of the opponents to the Constitution in your own. I trust, however, that we shall have the benefit of your counsels and exertions in the House of Representatives, notwithstanding Mr. Henry's[2] manœuvres to prevent it.

You may remember some conversation I once had with you on the subject of electing Mr. John Adams as Vice-President. I have ascertained, through General Knox,[3] that this gentleman, if chosen, will be a strenuous opposer against calling a Convention, which, in the present state of parties, I consider as a vital stab to the Constitution; and not only that, I have been informed, in a mode perfectly satisfactory, that he and his old coadjutor, R. H. Lee, will be altogether opposite in all measures relative to the establishment of the character and credit of the Government. I am therefore anxious that the Federalists to the southward may join in supporting his nomination. A greater knowledge of the world has cured him of his old party prejudices, and I am satisfied nothing is to be feared from that quarter; on the contrary, should he be elected to that station (which I am fully convinced is his wish), the weight of his State would be cast into the Federal scale.

Interested as I know you are in the welfare of the Union, I cannot omit giving you this information, on the authenticity of which you may rely, that you may (without committing my name) make such use of it as you think proper.

I am, with sentiments of great esteem,

Your obedient; humble servant, WILLIAM DUER.

P. S. I have no objection to Messrs. Robert and Gouverneur Morris seeing this letter.

[1] Alexander Hamilton. [2] Patrick Henry.

[3] Henry Knox, Secretary at War, in Washington's administration.

JAMES MADISON TO WILLIAM A. DUER.

Montpelier, May 5, 1835.

DEAR SIR,

I have received your letter of April 25, and, with the aid of a friend, an amanuensis, have made out the following answer.

On the subject of Mr. Pinckney's proposed plan of a Constitution, it is to be observed, that the plan printed in the journal was not the document actually presented by him to the Convention. That document was in no otherwise noticed in the proceedings of the Convention than by a reference of it, with Mr. Randolph's[1] plan, to a committee of the whole, and afterward to a committee of detail, with others; and not being found among the papers left with President Washington, and finally deposited in the Department of State, Mr. Adams,[2] charged with the publication of them, obtained from Mr. Pinckney[3] the document in the printed journal as a copy supplying the place of the missing one. In this there must be error; there being sufficient evidence, even on the surface of the journals, that the copy sent to Mr. Adams could not be the same with the document laid before the Convention. Take, for example, the article constituting the House of Representatives — the corner-stone of the fabric; the identity, even verbal, of which, with the adopted Constitution, has attracted so much notice. In the first place, the detail and phraseology of the Constitution appears to have been the result of successive discussions, and are too minute and exact to have been anticipated. In the next place, it appears that, within a few days after Mr. Pinckney presented his plan to the Convention, he moved to strike out from the resolution of Mr. Randolph the provision for the election of the House of Representatives by the people, and refer the choice of that House to the Legislatures of the States; and to this preference he appears to have adhered in the subsequent proceedings of the Convention. Other discrepancies might be

[1] Edmund Randolph, afterwards Attorney-General of the United States.

[2] John Quincy Adams.

[3] Charles Pinckney, of South Carolina.

found, in a source also within your reach, in a pamphlet published by Mr. Pinckney soon after the close of the Convention, in which he refers to parts of his plan which are at variance with the document in the printed journal.[1] Further evidence on this subject await a future, perhaps a posthumous disclosure. One conjecture explaining the phenomena has been, that Mr. Pinckney interwove with the draft sent to Mr. Adams passages as agreed on in the Convention in the progress of the work, and which, after a lapse of more than thirty years, were not separated by his recollection.

The resolutions of Mr. Randolph, the basis on which the deliberations of the committee proceeded, were the result of a consultation among the Virginia deputies, who thought it possible that, as Virginia had taken so leading a part in reference to the Federal Convention, some initiative propositions might be expected from them. They were understood not to commit any of the members, absolutely or definitively, on the tenor of them. The resolutions will be seen to present the characteristic provisions and features of a government as complete, in some respects, perhaps more so, than the plan of Mr. Pinckney, though without being thrown into a formal shape. The moment, indeed, a real Constitution was looked for as a substitute for the Confederacy, the distribution of the government into the usual departments became a matter of course with all who speculated on the prospective change, and the form of general resolutions was adopted, as most respectful to the Convention, and as the most convenient for discussion. It may be observed that, in reference to the powers to be given to the General Government, the resolutions comprehended as well the powers contained in the Articles of Confederation, without enumerating them, as others not overlooked in the resolutions, but left to be developed and defined by the Convention.

With regard to the plan proposed by Mr. Hamilton, I may

[1] *Observations on the Plan of Government submitted to the Federal Convention, on the 28th of May*, 1787, by Charles Pinckney, &c., &c. *Vide* "Select Facts," vol. ii., in the library of the Historical Society of New York.

say to you, that a Constitution such as you describe was never proposed in the Convention, but was communicated by him to me, at the close of it. The original draft being in the possession of his family, and their property, I have considered any publicity of it as lying with them. Mr. Yates's notes, as you observe, are very *inaccurate*; *they* are also, in some respects, grossly erroneous. The desultory manner in which he took them, catching sometimes but half the language, may in part account for it. Though said to be a respectable and honorable man, he brought with him to the Convention the strongest prejudices against the existence and objects of that body, in which he was strengthened by the course taken in its deliberations. He left the Convention long before the opinions and views of many members were finally developed into their practical application. The passion and prejudice of Mr. Luther Martin, betrayed in his public letter, could not fail to discolor his representations. He also left the Convention before the completion of their work. I have heard, but will not vouch for the fact, that he became sensible of, and admitted his error; certain it is that he joined the party who favored the Constitution in its most liberal construction.

I had, as you may recollect, an acquaintance with your father,[1] to which his talents and social accomplishments were very attractive; and there was an incidental correspondence between us, interchanging information at a critical moment, when the elections and State Conventions which were to decide the fate of the new Constitution were taking place. You are, I presume, not ignorant that your father was the author of several papers auxiliary to the numbers of "The Federalist." They appeared, I believe, in the Gazette of Mr. Childs.[2]

With great respect and cordial salutations, yours,

James Madison.

[1] Colonel William Duer.

[2] Under the signature of Philo-Publius, these papers treated of the financial questions and benefits arising from the New Constitution, in the

E, p. 25.

PROCLAMATION BY ANDREW JACKSON, PRESIDENT OF THE UNITED STATES.

Whereas a convention assembled in the State of South Carolina have passed an ordinance, by which they declare "that the several Acts and parts of Acts of the Congress of the United States, purporting to be laws for the imposing of duties and imposts on the importation of foreign commodities, and now having actual operation and effect within the United States, and more especially" two Acts, for the same purposes, passed on the 29th of May, 1828, and on the 14th of July, 1832, "are unauthorized by the Constitution of the United States, and violate the true meaning and intent thereof, and are null and void, and no law," nor binding on the citizens of that State or its officers; and by the said ordinance it is further declared to be unlawful for any of the constituted authorities of the State, or of the United States, to enforce the payment of the duties imposed by the said Acts within the same State, and that it is the duty of the Legislature to pass such laws as may be necessary to give full effect to the said ordinance:

And whereas, by the said ordinance it is further ordained that, in no case of law or equity, decided in the courts of said State, wherein shall be drawn in question the validity of the said ordinance, or of the Acts of the Legislature that may be passed to give it effect, or of the said laws of the United States, no appeal shall be allowed to the Supreme Court of the United States, nor shall any copy of the record be permitted or allowed for that purpose; and that any person attempting to take such appeal shall be punished as for a contempt of court:

And, finally, the said ordinance declares that the people of South Carolina will maintain the said ordinance at every hazard;

organization of an adequate and permanent system of revenue for the support of the Government, encouragement of domestic manufactures, and the establishment of public credit.

and that they will consider the passage of any Act by Congress abolishing or closing the ports of the said State, or otherwise obstructing the free ingress or egress of vessels to and from the said ports, or any other Act of the Federal Government to coerce the State, shut up her ports, destroy or harass her commerce, or to enforce the said Acts otherwise than through the civil tribunals of the country, as inconsistent with the longer continuance of South Carolina in the Union; and that the people of the said State will thenceforth hold themselves absolved from all further obligation to maintain or preserve their political connection with the people of the other States, and will forthwith proceed to organize a separate Government, and do all other acts and things which sovereign and independent States may of right do:

And whereas, the said ordinance prescribes to the people of South Carolina a course of conduct in direct violation of their duty as citizens of the United States, contrary to the laws of their country, subversive of its Constitution, and having for its object the destruction of the Union — that Union which, coeval with our political existence, led our fathers, without any other ties to unite them than those of patriotism and a common cause, through a sanguinary struggle to a glorious independence — that sacred Union, hitherto inviolate, which, perfected by our happy Constitution, has brought us, by the favor of Heaven, to a state of prosperity at home and high consideration abroad, rarely, if ever, equalled in the history of nations. To preserve this bond of our political existence from destruction, to maintain inviolate this state of national honor and prosperity, and to justify the confidence my fellow-citizens have reposed in me, I, Andrew Jackson, *President of the United States*, have thought proper to issue this my PROCLAMATION, stating my views of the Constitution and laws applicable to the measures adopted by the convention of South Carolina, and to the reasons they have put forth to sustain them, declaring the course which duty will require me to pursue, and, appealing to the understanding and patriotism of the people, warn them of the consequences that must inevitably result from an observance of the dictates of the convention.

Strict duty would require of me nothing more than the exercise of those powers with which I am now, or may hereafter be invested, for preserving the peace of the Union, and for the execution of the laws. But the imposing aspect which opposition has assumed in this case, by clothing itself with State authority, and the deep interest which the people of the United States must all feel in preventing a resort to stronger measures, while there is a hope that any thing will be yielded to reasoning and remonstrance, perhaps demand, and will certainly justify a full exposition to South Carolina, and the nation, of the views I entertain of this important question, as well as a distinct enunciation of the course which my sense of duty will require me to pursue.

The ordinance is founded, not on the indefeasible right of resisting Acts which are plainly unconstitutional, and too oppressive to be endured, but on the strange position that any one State may not only declare an Act of Congress void, but prohibit its execution; that they may do this consistently with the Constitution; that the true construction of that instrument permits a State to retain its place in the Union, and yet be bound by no other of its laws than those it may choose to consider as constitutional. It is true, they add, that, to justify this abrogation of a law, it must be palpably contrary to the Constitution; but it is evident that, to give the right of resisting laws of that description, coupled with the uncontrolled right to decide what laws deserve that character, is to give the power of resisting all laws. For as by the theory there is no appeal, the reasons alleged by the State, good or bad, must prevail. If it should be said that public opinion is a sufficient check against the abuse of this power, it may be asked why it is not deemed a sufficient guard against the passage of an unconstitutional Act by Congress. There is, however, a restraint in this last case, which makes the assumed power of a State more indefensible, and which does not exist in the other. There are two appeals from an unconstitutional Act passed by Congress — one to the Judiciary, the other to the people and the States. There is no appeal from the State decision in theory; and the practical illustration shows that the Courts are closed against an application to review it, both judges and jurors being sworn to decide in its favor. But reasoning on this subject is superfluous, when our social compact, in express terms, declares that the laws of the United States, its Constitution, and treaties made under it, are the supreme law of the land; and, for greater caution, adds, "that the Judges in every State shall be bound thereby, any thing in the Constitution or laws of any State to the contrary notwithstanding." And it may be asserted, without fear of refutation, that no Federative Government could exist without a similar provision. Look for a moment to the consequence. If South Carolina considers the revenue laws unconstitutional, and has a right to prevent their execution in the port of Charleston, there would be a clear constitutional objection to their collection in every other port, and no revenue could be collected anywhere; for all imposts must be equal. It is no answer to repeat that an unconstitutional law is no law, so long as the question of its legality is to be decided by the State itself; for every law operating injuriously upon any local interest will be perhaps thought, and certainly represented, as unconstitutional; and, as has been shown, there is no appeal.

If this doctrine had been established at an earlier day, the Union would have been dissolved in its infancy. The excise law in Pennsylvania, the embargo and non-intercourse law in the Eastern States, the carriage-tax in Virginia, were all deemed unconstitutional, and were more unequal in their operation than any of the laws now complained of; but, fortunately, none of those States discovered that they had the right now claimed by South Carolina. The war into which we were forced, to support the dignity of the nation and the rights of our citizens, might have ended in defeat and disgrace, instead of victory and honor, if the States, who supposed it a ruinous and unconstitutional measure, had thought they possessed the right of nullifying the Act by which it was declared, and denying supplies for its prosecution. Hardly and unequally as those measures bore upon several members of the Union, to the Legislatures of none did this efficient and peaceable remedy, as it is called, suggest itself. The discovery of this important feature in our Constitution was reserved to the present day. To the statesmen of South Carolina belongs the invention, and upon the citizens of that State will, unfortunately, fall the evils of reducing it to practice.

If the doctrine of a State *veto* upon the laws of the Union carries with it internal evidence of its impracticable absurdity, our constitutional history will also afford abundant proof that it would have been repudiated with indignation, had it been proposed to form a feature in our government.

In our colonial state, although dependent on another power, we very early considered ourselves as connected by common interest with each other. Leagues were formed for common defence, and before the Declaration of Independence, we were known in our aggregate character as THE UNITED COLONIES OF AMERICA. That decisive and important step was taken jointly. We declared ourselves a nation by a joint, not by several acts; and when the terms of our confederation were reduced to form, it was in that of a solemn league of several States, by which they agreed that they would, collectively, form one nation for the purpose of conducting some certain domestic concerns, and all foreign relations. In the instrument forming that union, is found an article which declares that "every State shall abide by the determinations of Congress on all questions which by that confederation should be submitted to them."

Under the Confederation, then, no State could legally annul a decision of the Congress, or refuse to submit to its execution; but no provision was made to enforce these decisions. Congress made requisitions, but they were not complied with. The Government could not operate on individuals. They had no judiciary, no means of collecting revenue.

But the defects of the Confederation need not be detailed. Under its operation, we could scarcely be called a nation. We had neither prosperity at home nor consideration abroad. This state of things could not be endured, and our present happy Constitution was formed; but formed in vain, if this fatal doctrine prevails. It was formed for important objects that are announced in the preamble made in the name and by the authority of the people of the United States, whose delegates framed, and whose conventions approved it. The most important among these objects, that which is placed first in rank, on which all the others rest, is, "*to form a more perfect union.*" Now, is it possible that, even if there were no express provision giving supremacy to the Constitution and laws of the United States over those of the States, it can be conceived that an instrument made for the purpose of "*forming a more perfect union*" than that of the Confederation, could be so constructed by the assembled wisdom of our country as to substitute for that Confederation a form of government dependent for its existence on the local interest, the party spirit of a State, or of a prevailing faction in a State? Every man of plain, unsophisticated understanding, who hears the question, will give such an answer as will preserve the Union. Metaphysical subtlety, in pursuit of an impracticable theory, could alone have devised one that is calculated to destroy it.

I consider, then, the power to annul a law of the United States, assumed by one State, INCOMPATIBLE WITH THE EXISTENCE OF THE UNION, CONTRADICTED EXPRESSLY BY THE LETTER OF THE CONSTITUTION, UNAUTHORIZED BY ITS SPIRIT, INCONSISTENT WITH EVERY PRINCIPLE ON WHICH IT WAS FOUNDED, AND DESTRUCTIVE OF THE GREAT OBJECT FOR WHICH IT WAS FORMED.

After this general view of the leading principle, we must

examine the particular application of it which is made in the ordinance.

The preamble rests its justification on these grounds: It assumes as a fact, that the obnoxious laws, although they purport to be laws for raising revenue, were, in reality, intended for the protection of manufactures, which purpose it asserts to be unconstitutional; that the operation of these laws is unequal; that the amount raised by them is greater than is required by the wants of the Government; and, finally, that the proceeds are to be applied to objects unauthorized by the Constitution. These are the only causes alleged to justify an open opposition to the laws of the country, and a threat of seceding from the Union, if any attempt should be made to enforce them. The first virtually acknowledges that the law in question was passed under a power expressly given by the Constitution to lay and collect imposts; but its constitutionality was drawn in question from the motives of those who passed it. However apparent this purpose may be in the present case, nothing can be more dangerous than to admit the position that an unconstitutional purpose, entertained by the members who assent to a law enacted under a constitutional power, shall make that law void; for how is that purpose to be ascertained? Who is to make the scrutiny? How often may bad purposes be falsely imputed? in how many cases are they concealed by false professions? in how many is no declaration of motive made? Admit this doctrine, and you give to the States an uncontrolled right to decide, and every law may be annulled under this pretext. If, therefore, the absurd and dangerous doctrine should be admitted that a State may annul an unconstitutional law, or one that it deems such, it will not apply to the present case.

The next objection is, that the laws in question operate unequally. This objection may be made with truth to every law that has been or can be passed. The wisdom of man never yet contrived a system of taxation that would operate with perfect equality. If the unequal operation of a law makes it unconstitutional, and if all laws of that description may be abrogated by any State for that cause, then, indeed, is the Federal Constitution unworthy of the slightest effort for its preservation. We have hitherto relied on it as the perpetual bond of our Union. We have received it as the work of the assembled wisdom of the nation. We have trusted to it as to the sheet-anchor of our safety, in the stormy times of conflict with a foreign or domestic foe. We have looked to it with sacred awe as the palladium of our liberties, and, with all the solemnities of religion, have pledged to each other our lives and fortunes here, and our hopes of happiness hereafter, in its defence and support. Were we mistaken, my countrymen, in attaching this importance to the Constitution of our country? Was our devotion paid to the wretched, inefficient, clumsy contrivance which this new doctrine would make it? Did we pledge ourselves to the support of an airy nothing — a bubble that must be blown away by the first breath of disaffection? Was this self-destroying, visionary theory, the work of the profound statesmen, the exalted patriots, to whom the task of a constitutional reform was intrusted? Did the name of Washington sanction, did the States deliberately ratify, such an anomaly in the history of fundamental legislation? No. We were not mistaken! The letter of this great instrument is free from this radical fault; its language directly contradicts the imputation; its spirit — its evident intent contradicts it. No, we did not err! Our Constitution does not contain the absurdity of giving power to make laws, and another power to resist them. The sages, whose memory will always be reverenced, have given us a practical, and, as they hoped, a permanent constitutional compact. The father of his country did not affix his revered name to so palpable an absurdity. Nor did the States, when they severally ratified it, do so under the impression that a *veto* on the laws of the United States was reserved to them, or that they could exercise it by implication. Search the debates in all their conventions — examine the speeches of the most zealous opposers of Federal authority—look at the amendments that were proposed. They are all silent—not a syllable uttered, not a vote given, not a motion made, to correct the explicit supremacy given to the laws of the Union over those of the States—or to show that implication, as is now contended, could defeat it. No, we have not erred! The Constitution is still the object of our reverence, the bond of our Union, our defence in danger, the source of our prosperity in peace. It shall descend, as we have received it, uncorrupted by sophistical construction, to our posterity; and the sacrifices of local interest, of State prejudices, of personal animosities, that were made to bring it into existence, will again be patriotically offered for its support.

The two remaining objections made by the ordinance to these laws are, that the sums intended to be raised by them are greater than are required, and that the proceeds will be unconstitutionally employed. The Constitution has given expressly to Congress the right of raising revenue, and of determining the sum the public exigencies will require. The States have no control over the exercise of this right, other than that which results from the power of changing the representatives who abuse it, and thus procure redress. Congress may undoubtedly abuse this discretionary power, but the same may be said of others with which they are vested. Yet the discretion must exist somewhere. The Constitution has given it to the representatives of all the people, checked by the representatives of the States, and by the Executive power. The South Carolina construction gives it to the Legislature or the convention of a single State, where neither the people of the different States, nor the States in their separate capacity, nor the Chief Magistrate elected by the people, have any representation. Which is the most discreet disposition of the power? I do not ask you, fellow-citizens, which is the constitutional disposition—that instrument speaks a language not to be misunderstood. But if you were assembled in General Convention, which would you think the safest depository of this discretionary power in the last resort? Would you add a clause giving it to each of the States, or would you sanction the wise provisions already made by your Constitution? If this should be the result of your deliberations when providing for the future, are you — can you — be ready to risk all that we hold dear, to establish, for a temporary and a local purpose, that which you must acknowledge to be destructive, and even absurd, as a general provision? Carry out the consequences of this right vested in the different States, and you must perceive that the crisis your conduct presents at this day would recur whenever any law of the United States displeased any of the States, and that we should soon cease to be a nation.

The ordinance, with the same knowledge of the future that characterizes a former objection, tells you that the proceeds of the tax will be unconstitutionally applied. If this could be ascertained with certainty, the objection would, with more propriety, be reserved for the law so applying the proceeds, but surely cannot be urged against the laws levying the duty.

These are the allegations contained in the ordinance. Examine them seriously, my fellow-citizens — judge for yourselves. I appeal to you to determine whether they are so clear, so convincing, as to leave no doubt of their correctness; and even if you should come to this conclusion, how far they justify the reckless, destructive course, which you are directed to pursue. Review these objections, and the conclusions drawn from them, once more. What are they? Every law, then, for raising revenue, according to the South Carolina ordinance, may be rightfully annulled, unless it be so framed as no law ever will or can be framed. Congress have a right to pass laws for raising revenue, and each State has a right to oppose their execution — two rights directly opposed to each other; and yet is this absurdity supposed to be contained in an instrument drawn for the express purpose of avoiding collisions between the States and the General Government, by an assembly of the most enlightened statesmen and purest patriots ever embodied for a similar purpose.

In vain have these sages declared that Congress shall have power to lay and collect taxes, duties, imposts, and excises; in vain have they provided that they shall have power to pass laws which shall be necessary and proper to carry those powers into execution; that those laws and that Constitution shall be the "supreme law of the land; and that the judges in every State shall be bound thereby, any thing in the Constitution or laws of any State to the contrary notwithstanding." In vain have the people of the several States solemnly sanctioned these provisions, made them their paramount law, and individually sworn to support them whenever they were called on to execute any office. Vain provisions! ineffectual restrictions! vile profanation of oaths! miserable mockery of legislation! if a bare majority of the voters in any one State may, on a real or supposed knowledge of the intent with which a law has been passed, declare themselves free from its operations — say here it gives too little, there too much, and operates unequally — here it suffers articles to be free that ought to be taxed, there it taxes those that ought to be free — in this case the proceeds are intended to be applied to purposes which we do not approve, in that the amount raised is more than is wanted. Congress, it is true, are invested by the Constitution with the right of deciding these questions according to their sound discretion. Congress is composed of the Representatives of all the States, and of all the people of all the States; but WE, part of the people of one State, to whom the Constitution has given no power on the subject, from whom it has expressly taken it away — *we*, who have solemnly agreed that this Constitution shall be our law — *we*, most of whom have sworn to support it — *we* now abrogate this law, and swear, and force others to swear, that it shall not be obeyed; and we do this, not because Congress have no right to pass such laws — this we do not allege — but because they have passed them with improper views. They are unconstitutional from the motives of those who passed them, which we can never with certainty know, from their unequal operation;

although it is impossible, from the nature of things, that they should be equal; and from the disposition which we presume may be made of their proceeds, although that disposition has not been declared. This is the plain meaning of the ordinance in relation to laws which it abrogates for alleged unconstitutionality. But it does not stop there. It repeals, in express terms, an important part of the Constitution itself, and of laws passed to give it effect, which have never been alleged to be unconstitutional. The Constitution declares that the Judicial powers of the United States extend to cases arising under the laws of the United States, and that such laws, the Constitution, and treaties, shall be paramount to the State Constitutions and laws. The Judiciary Act prescribes the mode by which the case may be brought before a court of the United States, by appeal, when a State tribunal shall decide against this provision of the Constitution. The ordinance declares there shall be no appeal; makes the State law paramount to the Constitution and laws of the United States; forces judges and jurors to swear that they will disregard their provisions; and even makes it penal in a suitor to attempt relief by appeal. It further declares that it shall not be lawful for the authorities of the United States, or of that State, to enforce the payment of duties imposed by the revenue laws within its limits.

Here is a law of the United States, not even pretended to be unconstitutional, repealed by the authority of a small majority of the voters of a single State. Here is a provision of the Constitution which is solemnly abrogated by the same authority.

On such expositions and reasonings the ordinance grounds, not only an assertion of the right to annul the laws of which it complains, but to enforce it by a threat of seceding from the Union, if any attempt is made to execute them.

This right to secede is deduced from the nature of the Constitution, which, they say, is a compact between sovereign States, who have preserved their whole sovereignty, and, therefore, are subject to no superior; that, because they made the compact, they can break it when, in their opinion, it has been departed from by the other States. Fallacious as this course of reasoning is, it enlists State pride, and finds advocates in the honest prejudices of those who have not studied the nature of our Government sufficiently to see the radical error on which it rests.

The people of the United States formed the Constitution, acting through the State Legislatures in making the compact, to meet and discuss its provisions, and acting in separate conventions when they ratified those provisions; but the terms used in its construction show it to be a government in which the people of all the States collectively are represented. We are ONE PEOPLE in the choice of the President and Vice-President. Here the States have no other agency than to direct the mode in which the votes shall be given. The candidates having the majority of all the votes are chosen. The electors of a majority of States may have given their votes for one candidate, and yet another may be chosen. The people, then, and not the States, are represented in the Executive branch.

In the House of Representatives there is this difference, that the people of one State do not, as in the case of President and Vice-President, all vote for the same officers. The people of all the States do not vote for all the members, each State electing only its own Representatives. But this creates no material distinction. When chosen, they are all Representatives of the United States, not Representatives of the particular State from which they come. They are paid by the United States, not by the State; nor are they accountable to it for any act done in the performance of their Legislative functions; and, however they may in practice, as it is their duty to do, consult and prefer the interests of their particular constituents when they come in conflict with any other partial or local interest, yet it is their first and highest duty, as Representatives of the United States, to promote the general good.

The Constitution of the United States, then, forms a *government*, not a league; and whether it be formed by compact between the States, or in any other manner, its character is the same. It is a Government in which all the people are represented, which operates directly on the people individually, not upon the States; they retained all the power they did not grant. But each State having expressly parted with so many powers as to constitute, jointly with the other States, a single nation, cannot from that period possess any right to secede, because such secession does not break a league, but destroys the unity of a nation; and any injury to that unity is not only a breach which would result from the contravention of a compact, but it is an offence against the whole Union. To say that any State may at pleasure secede from the Union, is to say that the United States are not a nation; because it would be a solecism to contend that any part of a nation might dissolve its connection with the other parts, to their injury or ruin, without committing any offence. Secession, like any other revolutionary act, may be morally justified by the extremity of oppression; but to call it a constitutional right is confounding the meaning of terms, and can only be done through gross error, or to deceive those who are willing to assert a right, but would pause before they make a revolution, or incur the penalties consequent on a failure.

Because the Union was formed by compact, it is said the parties to that compact may, when they feel themselves aggrieved, depart from it; but it is precisely because it is a compact that they cannot. A compact is an agreement or binding obligation. It may, by its terms, have a sanction or penalty for its breach, or it may not. If it contains no sanction, it may be broken with no other consequence than moral guilt; if it have a sanction, then the breach incurs the designated or implied penalty. A league between independent nations, generally, has no sanction other than a moral one; or, if it should contain a penalty, as there is no common superior, it cannot be enforced. A Government, on the contrary, always has a sanction, expressed or implied; and in our case, it is both necessarily implied and expressly given. An attempt by force of arms to destroy a Government, is an offence, by whatever means the constitutional compact may have been formed; and such Government has the right, by the law of self-defence, to pass Acts for punishing the offender, unless that right is modified, restrained, or resumed by the constitutional Act. In our system, although it is modified in the case of treason, yet authority is expressly given to pass all laws necessary to carry its powers into effect, and under this grant provision has been made for punishing acts which obstruct the due administration of the laws.

It would seem superfluous to add any thing to show the nature of that union which connects us; but, as erroneous opinions on this subject are the foundation of doctrines the most destructive to our peace, I must give some further development to my views on this subject. No one, fellow-citizens, has a higher reverence for the reserved rights of the States than the magistrate who now addresses you. No one would make greater personal sacrifices, or official exertions, to defend them from violation; but equal care must be taken to prevent, on their part, an improper interference with, or resumption of, the rights they have vested in the nation. The line has not been so distinctly drawn as to avoid doubts in some cases, of the exercise of power. Men of the best intentions and soundest views, may differ in their construction of some parts of the Constitution, but there are others on which dispassionate reflection can leave no doubt. Of this nature appears to be the assumed right of secession. It rests, as we have seen, on the alleged undivided sovereignty of the States, and on their having formed in this sovereign capacity a compact which is called the Constitution, from which, because they made it, they have the right to secede. Both of these positions are erroneous, and some of the arguments to prove them so have been anticipated.

The States severally have not retained their entire sovereignty. It has been shown that, in becoming parts of a nation, not members of a league, they surrendered many of their essential parts of sovereignty. The right to make treaties, declare war, levy taxes. exercise exclusive Judicial and Legislative powers, were all of them functions of sovereign power. The States, then, for all these important purposes, were no longer sovereign. The allegiance of their citizens was transferred, in the first instance, to the Government of the United States; they became American citizens, and owed obedience to the Constitution of the United States, and to laws made in conformity with the powers it vested in Congress. This last position has not been and cannot be denied. How, then, can that State be said to be sovereign and independent, whose citizens owe obedience to laws not made by it, and whose magistrates are sworn to disregard those laws when they come in conflict with those passed by another? What shows conclusively that the States cannot be said to have reserved an undivided sovereignty is, that they expressly ceded the right to punish treason — not treason against their separate power — but treason against the United States. Treason is an offence against *sovereignty*, and sovereignty must reside with the power to punish it. But the reserved rights of the States are not less sacred because they have for their common interest made the General Government the depository of these powers. The unity of our political character (as has been shown for another purpose) commenced with its very existence. Under the royal government we had no separate character — our opposition to its oppressions began as United Colonies. We were the United States under the Confederation, and the name was perpetuated, and the Union rendered more perfect by the Federal Constitution. In none of these stages did we consider ourselves in any other light than as forming one nation. Treaties and alliances were made in the name of all. Troops were raised for the joint defence. How, then, with all these proofs that, under all changes of our position, we had, for designated purposes and with defined powers, created national governments — how is it, that the most perfect of those several modes of union should now be considered as a mere league, that may be dissolved at pleasure? It is from an abuse of terms. Compact is used as synonymous with league, although the true term is not employed, because it would at once show the fallacy of the reasoning. It would not do to say that our Constitution was only a league; but it is labored to prove it a compact, (which in one sense it is,) and then to argue that, as a league is a compact, every compact between nations must of course be a league, and that from such an engagement every sovereign power has a right to recede. But it has been shown that in this sense the States are not sovereign, and that even if they were, and the National Constitution had been formed by compact, there would be no right in any one State to exonerate itself from its obligations.

So obvious are the reasons which forbid this secession, that it is necessary only to allude to them. The Union was formed for the benefit of all. It was produced by mutual sacrifices of interests and opinions. Can those sacrifices be recalled? Can the States who magnanimously surrendered their title to the territories of the West recall the grant? Will the inhabitants of the inland States agree to pay the duties that may be imposed without their assent by those on the Atlantic or the Gulf, for their own benefit? Shall there be a free port in one State, and onerous duties in another? No one believes that any right exists in a single State to involve all the others in these and countless other evils, contrary to the engagements solemnly made. Every one must see that the other States, in self-defence, must oppose, at all hazards.

These are the alternatives that are presented by the convention: a repeal of all the Acts for raising revenue, leaving the Government without the means of support; or an acquiescence in the dissolution of the Union by the secession of one of its members. When the first was proposed, it was known that it could not be listened to for a moment. It was known that, if force was applied to oppose the execution of the laws, that it must be repelled by force; that Congress could not, without involving itself in disgrace, and the country in ruin, accede to the proposition; and yet, if this is not done in a given day, or if any attempt is made to execute the laws, the State is, by the ordinance, declared to be out of the Union. The majority of a convention assembled for the purpose have dictated these terms, or rather this rejection of all terms, in the name of the people of South Carolina. It is true that the Governor of the State speaks of the submission of their grievances to a convention of all the States, which, he says, they "sincerely and anxiously seek and desire." Yet this obvious and constitutional mode of obtaining the sense of the other States on the construction of the Federal compact, and amending it, if necessary, has never been attempted by those who have urged the State on this destructive measure. The State might have proposed the call for a general convention to the other States; and Congress, if a sufficient number of them concurred, must have called it. But the first magistrate of South Carolina, when he expressed a hope that, "on a review by Congress and the functionaries of the General Government of the merits of the controversy," such a convention will be accorded to them, must have known that neither Congress nor any functionary of the General Government has authority to call such a convention, unless it be demanded by two thirds of the States. This suggestion, then, is another instance of the reckless inattention to the provisions of the Constitution with which this crisis has been madly hurried on, or of the attempt to persuade the people that a constitutional remedy has been sought and refused. If the Legislature of South Carolina "anxiously desire" a General Convention to consider their complaints, why have they not made application for it in the way the Constitution points out?

The assertion that they "earnestly seek" it is completely negatived by the omission.

This, then, is the position in which we stand. A small majority of the citizens of one State in the Union have elected delegates to a State Convention: that Convention has ordained that all the revenue laws of the United States must be repealed, or that they are no longer a member of the Union. The Governor of that State has recommended to the Legislature the raising of an army to carry the secession into effect, and that he may be empowered to give clearances to vessels in the name of the State. No act of violent opposition to the laws has yet been committed, but such a state of things is hourly apprehended; and it is the intent of this instrument to PROCLAIM, not only that the duty imposed on me by the Constitution "to take care that the laws be faithfully executed," shall be performed to the extent of the powers already vested in me by law, or of such other as the wisdom of Congress shall devise and intrust to me for that purpose, but to warn the citizens of South Carolina, who have been deluded into an opposition to the laws, of the danger they will incur by obedience to the illegal and disorganizing ordinance of the convention; to exhort those who have refused to support it to persevere in their determination to uphold the Constitution and laws of their country, and to point out to all the perilous situation into which the good people of that State have been led; and that the course they are urged to pursue is one of ruin and disgrace to the very State whose rights they affect to support.

Fellow-citizens of my native State! let me not only admonish you, as the first magistrate of our common country, not to incur the penalty of its laws, but use the influence that a father would over his children whom he saw rushing to certain ruin. In that paternal language, with that paternal feeling, let me tell you, my countrymen, that you are deluded by men who are either deceived themselves or wish to deceive you. Mark under what pretences you have been led on to the brink of insurrection and treason, on which you stand! First, a diminution of the value of your staple commodity, lowered by over-production in other quarters, and the consequent diminution in the value of your lands, were the sole effect of the tariff laws. The effect of those laws are confessedly injurious, but the evil was greatly exaggerated, by the unfounded theory you were taught to believe, that its burdens were in proportion to your exports, not to your consumption of imported articles. Your pride was roused by the assertion that a submission to those laws was a state of vassalage, and that resistance to them was equal, in patriotic merit, to the opposition our fathers offered to the oppressive laws of Great Britain. You were told that this opposition might be peaceably — might be constitutionally made; that you might enjoy all the advantages of the Union, and bear none of its burdens.

Eloquent appeals to your passions, to your State pride, to your native courage, to your sense of real injury, were used to prepare you for the period when the mask, which concealed the hideous features of DISUNION, should be taken off. It fell, and you were made to look with complacency on objects which, not long since, you would have regarded with horror. Look back at the arts which have brought you to this state — look forward to the consequences to which it must inevitably lead! Look back to what was first told you as an inducement to enter into this dangerous course. The great political truth was repeated to you, that you had the revolutionary right of resisting all laws that were palpably unconstitutional and intolerably oppressive: it was added that the right to nullify a law rested on the same principle, but that it was a peaceable remedy! This character which was given to it, made you receive, with too much confidence, the assertions that were made of the unconstitutionality of the law, and its oppressive effects. Mark, my fellow-citizens, that by the admission of your leaders, the unconstitutionality must be *palpable*, or it will not justify either resistance or nullification! What is the meaning of the word *palpable*, in the sense in which it is here used? — that which is apparent to every one; that which no man of ordinary intellect will fail to perceive. Is the unconstitutionality of these laws of that description? Let those among your leaders who once approved and advocated the principle of protective duties, answer the question; and let them choose whether they will be considered as incapable then of perceiving that which must have been apparent to every man of common understanding, or as imposing upon your confidence, and endeavoring to mislead you now. In either case, they are unsafe guides in the perilous path they urge you to tread. Ponder well on this circumstance, and you will know how to appreciate the exaggerated language they address to you. They are not champions of liberty, emulating the fame of our revolutionary fathers; nor are you an oppressed people, contending, as they repeat to you, against worse than colonial vassalage. You are free members of a flourishing and happy Union. There is no settled design to oppress you. You have, indeed, felt the unequal operation of laws which may have been unwisely, not unconstitutionally passed; but that inequality must necessarily be removed. At the very moment when you were madly urged on the unfortunate course you have begun, a change in public opinion had commenced. The nearly approaching payment of the public debt, and the consequent necessity of a diminution of duties, had already produced a considerable reduction, and that, too, on some articles of general consumption in your State. The importance of this change was understood, and you were authoritatively told that no further alleviation of your burdens was to be expected, at the very time when the condition of the country imperiously demanded such a modification of the duties as should reduce them to a just and equitable scale. But, as if apprehensive of the effect of this change in allaying your discontents, you were precipitated into the fearful state in which you now find yourselves.

I have urged you to look back to the means that were used

to hurry you on to the position you have now assumed, and forward to the consequences it will produce. Something more is necessary. Contemplate the condition of that country of which you still form an important part? Consider its Government, uniting in one bond of common interests and general protection so many different States, giving to all their inhabitants the proud title of AMERICAN CITIZENS, protecting their commerce, securing their literature and their arts, facilitating their intercommunication, defending their frontiers, and making their name respected in the remotest parts of the earth! Consider the extent of its territory, its increasing and happy population, its advance in arts, which render life agreeable, and the sciences, which elevate the mind! See education spreading the lights of religion, humanity, and general information into every cottage in this wide extent of our Territories and States! Behold it as the asylum where the wretched and the oppressed find a refuge and support! Look on this picture of happiness and honor, and say, WE, TOO, ARE CITIZENS OF AMERICA; Carolina is one of these proud States; her arms have defended, her best blood has cemented this happy Union! And then add, if you can, without horror and remorse, this happy Union we will dissolve; this picture of peace and prosperity we will deface; this free intercourse we will interrupt; these fertile fields we will deluge with blood; the protection of that glorious flag we renounce; the very names of Americans we discard. And for what, mistaken men! — for what do you throw away these inestimable blessings — for what would you exchange your share in the advantages and honor of the Union? For the dream of a separate independence — a dream interrupted by bloody conflicts with your neighbors, and a vile dependence on a foreign power. If your leaders could succeed in establishing a separation, what would be your situation? Are you united at home — are you free from the apprehension of civil discord, with all its fearful consequences? Do our neighboring republics, every day suffering some new revolution, or contending with some new insurrection — do they excite your envy? But the dictates of a high duty oblige me solemnly to announce that you cannot succeed.

The laws of the United States must be executed. I have no discretionary power on the subject — my duty is emphatically pronounced in the Constitution. Those who told you that you might peaceably prevent their execution, deceived you — they could not have been deceived themselves. They know that a forcible opposition could alone prevent the execution of the laws, and they know that such opposition must be repelled. Their object is disunion; but be not deceived by names; disunion, by armed force, is TREASON. Are you really ready to incur its guilt? If you are, on the heads of the instigators of the act be the dreadful consequences — on their heads be the dishonor, but on yours may fall the punishment — on your unhappy State will inevitably fall all the evils of the conflict you force upon the Government of your country. It cannot accede to the mad project of disunion of which you would be the first victims — its first magistrate cannot, if he would, avoid the performance of his duty — the consequence must be fearful for you, distressing to your fellow-citizens here, and to the friends of good government throughout the world. Its enemies have beheld our prosperity with a vexation they could not conceal: it was a standing refutation of their slavish doctrines, and they will point to our discord with the triumph of malignant joy. It is yet in your power to disappoint them. There is yet time to show that the descendants of the Pinckneys, the Sumpters, the Rutledges, and of the thousand other names which adorn the pages of your revolutionary history, will not abandon that Union to support which so many of them fought, and bled, and died. I adjure you, as you honor their memory — as you love the cause of freedom, to which they dedicated their lives — as you prize the peace of your country, the lives of its best citizens, and your own fair fame, to retrace your steps. Snatch from the archives of your State the disorganizing edict of its convention; bid its members to reassemble and promulgate the decided expressions of your will to remain in the path which alone can conduct you to safety, prosperity, and honor; tell them that, compared to disunion, all other evils are light, because that brings with it an accumulation of all; declare that you will never take the field unless the star-spangled banner of your country shall float over you; that you will not be stigmatized when dead, and dishonored and scorned while you live, as the authors of the first attack on the Constitution of your country! Its destroyers you cannot be. You may disturb its peace — you may interrupt the course of its prosperity — you may cloud its reputation for stability — but its tranquillity will be restored, its prosperity will return, and the stain upon its national character will be transferred, and remain an eternal blot on the memory of those who caused the disorder.

Fellow-citizens of the United States! The threat of unhallowed disunion — the names of those, once respected, by whom it is uttered — the array of military force to support it — denote the approach of a crisis in our affairs on which the continuance of our unexampled prosperity, our political existence, and perhaps that of all free governments, may depend. The conjunction demanded a free, a full, and explicit enunciation, not only of my intentions, but of my principles of action; and as the claim was asserted of a right by a State to annul the laws of the Union, and even to secede from it at pleasure, a frank exposition of my opinions in relation to the origin and form of our Government, and the construction I give to the instrument by which it was created, seemed to be proper. Having the fullest confidence in the justness of the legal and constitutional opinion of my duties which has been expressed, I rely with equal confidence on your undivided support in my determination to execute the laws — to preserve the Union by all constitutional means — to arrest, if possible, by moderate but firm measures, the necessity of a recourse to force; and, if it be the will of Heaven that the recurrence of its primeval curse on man for the shedding of a brother's blood should fall upon our land, that it be not called down by any offensive act on the part of the United States.

Fellow-citizens! The momentous case is before you. On your undivided support of your Government depends the decision of the great question it involves, whether your sacred Union will be preserved, and the blessings it secures to us as one people shall be perpetuated. No one can doubt that the unanimity with which that decision will be expressed, will be such as to inspire new confidence in Republican institutions; and that the prudence, the wisdom, and the courage which it will bring to their defence, will transmit them, unimpaired and invigorated, to our children.

May the great Ruler of nations grant that the signal blessings with which He has favored ours may not, by the madness of party or personal ambition, be disregarded and lost; and may His wise providence bring those who have produced this crisis to see the folly, before they feel the misery of civil strife; and inspire a returning veneration for that Union which, if we may dare to penetrate His designs, He has chosen as the only means of attaining the high destinies to which we may reasonably aspire.

In testimony whereof, I have caused the seal of the United States to be hereunto affixed, having signed the same with my hand.

Done at the city of Washington this 10th day of December, in the year of our Lord one thousand eight hundred and thirty-two, and of the Independence of the United States the fifty-seventh.

ANDREW JACKSON.

By the President:

EDW. LIVINGSTON, *Secretary of State.*

F. p. 465.

OPINION AS TO THE CONSTITUTIONAL VALIDITY OF THE LAWS OF NEW YORK GRANTING EXCLUSIVE PRIVILEGES OF STEAM NAVIGATION.

On considering the case submitted to me on behalf of Mr. Gibbons, I am of opinion that he has a perfect right founded on the documents, of which copies are appended to the case, to navigate his steamboats on all the waters of this State, which it enjoys in common with New Jersey, and which communicate either with a port or place in the State of New York, or empty into the Atlantic Ocean; and that such right is not taken away, affected, or impaired by the Legislative grant to Messrs. Livingston and Fulton. I should, therefore, advise Mr. Gibbons, instead of making the application he contemplates to the Legislature, to bring the questions at issue between him and its grantees, to trial in the courts of the United States. The reasons that govern my opinion I shall briefly state.

The case of *Livingston and Fulton* v. *Van Ingen and others*, (9 Johns. Rep. 507,) furnishes, as I humbly conceive, no inferences hostile to the claim of Mr. Gibbons; but, properly considered, strengthens the arguments which occur to me in support of this right. The great question in that cause was twofold, viz: Whether the grant to Livingston and Fulton was absolutely void, as made in contravention of the constitutional powers of Congress, *first*, "To promote the progress of science and the useful arts;" and, *secondly*, whether it were repugnant to the power vested in Congress "to regulate commerce."

I. On the first point, the Court decided that the grant was not absolutely void, on two grounds: *first*, that, considering Messrs. Livingston and Fulton as *inventors*, the State had a concurrent right with Congress to reward them as inventors, by the grant of exclusive privileges; *secondly*, that, considering them not as inventors, but as *possessors and importers* of a foreign invention, the State had an independent power to reward them as such; which power had not been ceded to Congress at all.

It must be borne in mind, that Van Ingen and his associates showed no right or title whatever; and, for aught that appears, their mode of applying the steam-engine in the navigation of their boats was the same that had already been introduced by Livingston and Fulton. Throughout the whole discussion, the powers of the State were assimilated to the powers of Congress; and two of the learned judges, by whom opinions were delivered, Mr. Justice Thompson and Mr. Justice Yates, explicitly admit that the State powers can only be legitimately exercised *in harmony with, and in subordination to, the superior power of Congress.* In strict reasoning, therefore, no more can be inferred from the decision of the Court of Errors than that the grant to Livingston and Fulton is so far valid as to secure to them, and their representatives, an exclusive right *to that peculiar mode of navigating vessels by steam or fire which they introduced into practice, and of which the Act of March,* 1798, *states Mr. Livingston to be in possession.* Such is the extent of the constitutional power of Congress, to which the State powers are resembled; and it is only by this limited construction of the grant that the reasoning of the learned judges can be rendered applicable and consistent, as it is, then, only that a "collision" between this exercise of the State sovereignty and the constitutional power of Congress can possibly be prevented. Certainly the Court of Errors has not said, nor is there any ground for supposing that it meant to say, that the State, by virtue, either of its concurrent power to reward inventors, or its independent power to reward the importers of foreign inventions, can prohibit the introduction and use, within its jurisdiction, of all future inventions, *although secured by patent,* in relation to the same object; or, by a still more violent stretch of authority, transfer the exclusive right to such inventions from the patentee to the Legislative favorite. Yet, if the terms of the original grant to Messrs. Livingston and Fulton, and of the various laws passed to enlarge and secure that grant, are to be taken in their literal extent, such was to be their operation.

By the Act of March, 1798, all the privileges granted before to John Fitch and his representatives were transferred to Mr. Livingston. These privileges were "the sole and exclusive right of constructing, making, using, employing, or navigating all, and every species or kind of boats or water-craft, which might be urged or propelled through the waters of this State, by force of fire or steam, in all creeks, rivers, &c., within the territory and jurisdiction of this State." It must be remembered, that the grant to Fitch was made *previously to the adoption of the present Federal Constitution,* and before the State had surrendered this portion of its sovereignty to the General Government; while it remained in full and acknowledged possession of the powers to reward genius and skill, and to encourage and foster navigation and commerce, by the means resorted to in favor of John Fitch. But she had ceded those powers, which, to be effectual, must be exclusive, to the United States, before the *monopoly* — for this is the proper, though odious term, by which such grants should be designated — was attempted to be vested in Messrs. Livingston and Fulton. The only limitation of this monopoly of navigation is, that *steam* or *fire* be made use of as the propelling force; and the general terms of the grant comprehend every possible mode of producing and applying that force, which human ingenuity has discovered or can invent.

By the Act of 1808, creating the forfeiture, it is declared that "no person or persons, without the license of the persons entitled to the exclusive right, shall navigate on the waters of this State, or within the jurisdiction thereof, any boat or vessel moved by steam or fire." Thus the introduction into this State of any future invention, however original or valuable, in navigating vessels by steam or fire, is in terms prohibited without the sanction of the individuals in whom the right to employ *all* such inventions is exclusively vested. The very ground on which invention is to work is seized upon and preoccupied, and an exclusive privilege given, which not only prevents the future reward of security to inventors, but, in one important region, would stop the progress of discovery itself. The very elements by which improvements can be made is monopolized, and the occasion snatched from Congress of exercising the power given to it by the Constitution. Now, if this can be done in one State in relation to any one subject, why may it not be done in all, and in relation to all? Where are we to fix the limit of State power? Why may not the States, respectively, grant monopolies embracing all the possible elements and materials, of which inventions can be framed, and every possible subject upon which ingenuity can operate, and thus anticipate and frustrate, *in toto*, the exercise of the constitutional power of Congress, *to secure an exclusive right to inventors?*

It may be said that this is an extreme and improbable supposition. I admit it to be improbable that the States will attempt such an exercise of power; but it is by extreme cases, or, to speak with more propriety, it is by pursuing a doctrine to its legitimate consequences, that we are frequently best enabled to detect or illustrate its absurdity. If the constitutional power of Congress can be taken away by the grant of a State monopoly in any case, I am at a loss to conceive why it may not, by similar means, be taken away in all cases. The principle once admitted, the consequence, of necessity, follows. It was affirmed in argument, by one of the learned counsel[1] by whom the claim of Messrs. Livingston and Fulton was so ably vindicated in the Court of Errors, that the only effect of a patent is to confer on the inventor *an exclusive right of property in his discovery;* that, at common law, an invention or discovery is converted into a chattel, a subject to which a right of property can attach. The exercise, however, of this right of property is, as it was said, still liable to be controlled and regulated by

[1] The late Thomas Addis Emmet.

the municipal laws of the several States, who may prohibit the use of any particular invention, as noxious to the health, injurious to the morals, or in any other respect prejudicial to the welfare of its citizens. When I declare that I cannot help entertaining the strongest doubts of the truth and soundness of this doctrine, I must be understood to speak with the utmost diffidence in my own judgment, and with the highest respect for the authority of those by whom the doctrine has been advanced or adopted. It seems to me that Congress possesses exclusively the power to determine whether an invention for which a patent is sought be useful or pernicious; in other words, whether it be one for which a patent ought or ought not to be granted. The object of the constitutional power of Congress to secure an exclusive right to inventions, is the promotion of the "*useful* arts." An invention useless or pernicious, it is evident, would not be a proper object for its exercise. Should a patent for such an invention unadvisedly have issued, there can be no doubt that Congress might repeal the patent, and interdict the use of the noxious discovery.

The grant of the power in question to Congress would, as it appears to me, be completely nugatory, by the admission that the States, in the exercise of an absolute discretion, may prohibit the introduction or use of any particular invention, for which a patent has been regularly obtained. Were this construction of the Constitution to prevail, the States, it seems to me, would retain, substantially, the very power they nominally have parted with. What is the Constitution? It is the instrument by which the States have severally ceded to the Federal Government a certain portion of their own sovereignty, to be exercised for the common good. The power of securing the exclusive right of inventors is thus given. But if the States not only possess a concurrent power of granting exclusive privileges within their respective limits, but may, in effect, repeal and annul, *ad libitum*, any and all patents which Congress may have issued, what power, I may ask, in relation to this subject, have they parted with? What portion of their sovereignty, *quoad hoc*, have they ceded? The whole value of a patent consists, I apprehend, in the exclusive privilege of using the invention, which it is meant to ascertain and secure. To strip the inventor of this, in order to confer upon him a barren metaphysical right, is not to reward, but to mock and insult him. It may be a good scholastic distinction, but it is very contradictory to common sense to say that a man's right of property is not invaded when his use and enjoyment of it are interdicted. Suppose a State Legislature, jealous of the overgrown and accumulating wealth of some unpopular landlord, should, on the common pretext of the public good, release his tenants, *in perpetuum*, from the payment of rents, would the lord of the manor of Clermont[1] consider this no invasion of the right of property, because the fee-simple, technically speaking, would still remain vested in the obnoxious proprietor?

It is admitted by those who urge the doctrine against which I am contending, that the States cannot, in direct terms, divest or take away an exclusive right secured by patent. But to prohibit the exercise of such a right within the jurisdiction of a State, and during the whole period for which the patent has been granted, is, in effect, so far as the power of the State extends, to take away the right itself. There may be a difference in the terms employed, but the injury to the patentee is in both cases precisely the same. Nor can I believe that the Federal Courts would listen to the verbal distinction by which such a usurpation of power is attempted to be justified. It is not my intention to deny that the States may, by their own laws, define and modify the rights of property within their respective jurisdictions, *when such rights have their origin in the State or municipal law.* I am free to allow, that not only the exercise of those rights may, by the same law, be controlled and regulated, but even that the rights themselves may be

[1] The property of Chancellor Livingston.

annulled and destroyed. But it seems to have been forgotten that the right of a patentee is not derived from State authority, but has its foundation in the Constitution and laws of the United States. As the State prohibition of its exercise, in whatever terms expressed, under whatsoever pretext made, however colored and disguised, would, in truth, be a violation of the right itself, I am forced to the conclusion that such a Legislative act would be wholly void, as repugnant to that law which is confessed by all to be *supreme and paramount*.

II. I consider the grant to Messrs. Livingston and Fulton as repugnant, also, to that clause of the Constitution of the United States which vests in Congress the power "to regulate commerce with foreign nations and among the several States;" which power I regard also as necessarily exclusive. It has been so treated by every department of the Government, and by all classes of citizens, in every quarter of the Union, ever since the adoption of the Federal Constitution. It was to effect this transfer of power that the Constitution owes its origin. This was the express motive for assembling the Federal Convention. The exclusive grant of this power was essentially requisite to give to our shipping its nationality and protection; and the surrender of this power was, in this State, the most formidable obstacle to the ratification of the new Constitution. It possessed the best harbor upon the Atlantic coast; the fertility of its western territory was known; the rapid increase of its population was confidently anticipated; the tide of immigration had begun to flow in upon it; and the consequent accession of wealth and power promised from these sources afforded the most seductive objects to the ambition of its statesmen and politicians. These were the causes, indeed, which combined to delay and resist the adoption of the Constitution in this State, until it became certain that, by the assent of "*nine States*," it would go into immediate operation among them, while this State and the other recusant members of the old Confederacy would thus be deprived of the benefits both of the former compact, and of the Government by which it was superseded.

It remains only to consider in what manner Mr. Gibbons may best avail himself of the rights conferred by his patents and coasting license under the Constitution and laws of the United States. My advice is, that he send his boat into those waters between this State and New Jersey which are claimed as lying within the territorial boundary, as well as the jurisdiction of the former, without confining her navigation to those waters which, though admitted to be within the limits of the latter, yet over which New York claims, nevertheless, exclusive jurisdiction. Nor need he be deterred by fear of having his boats seized under the Act of 1811, authorizing Messrs. Livingston and Fulton immediately to seize and keep possession of his property before condemnation, and without trial; thus giving them the benefit of an execution before the verdict of a jury or the judgment of a Court, and without the intervention of the sheriff; for I hold this monstrous provision to be so clearly repugnant to that fundamental law which man derives from his Creator, and which is paramount to all human authority, that no judge on earth will venture to execute it.[1]

W. A. Duer.

Albany, July 14, 1816.

G. p. 176.

AN ORDINANCE FOR THE GOVERNMENT OF THE TERRITORY OF THE UNITED STATES NORTHWEST OF THE RIVER OHIO.

Be *it ordained by the United States in Congress assembled*, that the said territory, for the purposes of temporary Government, be one District; subject, however, to be divided into two Districts, as future circumstances may, in the opinion of Congress, make it expedient.

[1] The application of the State Grantees to Chancellor Kent for an order of seizure of Mr. Gibbons's boat, under this statute, was denied, and the Common Law Injunction only was granted. See the case of Gibbons *v.* Ogden, 10 *Wheat.* 446.

Be it ordained by the authority aforesaid, that the estates both of resident and non-resident proprietors in the said Territory dying intestate, shall descend to, and be distributed among their children, and the descendants of a deceased child, in equal parts; the descendants of a deceased child or grandchild to take the share of their deceased parent in equal parts among them; and where there shall be no children or descendants, then in equal parts to the next of kin in equal degree; and among collaterals, the children of a deceased brother or sister of the intestate shall have in equal parts among them their deceased parents' share; and there shall in no case be a distinction between kindred of the whole and half blood; saving in all cases to the widow of the intestate her third part of the real estate for life, and one third part of the personal estate; and this law relative to descents and dower shall remain in full force until altered by the Legislature of the District. And until the Governor and judges shall adopt laws as hereinafter mentioned, estates in the said territory may be devised or bequeathed by wills in writing, signed and sealed by him or her in whom the estate may be (being of full age) and attested by three witnesses; and real estates may be conveyed by lease and release, or bargain and sale, signed, sealed, and delivered by the person, being of full age, in whom the estate may be, and attested by two witnesses, provided such wills be duly proved, and such conveyances be acknowledged, or the execution thereof duly proved, and be recorded within one year after proper magistrates, courts, and registers shall be appointed for that purpose; and personal property may be transferred by delivery; saving, however to the French and Canadian inhabitants, and other settlers, of the Kaskaskies, St. Vincent's, and the neighboring villages, who have heretofore professed themselves citizens of Virginia, their laws and customs now in force among them, relative to the descent and conveyance of property.

Be it ordained by the authority aforesaid, that there shall be appointed from time to time, by Congress, a Governor, whose commission shall continue in force for the term of three years, unless sooner revoked by Congress: he shall reside in the district, and have a freehold estate therein in one thousand acres of land, while in the exercise of his office.

There shall be appointed from time to time, by Congress, a Secretary, whose commission shall continue in force for four years, unless sooner revoked; he shall reside in the District, and have a freehold estate therein in five hundred acres of land, while in the exercise of his office; it shall be his duty to keep and preserve the Acts and laws passed by the Legislature, and the public records of the District, and the proceedings of the Governor in his Executive Department; and transmit authentic copies of such Acts and proceedings, every six months, to the Secretary of Congress; there shall also be appointed a Court, to consist of three judges, any two of whom to form a Court, who shall have a Common Law jurisdiction, and reside in the District, and have each therein a freehold estate in five hundred acres of land, while in the exercise of their offices; and their commissions shall continue in force during good behaviour.

The Governor and judges, or a majority of them, shall adopt and publish in the District such laws of the original States, criminal and civil, as may be necessary and best suited to the circumstances of the District, and report them to Congress from time to time; which laws shall be in force in the District until the organization of the General Assembly therein, unless disapproved of by Congress; but afterward the Legislature shall have authority to alter them as they shall think fit.

The Governor for the time being shall be Commander-in-Chief of the militia, appoint and commission all officers in the same below the rank of General officers; all General officers shall be appointed and commissioned by Congress.

Previous to the organization of the General Assembly, the Governor shall appoint such magistrates and other civil officers, in each county or township, as he shall find necessary for the preservation of the peace and good order in the same; after the General Assembly shall be organized, the powers and duties of magistrates and other civil officers shall be regulated and defined by the said Assembly; but all magistrates and other civil officers not herein otherwise directed shall, during the continuance of this temporary Government, be appointed by the Governor.

For the prevention of crimes and injuries, the laws to be adopted or made shall have force in all parts of the District, and for the execution of process, criminal and civil, the Governor shall make proper divisions thereof; and he shall proceed from time to time, as circumstances may require, to lay out the parts of the District in which the Indian titles shall have been extinguished into counties and townships, subject, however, to such alterations as may thereafter be made by the Legislature.

So soon as there shall be five thousand free male inhabitants, of full age, in the District, upon giving proof thereof to the Governor, they shall receive authority, with time and place to elect Representatives from their counties or townships to represent them in the General Assembly; provided that for every five hundred free male inhabitants, there shall be one Representative, and so on progressively with the number of free male inhabitants shall the right of representation increase, until the number of Representatives shall amount to twenty-five; after which the number and proportion of Representatives shall be regulated by the Legislature: provided that no person be eligible or qualified to act as a Representative unless he shall have been a citizen of one of the United States three years, and be a resident in the District, or unless he shall have resided in the District three years; and in either case, shall likewise hold in his own right, in fee-simple, two hundred acres of land within the same: provided, also, that a freehold in fifty acres of land in the District, having been a citizen of one of the States, and being resident in the District, or the like freehold, and two years' residence in the District, shall be necessary to qualify a man as an elector of a Representative.

The Representatives thus elected shall serve for the term of two years; and in case of the death of a Representative, or removal from office, the Governor shall issue a writ to the county or township for which he was a member to elect another in his stead, to serve for the residue of the term.

The General Assembly, or Legislature, shall consist of the Governor, Legislative Council, and a House of Representatives. The Legislative Council shall consist of five members, to continue in office five years, unless sooner removed by Congress, any three of whom to be a quorum; and the members of the Council shall be nominated and appointed in the following manner, to wit: As soon as Representatives shall be elected, the Governor shall appoint a time and place for them to meet together, and when met, they shall nominate ten persons, residents in the District, and each possessed of a freehold in five hundred acres of land, and return their names to Congress; five of whom Congress shall appoint and commission to serve as aforesaid; and whenever a vacancy shall happen in the Council, by death or removal from office, the House of Representatives shall nominate two persons, qualified as aforesaid for each vacancy, and return their names to Congress, one of whom Congress shall appoint and commission for the residue of the term. And every five years, four months at least before the expiration of the time of service of the members of Council, the said House shall nominate ten persons, qualified as aforesaid, and return their names to Congress; five of whom Congress shall appoint and commission to serve as members of the Council five years, unless sooner removed. And the Governor, Legislative Council, and House of Representatives shall have authority to make laws, in all cases, for the good government of the District, not repugnant to the principles and articles in this ordinance established and declared. And all bills having passed by a majority in the House, and by a majority in the Council, shall be referred to the Governor for his assent; but no bill or Legislative Act whatever shall be of any force without his assent. The Governor shall have power to convene, prorogue, and dissolve the General Assembly, when in his opinion it shall be expedient.

The Governor, Judges, Legislative Council, Secretary, and such other officers as Congress shall appoint in the District, shall take an oath or affirmation of fidelity, and of office; the Governor before the President of Congress, and all other officers before the Governor. As soon as a Legislature shall be formed in the District, the Council and House, assembled in one room, shall have authority, by joint ballot, to elect a delegate to Congress, who shall have a seat in Congress, with a right of debating, but not of voting, during this temporary Government.

And for extending the fundamental principles of civil and religious liberty, which form the basis whereon these republics, their laws and constitutions are erected; to fix and establish those principles as the basis of all laws, constitutions, and governments, which forever hereafter shall be formed in the said Territory; to provide also for the establishment of States, and permanent Government therein, and for their admission to a share in the Federal Councils, on an equal footing with the original States, at as early periods as may be consistent with the general interest:

It is hereby ordained and declared, by the authority aforesaid, that the following Articles shall be considered as Articles of compact between the original States, and the people and States in the said Territory, and forever remain unalterable, unless by common consent, to wit:

Article I. No person demeaning himself in a peaceable and orderly manner, shall ever be molested on account of his mode of worship or religious sentiments in the said Territory.

Art. II. The inhabitants of the said Territory shall always be entitled to the benefits of the writ of *habeas corpus*, and of a trial by Jury; of a proportionate representation of the people in the Legislature, and of Judicial proceedings according to the course of the Common Law. All persons shall be bailable, unless for capital offences, where the proof shall be evident, or the presumption great. All fines shall be moderate, and no cruel or unusual punishments shall be inflicted. No man shall be deprived of his liberty or property but by the judgment of his peers or the law of the land; and should the public exigencies make it necessary for the common preservation, to take any person's property, or to demand his particular services, full compensation shall be made for the same. And in the just preservation of rights and property, it is understood and declared that no law ought ever to be made, or have force in the said Territory, that shall in any manner whatever interfere with, or affect private contracts or engagements, *boná fide*, and without fraud previously formed.

Art. III. Religion, morality, and knowledge being necessary to good government and the happiness of mankind, schools and the means of education shall forever be encouraged. The utmost good faith shall always be observed towards the Indians; their lands and property shall never be taken from them without their consent; and in their property, rights, and liberty, they never shall be invaded or disturbed, unless in just and lawful wars authorized by Congress; but laws founded in justice and humanity shall from time to time be made, for preventing wrongs being done to them, and for preserving peace and friendship with them.

Art. IV. The said Territory, and the States which may be formed therein, shall forever remain a part of this Confederacy of the United States of America, subject to the Articles of Confederation, and to such alterations therein as shall be constitutionally made, and to all the Acts and ordinances of the United States in Congress assembled conformable thereto. The inhabitants and settlers in the said Territory shall be subject to pay a part of the Federal debts, contracted or to be contracted, and a proportional part of the expenses of Government, to be apportioned on them by Congress, according to the same common rule and measure by which apportionments thereof shall be made on the other States; and the taxes for paying their proportion shall be laid and levied by the authority and direction of the Legislatures of the District or Districts or new States, as in the original States, within the time agreed upon by the United States in Congress assembled. The Legislatures of those Districts or new States shall never interfere with the primary disposal of the soil by the United States in Congress assembled, nor with any regulations Congress may find necessary for securing the title in such soil to the *bonâ fide* purchasers. No tax shall be imposed on lands the property of the United States; and in no case shall non-resident proprietors be taxed higher than residents. The navigable waters leading into the Mississippi and St. Lawrence, and the carrying places between the same, shall be common highways, and forever free, as well to the inhabitants of the said Territory as to the citizens of the United States, and those of any other States that may be admitted into the Confederacy, without any tax, impost, or duty therefor.

Art. V. There shall be formed in the said Territory not less than three, nor more than five States; and the boundaries of the States, as soon as Virginia shall alter her Act of cession, and consent to the same, shall become fixed and established as follows, to wit: The western State in the said Territory shall be bounded by the Mississippi, the Ohio, and Wabash rivers; a direct line drawn from the Wabash and Post Vincent's due north to the territorial line between the United States and Canada; and by the said territorial line to the Lake of the Woods and Mississippi. The middle State shall be bounded by the said direct line, the Wabash from Post Vincent's to the Ohio; by the Ohio, by a direct line drawn due north from the mouth of the Great Miami to the said territorial line, and by the said territorial line. The eastern State shall be bounded by the last-mentioned District line, the Ohio, Pennsylvania, and the said territorial line: Provided, however, and it is further understood and declared, that the boundaries of these three States shall be subject so far to be altered, that if Congress shall hereafter find it expedient, they shall have authority to form one or two States in that part of the said Territory which lies north of an east and west line drawn through the southerly bend or extreme of Lake Michigan. And whenever any of the said States shall have sixty thousand free inhabitants therein, such State shall be admitted, by its delegates, into the Congress of the United States, on an equal footing with the original States, in all respects whatever, and shall be at liberty to form a permanent Constitution and State Government: Provided the Constitution and Government so to be formed shall be republican, and in conformity to the principles contained in these Articles; and so far as it can be consistent with the general interest of the Confederacy, such admission shall be allowed at an earlier period, and when there may be a less number of free inhabitants in the State than sixty thousand.

Art. VI. There shall be neither slavery nor involuntary servitude in the said Territory, otherwise than in punishment of crimes, whereof the party shall have been duly convicted: Provided, always, that any person escaping into the same, from whom labor or service is lawfully claimed in any one of the original States, such fugitive may be lawfully reclaimed, and conveyed to the person claiming his or her labor or service as aforesaid.

Done by the United States, in Congress assembled, the thirteenth day of July, in the year of our Lord one thousand seven hundred and eighty-seven, and of their sovereignty and independence the twelfth.

WILLIAM GRAYSON, *Chairman.*

CHARLES THOMSON, *Secretary.*

H.

VIRGINIA RESOLUTIONS OF 1798,

Pronouncing the Alien and Sedition Laws unconstitutional, and defining the rights of the States. Drawn by James Madison.

In the Virginia House of Delegates, Friday, Dec. 21, 1798.

Resolved, That the General Assembly of Virginia, doth unequivocally express a firm resolution to maintain and defend the Constitution of the United States, and the Constitution of this State against every aggression, either foreign or domestic; and that they will support the Government of the United States in all measures warranted by the former.

That this Assembly most solemnly declares a warm attachment to the Union of the States, to maintain which it pledges its powers; and that, for this end, it is their duty to watch over and oppose every infraction of those principles which constitute the only basis of that union, because a faithful observance of them can alone secure its existence and the public happiness.

That this Assembly doth explicitly and peremptorily declare, that it views the powers of the Federal Government, as resulting from the compact to which the States are parties, as limited by the plain sense and intention of the instrument constituting that compact, as no further valid than they are authorized by the grants enumerated in that compact; and that in case of a deliberate, palpable, and dangerous exercise of other powers, not granted by the said compact, the States, who are parties thereto, have the right, and are in duty bound, to interpose for arresting the progress of the evil, and for maintaining within their respective limits, the authorities, rights, and liberties appertaining to them.

That the General Assembly doth also express its deep regret, that a spirit has, in sundry instances, been manifested by the Federal Government, to enlarge its powers by forced constructions of the constitutional charter which defines them; and, that indications have appeared of a design to expound certain general phrases, (which, having been copied from the very limited grant of powers in the former Articles of Confederation, were the less liable to be misconstrued,) so as to destroy the meaning and effect of the particular enumeration which necessarily explains, and limits the general phrases, and so as to consolidate the States by degrees, into one sovereignty, the obvious tendency and inevitable result of which would be, to transform the present republican system of the United States into an absolute or at best a mixed monarchy.

That the General Assembly doth particularly protest against the palpable and alarming infractions of the Constitution in the two late cases of the "Alien and Sedition Acts," passed at the last session of Congress; the first of which exercises a power nowhere delegated to the Federal Government, and which, by uniting Legislative and Judicial powers to those of Executive, subverts the general principles of free government, as well as the particular organization and positive provisions of the Federal Constitution; and the other of which Acts exercises, in like manner, a power not delegated by the Constitution, but on the contrary, expressly and positively forbidden by one of the amendments thereto; a power which, more than any other, ought to produce universal alarm, because it is levelled against the right of freely examining public characters and measures, and of free communication among the people thereon, which has ever been justly deemed the only effectual guardian of every other right.

That this State having by its convention, which ratified the Federal Constitution, expressly declared, that among other essential rights, "the liberty of conscience and the press cannot be cancelled, abridged, restrained, or modified by any authority of the United States," and from its extreme anxiety to guard these rights from every possible attack of sophistry and ambition, having, with other States, recommended an amendment for that purpose, which amendment was in due time annexed to the Constitution, it would mark a reproachful inconsistency and criminal degeneracy, if an indifference were now shown to the most palpable violation of one of the rights thus declared and secured, and to the establishment of a precedent which may be fatal to the other.

That the good people of this Commonwealth, having ever felt, and continuing to feel the most sincere affection for their brethren of the other States; the truest anxiety for establishing and perpetuating the union of all; and the most scrupulous fidelity to that Constitution, which is the pledge of mutual friendship, and the instrument of mutual happiness; the General Assembly doth solemnly appeal to the like dispositions in the other States, in confidence, that they will concur with this Commonwealth in declaring, as it does hereby declare, that the Acts aforesaid are unconstitutional, and that the necessary and proper measures will be taken by each for coöperating with this State, in maintaining unimpaired the authorities, rights, and liberties, reserved to the States respectively, or to the people.

That the Governor be desired to transmit a copy of the foregoing resolutions to the Executive authority of each of the other States, with a request that the same may be communicated to the Legislature thereof; and that a copy be furnished to each of the Senators and Representatives representing this State in the Congress of the United States.

Attest, JOHN STEWART.

1798, December 24. Agreed to by the Senate.

H. BROOKE.

A true copy from the original deposited in the office of the General Assembly. JOHN STEWART,
Keeper of Rolls.

KENTUCKY RESOLUTIONS OF 1798 AND 1799.

THE ORIGINAL DRAFT PREPARED BY THOMAS JEFFERSON.

The following Resolutions passed the House of Representatives of Kentucky Nov. 10, 1798. *On the passage of the first Resolution, one dissentient;* 2*d,* 3*d,* 4*th,* 5*th,* 6*th,* 7*th,* 8*th, two dissentients;* 9*th, three dissentients.*

I. *Resolved,* That the several States composing the United States of America, are not united on the principle of unlimited submission to their General Government; but that by compact under the style and title of a Constitution for the United States, and of amendments thereto, they constituted a General Government for special purposes, delegated to that Government certain definite powers, reserving, each State to itself, the residuary mass of right to their own self-government; and that, whensoever the General Government assumes undelegated powers, its acts are unauthoritative, void, and of no force; that to this compact each State acceded as a State, and is an integral party; that this Government, created by this compact, was not made the exclusive or final judge of the extent of the powers delegated to itself; since that would have made its discretion, and not the Constitution, the measure of its powers; but that as in all other cases of compact, among parties having no common judge, each party has an equal right to judge for itself, as well of infractions as of the mode and measure of redress.

II. *Resolved,* That the Constitution of the United States having delegated to Congress a power to punish treason, counterfeiting the securities and current coin of the United States, piracies and felonies committed on the high seas, and offences against the laws of nations, and no other crimes whatever, and it being true, as a general principle, and one of the amendments to the Constitution having also declared, "that the powers not delegated to the United States by the Constitution, nor prohibited by it to the States, are reserved to the States respectively, or to the people," therefore, also, the same Act of Congress, passed on the 14th day of July, 1798, and entitled, "An Act in addition to the Act entitled an Act for the punishment of certain crimes against the United States," as also the Act passed by them on the 27th day of June, 1798, entitled "An Act to punish frauds committed on the Bank of the United States," (and all other their Acts which assume to create, define, or punish crimes other than those enumerated in the Constitution,) are altogether void and of no force, and that the power to create, define, and punish such other crimes is reserved, and of right appertains solely and exclusively to the respective States, each within its own territory.

III. *Resolved*, That it is true, as a general principle, and is also expressly declared by one of the amendments to the Constitution, that "the powers not delegated to the United States by the Constitution, nor prohibited by it to the States, are reserved to the States respectively or to the people;" and, that no power over the freedom of religion, freedom of speech, or freedom of the press, being delegated to the United States by the Constitution, nor prohibited by it to the States, all lawful powers respecting the same did of right remain, and were reserved to the States or to the people; that thus was manifested their determination to retain to themselves the right of judging how far the licentiousness of speech and of the press may be abridged without lessening their useful freedom, and how far those abuses which cannot be separated from their use, should be tolerated rather than the use be destroyed; and thus also they guarded against all abridgment by the United States of the freedom of religious principles and exercises, and retained to themselves the right of protecting the same, as this, stated by a law passed on the general demand of its citizens, had already protected them from all human restraint or interference; and that, in addition to this general principle and express declaration, another and more special provision has been made by one of the amendments to the Constitution, which expressly declares that "Congress shall make no laws respecting an establishment of religion, or prohibiting the free exercise thereof, or abridging the freedom of speech, or of the press," thereby guarding in the same sentence, and under the same words, the freedom of religion, of speech, and of the press, insomuch that whatever violates either, throws down the sanctuary which covers the others, and that libels, falsehood, and defamation, equally with heresy and false religion, are withheld from the cognizance of Federal tribunals. That therefore the Act of the Congress of the United States, passed on the 14th of July, 1798, entitled "An Act in addition to the Act entitled an Act for the punishment of certain crimes against the United States," which does abridge the freedom of the press, is not law, but is altogether void and of no force.

IV. *Resolved,* That alien friends are under the jurisdiction and protection of the laws of the State wherein they are; that no power over them has been delegated to the United States, nor prohibited to the individual States distinct from their power over citizens; and it being true, as a general principle, and one of the amendments to the Constitution having also declared, that "the powers not delegated to the United States by the Constitution, nor prohibited to the States, are reserved to the States respectively, or to the people," the Act of the Congress of the United States, passed the 22d day of June, 1798, entitled, "An Act concerning aliens," which assumes power over alien friends not delegated by the Constitution, is not law, but is altogether void and of no force.

V. *Resolved,* That in addition to the general principle as well as the express declaration, that powers not delegated are reserved, another and more special provision inferred in the Constitution, from abundant caution has declared, "that the migration or importation of such persons as any of the States now existing shall think proper to admit, shall not be prohibited by the Congress prior to the year 1808." That this Commonwealth does admit the migration of alien friends described as the subject of the said Act concerning aliens; that a provision against prohibiting their migration is a provision against all acts equivalent thereto, or it would be nugatory; that to remove them when migrated is equivalent to a prohibition of their migration, and is, therefore, contrary to the said provision of the Constitution and void.

VI. *Resolved*, That the imprisonment of a person under the protection of the laws of this Commonwealth on his failure to obey the simple order of the President, to depart out of the United States, as is undertaken by the said Act, entitled "An Act concerning Aliens," is contrary to the Constitution, one amendment in which has provided, that "no person shall be deprived of liberty without due process of law," and, that another having provided, "that in all criminal prosecutions, the accused shall enjoy the right to a public trial by an impartial jury, to be informed as to the nature and cause of the accusation, to be confronted with the witnesses against him, to have compulsory process for obtaining witnesses in his favor, and to have assistance of counsel for his defence," the same Act undertaking to authorize the President to remove a person out of the United States who is under the protection of the law, on his own suspicion, without jury, without public trial; without confrontation of the witnesses against him, without having witnesses in his favor, without defence, without counsel, is contrary to these provisions also of the Constitution, is therefore not law, but utterly void and of no force.

That transferring the power of judging any person who is under the protection of the laws, from the Courts to the President of the United States, as is undertaken by the same Act concerning aliens, is against the article of the Constitution which provides that "the Judicial power of the United States shall be vested in the Courts, the judges of which shall hold their office during good behavior," and that the said Act is void for that reason also; and it is further to be noted that this transfer of Judiciary power is to that magistrate of the General Government who already possesses all the Executive, and a qualified negative in all the Legislative powers.

VII. *Resolved,* That the construction applied by the General Government (as is evident by sundry of their proceedings) to those parts of the Constitution of the United States which delegate to Congress power to lay and collect taxes, duties, imposts, excises; to pay the debts and provide for the common defence and general welfare of the United States, and to make all laws which shall be necessary and proper for carrying into execution the powers vested by the Constitution in the Government of the United States, or any department thereof, goes to the destruction of all the limits prescribed to their power by the Constitution — That words meant by that instrument to be subsidiary only to the execution of the limited powers, ought not to be so construed as themselves to give unlimited powers, nor a part so to be taken as to destroy the whole residue of the instrument: That the proceedings of the General Government under color of those articles, will be a fit and necessary subject for revisal and correction at a time of greater tranquillity, while those specified in the preceding resolutions call for immediate redress.

VIII. *Resolved,* That the preceding resolutions be transmitted to the Senators and Representatives in Congress from this Commonwealth, who are enjoined to present the same to their respective Houses, and to use their best endeavors to procure at the next session of Congress, a repeal of the aforesaid unconstitutional and obnoxious Acts.

IX. *Resolved,* lastly, That the Governor of this Commonwealth be, and is hereby authorized and requested to communicate the preceding resolutions to the Legislatures of the several States, to assure them that this Commonwealth considers union for special national purposes, and particularly for those specified in their late Federal compact, to be friendly to the peace, happiness, and prosperity of all the States — that faithful to that compact, according to the plain intent and meaning in which it was understood and acceded to by the several parties, it is sincerely anxious for its preservation; that it does also believe that, to take from the States all the powers of self-government, and transfer them to a general and consolidated Government, without regard to the special delegations and reservations solemnly agreed to in that compact, is not for the peace, happiness, or prosperity of these States: And that, therefore, this Commonwealth is determined, as it doubts not its co-States are, to submit to undelegated and consequently unlimited powers in no man or body of men on earth; that if the Acts before specified should stand, these conclusions would flow from them; that the General Government may place any act they think proper on the list of crimes and punish it themselves whether enumerated or not enumerated by the Constitution as cognizable by them; that they may transfer its cognizance to the President or any other person, who may himself be the accuser, counsel, judge, and jury, whose suspicions may be the evidence, his order the sentence, his officer the executioner, and his breast the sole record of the transaction; that a very numerous and valuable description of the inhabitants of these States, being by this precedent reduced as outlaws to the absolute dominion of one man, and the barriers of the Constitution thus swept from us all; no rampart now remains against the passions and the power of a majority of Congress, to protect from a like exportation or other grievous punishment the minority of the same body, the Legislatures, Judges, Governors, and Counsellors of the States, nor their other peaceable inhabitants who may venture to reclaim the constitutional rights and liberties of the States and people, or who, for other causes, good or bad, may be obnoxious to the view or marked by the suspicions of the President, or to be thought dangerous to his or their elections or other interests, public or personal; that the friendless alien has been selected as the safest subject of a first experiment; but the citizen will soon follow, or rather has already followed, for already has a sedition Act marked him as a prey: That these and successive Acts of the same character, unless arrested on the threshold, may tend to drive these States into revolution and blood, and will furnish new calumnies against republican governments, and new pretexts for those who wish it to be believed that man cannot be governed but by a rod of iron; that it would be a dangerous delusion were a confidence in the men of our choice to silence our fears for the safety of our rights; that confidence is everywhere the parent of despotism: free government is founded in jealousy and not in confidence; it is jealousy and not confidence which prescribes limited Constitutions to bind down those whom we are obliged to trust with power; that our Constitution has accordingly fixed the limits to which and no further our confidence may go; and let the honest advocate of confidence read the alien and sedition Acts, and say if the Constitution has not been wise in fixing limits to the Government it created, and whether we should be wise in destroying those limits? Let him say what the Government is, if it be not a tyranny which the men of our choice have conferred on the President, and the President of our choice has assented to and accepted over the friendly strangers, to whom the mild spirit of our country and its laws had pledged hospitality and protection; that the men of our choice have more respected the bare suspicions of the President than the solid rights of innocence, the claims of justification, the sacred force of truth, and the forms and substance of law and justice. In questions of power, then, let no more be said of confidence in man, but bind him down from mischief by the chains of the Constitution. That this Commonwealth does therefore call on its co-States for an expression of their sentiments on the Acts concerning aliens, and for the punishment of certain crimes hereinbefore specified, plainly declaring whether these Acts are or are not authorized by the Federal compact. And it doubts not that their sense will be so announced as to prove their attachment to limited government, whether general or particular, and that the rights and liberties of their co-estates will be exposed to no dangers by remaining embarked on a common bottom with their own: But they will concur with this Commonwealth in considering the said Acts as so palpably against the Constitution as to amount to an undisguised declaration, that the compact is not meant to be the measure of the powers of the General Government, but that it will proceed in the exercise over these States of all powers whatsoever. That they will view this as seizing the rights of the States and consolidating them in the hands of the General Government, with a power assumed to bind the States (not merely in cases made Federal) but in all cases whatsoever, by laws made, not with their consent, but by others against their consent; that this would be to surrender the form of government we have chosen, and live under one deriving its powers from its own will, and not from our authority; and that the co-States recurring to their natural rights in cases not made Federal, will concur in declaring these void and of no force, and will each unite with this Commonwealth in requesting their repeal at the next session of Congress.

EDMUND BULLOCK, S. H. R.
JOHN CAMPBELL, S. S. P. T.

Passed the House of Representatives, Nov. 10, 1798.
Attest, THOS. TODD, C. H. R.

In Senate, Nov. 13, 1798 — Unanimously concurred in.
Attest, B. THURSTON, C. S.

Approved, Nov. 19th, 1798.

JAMES GARRARD, *Governor of Kentucky.*

By the Governor: HARRY TOULMAN, *Sec'y of State.*

INDEX.

PRESIDENT OF UNITED STATES.

State Records.

States.

Supreme Court.

ERRATA.

Page Line
ii, 13, for "judicial," read juridical.
viii, 31, for "amorphy," read atrophy.
xii, note 2, for "this," read the.
xiv, 13, between "the" and "work," insert original.
41, 12, for "authorize," read authorizes.
80, 15, for "costs," read evils.
96, 5, for "departments," read department.
171, note, for "Act," read Art.
182, 9, *for* "it," read they.
219, 31, *dele* "awkward."
247, note, for "19," read 10.
267, 4, for "repeated," read repealed.
279, —, *dele* 1st note.
297, 5, between "to" and "another," insert those of.
308, 2, before "or," insert N.
375, 29, between "that" and "the," insert if.
380, note 24, *dele* "not."
389, note *dele* "to xviii," and insert 18.

Reprints of the Legal Classics Published by The Lawbook Exchange, Ltd.

☙Admiralty & Maritime Law ☙

Flanders, Henry. [1824-1911]. *A Treatise on Maritime Law*. Boston: Little, Brown and Company, 1852. xvi, 444 pp. Reprinted 1999 by The Lawbook Exchange, Ltd. ISBN 1-886363-72-2. Cloth. $75.

Marsden. R.[eginald]. G.[odfrey], ed. *Documents Relating to Law and Custom of the Sea.* [n.p.]: The Navy Record Society, 1915-6. Two volumes. xxxiii, 561; xl, 457, [5] pp. Reprinted 1999 by The Lawbook Exchange, Ltd. LCCN 99-24138. ISBN 1-886363-96-X. Cloth. $175.

[Twiss, Sir Travers]. *The Black Book of the Admiralty, with an Appendix.* Monumenta Juridica. Edited by Sir Travers Twiss. Four volumes. 4, xciii, 491, [2]; 4, lxxxvii, 500, 31; 4, lxxxvi, 673, [1], 31; 4, clii, 559, 32 pp. LCCN 97-38809 ISBN 1-886363-39-0. 1871. Reprinted 1998 by The Lawbook Exchange, Ltd. Cloth. $495.

☙ Law & Literature ☙

Barton, Dunbar Plunket. *Shakespeare and the Law.* With a foreword by James M. Beck. Boston: Houghton Mifflin Company, 1929. xl, 167 pp. Reprint available October 1999 by The Lawbook Exchange, Ltd. LCCN 99-26602. ISBN 1-58477-000-7. Cloth. $60.

Darrow, Clarence. *A Persian Pearl. And Other Essays.* East Aurora, NY: The Roycroft Shop, 1899. 175 pp. Reprinted 1997 by The Lawbook Exchange, Ltd. ISBN 1-886363-27-7. Cloth. $50.

Darrow, Clarence S. *An Eye for an Eye.* New York: Fox Duffield & Company, 1905. 213 pp. Reprinted 1996 by The Lawbook Exchange, Ltd. ISBN 1-886363-07-2. Cloth. $40.

Davis, C.K. *The Law in Shakespeare.* Washington, D.C.: Washington Law Book Co., [1883]. 303 pp. Reprinted 1999 by The Lawbook Exchange, Ltd. ISBN 1-886363-75-7. Cloth. $60.

Gest, John Marshall. *The Lawyer in Literature.* London: Sweet & Maxwell, Limited, 1913. xii, 249 pp. Reprint available November 1999 by The Lawbook Exchange, Ltd. LCCN99-18365. ISBN 1-886363-90-0. Cloth. $60.

Holdsworth, William S. *Charles Dickens as a Legal Historian.* New Haven: Yale University Press, 1929. 157 pp. Reprinted 1995 by The Lawbook Exchange, Ltd. ISBN 1-886363-06-4. Cloth. $40.

☙ Legal Biography ☙

Foss, Edward. *A Biographical Dictionary of the Judges of England From the Conquest to the Present Time 1066-1870.* London: John Murray, 1870. xv, 792 pp. Reprint available December 1999 by The Lawbook Exchange, Ltd. LCCN 99-12577. ISBN 10886363-86-2. Cloth. $100.

Richards, John T. *Abraham Lincoln The Lawyer-Statesman.* Boston: Houghton Mifflin, 1916. Frontis. Illustrated. xii, 260 pp. Reprint available October 1999 by The Lawbook Exchange, Ltd. LCCN 99-20587. ISBN 1-886363-94-3. Cloth. $60.

☙ Legal Codes ☙

[Field Codes]. [New York 1850-1865]. New York Field Codes. 1850-1865.
Vol. I. *The Code of Civil Procedure of the State of New-York, Reported Complete by the Commissioners on Practice and Pleadings. 1850.*
Vol. II. *The Code of Criminal Procedure of the State of New York, Reported Complete by the Commissioners on Practice and Pleadings. 1850.*
Vol. III. *The Civil Code of the State of New York, Reported Complete by the Commissioners of the Code. 1865.*
Vol. IV. *The Penal Code of the State of New York, Reported Complete by the Commissioners of the Code. 1865.*
Vol. V. *The Political Code of the State of New York. 1860.*
With a new introduction by Michael Weber. Reprinted 1998 by The Lawbook Exchange, Ltd. Five volume series. [8], xcvi, 791; liii, [1], 486; cxii, 776; lxiv, 406, clxvii; xlvii, 607 pp. ISBN 1-886363-40-4 (set). Cloth. $495.

Livingston, Edward. *A System of Penal Law, for the State of Louisiana: Consisting of A Code of Crimes and Punishments, A Code of Procedure, A Code of Evidence, A Code of Reform and Prison Discipline, A Book of Definitions. Prepared Under the Authority of a Law of the Said State. To Which are Prefixed a Preliminary Report on the Plan of a Penal Code, and Introductory Reports to the Several Codes Embraced in the System of Penal Law.* Philadelphia: James Kay, Jun. & Brother, 1833. v, 745 pp. Reprint available November 1999 by The Lawbook Exchange, Ltd. LCCN 99-11403. ISBN 1-886363-83-8. Cloth. $95.

☙ Legal Dictionaries ☙

Anderson, William C. *A Dictionary of Law, Consisting of Judicial Definitions and Explanations of Words, Phrases, and Maxims, and an Exposition of the Principles of Law: Comprising a Dictionary and Compendium of American and English Jurisprudence.* Chicago: T.H. Flood and Company, 1889. viii, 1140pp. Reprinted 1996 by The Lawbook Exchange, Ltd. ISBN 1-886363-23-4. Cloth. $125.

Black, Henry Campbell. *A Law Dictionary. Containing Definitions of the Terms and Phrases of American and English Jurisprudence, Ancient and Modern. And Including the Principal Terms of International, Constitutional, Ecclesiastical and Commercial Law, and Medical Jurisprudence, with a Collection of Legal Maxims, Numerous Select Titles from the Roman, Modern Civil, Scotch, French, Spanish, and Mexican Law, and Other Foreign Systems, and a Table of Abbreviations.* St. Paul, Minn.: West Publishing, 1910. 1314 pp. Reprinted 1995 by The Lawbook Exchange, Ltd. ISBN 1-886363-10-2. Cloth. $125.

Black, Henry Campbell. *A Dictionary of Law. Containing Definitions of the Terms and Phrases of American and English Jurisprudence, Ancient and Modern. Including the Principal Terms of International, Constitutional, and Commercial Law; with a Collection of Legal Maxims and Numerous Select Titles from the Civil Law and Other Foreign Systems.* St. Paul, Minn.: West Publishing, 1891. x, 1253 pp. Reprinted 1991 by The Lawbook Exchange, Ltd. ISBN 0-9630106-0-3. $125.

Bouvier, John. *A Law Dictionary Adapted to the Constitution and Laws of the United States of America, and of the Several States of the American Union; with References to the Civil and Other Systems of Foreign Law.* Philadelphia: T. & J.W. Johnson, 1839. Two volumes. 559; 28 pp. Reprinted 1993 by The Lawbook Exchange, Ltd. ISBN 0-9630106-7-0. Cloth. $130.

Burrill, Alexander M. *A New Law Dictionary and Glossary: Containing Full Definitions of the Principal Terms of the Common and Civil Law, Together with Translations and Explanations of the Various Technical Phrases in Different Languages, Occurring in the Ancient and Modern Reports, and Standard Treatises; Embracing Also All the Principal Common and Civil Law Maxims. Compiled on the Basis of Spelman's Glossary, and Adapted to the Jurisprudence of the United States; with Copious Illustrations, Critical and Historical.* New York: John S. Voorhies, 1850. Two volumes. xviii, 1099 pp. Reprinted 1998 by The Lawbook Exchange, Ltd. LC 97-38481. ISBN 1-886363-32-3. Cloth. $175.

Holthouse, Henry James. *A New Law Dictionary, Containing Explanations of Such Technical Terms and Phrases As Defined in the Works of Legal Authors, in the Practice of the Courts, and in the Parliamentary Proceedings of the Houses of Lords and*

Commons, To Which Is Added An Outline of An Action at Law and of A Suit in Equity. Edited, from the Second and Enlarged London Edition, With Numerous Additions, by Henry Penington. Philadelphia: Lea and Blanchard, 1847. viii, [17]-495 pp. Reprinted 1999 by The Lawbook Exchange, Ltd. ISBN 1-886363-67-6. Cloth. $75.

Jacob, Giles. [1686-1744]. *The Law-Dictionary: Explaining the Rise, Progress, and Present State of the English Law; Defining and Interpreting the Terms or Words of Art; and Comprising Copious Information on the Subjects of Law, Trade, and Government. Corrected and Greatly Enlarged by T[homas] E[dlyne] Tomlins.* New York: Printed for, and Published by I. Riley, 1811. Originally six volumes, viii, 531; [2], 543; [2],618; [2], 472; [2], 553; [2], 471pp. Reprint available December 1999 by The Lawbook Exchange, Ltd. ISBN 1-886363-68-4. Cloth. $495.

Rapalje, Stewart and Lawrence, Robert L. *A Dictionary of American and English Law with Definitions of the Technical terms of the Canon and Civil Laws. Also, Containing a Full Collection of Latin Maxims, and Citations of Upwards of Forty Thousand Reported Cases, in which Words and Phrases Have Been Judicially Defined or Construed.* Jersey City: Frederick C. Linn & Co., 1888. Two volumes. xxxviii, 1380 pp. Reprinted 1997 by The Lawbook Exchange, Ltd. LC 97-38484. ISBN 1-886363-33-1. Cloth. $195.

Stimson, Frederic Jesup. *Glossary of Technical Terms, Phrases, and Maxims of the Common Law.* Boston: Little, Brown, and Company, 1881. iv, 305pp. Reprinted 1999 by The Lawbook Exchange, Ltd. ISBN 1-886363-70-6. Cloth. $60.

Tayler, Thomas. *The Law Glossary: Being a Selection of the Greek, Latin, Saxon, French, Norman and Italian Sentences, Phrases, and Maxims, Found in the Leading English and American reports, and Elementary Works.* New York: Lewis & Blood, 1856. 580 pp. Reprinted 1995 by The Lawbook Exchange, Ltd. ISBN 1-886363-12-9. Cloth. $65.

Legal History

Bar, Carl Ludwig von. *A History of Continental Criminal Law.* Boston: Little, Brown, and Company, 1916. lvi, 561 pp. Reprint available September 1999 by The Lawbook Exchange, Ltd. LCCN 99-32341. ISBN 1-58477-013-9. Cloth. $90.

[Brandeis, Louis D.]. [1856-1941]. *Brandeis on Zionism. A Collection of Addresses and Statements by Louis D. Brandeis with a Foreword by Mr. Justice Felix Frankfurter.* Washington, D.C.: Zionist Organization of America, [1942]. viii,

156 pp. Reprinted 1999 by The Lawbook Exchange, Ltd. ISBN 1-886363-60-9. Cloth. $65.

Corwin, Edward. *The Doctrine of Judicial Review: Its Legal and Historical Basis and Other Essays*. Princeton: Princeton University Press, 1914. ix, 178 pp. Reprint available December 1999 by The Lawbook Exchange, Ltd. LCCN 99-32362. ISBN 1-58477-011-2. Cloth. $60.

Darrow, Clarence and William J. Bryan. The *World's Most Famous Court Trial. Tennessee Evolution Case. A Complete Stenographic Report of the Famous Court Test of the Anti-Evolution Act, at Dayton July 10 to 21, 1925, Including Speeches and Arguments of Attorneys*. Cincinnati: National Book Company, [1925]. [4], 339 pp. Reprinted 1997 by The Lawbook Exchange, Ltd. LC 97-38485. ISBN 1-886363-31-5. Cloth. $65.

Dawson, John P. *A History of Lay Judges*. Cambridge, Mass.: Harvard University Press, 1960. viii, [2], 310 pp. Reprinted 1999 by The Lawbook Exchange, Ltd. ISBN 1-886363-69-2. Cloth. $75.

Evans, E.P. *The Criminal Prosecution and Capital Punishment of Animals.* New York: E.P. Dutton, 1906. x, 384pp. Reprinted 1998 by The Lawbook Exchange, Ltd. LC 98-12801. ISBN 1-886363-52-8. Cloth. $65.

Forsyth, William. *History of Trial by Jury* [*Second edition*]. Jersey City: Frederick D. Linn, [1875]. x, 388 pp. Reprinted 1994 by The Lawbook Exchange, Ltd. ISBN 0-9630106-8-9. Cloth. $65.

Forsyth, William. *The History of Lawyers. Ancient and Modern*. Boston: Estes & Lauriat, 1875. Illustrated. xvii, 404 pp. Reprinted 1996 by the Lawbook Exchange, Ltd. ISBN 1-886363-14-5. Cloth. $60.

Fortescue, Sir John. [?1394-1476?]. *The Governance of England: Otherwise Called The Difference between an Absolute and a Limited Monarchy. A Revised Text edited with Introduction, Notes, and Appendices by Charles Plummer.* London: Oxford University Press, 1885. xxiii, 387pp. Reprinted 1999 by The Lawbook Exchange, Ltd. ISBN 1-886363-79-X. Cloth. $65.

Futrell, William H. *The History of American Customs Jurisprudence.* New York: Published privately, 1941. 314pp. Reprinted 1998 by The Lawbook Exchange, Ltd. LC 98-11342. ISBN 1-886363-51-X. Cloth. $60.

Greenidge, A.H.J. *The Legal Procedure of Cicero's Time*. Oxford: The Clarendon Press, 1901. xiii, 599 pp. Reprint available December 1999 by The Lawbook Exchange, Ltd. LCCN 99-26771. ISBN 1-886363-99-4. Cloth. $85.

Harris, Virgil M. *Ancient, Curious, and Famous Wills.* Boston: Little, Brown, and Company, 1911. xiv, 472 pp. Reprinted 1999 by The Lawbook Exchange, Ltd. LCCN 99-20588. ISBN 1-886363-93-5. Cloth. $75.

Henderson, Gerard Carl. *The Position of Foreign Corporations in American Constitutional Law. A Contribution to the History and Theory of Juristic Persons in Anglo-American Law.* Cambridge: Harvard University Press, 1918. xix, 199 pp. Reprint available November 1999 by The Lawbook Exchange, Ltd. LCCN 99-18233. ISBN 1-886363-89-7. Cloth. $50.

Holdsworth, William S. *Essays in Law and History.* Edited by A.L. Goodhart and H.G. Hanbury. Oxford: At the Clarendon Press, 1946. xv, 302 pp. Reprinted 1995 by The Lawbook Exchange, Ltd. ISBN 1-886363-13-7. Cloth. $50.

Holdsworth, W.S. *The Historians of Anglo-American Law.* New York: Columbia University Press, 1928. 175 pp. Reprinted 1994 by The Lawbook Exchange, Ltd. ISBN 0-9630106-9-7. Cloth. $50.

Langdell, C.C. [1826-1906]. *A Selection of Cases on the Law of Contracts. with References and Citations. Prepared for Use as a Text-book in Harvard Law School.* Boston: Little, Brown & Co., 1871. xvi, 1022 pp. Reprint available September 1999 by The Lawbook Exchange, Ltd. LCCN 99-28293. ISBN 1-58477-001-5. Cloth. $120.

[MacDonell, Sir John and Edward Manson]. *Great Jurists of the World.* Edited by Sir John MacDonell and Edward Manson. With an Introduction by Van Vechten Veeder. Boston: Little, Brown, and Company, 1914. Illustrated. xxxii, 607 pp. Reprinted 1997 by The Lawbook Exchange, Ltd. ISBN 1-886363-28-5. Cloth. $95.

Maitland, Frederick W., et.al. *A General Survey of Events, Sources, Persons & Movements in Continental Legal History. By Various European Authors.* With an introduction by Albert Kocourek. Boston: Little, Brown, 1912. liii, 754pp. Reprinted 1998 by The Lawbook Exchange, Ltd. LC 98-11159. ISBN 1-886363-47-1. Cloth. $110.

Maitland, Frederic William. *Roman Canon Law in the Church of England: Six Essays.* London: Methuen & Co., 1898. vii, 184 pp. Reprinted 1998 by The Lawbook Exchange, Ltd. LC 98-22357. ISBN 1-886363-57-9. Cloth. $65.

Maitland, Frederick W., et.al. *Select Essays in Anglo-American Legal History. By Maitland, Pollock, Holmes, Beale, Holdsworth and Others.* Boston: Little, Brown, and Company, 1907. Three volumes. 847; 823; 862 pp. Reprinted 1992 by The Lawbook Exchange, Ltd. LCCN 91-77977. ISBN 0-9630106-0-1. Cloth. $195.

Maitland, Frederick W., Montague, Francis C., *A Sketch of English Legal History.* Edited with Notes and Appendices by James F. Colby. New York: G.P. Putnam's Sons, 1915. x, 234pp. LCCN 98-11337. ISBN 1-886363-50-1. Reprinted 1998 by The Lawbook Exchange, Ltd. Cloth. $50.

[Nichols, J.]. *A Collection of all the Wills, Now Known to Be Extant, of the Kings and Queens of England, Princes and Princesses of Wales, and every Branch of the Blood Royal, from the Reign of William the Conqueror, to that of Henry the Seventh Exclusive: With Explanatory Notes and a Glossary.* London: J. Nichols, 1780. x, 434 pp. Reprinted 1999 by The Lawbook Exchange, Ltd. LCCN 99-17114. ISBN 1-886363-87-0. Cloth. $75.

Pollock, Frederick and Frederic William Maitland. *The History of English Law before the Time of Edward I.* Cambridge: Cambridge University Press, 1898. Two volumes. xxxviii, 688; xiv, 691 pp. Reprinted 1996 by The Lawbook Exchange, Ltd. ISBN 1-886363-22-6. Cloth. $165.

Merriam, C.E., Jr. *History of the Theory of Sovereignty Since Rousseau.* New York: Columbia University Press, [1900]. x, [11]-233 pp. Reprinted 1999 by The Lawbook Exchange, Ltd. LCCN 98-32385. ISBN 1-886363-76-5. Cloth. $65.

Reeve, Tapping. [1744-1823]. *The Law of Baron and Femme, of Parent and Child, Guardian and Ward, Master and Servant, and of the Powers of the Courts of Chancery; with an Essay on the Terms Heir, Heirs, Heirs of the Body. Third Edition, With Notes and References to English and American Cases by Amasa J. Parker and Charles E. Baldwin, Counselors-At-Law.* Albany: William Gould, 1862. xlvi, 677pp. LCCN 98-36057. ISBN 1-886363-58-7. Reprinted 1998 by The Lawbook Exchange, Ltd. Cloth. $75.

Schwartz, Bernard, editor. *The Code Napoleon and the Common-Law World. The Sesquicentennial Lectures Delivered at The Law Center of New York University December 13-15, 1954.* New York: New York University Press, 1956. x, 438pp. LCCN 98-34100. ISBN 1-886363-59-5. Reprinted 1998 by The Lawbook Exchange, Ltd. Cloth. $65.

Schwarz, Philip J. *Twice Condemned: Slaves and the Criminal Laws of Virginia, 1705-1865.* [Baton Rouge: Louisiana State University Press]. [1988]. xvi, 354pp. Reprinted 1998 by The Lawbook Exchange, Ltd. LCCN 98-4424 ISBN 1-886363-54-4. Cloth. $75.

Tucker, Henry St. George. *Commentaries on the Laws of Virginia. Comprising the Substance of a Course of Lectures Delivered to the Winchester Law School. With an Introduction by David Cobin and Paul Finkelman.* Richmond: Shepherd and Colin, 1846. Two volumes. 34, 468; 24, 512 pp. Reprinted 1998 by The

Lawbook Exchange, Ltd. LCCN 97-10313. ISBN 1-886363-26-9. Cloth. $175.

Vinogradoff, Sir Paul. *Outlines of Historical Jurisprudence.* London: Oxford University Press, 1920. Two volumes. 428; x, 315 pp. Reprinted 1999 by The Lawbook Exchange, Ltd. LCCN 98-42298. ISBN 1-886363-64-1. Cloth. $150.

Walker, James. *The Theory of the Common Law.* Boston: Little, Brown and Co., 1852. xxiv, 130pp. Reprinted 1998 by The Lawbook Exchange, Ltd. LCCN 98-9522. ISBN 1-886363-45-5. Cloth. $65.

Warren, Charles. *History of the Harvard Law School and of Early Legal Conditions in America.* New York: Lewis Publishing Company, 1908. Three volumes. xiv, 543; iv, 560; 397 pp. Illustrated. Reprint available September 1999 by The Lawbook Exchange, Ltd. LCCN 99-29193. ISBN 1-58477-006-6. Cloth. $275.

Wiener, Leo. *Commentary to the Germanic Laws and Mediaeval Documents.* Cambridge: Harvard University Press, 1915. lxi, 224 pp. Reprint available October 1999 by The Lawbook Exchange, Ltd. LCCN 99-23969. ISBN 1-58477-005-8. Cloth. $60.

Legal Reference and Bibliography

Benedict, Russell. *Acts and Laws of the Thirteen Original Colonies and States: Constituting the extraordinary collection of Hon. Russell Benedict.* New York: American Art Association, 1922. [272]pp. Reprinted 1998 The Lawbook Exchange, Ltd. LCCN 98-20196 ISBN 1-886363-56-0. Cloth. $85.

Eller, Catherine Spicer. *The William Blackstone Collection in the Yale Law Library. A Bibliographical Catalogue.* New Haven: Yale University Press, 1938. Reprinted 1993 by the Lawbook Exchange, Ltd. xvii, 113 pp. Cloth. LCCN 99-38826. ISBN 0-9630106-5-4. $40.

Finkelman, Paul. *Slavery in the Courtroom. An Annotated Bibliography of American Cases.* Washington:Library of Congress, 1985. Illustrated. xxvii, 312pp. Reprinted 1998 by The Lawbook Exchange, Ltd. LCCN 98-11284. ISBN 1-886363-48-X. Cloth. $85.

Friend, William L. *Anglo-American Legal Bibliographies. An Annotated Guide.* Washington, D.C.: United States Government Printing Office, 1944. xii, 166 pp. Reprinted 1996 by The Lawbook Exchange, Ltd. ISBN 1-886363-21-8. Cloth. $65.

Hicks, Frederick. *Men and Books Famous in the Law. With an introduction by Harlan F. Stone.* Rochester, New York: Lawyers Co-operative Publishing, 1921. 259 pp. Reprinted 1992 by The Lawbook Exchange, Ltd. LCCN 92-070809. ISBN 0-9630106-2-X. Cloth.$50.

Jackson, E. Hilton. *Latin for Lawyers. Containing I: A Course in Latin, with Legal Maxims and Phrases As a Basis of Instruction. II. A Collection of Over One Thousand Latin Maxims, with English Translations, Explanatory Notes, and Cross-References. III. A Vocabulary of Latin Words.* London: Sweet & Maxwell, 1915. viii, 300 pp. Reprinted 1992 by The Lawbook Exchange, Ltd. LCCN 92-074408. ISBN 0-9630106-4-6. Cloth. $50.

McNamara, M. Frances. *Ragbag of Legal Quotations*. Albany: Matthew Bender & Company, 1960. xi, 334 pp. Reprinted 1992 by The Lawbook Exchange, Ltd. LC 92-074141. ISBN 0-9630106-3-8. Cloth. $50.

Maxwell, W. Harold and C.R. Brown. *A Complete List of British and Colonial Law Reports and Legal Periodicals. Arranged in Alphabetical and in Chronological Order with Bibliographical Notes.* **[With]:** *Check List of Canadian and Newfoundland Statutes.*[Third Edition]. Toronto: The Carswell Company, Limited, 1937. viii, 141, 49 pp. Reprinted 1995 by The Lawbook Exchange, Ltd. ISBN 1-886363-11-0. Cloth. $70.

[Worrall, John and Edward Brooke]. *Bibliotheca Legum Angliae. Or, a Catalogue of the Common and Statute Law Books of This Realm, and Some Others Relating Thereto: Giving an Account of Their Several Editions, Ancient Printers, Dates, and Prices, and Wherein They Differ. [With a Supplement to 1800]. Part I Compiled by John Worrall, Part II and Supplement Compiled by Edward Brooke. Parts I, II and Supplement bound in one volume.* London: Printed for Edward Brooke, 1788-1800. 316; 264; 48 pp. 1788-1800. Reprinted 1997 by The Lawbook Exchange, Ltd. ISBN 1-886363-29-3. Cloth. $110.

☙ Legal Sources ☙

Bouvier, John. [1787-1851]. *Institutes of American Law. New Edition by Daniel A. Gleason. In Two Volumes.* Boston:Little, Brown, & Company, 1880. Two volumes. lxviii, 651; iv, 798pp. Reprint available December 1999 by The Lawbook Exchange, Ltd. LCCN 98-54288. ISBN 1-886363-80-3. Cloth. $265.

[Cardozo, Benjamin]. *Law is Justice. Notable Opinions of Mr. Justice Cardozo.* Foreword by Robert F. Wagner. Edited by A.L. Sainer. New York: Ad Press Ltd., [1938]. xvii, 441 pp. Frontis. Reprint available September 1999 by The

Lawbook Exchange, Ltd. LCCN 99-34154. ISBN 1-58477-010-4. Cloth. $75.

[Cherokee Laws]. *Compiled Laws of the Cherokee Nation.* Tahlequah, I.T.: National Advocate Print, 1881. 370pp. LC 98-12741. ISBN 1-886363-42-0. Reprinted 1998 by The Lawbook Exchange, Ltd. With a new introduction by Michael Weber. Cloth. $60.

Fortescue, John. *DeLaudibus Legum Angliae. A Treatise in Commendation of the Laws of England.* With Translation by Francis Gregor. Notes by Andrew Amos and a Life of the Author by Thomas (Fortescue) Lord Clermont. Cincinnati: Robert Clarke & Co., 1874. Reprint available September 1999 by The Lawbook Exchange, Ltd. LCCN 99-16485. ISBN 1-58477-019-8. Cloth. $65.

[St. Germain, Christopher]. [1460-1540]. *The Doctor and Student or Dialogues Between a Doctor of Divinity and a Student in the Laws of England Containing the Grounds of Those Laws Together with Questions and Cases Concerning the Equity Thereof Revised and Corrected by William Muchall, Gent. to which are added two pieces concerning Suits in Chancery by Subpoena.* Cincinnati:Robert Clarke & Co., 1874. xiv, 401pp. Reprinted 1998 by The Lawbook Exchange, Ltd. LCCN 98-11338. ISBN 1-886363-49-8. Cloth. $65.

Woodbine, George E. *Four Thirteenth Century Law Tracts. A Thesis Presented to the Faculty of the Graduate Schol of Yale University in Candidacy for the Degree of Doctor of Philosophy.* New Haven: Yale University Press, 1910. vi, 183 pp. Reprint available October 1999 by The Lawbook Exchange, Ltd. LCCN 99-29294. ISBN 1-58477-007-4. Cloth. $50.

Legal Treatises

Beck, Theodric Romeyn. *Elements of Medical Jurisprudence.* Albany: Websters and Skinners, 1823. Two volumes. xxxiv, 418; viii, [9]-471 pp. Reprinted 1997 by The Lawbook Exchange, Ltd. ISBN 1-886363-24-2. Cloth. $125.

Freeman, A.C. *A Treatise of the Law of Judgments. Including All Final Determinations of the Rights of Parties in Actions or Proceedings at Law or in Equity. Revised, and Greatly Enlarged by Edward W. Tuttle.* San Francisco: Bancroft-Whitney, 1925. Three volumes. 1216; 1280; 1264 pp. Reprinted 1993 by The Lawbook Exchange, Ltd. ISBN 0-9630106-6-2. Cloth. $295.

Gilmore, Grant. *Security Interests in Personal Property.* Boston: Little, Brown & Company, 1965. Two volumes. xxxiv, 651; xiii, 653-1508 pp. Reprinted

1999 by The Lawbook Exchange, Ltd. LCCN 99-10258. ISBN 1-886363-81-1. Cloth. $195.

Pomeroy, John N. *A Treatise on Equity Jurisprudence As Administered in the United States of America. Adapted for All the States and to the Union of Legal and Equitable Remedies under the Reformed Procedure.* San Francisco and New York: Bancroft-Whitney and Lawyers Cooperative, 1941. Five volumes. 914; 1134; 1063; 1104; 716 pp. Reprinted 1995 by The Lawbook Exchange, Ltd. ISBN 1-886363-05-6. Cloth. $450.

Pothier, Robert Joseph [1699-1772]. *A Treatise on Obligations, Considered in a Moral and Legal View. Translated from the French of Pothier. Translated by Francois-Xavier Martin.* Newburn, N.C.: Martin & Ogden, 1802. Reprint available December 1999 by The Lawbook Exchange, Ltd. With a new introduction by Warren M. Billings. LC 98-38360. ISBN 1-886363-62-5. Cloth. $75.

Sears, John H. *Trust Estates as Business Companies. [Second Edition].* Kansas City, Mo.:Vernon Law Book Company, 1921. xx, 782 pp. [1921]. Reprinted June 1998 by The Lawbook Exchange, Ltd. LCCN 97-32423 ISBN 1-886363-41-2. Cloth. $95.

Philosophy of Law

Fuller, Lon L. *The Law in Quest of Itself.* Boston: Beacon Press, 1966. [vi], 150 pp. Reprint available October 1999 by The Lawbook Exchange, Ltd. LCCN 99-32863. ISBN 1-58477-016-3. Cloth. $45.

Jhering, Rudolf Von. *Law as a Means to an End.* Translated from the German by Isaac Husik with an Editorial Preface by Joseph H. Drake and with Introductions by Henry Lamm and W.M. Geldart. Boston: The Boston Book Company, 1913. lxi, 483 pp. Reprint available September 1999 by The Lawbook Exchange, Ltd. LCCN 99-23754. ISBN 1-58477-009-0. Cloth. $80.

Jhering, Rudolph von. *The Struggle for Law. Translated from the Fifth German Edition by John J. Lalor. Second Edition, with an Introduction by Albert Kocourek.* Chicago: Callaghan and Company, 1915. lii, 138 pp. Reprinted 1997 by The Lawbook Exchange, Ltd. ISBN 1-886363-25-0. Cloth. $60.

Kelsen, Hans. [1881-1973]. *General Theory of Law and State.* Translated by Anders Wedberg. Cambridge: Harvard University Press, 1945. xxxiii, 516pp. LCCN 98-32334. ISBN 1-886363-74-9. Reprinted 1999 by The Lawbook Exchange, Ltd. Cloth. $75.

ঞ Special Editionsঞ

Stokes, I.N. Phelps. *The Iconography of Manhattan Island 1498-1909.* New York: Robert H. Dodd, 1915. Six volumes. Reprinted 1998 by The Lawbook Exchange, Ltd. LCCN 97-30604. ISBN 1-886363-30-7. Cloth. $750.

ঞ U.S. Constitutional History ঞ

Bauer, Elizabeth Kelley. *Commentaries on the Constitution 1790-1860.* New York: Columbia University Press, 1952. 400 pp. Reprinted 1999 by The Lawbook Exchange, Ltd. LCCN 98-45409. ISBN 1-886363-66-8. Cloth. $75.

Beard, Charles A. *The Supreme Court and the Constitution.* New York: The Macmillan Company, 1912. vii, 127 pp. Reprinted 1999 by The Lawbook Exchange, Ltd. LCCN 98-50368. ISBN 1-886363-78-1. Cloth. $45.

Bondy, William. *Separation of Governmental Powers in History, in Theory, and in the Constitutions.* New York: Columbia College, 1896. Reprinted 1999 by The Lawbook Exchange, Ltd. vi,[7]-185, [1] pp. LCCN 98-44994. ISBN 1-886363-65-X. Cloth. $65.

Cooley, Thomas McIntyre. *A Treatise on the Constitutional Limitations Which Rest Upon the Legislative Power of the States of the American Union.* [*1st edition*]. Boston: Little, Brown, and Co., 1868. xlvii, 720pp. Reprinted 1999 by The Lawbook Exchange, Ltd. LCCN 99-20589. ISBN 1-886363-92-7. Cloth. $95.

Cooley, Thomas M. *A Treatise on the Constitutional Limitations which Rest Upon the Legislative Power of the States of the American Union. Fifth edition.* Boston: Little, Brown, and Co., 1883. lxxxi, 886pp. Reprinted October 1998 by The Lawbook Exchange, Ltd. LCCN 98-12730. ISBN 1-886363-53-6. Cloth. $120.

Dodd, Walter Fairleigh. *The Revision and Amendment of State Constitutions.* Baltimore: The Johns Hopkins Press, 1910. xvii, 350 pp. Reprinted 1999 by The Lawbook Exchange, Ltd. ISBN 1-886363-73-0. Cloth. $65.

Fisher, Sydney George. *The Evolution of the Constitution of the United States. Showing That It Is a Development of Progressive History and Not an Isolated Document Struck Off at a Given Time or an Imitation of English or Dutch Forms of*

Government. Philadelphia: J.B. Lippincott, 1897. 398 pp. Reprinted 1996 by The Lawbook Exchange, Ltd. LCCN 97-41054. ISBN 1-886363-08-0. Cloth. $65.

Flanders, Henry. *An Exposition of the Constitution of the United States. Designed as a Manual of Instruction.* Philadelphia: E.H. Butler & Co., 1860. xii, 311 pp. Reprint available October 1999 by The Lawbook Exchange, Ltd. LCCN 99-31594. ISBN 1-58477-014-7. Cloth. $60.

[Madison, James]. Hunt, Gaillard, Scott, James Brown. *The Debates in The Federal Convention of 1787 Which Framed the Constitution of the United States of America.* New York: Oxford University Press, 1920. xcvii, [1], 731 pp. Reprinted 1999 by The Lawbook Exchange, Ltd. LCCN 98-51911. ISBN 1-886363-77-3. Cloth. $110.

Minor, Raleigh C. *Notes on the Science of Government and the Relations of the States to the United States.* [Charlottesville]: University of Virginia, 1913. x, 171 pp. Reprinted 1995 by The Lawbook Exchange,Ltd. ISBN 1-886363-09-9. Cloth. $40.

Story, Joseph. [1779-1845]. *A Familiar Exposition of the Constitution of the United States: Containing a Brief Commentary on Every Clause, Explaining the True Nature, reasons, and Objects Thereof; Designed for the Use of School, Libraries and General Readers. With an Appendix, Containing Important Public Documents, Illustrative of the Constitution.* New York: Harper & Brothers: 1865. 372 pp. Reprinted 1999 by The Lawbook Exchange, Ltd. ISBN 1-886363-71-4. Cloth. $60.

[Taylor, John]. [1753-1824]. *A Defence of the Measures of the Administration of Thomas Jefferson. By Curtius.* Washington: Samuel H. Smith, 1804. 136 pp. Reprinted 1999 by The Lawbook Exchange, Ltd. LCCN 99-24139. ISBN 1-886363-97-8. Cloth. $60.

Taylor, John. *Construction Construed and Constitutions Vindicated.* Richmond:printed by Shepherd & Pollard, 1820. iv, 344pp. Reprinted 1998 by The Lawbook Exchange, Ltd. LCCN 97-49411. ISBN 1-886363-43-9. Cloth. $65.

Taylor, John. *An Inquiry into the Principles and Policy of the Government of the United States.* Fredericksburg:Green and Cady, 1814. With an introduction by Roy Franklin Nichols, Yale University Press, 1950. 562pp. Reprinted 1998 by The Lawbook Exchange, Ltd. LCCN 98-11147. ISBN 1-886363-46-3. Cloth. $75.

Tucker, St. George. *Blackstone's Commentaries. With Notes of Reference to the Constitution and Laws, of the Federal Government of the United States, and of the*

Commonwealth of Virginia. In Five Volumes, with an Appendix to Each volume, Containing Short Tracts upon Such Subjects As Appeared Necessary to Form a Connected View of the Laws of Virginia As a Member of the Federal Union. Philadelphia: William Young Birch and Abraham Small, 1803. Five volumes. Reprinted 1996 by The Lawbook Exchange, Ltd. ISBN 1-886363-15-3. Cloth. $450.

[Upshur, Abel Parker]. *A Brief Enquiry Into the True Nature and Character of Our Federal Government, being a review of Judge Story's Commentaries on the Constitution of the United States. By a Virginian.* Petersburg: Printed by Edmund and Julian C. Ruffin, 1840. 132pp. Reprinted 1998 by The Lawbook Exchange, Ltd. LCCN 97-11151. ISBN 1-886363-44-7. Cloth. $45.

Wright, John S. *Citizenship Sovereignty.* Chicago: Published for American Citizens, the True Maintainers of State Sovereignty, 1864. Reprinted 1998 by The Lawbook Exchange, Ltd. LCCN 98-15940 ISBN 1-886363-55-2. Cloth. $65.